Cold War
Biographies

Cold War Biographies

Volume 2: K-Z

Sharon M. Hanes
and Richard C. Hanes

Lawrence W. Baker,
Project Editor

Detroit • New York • San Diego • San Francisco • Cleveland • New Haven, Conn. • Waterville, Maine • London • Munich

Cold War: Biographies

Sharon M. Hanes and Richard C. Hanes

Project Editor
Lawrence W. Baker

Editorial
Matthew May, Diane Sawinski

Permissions
Margaret Chamberlain, Shalice Shah-Caldwell

Imaging and Multimedia
Lezlie Light, Mike Logusz, Dave Oblender, Kelly A. Quin

Product Design
Pamela A. E. Galbreath, Jennifer Wahi

Composition
Evi Seoud

Manufacturing
Rita Wimberley

LIBRARY OF CONGRESS CATALOGING-IN-PUBLICATION DATA

Hanes, Sharon M.

Cold War : biographies / Sharon M. Hanes and Richard C. Hanes ; Lawrence W. Baker, editor.

v. cm. — (UXL Cold War reference library)

Includes bibliographical references and index.

Contents: v. 1. A–J. Dean G. Acheson. Konrad Adenauer. Salvador Allende. Clement R. Attlee. Ernest Bevin. Leonid Brezhnev. George Bush. James F. Byrnes. Jimmy Carter. Fidel Castro. Chiang Kai-shek. Winston Churchill. Clark M. Clifford. Deng Xiaoping. John Foster Dulles. Dwight D. Eisenhower. Mikhail Gorbachev. Andrey Gromyko. W. Averell Harriman. Ho Chi Minh. J. Edgar Hoover. Lyndon B. Johnson — v. 2. K–Z. George F. Kennan. John F. Kennedy. Nikita Khrushchev. Kim Il Sung. Jeane Kirkpatrick. Henry Kissinger. Helmut Kohl. Aleksey Kosygin. Igor Kurchatov. Douglas MacArthur. Harold Macmillan. Mao Zedong. George C. Marshall. Joseph R. McCarthy. Robert S. McNamara. Vyacheslav Molotov. Richard M. Nixon. J. Robert Oppenheimer. Ayn Rand. Ronald Reagan. Condoleezza Rice. Andrey Sakharov. Eduard Shevardnadze. Joseph Stalin. Margaret Thatcher. Josip Broz Tito. Harry S. Truman. Zhou Enlai.

ISBN 0-7876-7663-2 (alk. paper) — ISBN 0-7876-7664-0 (v. 1 : alk. paper) — ISBN 0-7876-7665-9 (v. 2 : alk. paper)

1. Cold War—Biography—Juvenile literature. 2. History, Modern—1945–1989—Juvenile literature. 3. Biography—20th century —Juvenile literature. [1. Cold War—Biography. 2. History, Modern—1945–1989. 3. Biography—20th century.] I. Hanes, Richard Clay, 1946– . II. Baker, Lawrence W. III. Title. IV. Series.

D839.5.H36 2003
909.82'5'0922—dc22

2003018989

Contents

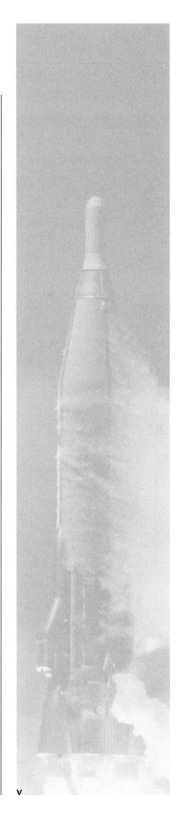

Introduction vii

Reader's Guide xi

Cold War Timeline xv

Volume 1

Dean G. Acheson 1

Konrad Adenauer 9

Salvador Allende 17

Clement R. Attlee 25

Ernest Bevin 33

Leonid Brezhnev 41

George Bush 53

James F. Byrnes 62

Jimmy Carter 70

Fidel Castro 82

Chiang Kai-shek 92

Winston Churchill 100

Clark M. Clifford 109

Deng Xiaoping 116

John Foster Dulles 124
Dwight D. Eisenhower 134
Mikhail Gorbachev 146
Andrey Gromyko 159
W. Averell Harriman 168
Ho Chi Minh 176
J. Edgar Hoover 185
Lyndon B. Johnson 194

Volume 2

George F. Kennan 207
John F. Kennedy 218
Nikita Khrushchev 230
Kim Il Sung 241
Jeane Kirkpatrick 249
Henry Kissinger 255
Helmut Kohl 268
Aleksey Kosygin 277
Igor Kurchatov 283
Douglas MacArthur 293
Harold Macmillan 303
Mao Zedong 312
George C. Marshall 321
Joseph R. McCarthy 329
Robert S. McNamara 337
Vyacheslav Molotov 345
Richard M. Nixon 354
J. Robert Oppenheimer 366
Ayn Rand 379
Ronald Reagan 387
Condoleezza Rice 401
Andrey Sakharov 408
Eduard Shevardnadze 416
Joseph Stalin 425
Margaret Thatcher 437
Josip Broz Tito 444
Harry S. Truman 452
Zhou Enlai 463

Where to Learn More xxxix

Index xliii

Introduction

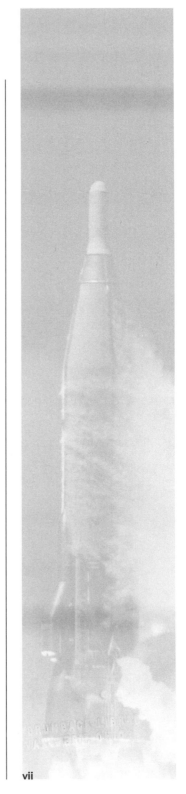

Sometimes single events alter the course of history; other times, a chain reaction of seemingly lesser occurrences changes the path of nations. The intense rivalry between the United States and the Soviet Union that emerged immediately after World War II (1939–45) followed the second pattern. Known as the Cold War, the rivalry grew out of mutual distrust between two starkly different societies: communist Soviet Union and the democratic West, which was led by the United States and included Western Europe. Communism is a political and economic system in which the Communist Party controls all aspects of citizens' lives and private ownership of property is banned. It is not compatible with America's democratic way of life. Democracy is a political system consisting of several political parties whose members are elected to various government offices by vote of the people. The rapidly growing rivalry between the two emerging post–World War II superpowers in 1945 would dominate world politics until 1991. Throughout much of the time, the Cold War was more a war of ideas than one of battlefield combat. Yet for generations, the Cold War affected almost every aspect of American life and those who lived in numerous other countries around the world.

The global rivalry was characterized by many things. Perhaps the most dramatic was the cost in lives and public funds. Millions of military personnel and civilians were killed in conflicts often set in Third World countries. This toll includes tens of thousands of American soldiers in the Korean War (1950–53) and Vietnam War (1954–75) and thousands of Soviet soldiers in Afghanistan. National budgets were stretched to support the nuclear arms races, military buildups, localized wars, and aid to friendly nations. On the international front, the United States often supported oppressive but strongly anticommunist military dictatorships. On the other hand, the Soviets frequently supported revolutionary movements seeking to overthrow established governments. Internal political developments within nations around the world were interpreted by the two superpowers—the Soviet Union and the United States—in terms of the Cold War rivalry. In many nations, including the Soviet-dominated Eastern European countries, basic human freedoms were lost. New international military and peacekeeping alliances were also formed, such as the United Nations (UN), the North Atlantic Treaty Organization (NATO), the Organization of American States (OAS), and the Warsaw Pact.

Effects of the Cold War were extensive on the home front, too. The U.S. government became more responsive to national security needs, including the sharpened efforts of the Federal Bureau of Investigation (FBI). Created were the Central Intelligence Agency (CIA), the National Security Council (NSC), and the Department of Defense. Suspicion of communist influences within the United States built some individual careers and destroyed others. The national education priorities of public schools were changed to emphasize science and engineering after the Soviets launched the satellite *Sputnik,* which itself launched the space race.

What would cause such a situation to develop and last for so long? One major factor was mistrust for each other. The communists were generally shunned by other nations, including the United States, since they gained power in Russia in 1917 then organized that country into the Soviet Union. The Soviets' insecurities loomed large. They feared another invasion from the West through Poland, as had happened through the centuries. On the other hand, the West was highly suspicious of the harsh closed society of Soviet communism. As a result, a move by one nation would bring a response by the other. Hard-liners on both sides believed long-term coexistence was not feasible.

A second major factor was that the U.S. and Soviet ideologies were dramatically at odds. The political, social, and economic systems of democratic United States and communist Soviet Union were essentially incompatible. Before the communist (or Bolshevik) revolution in 1917, the United States and Russia competed as they both sought to expand into the Pacific Northwest. In addition, Americans had a strong disdain for Russian oppression under their monarchy of the tsars. Otherwise, contact between the two growing powers was almost nonexistent until thrown together as allies in a common cause to defeat Germany and Japan in World War II.

It was during the meetings of the allied leaders in Yalta and Potsdam in 1945 when peaceful postwar cooperation was being sought that the collision course of the two new superpowers started becoming more evident. The end of World War II had brought the U.S. and Soviet armies face-to-face in central Europe in victory over the Germans. Yet the old mistrusts between communists and capitalists quickly dominated diplomatic relations. Capitalism is an economic system in which property and businesses are privately owned. Prices, production, and distribution of goods are determined by competition in a market relatively free of government intervention. A peace treaty ending World War II in Europe was blocked as the Soviets and the U.S.-led West carved out spheres of influence. Western Europe and Great Britain aligned with the United States and collectively was referred to as the "West"; Eastern Europe would be controlled by the Soviet Communist Party. The Soviet Union and its Eastern European satellite countries were collectively referred to as the "East." The two powers tested the resolve of each other in Germany, Iran, Turkey, and Greece in the late 1940s.

In 1949, the Soviets successfully tested an atomic bomb and Chinese communist forces overthrew the National Chinese government, and U.S. officials and American citizens feared a sweeping massive communist movement was overtaking the world. A "red scare" spread through America. The term "red" referred to communists, especially the Soviets. The public began to suspect that communists or communist sympathizers lurked in every corner of the nation.

Meanwhile, the superpower confrontations spread from Europe to other global areas: Asia, Africa, the Middle East, and Latin America. Most dramatic were the Korean and Vietnam wars, the Cuban Missile Crisis, and the military standoffs in Berlin, Germany. However, bloody conflicts erupted in many other areas as the United States and Soviet Union sought to expand their influence by supporting or opposing various movements.

In addition, a costly arms race lasted decades despite sporadic efforts at arms control agreements. The score card for the Cold War was kept in terms of how many nuclear weapons one country had aimed at the other. Finally, in the 1970s and 1980s, the Soviet Union could no longer keep up with the changing world economic trends. Its tightly controlled and highly inefficient industrial and agricultural systems could not compete in world markets while the government was still focusing its wealth on Cold War confrontations and the arms race. Developments in telecommunications also made it more difficult to maintain a closed society. Ideas were increasingly being exchanged despite longstanding political barriers. The door was finally cracked open in the communist European nations to more freedoms in the late 1980s through efforts at economic and social reform. Seizing the moment, the long suppressed populations of communist Eastern European nations and fifteen Soviet republics demanded political and economic freedom.

Through 1989, the various Eastern European nations replaced long-time communist leaders with noncommunist officials. By the end of 1991, the Soviet Communist Party had been banned from various Soviet republics, and the Soviet Union itself ceased to exist. After a decades-long rivalry, the end to the Cold War came swiftly and unexpectedly.

A new world order dawned in 1992 with a single superpower, the United States, and a vastly changed political landscape around much of the globe. Communism remained in China and Cuba, but Cold War legacies remained elsewhere. In the early 1990s, the United States was economically burdened with a massive national debt, the former Soviet republics were attempting a very difficult economic transition to a more capitalistic open market system, and Europe, starkly divided by the Cold War, was reunited once again and sought to establish a new union including both Eastern and Western European nations.

Reader's Guide

Cold War: Biographies presents biographies of fifty men and women who participated in or were affected by the Cold War, the period in history from 1945 until 1991 that was dominated by the rivalry between the world's superpowers, the United States and the Soviet Union. These two volumes profile a diverse mix of personalities from the United States, the Soviet Union, China, Great Britain, and other regions touched by the Cold War. Detailed biographies of major Cold War figures (such as Fidel Castro, Winston Churchill, Mikhail Gorbachev, John F. Kennedy, Nikita Khrushchev, and Joseph R. McCarthy) are included. But Cold War: Biographies also provides biographical information on lesser-known but nonetheless important and fascinating men and women of that era. Examples include nuclear physicist Igor Kurchatov, the developer of the Soviet atomic bomb; U.S. secretary of state George C. Marshall, a former Army general who unveiled the Marshall Plan, a major U.S. economic aid program for the war-torn countries of Western Europe; Kim Il Sung, the communist dictator of North Korea throughout the Cold War; and Condoleezza Rice, the top U.S. advisor on the Soviet Union when the Cold War ended in November 1990.

Cold War: Biographies also features sidebars containing interesting facts about people and events related to the Cold War. Within each full-length biography, boldfaced cross-references direct readers to other individuals profiled in the two-volume set. Finally, each volume includes photographs and illustrations, a "Cold War Timeline" that lists significant dates and events of the Cold War era, and a cumulative subject index.

U•X•L Cold War Reference Library

Cold War: Biographies is only one component of the three-part U•X•L Cold War Reference Library. The other two titles in this set are:

- *Cold War: Almanac* (two volumes) presents a comprehensive overview of the period in American history from the end of World War II until the fall of communism in Eastern Europe and the Soviet Union and the actual dissolution of the Soviet Union itself. Its fifteen chapters are arranged chronologically and explore such topics as the origins of the Cold War, the beginning of the nuclear age, the arms race, espionage, anticommunist campaigns and political purges on the home fronts, détente, the Cuban Missile Crisis, the Berlin Airlift and the Berlin Wall, the Korean and Vietnam wars, and the ending of the Cold War. The *Almanac* also contains more than 140 black-and-white photographs and maps, "Words to Know" and "People to Know" boxes, a timeline, and an index.

- *Cold War: Primary Sources* (one volume) tells the story of the Cold War in the words of the people who lived and shaped it. Thirty-one excerpted documents provide a wide range of perspectives on this period of history. Included are excerpts from presidential press conferences; addresses to U.S. Congress and Soviet Communist Party meetings; public speeches; telegrams; magazine articles; radio and television addresses; and later reflections by key government leaders.

- A cumulative index of all three titles in the U•X•L Cold War Reference Library is also available.

Acknowledgments

Kelly Rudd and Meghan O'Meara contributed importantly to *Cold War: Biographies*. Special thanks to Catherine

Filip, who typed much of the manuscript. Much appreciation also goes to copyeditors Christine Alexanian, Taryn Benbow-Pfalzgraf, and Jane Woychick; proofreader Wyn Hilty; indexer Dan Brannen; and typesetter Marco Di Vita of the Graphix Group for their fine work.

Dedication

To Aaron and Kara Hanes, that their children may learn about the events and ideas that shaped the world through the latter half of the twentieth century.

Comments and suggestions

We welcome your comments on *Cold War: Biographies* and suggestions for other topics to consider. Please write: Editors, *Cold War: Biographies,* U•X•L, 27500 Drake Rd., Farmington Hills, Michigan 48331-3535; call toll free: 1-800-877-4253; fax to 248-699-8097; or send e-mail via http://www.gale.com.

Cold War Timeline

September 1, 1939 Germany invades Poland, beginning World War II.

June 30, 1941 Germany invades the Soviet Union, drawing the Soviets into World War II.

December 7, 1941 Japan launches a surprise air attack on U.S. military installations at Pearl Harbor, Hawaii, drawing the United States into World War II.

November 1943 The three key allied leaders—U.S. president Franklin D. Roosevelt, British prime minister **Winston Churchill**, and Soviet premier **Joseph Stalin**—meet in Tehran, Iran, to discuss war strategies against Germany and Italy.

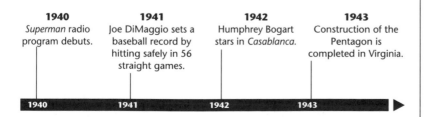

1940	**1941**	**1942**	**1943**
Superman radio program debuts.	Joe DiMaggio sets a baseball record by hitting safely in 56 straight games.	Humphrey Bogart stars in *Casablanca*.	Construction of the Pentagon is completed in Virginia.

| 1940 | 1941 | 1942 | 1943 |

August-October 1944 An international conference held at Dumbarton Oaks in Washington, D.C., creates the beginning of the United Nations.

February 1945 The Yalta Conference is held in the Crimean region of the Soviet Union among the three key allied leaders, U.S. president Franklin D. Roosevelt, British prime minister Winston Churchill, and Soviet premier Joseph Stalin to discuss German surrender terms, a Soviet attack against Japanese forces, and the future of Eastern Europe.

April-June 1945 Fifty nations meet in San Francisco to write the UN charter.

April 12, 1945 U.S. president Franklin D. Roosevelt dies suddenly from a brain hemorrhage, leaving Vice President **Harry S. Truman** as the next U.S. president.

April 23, 1945 U.S. president Harry S. Truman personally criticizes Soviet foreign minister **Vyacheslav Molotov** for growing Soviet influence in Eastern Europe, setting the tone for escalating Cold War tensions.

May 7, 1945 Germany surrenders to allied forces, leaving Germany and its capital of Berlin divided into four military occupation zones with American, British, French, and Soviet forces.

July 16, 1945 The United States, through its top-secret Manhattan Project, successfully detonates the world's first atomic bomb under the leadership of nuclear physicist **J. Robert Oppenheimer.**

July-August 1945 The Big Three—U.S. president Harry S. Truman, British prime minister Winston Churchill, and Soviet premier Joseph Stalin meet in Potsdam, Ger-

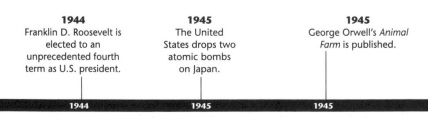

1944
Franklin D. Roosevelt is elected to an unprecedented fourth term as U.S. president.

1945
The United States drops two atomic bombs on Japan.

1945
George Orwell's *Animal Farm* is published.

1944   1945   1945

many, to discuss postwar conditions. On August 2, newly elected **Clement R. Attlee** replaces Churchill.

August 14, 1945 Japan surrenders, ending World War II, after the United States drops two atomic bombs on the cities of Hiroshima and Nagasaki.

November 29, 1945 Josip Broz Tito assumes leadership of the new communist government in Yugoslavia.

December 1945 U.S. secretary of state **James F. Byrnes** travels to Moscow to make a major effort to establish friendly relations with the Soviets, making agreements regarding international control of atomic energy and the postwar governments of Bulgaria, Hungary, and Japan; the agreements proved highly unpopular in the United States.

January 12, 1946 Nuclear physicist J. Robert Oppenheimer is awarded the "United States of America Medal of Merit" for his leadership on the Manhattan Project.

February 9, 1946 Soviet leader Joseph Stalin delivers the "Two Camps" speech, declaring the incompatibility of communist Soviet Union with the West.

February 22, 1946 U.S. diplomat **George F. Kennan** sends the "Long Telegram" from Moscow to Washington, D.C., warning of the Soviet threat.

March 5, 1946 Former British prime minister Winston Churchill delivers the "Iron Curtain Speech" at Westminster College in Fulton, Missouri.

September 1946 Clark M. Clifford, special counsel to U.S. president Harry S. Truman, coauthors an influential secret report titled "American Relations with the Soviet Union," warning of the threat of Soviet aggression

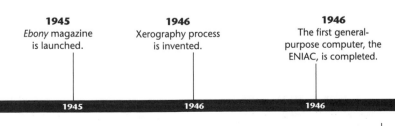

1945
Ebony magazine is launched.

1946
Xerography process is invented.

1946
The first general-purpose computer, the ENIAC, is completed.

1945   1946   1946

and calling for a policy of containment of further communist expansion.

September 6, 1946 U.S. secretary of state James F. Byrnes announces in a major speech that it is now U.S. policy to reestablish an independent Germany, something the Soviets strongly opposed; many consider this speech the end of the wartime alliance between the West and the Soviet Union.

October 7, 1946 W. Averill Harriman begins a stint as secretary of commerce, a position in which Harriman greatly influences later passage of the Marshall Plan, a plan to rebuild European economies devastated by World War II.

December 2, 1946 The United States, Great Britain, and France merge their German occupation zones to create what would become West Germany.

February 1947 After British foreign minister **Ernest Bevin** announces the withdrawal of long-term British support for Greece and Turkey, he approaches the U.S. government to seek its expansion in its international commitment to European security.

March 12, 1947 U.S. president Harry S. Truman announces the Truman Doctrine, which states that the United States will assist any nation in the world being threatened by communist expansion.

June 5, 1947 U.S. secretary of state **George C. Marshall** announces the Marshall Plan, an ambitious economic aid program to rebuild Western Europe from World War II destruction.

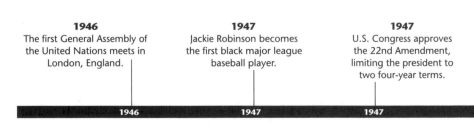

1946
The first General Assembly of the United Nations meets in London, England.

1947
Jackie Robinson becomes the first black major league baseball player.

1947
U.S. Congress approves the 22nd Amendment, limiting the president to two four-year terms.

1946   1947   1947

July 1947 U.S. diplomat George F. Kennan introduces the containment theory in the "X" article in *Foreign Affairs* magazine.

July 26, 1947 Congress passes the National Security Act, creating the Central Intelligence Agency (CIA) and the National Security Council (NSC).

October 1947 Actor **Ronald Reagan** and author **Ayn Rand** testify before the House Un-American Activities Committee (HUAC), a congressional group investigating communist influences in the United States.

December 5, 1947 The Soviets establish the Communist Information Bureau (Cominform) to promote the expansion of communism in the world.

February 25, 1948 A communist coup in Czechoslovakia topples the last remaining democratic government in Eastern Europe.

March 14, 1948 Israel announces its independence as a new state in the Middle East.

June 24, 1948 The Soviets begin a blockade of Berlin, leading to a massive airlift of daily supplies by the Western powers for the next eleven months.

January 21, 1949 At the beginning of his second term of office, President Harry S. Truman appoints **Dean G. Acheson** secretary of state.

April 4, 1949 The North Atlantic Treaty Organization (NATO), a military alliance involving Western Europe and the United States, comes into existence.

May 5, 1949 The West Germans establish the Federal Republic of Germany government.

1947
Tennessee Williams's *A Streetcar Named Desire* opens on Broadway.

1948
The Baskin-Robbins ice cream chain opens.

1949
The first Emmy Awards ceremony is held.

1947   1948   1949

May 12, 1949 The Soviet blockade of access routes to West Berlin is lifted.

May 30, 1949 Soviet-controlled East Germany establishes the German Democratic Republic.

August 1949 Konrad Adenauer becomes the first chancellor of West Germany in the first open parliamentary elections of the newly established Federal Republic of Germany (FRG).

August 29, 1949 Under the leadership of Soviet nuclear physicist **Igor Kurchatov**, the Soviet Union conducts its first successful atomic bomb test at the Semipalatinsk Test Site in northeastern Kazakhstan.

October 1, 1949 Communist forces under **Mao Zedong** gain victory in the Chinese civil war, and the People's Republic of China (PRC) is established, with **Zhou Enlai** its leader.

January 1950 Former State Department employee Alger Hiss is convicted of perjury but not of spy charges.

February 3, 1950 Klaus Fuchs is convicted of passing U.S. atomic secrets to the Soviets.

February 9, 1950 U.S. senator **Joseph R. McCarthy** of Wisconsin publicly claims in a speech in Wheeling, West Virginia, to have a list of communists working in the U.S. government.

March 1, 1950 Chiang Kai-shek, former leader of nationalist China, which was defeated by communist forces, establishes the Republic of China (ROC) on the island of Taiwan.

April 7, 1950 U.S. security analyst Paul Nitze issues the secret National Security Council report 68 (NSC-68), calling

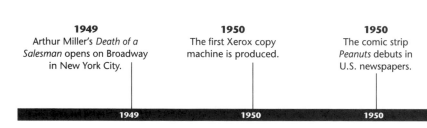

1949
Arthur Miller's *Death of a Salesman* opens on Broadway in New York City.

1950
The first Xerox copy machine is produced.

1950
The comic strip *Peanuts* debuts in U.S. newspapers.

1949   1950   1950

for a dramatic buildup of U.S. military forces to combat the Soviet threat.

June 25, 1950 North Korean communist leader **Kim Il Sung** launches his armed forces against South Korea in an attempt to reunify Korea under his leadership, leading to the three-year Korean War.

October 24, 1950 U.S. forces push the North Korean army back to the border with China, sparking a Chinese invasion one week later and forcing the United States into a hasty retreat.

April 11, 1951 U.S. president Harry S. Truman fires General **Douglas MacArthur**, the U.S. military commander in Korea, for publicly attacking the president's war strategy.

April 19, 1951 General Douglas MacArthur delivers his farewell address to a joint session of Congress.

June 21, 1951 The Korean War reaches a military stalemate at the original boundary between North and South Korea.

September 1, 1951 The United States, Australia, and New Zealand sign the ANZUS treaty, creating a military alliance to contain communism in the Southwest Pacific region.

October 25, 1951 Winston Churchill wins reelection as British prime minister over Clement R. Attlee.

October 3, 1952 Great Britain conducts its first atomic weapons test.

November 1, 1952 The United States tests the hydrogen bomb on the Marshall Islands in the Pacific Ocean.

1950
The Korean War begins.

1951
I Love Lucy debuts
on CBS-TV.

1952
NBC-TV's *The Today
Show* debuts.

1950   1951   1952

November 4, 1952 Former military general **Dwight D. Eisenhower** is elected U.S. president.

March 5, 1953 After leading the Soviet Union for thirty years, Joseph Stalin dies of a stroke; Georgy Malenkov becomes the new Soviet leader.

June 27, 1953 An armistice is signed, bringing a cease-fire to the Korean War.

August 12, 1953 The Soviet Union announces its first hydrogen bomb test.

May 7, 1954 The communist Viet Minh forces of **Ho Chi Minh** capture French forces at Dien Bien Phu, leading to a partition of Vietnam and independence for North Vietnam under Ho's leadership.

June 29, 1954 Nuclear physicist J. Robert Oppenheimer's security clearance is not renewed due to his opposition of the development of the hydrogen bomb; his stance leads anticommunists to question his loyalty to the United States.

September 8, 1954 The Southeast Asia Treaty Organization (SEATO) is formed.

December 2, 1954 The U.S. Senate votes to censure U.S. senator Joseph R. McCarthy of Wisconsin after his communist accusations proved to be unfounded.

January 12, 1955 U.S. secretary of state **John Foster Dulles** announces the "New Look" policy, promoting massive nuclear retaliation for any hostile actions.

February 8, 1955 Nikolai Bulganin replaces Georgy Malenkov as Soviet premier.

May 14, 1955 The Warsaw Pact, a military alliance of Soviet-controlled Eastern European nations, is established;

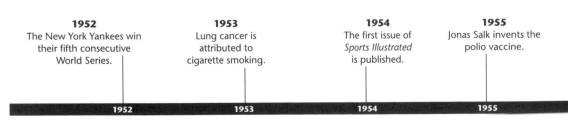

1952
The New York Yankees win their fifth consecutive World Series.

1953
Lung cancer is attributed to cigarette smoking.

1954
The first issue of *Sports Illustrated* is published.

1955
Jonas Salk invents the polio vaccine.

1952   1953   1954   1955

the countries include Albania, Bulgaria, Czechoslovakia, East Germany, Hungary, Poland, and Romania.

November 22, 1955 Under the guidance of nuclear physicist **Andrey Sakharov**, the Soviets detonate their first true hydrogen bomb at the Semipalatinsk Test Site; Sakharov would be awarded several of the Soviet Union's highest honors.

February 24, 1956 Soviet leader **Nikita Khrushchev** gives his "Secret Speech," attacking the past brutal policies of the late Soviet leader Joseph Stalin.

October 31, 1956 British, French, and Israeli forces attack Egypt to regain control of the Suez Canal.

November 1, 1956 In Hungary, the Soviets crush an uprising against strict communist rule, killing many protestors.

January 10, 1957 **Harold Macmillan** becomes the new British prime minister.

February 1957 Soviet leader Nikita Khrushchev appoints **Andrey Gromyko** foreign minister, replacing Vyacheslav Molotov; Gromyko will hold the position for the next twenty-eight years.

March 7, 1957 The Eisenhower Doctrine, offering U.S. assistance to Middle East countries facing communist expansion threats, is approved by Congress.

October 5, 1957 Shocking the world with their new technology, the Soviets launch into space *Sputnik,* the first man-made satellite.

1958 FBI director J. Edgar Hoover (1895–1972) writes *Masters of Deceit,* a book that educates the public about the threat of communism within the United States.

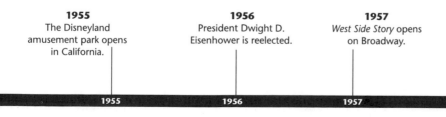

1955
The Disneyland amusement park opens in California.

1956
President Dwight D. Eisenhower is reelected.

1957
West Side Story opens on Broadway.

1955   1956   1957

March 27, 1958 Nikita Khrushchev replaces Nikolai Bulganin as Soviet premier while remaining head of the Soviet Communist Party.

November 10, 1958 Soviet leader Nikita Khrushchev issues an ultimatum to the West to pull out of Berlin, but later backs down.

January 2, 1959 Revolutionary **Fidel Castro** assumes leadership of the Cuban government after toppling pro-U.S. dictator Fulgencio Batista y Zaldivar.

September 17, 1959 Soviet leader Nikita Khrushchev arrives in the United States to tour the country and meet with U.S. president Dwight D. Eisenhower.

May 1, 1960 The Soviets shoot down a U.S. spy plane over Russia piloted by Francis Gary Powers, leading to the cancellation of a planned summit meeting in Paris between Soviet leader Nikita Khrushchev and U.S. president Dwight D. Eisenhower.

November 8, 1960 U.S. senator **John F. Kennedy** of Massachusetts defeats Vice President **Richard M. Nixon** in the presidential election.

January 1961 Robert S. McNamara becomes secretary of defense in the new Kennedy administration, a position he would hold until 1968 throughout the critical years of the Vietnam War.

March 1, 1961 U.S. president John F. Kennedy establishes the Peace Corps.

April 15, 1961 A U.S.-supported army of Cuban exiles launches an ill-fated invasion of Cuba, leading to U.S. humiliation in the world.

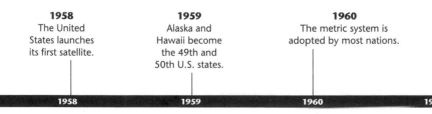

1958
The United States launches its first satellite.

1959
Alaska and Hawaii become the 49th and 50th U.S. states.

1960
The metric system is adopted by most nations.

| 1958 | 1959 | 1960 | 1961 |

June 3, 1961 U.S. president John F. Kennedy meets with Soviet leader Nikita Khrushchev at a Vienna summit meeting to discuss the arms race and Berlin; Kennedy comes away shaken by Khrushchev's belligerence.

August 15, 1961 Under orders from Soviet leader Nikita Khrushchev, the Berlin Wall is constructed, stopping the flight of refugees from East Germany to West Berlin.

October 1962 The Cuban Missile Crisis occurs as the United States demands the Soviets remove nuclear missiles from Cuba.

1963 Longtime U.S. diplomat W. Averell Harriman heads the U.S. team for negotiating with the Soviet Union the Limited Test Ban treaty, which bans above-ground testing of nuclear weapons.

January 1, 1963 Chinese communist leaders Mao Zedong and Zhou Enlai denounce Soviet leader Nikita Khrushchev's policies of peaceful coexistence with the West; the Soviets respond by denouncing the Chinese Communist Party.

August 5, 1963 The first arms control agreement, the Limited Test Ban Treaty, banning above-ground nuclear testing, is reached between the United States, Soviet Union, and Great Britain.

November 22, 1963 U.S. president John F. Kennedy is assassinated in Dallas, Texas, leaving Vice President **Lyndon B. Johnson** as the new U.S. president.

August 7, 1964 U.S. Congress passes the Gulf of Tonkin Resolution, authorizing U.S. president Lyndon B. Johnson to conduct whatever military operations he thinks appropriate in Southeast Asia.

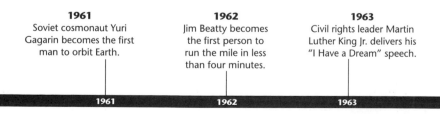

1961
Soviet cosmonaut Yuri Gagarin becomes the first man to orbit Earth.

1962
Jim Beatty becomes the first person to run the mile in less than four minutes.

1963
Civil rights leader Martin Luther King Jr. delivers his "I Have a Dream" speech.

1961   1962   1963

October 15, 1964 Soviet leader Nikita Khrushchev is removed from Soviet leadership and replaced by **Leonid Brezhnev** as leader of the Soviet Communist Party and **Aleksey Kosygin** as Soviet premier.

October 16, 1964 China conducts its first nuclear weapons test.

November 3, 1964 Lyndon B. Johnson is elected U.S. president.

March 8, 1965 U.S. president Lyndon B. Johnson sends the first U.S. ground combat units to South Vietnam.

June 23, 1967 U.S. president Lyndon B. Johnson and Soviet premier Aleksey Kosygin meet in Glassboro, New Jersey, to discuss a peace settlement to the Vietnam War.

January 23, 1968 Forces under the orders of North Korean communist leader Kim Il Sung capture a U.S. spy ship, the USS *Pueblo,* off the coast of North Korea and hold the crew captive for eleven months.

January 31, 1968 Communist forces inspired by the leadership of the ailing Ho Chi Minh launch the massive Tet Offensive against the U.S. and South Vietnamese armies, marking a turning point as American public opinion shifts in opposition to the Vietnam War.

July 15, 1968 Soviet leader Leonid Brezhnev announces the Brezhnev Doctrine, which allows for the use of force where necessary to ensure the maintenance of communist governments in Eastern European nations.

August 20, 1968 The Warsaw Pact forces a crackdown on a Czechoslovakia reform movement known as the "Prague Spring."

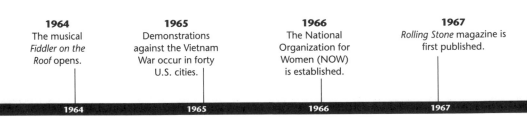

1964
The musical
Fiddler on the Roof opens.

1965
Demonstrations against the Vietnam War occur in forty U.S. cities.

1966
The National Organization for Women (NOW) is established.

1967
Rolling Stone magazine is first published.

1964   1965   1966   1967

August 27, 1968 Antiwar riots rage in Chicago's streets outside the Democratic National Convention.

November 5, 1968 Richard M. Nixon defeats Vice President Hubert Humphrey in the U.S. presidential election.

March 18, 1969 The United States begins secret bombing of Cambodia to destroy North Vietnamese supply lines.

July 20, 1969 The United States lands the first men on the moon.

October 15, 1969 Former West Berlin mayor Willy Brandt is elected chancellor of West Germany.

April 16, 1970 Strategic arms limitation talks, SALT, begin.

April 30, 1970 U.S. president Richard M. Nixon announces an invasion by U.S. forces of Cambodia to destroy North Vietnamese supply camps.

May 4, 1970 Four students are killed at Kent State University as Ohio National Guardsmen open fire on antiwar demonstrators.

November 3, 1970 Salvador Allende becomes president of Chile.

October 20, 1971 West German chancellor Willy Brandt is awarded the Nobel Peace Prize for seeking greater political and military stability in Europe.

October 25, 1971 The People's Republic of China (PRC) is admitted to the United Nations as the Republic of China (ROC) is expelled.

February 20, 1972 U.S. president Richard M. Nixon makes an historic trip to the People's Republic of China to discuss renewing relations between the two countries.

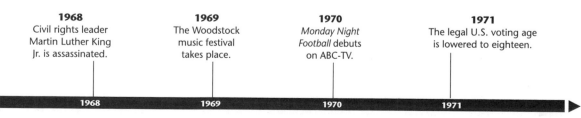

1968
Civil rights leader Martin Luther King Jr. is assassinated.

1969
The Woodstock music festival takes place.

1970
Monday Night Football debuts on ABC-TV.

1971
The legal U.S. voting age is lowered to eighteen.

1968   1969   1970   1971

May 26, 1972 U.S. president Richard M. Nixon travels to Moscow to meet with Soviet leader Leonid Brezhnev to reach an agreement on the strategic arms limitation treaty, SALT I.

January 27, 1973 After intensive bombing of North Vietnamese cities the previous month, the United States and North Vietnam sign a peace treaty, ending U.S. involvement in Vietnam.

June 27, 1973 Soviet leader Leonid Brezhnev journeys to Washington, D.C., to meet with U.S. president Richard M. Nixon to pursue détente.

August 22, 1973 U.S. national security advisor **Henry Kissinger** is nominated by U.S. president Richard M. Nixon to also serve as secretary of state.

September 11, 1973 Chilean president Salvador Allende is ousted in a coup and is replaced by pro-U.S. dictator Augusto Pinochet Ugarte.

May 16, 1974 Helmut Schmidt becomes the new West German chancellor.

June 27, 1974 U.S. president Richard M. Nixon travels to Moscow for another summit conference with Soviet leader Leonid Brezhnev.

August 9, 1974 Under threats of impeachment due to a political scandal, U.S. president Richard M. Nixon resigns as U.S. president and is replaced by Vice President Gerald R. Ford.

September 4, 1974 George Bush is sent as an envoy to the People's Republic of China.

1972
The Watergate scandal begins.

1973
U.S. troops pull out of Vietnam.

1974
Hank Aaron passes Babe Ruth as baseball's all-time home run hitter.

1972   1973   1974

November 23, 1974 U.S. president Gerald R. Ford and Soviet leader Leonid Brezhnev meet in the Soviet city of Vladivostok.

1975 Nuclear physicist Andrey Sakharov receives the Nobel Peace Prize for his brave opposition to the nuclear arms race in the Soviet Union.

April 30, 1975 In renewed fighting, North Vietnam captures South Vietnam and reunites the country.

August 1, 1975 Numerous nations sign the Helsinki Accords at the end of the Conference on Security and Cooperation in Europe.

January 27, 1976 George Bush is confirmed by the U.S. Senate as the director of the Central Intelligence Agency (CIA).

September 9, 1976 Mao Zedong dies and Hua Guofeng becomes the new leader of the People's Republic of China.

November 2, 1976 Former Georgia governor **Jimmy Carter** defeats incumbent U.S. president Gerald R. Ford in the presidential election.

December 16, 1976 U.S. president-elect Jimmy Carter names Zbigniew Brzezinski as the new national security advisor.

June 16, 1977 Soviet leader Leonid Brezhnev is elected president of the Soviet Union in addition to leader of the Soviet Communist Party.

December 25, 1977 Israeli prime minister Menachim Begin and Egyptian president Anwar Sadat begin peace negotiations in Egypt.

February 24, 1978 Deng Xiaoping is elected head of the Chinese Communist Party.

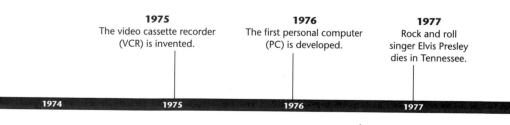

1975
The video cassette recorder (VCR) is invented.

1976
The first personal computer (PC) is developed.

1977
Rock and roll singer Elvis Presley dies in Tennessee.

1974   1975   1976   1977

September 17, 1978 Israeli prime minister Menachim Begin and Egyptian president Anwar Sadat, meeting with U.S. president Jimmy Carter at Camp David, reach an historic peace settlement between Israel and Egypt.

January 1, 1979 The United States and the People's Republic of China (PRC) establish diplomatic relations.

January 16, 1979 The shah of Iran is overthrown as the leader of Iran and is replaced by Islamic leader Ayatollah Ruhollah Khomeini.

May 4, 1979 Margaret Thatcher becomes the new British prime minister.

June 18, 1979 U.S. president Jimmy Carter and Soviet leader Leonid Brezhnev sign the SALT II strategic arms limitation agreement in Vienna, Austria.

July 19, 1979 Sandinista rebels seize power in Nicaragua with Daniel Ortega becoming the new leader.

November 4, 1979 Islamic militants seize the U.S. embassy in Tehran, Iran, taking U.S. staff hostage.

December 26, 1979 Soviet forces invade Afghanistan to prop up an unpopular pro-Soviet government, leading to a decade of bloody fighting.

January 1980 Nuclear physicist Andrey Sakharov is seized by the secret police, sentenced, and sent into exile to the closed city of Gorky for the next six years.

April 24, 1980 An attempted military rescue of American hostages in Iran ends with eight U.S. soldiers dead.

August 14, 1980 The Solidarity labor union protests the prices of goods in Poland.

November 4, 1980 Former California governor Ronald Reagan is elected president of the United States.

1978
Pope John Paul II begins reign as the leader of the Catholic Church.

1979
The Three Mile Island nuclear reactor accident occurs in Pennsylvania.

1980
Former Beatle John Lennon is murdered.

1978   1979   1980

January 20, 1981 Iran releases the U.S. hostages as Ronald Reagan is being sworn in as the new U.S. president.

January 29, 1981 U.S. president Ronald Reagan appoints **Jeane Kirkpatrick** as U.S. representative to the United Nations where she acts a key architect of Reagan's strong anticommunist position early in his presidency.

October 1, 1982 Helmut Kohl is elected West German chancellor.

November 12, 1982 Yuri Andropov becomes the new Soviet leader after the death of Leonid Brezhnev two days earlier.

March 8, 1983 U.S. president Ronald Reagan calls the Soviet Union the "Evil Empire."

March 23, 1983 U.S. president Ronald Reagan announces the Strategic Defense Initiative (SDI).

September 1, 1983 A Soviet fighter shoots down Korean Airlines Flight 007 as it strays off-course over Soviet restricted airspace.

October 25, 1983 U.S. forces invade Grenada to end fighting between two pro-communist factions.

February 13, 1984 Konstantin Chernenko becomes the new Soviet leader after the death of Yuri Andropov four days earlier.

May 2, 1984 Nuclear physicist Andrey Sakharov begins a hunger strike.

February 1985 The United States issues the Reagan Doctrine, which offers assistance to military dictatorships in defense against communist expansion.

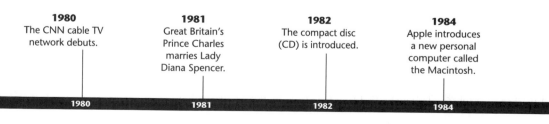

1980
The CNN cable TV network debuts.

1981
Great Britain's Prince Charles marries Lady Diana Spencer.

1982
The compact disc (CD) is introduced.

1984
Apple introduces a new personal computer called the Macintosh.

1980   1981   1982   1984

March 11, 1985 Mikhail Gorbachev becomes the new Soviet leader after the death of Konstantin Chernenko the previous day.

July 2, 1985 Eduard Shevardnadze is named the new foreign minister by Soviet leader Mikhail Gorbachev, replacing Andrey Gromyko.

October 11–12, 1986 Soviet leader Mikhail Gorbachev and U.S. president Ronald Reagan meet in Reykjavik, Iceland, and agree to seek the elimination of nuclear weapons.

October 17, 1986 Congress approves aid to Contra rebels in Nicaragua.

November 3, 1986 The Iran-Contra affair is uncovered.

June 11, 1987 Margaret Thatcher wins an unprecedented third term as British prime minister.

December 8–10, 1987 U.S. president Ronald Reagan and Soviet leader Mikhail Gorbachev meet in Washington to sign the Intermediate Nuclear Forces Treaty (INF), removing thousands of missiles from Europe.

February 8, 1988 Soviet leader Mikhail Gorbachev announces the decision to begin withdrawing Soviet forces from Afghanistan.

May 29, 1988 U.S. president Ronald Reagan journeys to Moscow for a summit meeting with Soviet leader Mikhail Gorbachev.

November 8, 1988 U.S. vice president George Bush is elected president of the United States.

January 11, 1989 The Hungarian parliament adopts reforms granting greater personal freedoms to Hungarians, including allowing political parties and organizations.

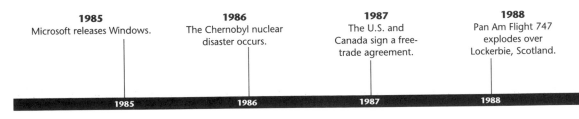

1985
Microsoft releases Windows.

1986
The Chernobyl nuclear disaster occurs.

1987
The U.S. and Canada sign a free-trade agreement.

1988
Pan Am Flight 747 explodes over Lockerbie, Scotland.

1985   1986   1987   1988

January 18, 1989 The labor union Solidarity gains formal acceptance in Poland.

March 26, 1989 Open elections are held for the new Soviet Congress of People's Deputies, with the communists suffering major defeats; Boris Yeltsin wins the Moscow seat.

May 11, 1989 Soviet leader Mikhail Gorbachev announces major reductions of nuclear forces in Eastern Europe.

June 3–4, 1989 Chinese communist leaders order a military crackdown on pro-democracy demonstrations in Tiananmen Square, leading to many deaths.

June 4, 1989 The first Polish free elections lead to major victory by Solidarity.

October 7, 1989 The Hungarian communist party disbands.

October 23, 1989 Massive demonstrations begin against the East German communist government, involving hundreds of thousands of protesters and leading to the resignation of the East German leadership in early November.

November 10, 1989 East Germany begins dismantling the Berlin Wall; Bulgarian communist leadership resigns.

November 24, 1989 Czechoslovakia communist leaders resign.

December 1, 1989 Soviet leader Mikhail Gorbachev and U.S. president George Bush, assisted by **Condoleezza Rice** of the National Security Council, begin a three-day meeting on a ship in a Malta harbor to discuss rapid changes in Eastern Europe and the Soviet Union.

December 20, 1989 Lithuania votes for independence from the Soviet Union.

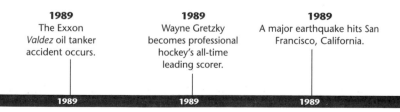

1989	1989	1989
The Exxon *Valdez* oil tanker accident occurs.	Wayne Gretzky becomes professional hockey's all-time leading scorer.	A major earthquake hits San Francisco, California.

1989   1989   1989

December 22, 1989 Romanian communist leader Nicolae Ceausescu is toppled and executed three days later.

March 1990 Lithuania declares independence from Moscow.

March 14, 1990 Mikhail Gorbachev is elected president of the Soviet Union.

March 18, 1990 Open East German elections lead to a major defeat of Communist Party candidates.

May 29, 1990 Boris Yeltsin is elected president of the Russian republic.

May 30, 1990 Soviet leader Mikhail Gorbachev begins a summit meeting with U.S. president George Bush in Washington, D.C.

June 1990 Russia declares independence as the Russian Federation.

October 15, 1990 Soviet leader Mikhail Gorbachev is awarded the Nobel Peace Prize for his reforms that ended the Cold War.

November 14, 1990 Various nations sign the Charter of Paris for a New Europe, ending the economic and military division of Europe created by the Cold War.

July 1, 1991 The Warsaw Pact disbands.

August 19, 1991 Soviet communist hardliners attempt an unsuccessful coup of Soviet leader Mikhail Gorbachev, leading to the banning of the Communist Party in Russia and other Soviet republics.

August 20–September 9, 1991 The various Soviet republics declare their independence from the Soviet Union, including Estonia, Latvia, Lithuania, Ukraine, Belorussia, Moldovia, Azerbaijan, Uzbekistan, Kirgizia, and Tadzhikistan.

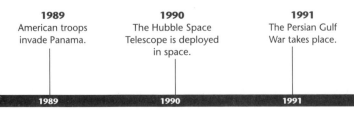

1989
American troops invade Panama.

1990
The Hubble Space Telescope is deployed in space.

1991
The Persian Gulf War takes place.

1989   1990   1991

October 3, 1991 East and West Germany reunite as one nation.

December 8, 1991 Russia, Ukraine, and Belorussia create the Commonwealth of Independent States organization as an alliance replacing the Soviet Union.

December 25, 1991 Mikhail Gorbachev resigns as the Soviet president, and the Soviet Union ceases to exist.

January 28, 1992 In his State of the Union Address, U.S. president George Bush declares victory in the Cold War.

1991
Clarence Thomas
becomes a U.S.
Supreme Court justice.

1992
Hurricane Andrew
causes $15 billion
in damage
in Florida.

1991   1992

Cold War
Biographies

George F. Kennan

Born February 16, 1904
Milwaukee, Wisconsin

U.S. diplomat, historian, and author

George F. Kennan is considered one of the greatest diplomats and statesmen of the United States. Kennan played a major role in formulating U.S. foreign policy, especially on the issue of Soviet-U.S. relations during the early stages of the Cold War. The Cold War was an intense political and economic rivalry between the United States and the Soviet Union that lasted from 1945 to 1991. After World War II (1939–45), Kennan was the person who first suggested the policy of containment to control Soviet expansion. Kennan continued to have an important impact on foreign policy into the 1980s. His ideas frequently spurred considerable public debate. A historian, he authored many books of exceptional scholarly standards.

> "Russia, Russia—unwashed, backward appealing Russia, so ashamed of your own backwardness, so orientally determined to conceal it from us by clever deceit."

Princeton grad

George Frost Kennan was born into an affluent family on the east side of Milwaukee, Wisconsin. His father was a prosperous lawyer of Scotch-Irish descent, and his mother's heritage was German. George's mother died shortly after his birth, and his relationship with his father was not close.

George F. Kennan.
Reproduced by permission of the Corbis Corporation.

George, a quiet and bookish child, was enrolled in St. John's Military Academy in 1916 at the age of twelve; he graduated in 1921. He entered Princeton University that same year and chose to major in history, specializing in modern European diplomacy and international relations. He graduated in 1925 with a bachelor of arts degree.

Foreign service

Young Kennan had been a mediocre student at Princeton, but in 1926 he managed to score high marks on the newly instituted exams for entrance into the Foreign Service diplomatic corps, which was part of the U.S. State Department. Thrilled at being selected by the Foreign Service, Kennan drew his first posting in Geneva, Switzerland. This posting began a career that would span decades of American diplomacy. Between 1927 and 1953, and again from 1961 to 1963, Kennan served in many European nations. By the fall of 1927, he was off to Hamburg, Germany; next, he went to Tallinn, Estonia; and in early 1929, he left for Riga, Latvia. At the time, the United States had no official foreign ministry in the Soviet Union, but the proximity of Latvia to Russia allowed the United States to be involved with diplomatic efforts with the Soviet Union.

Kennan already had a special interest in Russia through his grandfather's cousin, also named George Kennan (1845–1924). The earlier George Kennan first experienced the Russian culture in 1865 as a member of the Russian-American Telegraph Expedition, which was sponsored by Western Union, an American communication company. The goal of the expedition was to establish telegraph service between the United States and Russia. This cousin made numerous visits to Russia through 1901 and wrote about his experiences. He became the foremost American expert on Russian life before the Russian Revolution of 1917. To honor this man, the later George Kennan helped establish the Kennan Institute for Advanced Russian Studies in 1974. The institute is located in the Woodrow Wilson International Center for Scholars in Washington, D.C.

Hoping for a future assignment in the Soviet Union, young George Kennan seized the opportunity to learn the Russian language at Berlin Seminary for Oriental Languages in Germany. He received his diploma in 1930. In Berlin, he met and married Annelise Sorenson, and they returned to Riga in 1931.

To Moscow

President Franklin D. Roosevelt (1882–1945; served 1933–45) decided shortly after taking office that the United States needed to formally recognize the government of the Soviet Union; he soon announced that a U.S. embassy would be established in Moscow. The United States had gone sixteen years with no representation in the Soviet Union because the United States had refused to extend diplomatic relations to the new Soviet government following the communist takeover in 1918. Roosevelt appointed William C. Bullitt (1891–1967) as America's first ambassador to Moscow, and Bullitt chose Kennan to serve on the embassy staff.

Kennan's three-year stay in Moscow allowed him to assess the character of Soviet leader **Joseph Stalin** (1879–1953; see entry) and observe the terror tactics Stalin used against the Soviet people. Kennan expanded his knowledge of Russian language, history, and culture, all of which helped him communicate with and understand Soviet leadership. In an interview in 1996 for the CNN "Cold War" series, Kennan described the Stalin he witnessed in the 1930s as a man with several faces: "Stalin was an excellent actor, and when he did meet with leading people at these various conferences, he was magnificent: quiet, affable, reasonable. He sent them all away thinking, 'This really is a great leader.' And yes, but behind that there lay something entirely different." Kennan related that when Stalin was displeased with the actions of his assistants, "he turned on them and then the yellow eyes lit up— you suddenly realized what sort of animal you had by the tail there." Kennan realized that Stalin was doing away with, or purging, many of his own people in government positions. Describing a 1937 Soviet purge trial that he attended, Kennan related, "I could see [purge trial defendants] there, and their pale faces, their twitching lips, their evasive eyes. These were the faces of men who had been, if not tortured, then terrified in many ways, and often by threats to take it out on their families if they didn't confess."

Because he had an up-close understanding of the Stalin regime, Kennan urged President Roosevelt's administration to be tough and firm with the Soviet leader. He was dismayed when Ambassador Bullitt was replaced in 1937 by Joseph Davies (1876–1958), who had been instructed to develop goodwill with Stalin. U.S. leaders thought this was the safest strategy in case they needed Soviet support in future alliances. (As it turned out, the Soviet Union did join the United States and the rest of the Allies in fighting Germany during World War II.) Unwilling to support this strategy, Kennan resigned and was sent to a post in Prague, Czechoslovakia. In the 1996 CNN interview, Kennan remarked, "I don't think FDR [President Roosevelt] was capable of conceiving of a man of such profound iniquity [wickedness], coupled with enormous strategic cleverness, as Stalin. He [Roosevelt] had never met such a creature."

World War II

In 1939, World War II began in Europe. Kennan was transferred to the U.S. wartime embassy in Berlin, the capital of Germany. The United States did not enter the war until December 1941; at that point, Germany and the United States formally became enemies. Kennan briefly found himself a detainee and was unable to leave Germany until May 1942. After a short posting to Lisbon, Portugal, in 1943, Kennan joined the European Advisory Commission in London; this group was in charge of creating a plan to deal with postwar Germany. In 1944, Kennan was reassigned to Moscow as an aide to Ambassador **W. Averell Harriman** (1891–1986; see entry). Kennan urged the United States not to form too close an alliance with the Soviet Union. He was dismayed as he watched the United States make concession after concession to the Soviet government for wartime reasons. Kennan fretted that his country was entirely too eager to please Stalin.

After the war, when the Soviets occupied Eastern European countries with the apparent intention of staying there indefinitely, Kennan pushed for the United States to cut off all economic aid to the Soviets to force them to withdraw. Almost no other U.S. official agreed with Kennan—but then none of them understood Stalin as Kennan did.

The "Long Telegram"

In February 1946, Stalin made a speech the night before elections of the Supreme Soviet, the Soviet legislative body. The speech denounced capitalism, the economic system of the United States and Western Europe. Capitalism is based on private ownership of property. Prices—and individual profits—are determined by competition in a free market, with relatively little government intervention. In contrast, the Soviets had a communist economy and government. Private ownership of property was not allowed. Instead the government controlled all economic production, ensuring that goods and profits would be divided equally among all Soviet citizens. Stalin's pronouncements strongly suggested that a war between communist and capitalist countries was inevitable.

Confused American officials turned to their embassy in Moscow, hoping someone there could explain what the Soviets were thinking. The task fell to Kennan. He sent his response, an eight-thousand-word telegram, to Washington, D.C., on February 22, 1946. In the now famous "Long Telegram," Kennan took U.S. leaders back to step one in understanding the Soviets. He spoke of Moscow's traditional "neurotic view of world affairs" and "instinctive Russian sense of insecurity." He asserted that Stalin intended to occupy countries surrounding the Russian homeland to provide a security buffer between Russia and its traditional enemies, the capitalist Western European nations. Then, according to Kennan, the Soviet communists hoped to overthrow those Western European nations. This would eventually leave the United States politically and economically isolated.

In the telegram, Kennan went on to state that for the Soviet Union it was "desirable and necessary that the internal harmony of our [U.S.] society be disrupted, our traditional way of life be destroyed, the international authority of our state be broken." This, Keegan said, was the only way the Soviet Union would ever feel secure. Kennan noted that the Soviet Union was in a weakened state, but he also remarked that the resolve and strength of the Western world would determine the fate of capitalism. Kennan stressed that the United States must abandon any isolationist attitudes (policies of avoiding official agreements with other nations in order to remain neutral) and take a strong, active position on the international political stage.

The telegram was quickly circulated throughout the State Department and all the important political circles of Washington, D.C. The press caught hold of it, and the telegram was widely distributed. Although it was both criticized and praised, the message was clearly one that rang true to government officials, U.S. foreign policy makers, and everyday Americans. Lost amid urgent discussions of the telegram was at least one important point: Kennan's position on atomic weapons. In the telegram, he urged President **Harry S. Truman** (1884–1972; served 1945–53; see entry) not to relentlessly pursue development of such weapons, because, as Kennan saw it, atomic bomb development was a dangerous and unnecessary path to take.

The Long Telegram became a cornerstone of President Truman's foreign policy; the U.S. position regarding the Soviet Union immediately became much tougher. Introducing the Truman Doctrine, the president promised U.S. aid to all countries that were engaged in resisting communist influence or invasion. This announcement created more animosity between the United States and the Soviet Union. Though it was never declared or officially launched, the Cold War had begun.

Containment policy

In the fall of 1946, Kennan accepted a lecturer's position at the Naval War College, but in the spring of 1947, Secretary of State **George C. Marshall** (1880–1959; see entry) made Kennan director of the new Policy Planning Staff (PPS), a group whose chief focus was U.S. diplomacy. In the July 1947 issue of *Foreign Affairs* an article titled "The Sources of Soviet Conduct" appeared; it was written by "X." "X" was Kennan; he did not want to reveal his identity, because he was part of the State Department and what he had written did not conform with U.S foreign policy on the Soviet Union. At the time, officially, the U.S. policy was not anti-Soviet. Nevertheless, Kennan's article expanded on ideas in the "Long Telegram" and developed the idea of "containing" Soviet expansion. The policy of containment involved drawing geographic lines to establish a boundary beyond which Soviet influence would not be tolerated but rather confronted.

Containment misunderstood

Kennan soon realized that his containment ideas had been misunderstood by U.S. government officials and military leaders. As he later explained in a PBS interview with David Gergen, editor-at-large for the magazine *U.S. News and World Report,* it was Kennan's fault that containment was misunderstood. "It all came down to one sentence in the 'X' article where I said that wherever these people, meaning the Soviet leadership, confronted us with dangerous hostility anywhere in the world, we should do everything possible to contain it and not let them expand any further. I should have explained that I didn't suspect them of any desire to launch an attack on us. This was right after the war, and it was absurd to suppose that they were going to turn around and attack the United States. I didn't think I needed to explain that, but I obviously should have done it." In the interview, Kennan stressed that he had meant *political* containment, not military containment. He knew the Soviets would use political subversion to try to shift other countries to communism, but he never thought they would use military action. Stalin and his communist loyalists were a crafty and dangerous group, but they did not have the military strength after World War II to fight new wars.

Kennan believed that the United States could contain the Soviets with tough diplomacy. He knew that Stalin tended to back down when confronted with firm warnings. However, Kennan also predicted that a major U.S. atomic weapons development program and weapons buildup would cause extreme insecurity in the Soviet Union and probably lead to an arms race. Historians look back at Kennan's 1947 assessments and note that events proceeded much as Kennan warned: Because the United States continued to pursue atomic weapons, the Soviets felt they had to do the same. Because the United States maintained a military force in Japan, the Soviets wanted a communist presence in Korea. As the Cold War continued, this competition and military maneuvering overshadowed Kennan's original idea of containment.

Ambassador to the Soviet Union

Kennan left the Policy Planning Staff in June 1950, and that fall he moved to Princeton, New Jersey, to join the Institute for Advanced Study (IAS). **J. Robert Oppenheimer** (1904–1967; see entry), the U.S. atomic physicist who successfully coordinated the development of the U.S. atomic bomb,

U.S. ambassador to Yugoslavia George Kennan (left) meets with Yugoslav leader Josip Broz Tito in May 1961. *Reproduced by permission of AP/Wide World Photos.*

headed this new research organization. By this time, Oppenheimer had come to believe that atomic energy should only be used for peaceful purposes.

In December 1951, not long after Kennan joined the IAS, Secretary of State **Dean G. Acheson** (1893–1971; see entry) appointed him as ambassador to the Soviet Union. He took this position at a time when anticommunist hysteria consumed the United States, and in the Soviet Union, an aging Stalin became ever more paranoid. Kennan was restricted to the Moscow area. He protested to Soviet officials, and he criticized the internal politics of Stalin. By October 1952, Kennan was forced to leave Moscow.

Writer, lecturer, commentator

Kennan retired from government service at the end of 1952 and returned to the IAS, which would remain his home

The Writings of George Kennan

George Frost Kennan was a prolific writer on U.S. history. Two of his books received the Pulitzer Prize:

Soviet-American Relations, 1917–1920. Vol. 1. *Russia Leaves the War.* Princeton, NJ: Princeton University Press, 1956.

Memoirs, 1925–1950. Boston: Little, Brown, 1968.

Some of Kennan's other articles and books include the following:

"Sources of Soviet Conduct." *Foreign Affairs* 25 (July 1947): 566–82 (written under the name "X").

American Diplomacy, 1900–1950. Chicago: University of Chicago Press, 1951.

Soviet-American Relations, 1917–1920. Vol. 2. *The Decision to Intervene.* Princeton, NJ: Princeton University Press, 1958.

Russia and the West under Lenin and Stalin. Boston: Little, Brown, 1961.

Memoirs, 1950–1963. New York: Pantheon, 1973.

The Nuclear Delusion: Soviet-American Relations in the Atomic Age. New York: Pantheon, 1984.

Sketches from a Life. New York: Pantheon, 1989.

At a Century's Ending: Reflections, 1982–1995. New York: W. W. Norton, 1996.

base for decades to come. He was made the Permanent Professor in the School of Historical Studies. There, he found a supportive environment and resources in which to write and develop lectures and commentary on global issues. He opposed the nuclear arms buildup during the administration of President **Dwight D. Eisenhower** (1890–1969; served 1953–61; see entry). Kennan advocated mutual disengagement of U.S. and Soviet forces in Europe and the abolishment of nuclear weapons by both powers. Throughout the second half of the twentieth century, he staunchly criticized nuclear weapons stockpiling as immoral and counterproductive to diplomacy.

Kennan returned to government one last time in 1961. When **John F. Kennedy** (1917–1963; served 1961–63; see entry) became president in January 1961, he appointed Kennan as ambassador to Yugoslavia. There, Kennan developed a political relationship with Yugoslav leader **Josip Broz Tito** (1892–1980; see entry), a communist who had successfully broken away from Soviet domination. Disregarding Tito's relatively independent communist position, the U.S. Congress passed legislation denying Yugoslavia most-favored-nation trade status. (Most-favored-nation trade status lowers taxes on goods exported to the United States, making it much easier for a foreign country to sell goods to American consumers and U.S. businesses.) In disgust, Kennan resigned in 1963 and returned to the IAS. He also spent time at his Pennsylvania farm. He concentrated on traveling and writing numerous books and articles.

Throughout the 1960s, Kennan was an outspoken opponent of America's involvement in Vietnam. He argued that participating in the Vietnam War (1954–75) was causing a greater rift between the United States, the Soviet Union, and communist China and that European diplomacy was being ignored. However, when Soviet communist forces suppressed a political reform movement in communist Czechoslovakia in 1968, he favored sending additional U.S. troops to West Germany, so that soldiers would be as near the Soviet communist forces in Eastern Europe as possible to perturb and distract the Soviets. Some officials charged Kennan with focusing on Europe to the exclusion of the rest of the world.

Between 1965 and 1969, Kennan served as a university fellow at Harvard. During the 1970s and 1980s, he continued to lecture and write, always emphasizing U.S.-Soviet relations. From 1974 to 1975, Kennan was a fellow of the Woodrow Wilson Center in Washington, D.C. Also in 1974, he became a professor emeritus at the IAS. In 1981, he was awarded the Albert Einstein Peace Prize of $50,000 for his work in U.S.-Soviet relations.

In the 1980s, Kennan strongly criticized the policies of President **Ronald Reagan** (1911–; served 1981–89; see entry) toward the Soviet Union; Kennan thought the policies were extreme and not based on the reality of the situation inside the Soviet Union. However, in retrospect, Kennan said that the two individuals who contributed most to the end of the Cold War were Reagan and former Soviet leader **Mikhail Gorbachev** (1931–; see entry). In his PBS interview, Kennan stated, "I would put first of all Gorbachev ... but also Ronald Reagan, who was, in his own inimitable [incapable of being copied] way, probably not even quite aware of what he was really doing! He did what few other people would have been able to do in breaking this logjam [in U.S.-Soviet relations].

Celebration of stature

As Kennan grew older, his stature as a former statesman continued to grow. Gorbachev greeted Kennan warmly at their only meeting, which occurred in Washington, D.C., in 1987. Gorbachev expressed his admiration for Kennan, saying that Kennan understood that it was possible to embrace other peoples and still remain a devoted American. Honor and recognition culminated in 1989, when President **George Bush** (1924–; served 1989–93; see entry) awarded Kennan the Presidential Medal of Freedom. In the late 1990s, Kennan, by then in his nineties, continued to write and comment on U.S. history. He is widely recognized as one of America's great statesmen.

For More Information

Books

Isaacson, Walter, and Evan Thomas. *The Wise Men: Six Friends and the World They Made: Acheson, Bohlen, Kennan, Harriman, Lovett, McCloy.* New York: Simon and Schuster, 1986.

Kennan, George F., and John Lukacs. *George F. Kennan and the Origins of Containment, 1944–1946: The Kennan-Lukacs Correspondence.* Columbia: University of Missouri Press, 1997.

Mayers, David A. *George Kennan and the Dilemmas of U.S. Foreign Policy.* New York: Oxford University Press, 1989.

Miscamble, Wilson D. *George F. Kennan and the Making of American Foreign Policy, 1947–1950.* Princeton, NJ: Princeton University Press, 1992.

Web Sites

CNN Cold War. http://www.cnn.com/specials/cold.war/episodes/01/interviews/kennan (accessed on September 5, 2003).

"George Kennan." *Public Broadcasting Service: Essays and Dialogues.* http://www.pbs.org/newshour/gergen/kennan.html (accessed on September 5, 2003).

Kennan Institute for Advanced Russian Studies. http://www.kennan.yar.ru/news/25anniv/gfk.htm (accessed on September 5, 2003).

John F. Kennedy

Born May 29, 1917
Brookline, Massachusetts
Died November 22, 1963
Dallas, Texas

U.S. president, senator

"All free men, wherever they may live, are citizens of Berlin, and, therefore, as a free man, I take pride in the words 'Ich bin ein Berliner.'"

In 1960, John F. Kennedy became the youngest person elected to the presidency of the United States. He was forty-three years old. He assumed the office in the midst of the Cold War, an intense political and economic rivalry between the United States and the Soviet Union that lasted from 1945 to 1991. Kennedy successfully led the country through two of the most alarming Cold War crises: the Cuban Missile Crisis and the Soviet construction of the Berlin Wall. The Kennedy administration also crafted sweeping civil rights legislation that was signed into law in 1964. Kennedy's presidency came to a shocking end on November 22, 1963, when he was assassinated in Dallas, Texas.

Young Kennedy

John Fitzgerald Kennedy was the second of nine children born to Joseph Patrick Kennedy (1888–1969) and Rose Fitzgerald Kennedy (1890–1995); he was born at the family home, 83 Beals Street in Brookline, Massachusetts. The Kennedys were a politically prominent Irish Catholic family. John's grandfather on his father's side was a state senator and ac-

John F. Kennedy. *Courtesy of the Library of Congress.*

tive in Boston political circles. His grandfather on his mother's side had served as mayor of Boston, state senator, and U.S. congressman. John's father was a tough, successful businessman.

Kennedy attended elementary schools in Brookline and then in Riverdale, New York, where his prosperous family had moved. He attended high school at the private Choate Academy in Wallingford, Connecticut. Kennedy was not an outstanding student, but he had many friends and in his senior year was voted the student "most likely to succeed" in the future.

Kennedy entered Harvard University in 1936 and graduated with honors in 1940. In the spring and summer of 1939, between his junior and senior years, his father sent him on a tour of Europe and put him in touch with various government officials. The young Kennedy carefully studied the conflicts that were building in Europe as Germany's Adolf Hitler (1889–1945) and his Nazi Party (known primarily for its brutal policies of racism) grew more and more threatening. In young Kennedy's view, England was not well prepared for war; when he returned to Harvard, he wrote his senior thesis on this subject. The thesis later became a best-selling book titled *Why England Slept* (1940).

Kennedy, who loved the sea and sailing, joined the U.S. Navy as a seaman in 1941. When Pearl Harbor, a U.S. naval base in Hawaii, was bombed on December 7, 1941, the United States entered World War II (1939–45). In the war, Kennedy commanded a boat known as PT-109. Kennedy and his crew were patrolling near the Solomon Islands on August 2, 1943, when a Japanese destroyer sliced right through PT-109. Two of the crew were killed, but Kennedy managed to rescue the others—some injured—and get them to a nearby island. He then swam to other nearby islands for help. He and his crew were rescued on August 7. Kennedy received the Purple Heart because his back had been injured in the incident; he also received navy and marine honors for his heroics. Returning to the United States in December, he recuperated, but he would suffer from his back injury the rest of his life.

Congressman and U.S. senator

When Kennedy's older brother, Joseph Jr., whom his father had groomed to enter politics, was killed in the war,

Joseph Sr. turned to John, his second son, to fulfill the family's political ambition. A determined and articulate young man, John Kennedy was also very handsome and readily liked by those with whom he came in contact. He had all the makings of a politician. In 1946, he made a successful run for the U.S. House of Representatives, representing the eleventh congressional district of Massachusetts. Kennedy entered the House in January 1947 as a twenty-nine-year-old congressman. Easily reelected in 1948 and 1950, Kennedy supported the social programs of President **Harry S. Truman** (1884–1972; served 1945–53; see entry). In 1952, Kennedy successfully ran for the U.S. Senate.

On September 12, 1952, Senator Kennedy married a Vassar College graduate, Jacqueline "Jackie" Lee Bouvier (1929–1994), who was the daughter of a wealthy New York City financier. They would have four children, but only two survived infancy, a daughter and a son—Caroline and John Jr.

Young Senator Kennedy served on the Senate Labor Committee investigating charges of corruption. Fighting for the average union worker and local unions, he fought alleged corruption of national labor union leaders, such as racketeering between labor and management, in which top leaders obtained money illegally from management in exchange for agreeing not to strike. Kennedy also served on the Government Operations Committee, which was headed by U.S. senator **Joseph R. McCarthy** (1908–1957; see entry) of Wisconsin. McCarthy had also led a witch-hunt for communists he thought were lurking within the U.S. government and among the general public. By making unfounded accusations against various government workers and questioning the loyalty of certain private citizens, McCarthy had destroyed the careers of many innocent Americans. By 1954, McCarthy's lack of evidence was exposed and the Senate voted to censure him (publicly and officially disapprove of his behavior). Kennedy had never outwardly opposed or confronted McCarthy, and he missed the actual roll call vote on censure because he was ill that day. But Kennedy agreed with the censure vote.

Kennedy easily won reelection to the Senate in 1958, but since the mid-1950s he had had his sights set on the U.S. presidency. His main drawbacks were being Roman Catholic (a

Catholic had never been elected president) and being young. Nevertheless, at the 1960 Democratic National Convention, Kennedy won the party's nomination on the first ballot. He chose U.S. senator **Lyndon B. Johnson** (1908–1973; see entry) of Texas, who also had run for president that year, as his vice presidential running mate. The Republican candidate was Vice President **Richard M. Nixon** (1913–1994; see entry), whose running mate was Henry Cabot Lodge (1902–1985), a U.S. representative to the United Nations. (Kennedy had defeated Lodge in the U.S. Senate race of 1952.) As in previous elections, Kennedy's very large and influential family campaigned tirelessly. After a series of televised debates between the presidential candidates—the first such debates ever shown on television—Kennedy eked out a narrow victory over Nixon.

The thirty-fifth president

The Kennedys brought youth, vitality, and style to the White House. John Jr. and Caroline often played in the Oval Office as their father worked. Jackie Kennedy, only in her early thirties, set the standards for fashions of the day. She brought many performing artists to the White House. Mrs. Kennedy also redecorated the White House, placing furnishings and articles long in storage from past presidents back into the many different rooms.

One of President Kennedy's earliest actions was establishing the Peace Corps by executive order on March 1, 1961. The goal of the Peace Corps was to promote world peace and friendship by aiding people in countries around the world through improved education, health care, and public facilities. A program that remained successful into the twenty-first century, the Peace Corps sent five hundred volunteers to eight developing countries in its first year. By 1966, over fifteen thousand volunteers were working in fifty-two countries.

The dominant domestic issue for President Kennedy was civil rights—making the civil and economic rights of black Americans equal to the rights white Americans already possessed. Large racial demonstrations—both for and against civil rights—occurred across the South and throughout the nation. Courts ordered an end to segregation in public

Famous Words from John F. Kennedy's Inaugural Address

On January 20, 1961, the thirty-fifth U.S. president, John F. Kennedy, gave his first and only inaugural address to the nation. The address contained a number of highly memorable segments that served to rally Americans to actively support the American way of life and oppose the potential spread of communism in the world. A few of those historic passages follow:

> And so, my fellow Americans: ask not what your country can do for you—ask what you can do for your country.

> Let the word go forth from this time and place, to friend and foe alike, that the torch has been passed to a new generation of Americans ... unwilling to witness or permit the slow undoing of those human rights to which this nation has always been committed and to which we are committed today at home and around the world. Let every nation know, whether it wishes us well or ill, that we shall pay any price, bear any burden, meet any hardship, support any friend, oppose

New U.S. president John F. Kennedy gives his inaugural speech on January 20, 1961. Vice President Lyndon B. Johnson (right) looks on. *Reproduced by permission of Getty Images.*

> any foe to assure the survival and the success of liberty.

> Let us never negotiate out of fear. But let us never fear to negotiate.

schools. (Segregation means separating people by their race so that they cannot use the same public facilities.) President Kennedy had to call out the National Guard to maintain order and enforce desegregation at the University of Mississippi in 1962 and at the University of Alabama in 1963. In August 1963, over two hundred thousand people marched to Washington, D.C., to demand equal rights for black Americans; this event was known as the Freedom March. Kennedy had been planning sweeping civil rights legislation, but he was assassinated before it was passed into law. When Kennedy died in November, Lyndon B. Johnson took office; Johnson would sign the Civil Rights Act a year later.

The Bay of Pigs

When President Kennedy took office on January 20, 1961, he inherited the "Cuban problem." **Fidel Castro** (1926–; see entry) had taken power in Cuba in early 1959. His relationship with the United States had quickly gone downhill; Castro, with his communist leanings, naturally looked to the communist Soviet Union for trade agreements. To the dismay of U.S. government leaders, Soviet premier **Nikita Khrushchev** (1894–1971; see entry) gloated that communism had gained a toehold in the Americas. Communism is a system of government in which a single political party, the Communist Party, controls almost all aspects of people's lives. In a communist economy, private ownership of property and businesses is prohibited so that goods produced and wealth accumulated can be shared equally by all.

As communism infiltrated the Castro-led Cuba, many middle-class and wealthy Cubans left their country for America. However, some hoped to return; they hoped that another leader or group might overthrow Castro and restore the old Cuban economy. President Kennedy's predecessor, **Dwight D. Eisenhower** (1890–1969; served 1953–61; see entry), had allowed the U.S. Central Intelligence Agency (CIA) to train fifteen hundred Cuban exiles to invade Cuba and overthrow Castro. Although skeptical of the plan, Kennedy allowed the invasion to proceed. The army of CIA-trained Cuban exiles landed on the south coast of Cuba at an area known as the Bay of Pigs; they were promptly defeated by Castro's forces, who were armed with Soviet tanks. After this embarrassment, Kennedy vowed that in the future he would consider more carefully the advice he received and the way he acted on that advice.

Vienna summit

In June 1961, two months after the Bay of Pigs fiasco, Kennedy met with Khrushchev in Vienna, Austria, for summit talks. Kennedy was still smarting from the embarrassment of the incident; Khrushchev was gloating over the United States' failure. Before the summit meeting, Khrushchev had decided to test the young American president's strength and statesmanship. Kennedy had been warned that Khrushchev could talk very tough, but he was not ready for the blustery, explosive behavior that Khrushchev would display.

U.S. president John F. Kennedy (left) meets with Soviet leader Nikita Khrushchev at the Vienna summit in June 1961.
Reproduced by permission of the Corbis Corporation.

Khrushchev's topic of choice was Berlin, long a sore spot with the Soviet Union. After Germany's defeat in World War II, Germany was divided among the victorious Allies into four sectors—American, French, British, and Soviet. The Soviet sector was known as East Germany; the other three occupying powers soon agreed to rule their sectors jointly and called the combined territory West Germany. Berlin, Germany's capital city, was similarly divided: East Berlin was under Soviet control; French, British, and American forces occupied West Berlin. Since the division of Germany, no peace treaty had ever been signed between the powers to determine Germany's and Berlin's future. The entire city of Berlin was located well within Soviet-controlled East Germany. Therefore, West Berlin—operating under a democratic, capitalist government—sat in the middle of communist-controlled territory.

The awkward Berlin situation spurred Khrushchev to demand that all Western powers leave West Berlin by the year's end and that East Germany be recognized as a sovereign country. Khrushchev fiercely warned Kennedy that any violation of East German territory (that is, crossing through or over East Germany to get to Berlin without East German permission) would be considered an act of aggression, a precursor to war—nuclear war. Taken aback, Kennedy refused Khrushchev's demands. The two never met again. On his way home, a shaken Kennedy stopped in Britain. He confided to British prime minister **Harold Macmillan** (1894–1986; see entry) that perhaps it was possible the Soviet Union could win the Cold War. When the young president returned home, he ordered a thorough probing of the Berlin issue to find strategies the United States could pursue. Kennedy also announced a buildup of conventional, nonnuclear weapons and the armed services.

Berlin

Kennedy could not have realized that Khrushchev had no intention of actually starting a war. Khrushchev had decided to make an issue of the capital city because thousands of East Germans, many of them highly skilled and well educated, were leaving East Germany for economic opportunities and political freedom in West Germany. They all made their exodus through Berlin, where anyone could travel freely among the four sectors. East Germans could go to Berlin, enter one of the Western sectors, and from there slip into West Germany, escaping communist rule. East Germany could not afford to lose its best people to the West; the East German economy was already struggling. Walter Ulbricht (1893–1973), East Germany's leader, had been demanding for some time that Khrushchev do something to stop the exodus.

In the early-morning hours of Sunday, August 13, 1961, East German crews began erecting a barbed wire fence along the boundary of the Soviet East Berlin sector. U.S. intelligence informed President Kennedy about the construction of the fence by midmorning Sunday as he set out for a family picnic near Hyannis Port, Massachusetts. The development had caught top U.S. officials completely off guard. Khrushchev was testing the Western powers, trying to see if they would challenge him. Because Khrushchev had not touched West Berlin and had left access routes from East Germany to

West Germany open and unchanged, Kennedy decided it was best not to risk war. The fence—better known as the Berlin Wall—was an ugly statement, but even so, in Kennedy's view, a wall was better than a war. The wall accomplished Khrushchev's goal: It stopped the flow of East Germans moving to the West. However, the wall was also a defeat for communism. Its existence seemed to prove that people would stay in a communist country only if they were physically prevented from leaving.

In June 1963, President Kennedy went on a European tour. When he arrived in West Berlin, he looked at the wall from a viewing stand. Back at West Berlin city hall, he addressed 250,000 Berliners. Throwing out a speech that had been prepared for him, he instead spoke from the heart. Kennedy said that if there were people who did not understand the issues between the free world and a communist one, they should come to Berlin; with the crowd cheering wildly, Kennedy thundered again and again, "Let them come to Berlin." He ended the speech with a now-famous line that expressed the unity of the Western world: "Ich bin ein Berliner (I am a Berliner)."

Cuba

The "Cuban problem" had not reared its head again since the Bay of Pigs incident in early 1961. However, President Kennedy had ordered a top-secret operation—Operation Mongoose—to oust Cuban leader Fidel Castro. U.S. intelligence had considered various plots, from lacing Castro's water with drugs to assassinating Castro. Despite careful planning, Operation Mongoose never materialized.

Behind the scenes, the Soviet Union had been helping Cuba build up its armaments, or military equipment. By the end of 1961, Soviet military advisors had arrived in Cuba. The Soviet investment in the tiny island was considerable. Khrushchev's plan was to place both medium- and long-range missiles with nuclear warheads in Cuba. He had long fumed over U.S. nuclear missiles openly located in Turkey, Italy, and the United Kingdom—within easy striking distance of the Soviet Union. The Soviets had warheads targeting Western Europe, but none of them was located outside the Soviet Union.

Khrushchev wanted to even the score by placing Soviet nuclear weapons close to the United States.

By October 1962, the nuclear missile sites in Cuba were almost complete. On October 14, 1962, a high-flying U.S. intelligence aircraft on a mission over Cuba returned with photographs of the missile sites. The photographs were processed, analyzed, and presented to President Kennedy on the morning of October 16. It was clear from the photos that most parts of the United States would be easy prey for the Cuban missiles.

President Kennedy spoke to the American people by way of television on Monday evening, October 22. He informed them of the crisis and told them that the U.S. military was on full alert and ready for any possibility. He also announced that he would institute a naval blockade, or "quarantine," to prevent Soviet ships from bringing any more missiles to Cuba. The blockade would go into effect on Wednesday, October 24. Kennedy demanded that Khrushchev dismantle and remove all the missiles already in Cuba. The Soviet ships carrying missiles stopped and turned around, but as of October 27 the missiles already in Cuba remained.

Many top U.S. officials believed a nuclear war would start at any moment. But fortunately President Kennedy's brother, U.S. attorney general Robert Kennedy (1925–1968), came up with a compromise that satisfied both sides: The United States would halt the blockade and promise not to invade Cuba if the Soviets would agree to remove the missiles from the island. U.S. leaders also secretly promised Khrushchev that they would remove the U.S. missiles in Turkey after the crisis ended. Kennedy insisted on secrecy so that the United States would not appear to withdraw protection for Western Europe for its own purposes. (Soviet leaders did not realize that the United States considered the missiles in Turkey outdated and had intended to remove them soon anyway.) Khrushchev agreed to the U.S. plan, and the crisis came to an end on Sunday morning, October 28. Kennedy won widespread praise for his handling of the crisis and for averting a military engagement.

Having taken the world to the brink of nuclear war, a sobered Kennedy and Khrushchev soon began talks on nuclear weapons control. Although they could not agree on a broad test-ban treaty, they did agree to ban nuclear testing in the atmosphere, in outer space, and beneath the ocean. The Limited Test-Ban Treaty went into effect on October 11, 1963, and provided an important foundation for future arms control.

Assassination

Just before Thanksgiving, on November 22, 1963, President and Mrs. Kennedy, along with Vice President and Mrs. Johnson, visited San Antonio and Houston, Texas, and then continued on to Dallas. The purpose of Kennedy's visit was to repair a rift in the Texas Democratic Party before the 1964 presidential election. Advisors had actually warned Kennedy about visiting Dallas at that time. Texas was a strongly Democratic state, but Dallas was the center and hotbed for radically conservative Republicans. Nevertheless, Kennedy went ahead with the Dallas visit. In the presidential motorcade, Kennedy sat next to his wife, Jackie; Texas governor John B. Connally (1917–1993) rode in the seat in front of them. Near the end of the downtown procession, shots rang out from the Texas School Book Depository Building, hitting both Connally and Kennedy. Connally was hit in the back

U.S. president John F. Kennedy (right) discusses the Cuban Missile Crisis with his brother, Attorney General Robert F. Kennedy, at the White House on October 1, 1962. *Reproduced by permission of the Corbis Corporation.*

but recovered; the president was hit in the head and neck and had no chance of survival. Vice President Johnson, whose home state was Texas, succeeded Kennedy as U.S. president.

The accused assassin, Lee Harvey Oswald (1939–1963), was murdered two days later by local nightclub owner Jack Ruby (1911–1967). Oswald was an avowed Marxist and once attempted to become a Soviet citizen. (Marxism promoted a system in which workers would own industry and other means of production and share equally in the wealth.) Oswald had a Soviet wife, and he was a supporter of Cuba's Fidel Castro. The official government investigation—called the Warren Commission (named after the commission chairman, U.S. Supreme Court chief justice Earl Warren (1891–1974)—concluded that Oswald probably acted alone, but for years others have speculated on possible conspiracy theories (in which two or more persons agree to commit a crime). In 1977, a congressional panel concluded that there was probably a conspiracy and recommended further investigation.

President Kennedy's body lay in state in the U.S. Capitol Rotunda as hundreds of thousands paid their respects. In a long solemn procession, his body was carried to Arlington National Cemetery, where he was buried.

For More Information

Books

FitzSimons, Louise. *The Kennedy Doctrine*. New York: Random House, 1972.

Gelb, Norman. *The Berlin Wall: Kennedy, Khrushchev, and a Showdown in the Heart of Europe*. New York: Times Books, 1986.

Higgins, Trumbull. *The Perfect Failure: Kennedy, Eisenhower, and the CIA and the Bay of Pigs*. New York: Norton, 1987.

Paterson, Thomas G., ed. *Kennedy's Quest for Victory: American Foreign Policy, 1961–1963*. New York: Random House, 1995.

Web Site

John F. Kennedy Library and Museum. http://www.cs.umb.edu/jfklibrary/index.htm (accessed on September 6, 2003).

Nikita Khrushchev

Born April 17, 1894
Kalinovka, Russia
Died September 11, 1971
Petrovo-Dalneye, Soviet Union

Soviet premier and first secretary of Communist Party

"Do you think when two representatives holding diametrically opposing views get together and shake hands, the contradictions between our systems will simply melt away? What kind of a daydream is that?"

Nikita Khrushchev. *Courtesy of the United Nations.*

Nikita Khrushchev was the most colorful Soviet leader during the Cold War. After being a loyal supporter of Soviet leader **Joseph Stalin** (1879–1953; see entry) through his early political career, Khrushchev denounced Stalin's policies when he assumed Soviet leadership in the mid-1950s. Khrushchev had a loud and blunt personality that took other leaders by surprise. His efforts to introduce major domestic reforms within the Soviet Union during his long period of leadership while fending off pressures from old guard Soviet communists led to erratic foreign policies that confounded U.S. leaders, including presidents **Dwight D. Eisenhower** (1890–1969; served 1953–61; see entry) and **John F. Kennedy** (1917–1963; served 1961–63; see entry), and took the world to the brink of nuclear war during the Cuban Missile Crisis of 1962.

A humble beginning

Nikita Sergeyevich Khrushchev was born in southern Russia, in the village of Kalinovka, near the Ukrainian border. His father was a poor peasant who farmed in the summer and worked in the Ukrainian coal mines in the winter. When Nikita was a teenager, the family moved close to Yuzovka, Ukraine, to be nearer the mines. Although he was a bright student, Khrushchev attended school sporadically for several years because he was busy working. He took jobs herding cattle and working in a factory and finally became a mechanic in the coal mines. Working under dismal conditions in the factory and mine, Khrushchev saw first-hand that his country needed social and economic change to help the working classes.

In 1914, Khrushchev married Galina Yefronsinya. The Bolshevik Revolution occurred in 1917, when Khrushchev was twenty-three years old. During the revolution, the communist Bolsheviks took control of Russia's government. Communism is a system of government in which a single political party, the Communist Party, controls almost all aspects of people's lives. In a communist economy, private ownership of property and businesses is prohibited so that goods produced and wealth accumulated can be shared equally by all. Khrushchev apparently did not take part in the revolution but did join the Communist Party in early 1918.

Khrushchev served in the Red Army in 1919, successfully defending the new communist regime against forces trying to regain control of the government. Following the war, Khrushchev returned to work in the Ukrainian mines in 1920. By 1921, he was put in charge of political affairs at the mine. In the winter of 1921–22, his wife died from a famine, or a shortage of food, leaving him with two young children. He returned to his hometown of Yuzovka in 1922. Through the 1920s, he was able to attend educational institutions established by the Communist Party. These schools gave young workers basic education and political instruction. At Donbass Technical College, he was elected to a top Communist Party position.

A Stalin supporter

Khrushchev remarried in 1924. He and his new wife, schoolteacher Nina Petrovna, had three children together. A staunch supporter of Soviet premier Joseph Stalin, Khrushchev moved up rapidly through various posts in the Ukrainian Communist Party bureaucracy. The first secretary of the Ukrainian Communist Party, Lazar Kaganovich (1893–1991), became a mentor for Khrushchev. Both Khrushchev and Kaganovich left for Moscow in 1929.

In Moscow, Khrushchev enrolled in the city's Industrial Academy. One of his classmates and friends was Joseph Stalin's wife, Nadezhada Allilueva. While at the academy, Khrushchev spent most of his energy on political work. By 1931, Kaganovich had become head of Moscow's Communist Party, and he brought Khrushchev into the city's political administration. Continuing to move up rapidly, Khrushchev became Kaganovich's assistant, the second secretary of the Moscow Central Committee, in 1933. (In both local and national branches of the Communist Party, the Central Committee is an important administrative body that oversees day-to-day party activities.) In 1935, at age forty, Khrushchev succeeded Kaganovich as first secretary of the Moscow city party. He was also elected to the Soviet Central Committee. Khrushchev was a major figure in Moscow economic developments, including construction of the city's highly regarded subway system.

During the late 1930s, Khrushchev took an active role in Stalin's purges of party leadership. Stalin executed or exiled millions of Soviet citizens, including his opponents and some supporters. Khrushchev was one of the few to survive among his colleagues at the higher levels of office, perhaps because of his close connections to Kaganovich and his past friendship with Stalin's wife. Stalin rewarded Khrushchev for his loyalty during the purges by taking an active role in getting Khrushchev elected to the Supreme Soviet in late 1937. Khrushchev was also elected to the Politburo. The Politburo was the executive body for the Central Committee and was responsible for making policy decisions. In 1938, Khrushchev was elected first secretary of the Ukrainian Communist Party. The Ukraine was the most important agricultural region in the Soviet Union and also an area that had strongly resisted Stalin's collective farming policies, which would provide more local control. In 1937 alone, 150,000 Ukrainian party members had been purged. Khrushchev focused on improving agricultural production under the new Soviet system. By the end of the decade, Khrushchev had risen to national prominence.

In June 1941, Germany's Nazi Party, known primarily for its brutal policies of racism, launched a massive invasion against the Soviet Union, drawing the Soviets into

World War II (1939–45). Khrushchev became an officer in the Soviet army, serving in the thick of the fighting. He was at the Battle of Stalingrad, in which the Soviets turned back a major German invasion. Hundreds of thousands were killed. Khrushchev rose to the rank of lieutenant general. By late 1943, when the momentum of the war shifted in favor of the Soviet troops, Khrushchev returned to Ukrainian politics. He regained his position as first secretary of the Ukrainian Communist Party and was also appointed chairman of the Ukrainian Council of Ministers in charge of economic affairs. Khrushchev led the postwar reconstruction of the Ukraine's economy.

Rise to power in Moscow

In 1949, Khrushchev returned to Moscow to once again serve as first secretary of the Moscow Central Committee. He regularly dined with Stalin. In March 1953, Stalin died of a stroke, and a prolonged power struggle followed. By September 1953, Khrushchev was named first secretary of the Soviet Central Committee. His chief rival, Georgy Malenkov (1902–1988), remained premier (head of state) of the Soviet Union. He and Khrushchev fought over domestic economic policies. The power struggle came to an end in 1955, when Khrushchev was able to replace Malenkov with a close associate, Nikolay Bulganin (1895–1975).

Khrushchev took the Soviet Union in a distinctly different direction than Stalin had charted. He openly criticized some of Stalin's policies and began a Communist Party reform movement known as de-Stalinization, a plan to introduce reforms to the Soviet Union. These reforms included allowing greater personal freedoms for Soviet citizens, lessening the powers of the secret police, closing concentration and hard-labor camps, and restoring certain legal processes. Khrushchev's criticism of Stalin was courageous; few in the Soviet Union dared to make such statements. Khrushchev freed many of the people imprisoned by Stalin. Unlike previous Soviet leaders, he traveled freely to foreign countries, including Great Britain and the United States. Khrushchev's behavior was often flamboyant, unconventional, and rude. For example, he drew a $10,000 fine from the United Nations (UN) for banging his shoe on a table at a UN meeting on October 13, 1960; he was using the shoe for emphasis as he responded angrily to a speech that sharply criticized the Soviet Union.

Though he had little formal education, Khrushchev had a quick mind and learned rapidly from experience, exhibiting considerable energy and enthusiasm. Khrushchev was often ruthless and independent, but he could also be warm and showed genuine care for common people; he was always interested in the Soviet farming population. Yet Khrushchev took a hard-line communist approach against religion and closed many churches. The communists looked at religion as an anticommunist concept that gave people false ideas of life. Many churches were destroyed, but underground religious worship survived.

Although the Communist Party controlled such forms of expression as the arts, Khrushchev was inconsistent in enforcing that policy. For example, he approved the publication of *One Day in the Life of Ivan Denisovich* (1962), by Aleksandr Solzhenitsyn (1918–), which describes the brutality of Soviet life under Stalin. At the same time, Khrushchev did not allow *Doctor Zhivago*, by Boris Pasternak (1890–1960), to be published in Russia (the book was published elsewhere in 1957). *Doctor Zhivago* is a novel about a Russian poet's life in conflict with the times in which he lives (1902 to 1953).

Khrushchev's campaign to reform the Communist Party was not entirely well received. In 1957, members of the Politburo moved to dismiss Khrushchev. However, he forced the Politburo to seek final approval from the larger Central Committee, where he had strong support. The Central Committee reversed the Politburo decision by voting to retain Khrushchev as Soviet leader. As a result, he was able to remove those who opposed his leadership and bring in his supporters to strengthen his position. Those who led the effort to dismiss him, including Malenkov, his old mentor Kaganovich, and former Soviet foreign minister **Vyacheslav Molotov** (1890–1986; see entry), were demoted or expelled from the Communist Party because they disagreed with Khrushchev's reform and de-Stalinization efforts. To complete his hold on power, Khrushchev removed Bulganin as head of state in 1958. Khrushchev was now leader of the Communist Party and the Soviet government.

An erratic Cold War path

Khrushchev's prestige at home and abroad was enhanced by the stunning success of the Soviet space program. In early October 1957, the Soviets launched *Sputnik,* the first man-made satellite to orbit Earth. The Western world was shocked; it seemed that the Soviets had passed the United States in technological development. However, *Sputnik* brought unexpected consequences for the Soviets. The United States began a massive space program, which forced the Soviets to continue with costly research and development in order to keep up. This expensive "space race" was another component of the Cold War rivalry between the two superpowers.

Despite the continuing rivalry between the Soviet Union and the United States, one of Khrushchev's stated goals was to "peacefully coexist" with the West. His de-Stalinization program was part of an effort to give the Soviet Union better international standing. Perhaps trying to demonstrate goodwill toward the West, Khrushchev refused to share space technology information with communist China, even though Chinese leaders eagerly sought this information. Khrushchev also refused to share nuclear technology with the Chinese. China's leadership thought Khrushchev's policies weakened the original principles of communism. His decisions seemed to indicate that Khrushchev was willing to forgo communist loyalties in order to promote better relations with Western countries.

Despite Khrushchev's promotion of peaceful coexistence, his foreign policy decisions often seemed erratic. For example, at a press conference in 1958 Khrushchev surprisingly announced that the United States and other Western countries must withdraw from West Berlin. The situation in West Berlin had been bothering the Soviets for a long time. During World War II, the Soviet Union fought on the side of the Western allies—the United States, Great Britain, and France. When the Allies defeated Germany and brought the war to a close, they agreed to divide Germany into two parts: West Germany, which was to be a democratic nation, and East Germany, which would be controlled by the communist Soviets. They also agreed to divide Berlin, the capital of Germany, into four sectors; each country would control one sector of the city. The three Western countries then agreed to rule jointly over their

De-Stalinization

Nikita Khrushchev's most dramatic moment as Communist Party leader came in February 1956 during a speech commonly known as the "Crimes of Stalin" speech. From 1924 to 1953, Joseph Stalin had ruled the Soviet Union with an iron hand. His legacy as a dictator included the Great Terror, a series of massive purges involving the execution or exile of millions of Soviet citizens—both opponents and supporters of the Communist Party. Khrushchev had been a key Stalin supporter for many years and apparently assisted in the purges. Therefore, it was an incredible moment in Soviet history when, three years after Stalin's death, Khrushchev denounced the policies of Stalin in a secret speech in the concluding session of the Twentieth Communist Party Congress.

For the first time, a Soviet leader boldly pointed out the flaws of the Communist past. Khrushchev recounted Stalin's crimes against the Communist Party, particularly the Great Terror purges of the 1930s. He accused Stalin of key strategy errors in World War II. He said Stalin had sought glory for himself rather than promoting the Communist Party. He also called Stalin's rule a "cult of personality," in which an individual becomes more important than the political movement itself, which is counter to pure communist beliefs in which everyone shares

in the system. This act of discrediting Stalin is referred to as de-Stalinization. Throughout the Soviet Union, special Communist Party meetings followed Khrushchev's epic speech, as party leaders discussed the best way to initiate de-Stalinization.

Historians have long pondered what led Khrushchev to make the speech. Many believe he was trying to strengthen his leadership against staunch Stalin supporters, including Georgy Malenkov, Vyacheslav Molotov, and Lazar Kaganovich. It is also possible that he wanted to formally recognize the many Soviet citizens who had been victims of the Stalin reign. He may have been trying to revitalize the Communist Party, hoping to turn de-Stalinization into a reform movement. Whatever Khrushchev's intentions, his bold words brought unintended results. The "Crimes of Stalin" speech caused great shock in Eastern European countries. It fed a mood of rebellion against communist rule and leftover communist hard-liners from the Stalin era. The most dramatic consequence was a widespread rebellion in Hungary in November 1956. Seeking to reestablish some order, Khrushchev ruthlessly crushed the revolt, killing thousands of soldiers and civilians. Through his actions in Hungary, Khrushchev lost international prestige and caused many to leave the Communist Party.

sectors, which were collectively referred to as West Berlin. The Soviets occupied East Berlin. However, the entire city of Berlin was located well within communist-controlled East Germany.

It was a nagging irritation to the Soviets to have West Berlin—an island of capitalism—existing within a communist country. Capitalism is an economic system in which property and businesses can be privately owned. Production, distribution, and prices of goods are determined by competition in a market relatively free of government intervention. Capitalism is incompatible with communism.

U.S. president Dwight D. Eisenhower decided to ignore Khrushchev's demand, and Khrushchev backed down. Khrushchev again demanded Western withdrawal from West Berlin in 1961, but he backed down a second time. However, he then ordered the construction of the Berlin Wall to stop East German residents from fleeing communist rule via West Berlin. Heavily guarded on the East Berlin side, the Wall would stand as a barrier between the capitalist West and the communist East for three decades. Historians believe that Khrushchev's demands and his decision to erect the Wall were intended to quiet his hard-line communist critics.

Unfriendly era with the United States

In July 1959, Vice President **Richard M. Nixon** (1913–1994; see entry) visited Khrushchev during an international trade fair in the Soviet Union. While in front of an exhibit featuring a typical American kitchen, the two leaders got into a much publicized discussion over the merits of communism and capitalism, which became known as the "kitchen debate." In September 1959, Khrushchev became the first Soviet leader to visit the United States. He was not warmly received on a brief tour around the country. Relations between Khrushchev and President Eisenhower cooled even further when the Soviets shot down an American spy plane that was flying over the Soviet Union. Khrushchev did not participate in a previously scheduled Paris summit meeting with Eisenhower in May 1960. In September 1960, Khrushchev returned uninvited to the United States to attend a United Nations meeting. There, he staged his famous outburst that included banging his shoe on a table in anger.

Khrushchev placed a strong emphasis on domestic issues such as housing and agricultural expansion. One massive project, the "Virgin Lands" program, involved 9 million acres of uncultivated land in Kazakhstan; the acreage was to be converted to grain crops. Khrushchev appointed **Leonid Brezhnev** (1906–1982; see entry) to direct the ambitious program. Brezhnev would later succeed Khrushchev as Soviet leader. The Virgin Lands program was somewhat successful but fell far short of meeting Soviet needs.

In 1962, lacking nuclear missiles capable of reaching the North American continent, Khrushchev decided to place some in pro-Soviet Cuba, located only 90 miles (145 kilometers) from the U.S. mainland. President John F. Kennedy responded by ordering a quarantine of Cuba to prevent Soviet ships from delivering more missiles. (Because blockades were against international law, the term "quarantine" was used instead.) Kennedy demanded that the Cuban missiles already in place be removed. During the brief but intense standoff, the dire threat of nuclear war loomed over both superpowers—and the entire world. This incident, known as the Cuban Missile Crisis, was the most dramatic Cold War confrontation between the United States and the Soviet Union. Again, Khrushchev backed down. He agreed to remove the missiles if the United States would promise not to invade Cuba in the future.

The scare of coming so close to nuclear war actually led to an improved relationship between the two countries. A hot line was established between Moscow and Washington, D.C., to improve direct communications during times of crisis. In addition, Khrushchev signed a nuclear test-ban treaty in August 1963, which prohibited nuclear testing in the atmosphere. With a poor harvest in 1963, Khrushchev also began purchasing large amounts of food from the United States; this was an embarrassment to the Soviet leader. To make matters worse, he still had to ration basics such as bread and flour.

Besides his setbacks in Berlin and Cuba, Khrushchev had problems at home in the Soviet Union. He irritated other Communist Party leaders with his efforts to reorganize the party and the state government. For instance, he created regional economic councils in the government in an effort to replace the higher bureaucracies and their ministers overseeing industrial production. This threatened the existing Soviet system created under Stalin. With his greater reliance on nu-

Communist leaders from around the world meet in Moscow on November 7, 1961. Included here are (left to right) Cuban delegate Blas Roca, North Vietnamese leader Ho Chi Minh, Soviet leader Nikita Khrushchev, Hungarian premier János Kádár, and Soviet official Leonid Brezhnev. *Courtesy of the National Archives and Records Administration.*

clear weapons, Khrushchev also reduced the size of the Soviet army and reduced the powers of the secret police, known as the KGB. This change caused the Soviet Union's top military leaders to withdraw their support for Khrushchev. Khrushchev's vigor in pursuing these changes, along with the unpredictability of his actions and policies, caused increasing concern among party leaders and others.

In October 1964, while Khrushchev was on vacation in the Crimean region of southern Russia, he was suddenly summoned back to the Kremlin, or Communist headquarters, in Moscow. There, the Politburo members removed him from leadership as first secretary of the Soviet Communist Party; they also removed him as chairman of the Council of Ministers, a position he had held since 1958. Khrushchev did not resist removal as he had in 1957. Instead, he peacefully accepted his fate. Party leaders instituted a collective leadership structure, with Brezhnev, much less colorful and more predictable than Khrushchev, in the key role of first secretary.

Khrushchev became practically nonexistent in Soviet society. Living both in Moscow and at a country house, he spent the rest of his life in peace, though under guard. He enjoyed working in gardens and playing with his grandchildren. He was rarely seen in public or even mentioned in newspapers and books. He did try to establish his place in history by dictating two volumes of memoirs that were published abroad. Khrushchev died in September 1971 at age seventy-seven. It was not until the late 1980s that historians would begin to study Khrushchev's role in Soviet history.

For More Information

Books

Crankshaw, Edward. *Khrushchev: A Career.* New York: Viking, 1966.

Frankland, Mark. *Khrushchev.* New York: Stein and Day, 1979.

Khrushchev, Nikita S. *Khrushchev Remembers.* Boston: Little, Brown, 1970.

Khrushchev, Nikita S. *Khrushchev Remembers: The Glasnost Tapes.* Boston: Little, Brown, 1990.

Khrushchev, Nikita S. *Khrushchev Remembers: The Last Testament.* Boston: Little, Brown, 1974.

Linden, Carl A. *Khrushchev and the Soviet Leadership.* Baltimore, MD: Johns Hopkins University Press, 1990.

Kim Il Sung

Born April 15, 1912
Man'gyondae, Korea
Died July 8, 1994
P'yongyang, North Korea

Premier of North Korea

Kim Il Sung was a communist dictator who ruled North Korea throughout the Cold War. The Cold War was an intense political and economic rivalry between the United States and the Soviet Union that lasted from 1945 to 1991. Asserting his rule with an iron hand, Kim Il Sung was the longest-serving leader of a communist government in the twentieth century. He created an almost mythical cult status for himself within North Korea, but he was little known elsewhere because he purposely kept North Korea isolated from the outside world.

Early years

Kim Il Sung was born Kim Sung Ju in April 1912 to a middle-class Korean family in the village of Man'gyondae, located in northwestern Korea. He was the oldest of three sons. His father, Kim Hyung-jik, was a schoolteacher. Korea had long been isolated from outside influences, but it was annexed by Japan shortly before Kim Sung Ju's birth. The family moved to Chinese-controlled Manchuria in 1919 to escape

"The essential excellence of the socialist system lies in the fact that the working people, freed from exploitation and oppression, work with conscious enthusiasm and creative initiative for the country and the people ... as well as their own welfare."

Kim Il Sung. *Reproduced by permission of AP/Wide World Photos.*

241

the harsh Japanese rule. In Manchuria, young Kim attended Chinese primary and secondary schools. In 1931, he joined the Chinese Communist Youth League and began leading small Chinese guerrilla forces on raids against remote Japanese outposts in northern Korea along the Manchurian border.

By 1939, the Japanese forces had gained the upper hand, and Kim fled from Manchuria to the far eastern part of Siberia in the Soviet Union. The Soviets gave Kim military and political training in Khabarovsk, and he served in the Soviet army during World War II (1939–45). At this time, he married a fellow revolutionary. In mid-1945, the Soviets attacked Japanese forces and captured northern Korea. The United States gained control of southern Korea. Kim was reportedly a Soviet army officer at the time. Japan surrendered to the United States and the Soviet Union in August 1945.

North Korean leader

U.S. president **Harry S. Truman** (1884–1972; served 1945–53; see entry) recommended to the Soviets that Korea be temporarily divided into northern and southern regions along the thirty-eighth parallel; later, the Koreans could hold elections to determine what type of government the unified nation should have. Most Korean political leaders were in Seoul, the traditional capital of Korea, which was located in South Korea and controlled by the United States. Therefore, the Soviets turned to Kim to be the provisional North Korean leader. With Soviet assistance, he built up a large military. He also changed his name to Kim Il Sung, the name of a legendary Korean hero, a guerrilla fighter who fought the Japanese.

To stabilize the new North Korean government, the Soviets quieted Kim's potential political rivals through intimidation and other means. Only one political party was allowed, the Korean Workers' Party. By 1947, the new political structure was taking shape; operating under communist economic principles, all businesses and farms were either owned by the state or assigned to groups of workers. The legislative body was called the Supreme People's Assembly; the executive branch, which Kim headed, was known as the Central People's Committee.

From 1945 through 1947, the United States sent various government officials to Korea, including General **George C. Marshall** (1880–1959; see entry), to negotiate for the reunification of Korea. After failure to make any diplomatic progress, the United States turned to the United Nations (UN), an international organization composed of most of the nations of the world, created to preserve world peace and security. The UN proposed national elections throughout Korea to establish a new unified government. However, Kim balked at the proposal. South Korea proceeded with elections in May 1948 and formed the Republic of Korea. In August, North Korea held elections for the Supreme People's Assembly and proclaimed the Democratic People's Republic of Korea with Kim as premier. Kim would hold that position for the next forty-six years. Kim claimed authority over all of Korea. However, in December 1948 the UN recognized the Republic of Korea as the only legitimate government of Korea.

Korean War

From the beginning, Kim was committed to reunifying Korea by militarily gaining control of the southern part of the country. The Soviet Union continued to supply North Korea with weapons. In June 1950, Kim's North Korean forces swept into South Korea. Within only three days, he had captured Seoul and pushed South Korean forces southward down the peninsula. In immediate response, the UN passed a resolution condemning the attack. The UN also approved the launch of a counterattack by an international coalition force primarily made up of U.S. soldiers commanded by General **Douglas MacArthur** (1880–1964; see entry). UN forces pushed North Korean troops back northward across the thirty-eighth parallel, all the way to the Korean border with China. In response, Stalin withdrew his support of Kim, and Kim's political career appeared over.

In 1949, a year before North Korea's forced retreat, communist Chinese forces led by **Mao Zedong** (1893–1976; see entry) had captured the Chinese government and formed the People's Republic of China (PRC). Mao felt threatened by the U.S. forces on his border. Therefore, in October 1950, the PRC launched a massive attack involving three hundred thousand

U.S. Army trucks cross the 38th Parallel, the border that separates North and South Korea. *Courtesy of the National Archives and Records Administration.*

troops. These troops pushed U.S. forces south, back across the thirty-eighth parallel. Continued fighting led to a stalemate.

After over two years of negotiations, a cease-fire agreement was finally reached on July 25, 1953. The agreement formalized the split between North and South Korea. The United States would continue supporting South Korea; North Korea would be backed by the Soviet Union and the PRC. No peace treaty was ever signed. The 155-mile-long (250-kilometer-long) boundary between North and South Korea became known as the Demilitarized Zone (DMZ). However, despite the name, there was an unusually high concentration of military forces stationed along the boundary on both sides.

Building a cult of personality

The war left North Korea's economy in shambles. Kim focused on rebuilding the economy and firming up his control. He closed North Korea to most outside contacts and purged all his internal enemies. No foreign newspapers were allowed, and radios could only receive state-owned stations. By 1959, all private land holdings had been abolished, and all agricultural land was collectivized, or placed under control of a group of local farmers. The state owned 90 percent of industry, and cooperatives, an organization of workers who share in the ownership and operation of a factory for their own benefit, owned the remainder. Using Soviet leader Joseph Stalin's "cult of personality" as a guide, Kim began creating a mythology around himself (he sought to make himself more important than the communist movement). He used fear, ignorance, and isolation to further establish his control. He promoted a doctrine of national self-sufficiency, known as Juche, and proclaimed himself the absolute ruler and leader of the North Korean people. In reality, however, North Korea remained highly reliant on the Soviets and the PRC for support. North Korea's economic recovery proceeded well through the 1960s. Through a combination of heavy industry and collective farming, North Korea surpassed South Korea in its economic achievements. For a time, North Korea was a model of state-controlled economic development.

North Korea also became the most regimented society in the world. Kim's government classified each of North Korea's twenty-two million citizens into categories based on their allegiance to Kim. People placed in the top category received better education and better jobs. People in the lowest category were sent to hard labor camps in remote areas. By some estimates, this category included tens of thousands of citizens. Some were executed in the labor camps, but no one knows how many. Kim also personally controlled the secret police, known as the Protection and Security Bureau, which tracked the movements of all individuals, even within each village. Each person had an identification card and needed a travel permit before leaving a residential or work area.

A confrontational foreign policy

Through the 1950s and 1960s, Kim had a difficult time balancing his relations with the Soviet Union and the PRC, because those two major communist nations had increasingly strained relations with each other. Kim would favor one and then the other. Finally in the late 1960s, Kim was targeted in the PRC's Cultural Revolution, a campaign launched by Mao Zedong to purge thousands of communist government leaders and others. He turned to the Soviets for protection, and they would be his primary arms supplier thereafter. However, Kim became increasingly independent overall.

To build North Korea's international standing, Kim successfully established ties with Third World countries. The term *Third World* refers to poor underdeveloped or economically developing nations in Africa, Asia, and Latin America. In the 1960s and 1970s, many Third World countries were seeking independence from the political control of Western European nations. In all, Kim established diplomatic relations with over 130 nations. North Korea became a major arms supplier to governments and revolutionaries in Africa, Asia, and Latin America. In the 1980s, Kim supplied Iran with weapons during Iran's war with Iraq. He also provided arms to Libya and Syria.

Kim's relations with the United States and other Western countries were strained. His political positions, economic policies, and overall style of government conflicted with Western political goals and ideals. To make matters worse, in 1968, North Korea captured a U.S. spy ship, the USS *Pueblo,* in international waters; North Korea claimed the U.S. ship was in North Korean waters. North Korea held the crew for eleven months before the United States finally apologized for spying. In 1976, North Korean soldiers killed two American officers, and in July 1977 North Korea shot down an unarmed U.S. Army helicopter.

Since the late 1960s, Kim had been promoting international terrorism, primarily aimed at South Korea. Kim supported spy rings and underground organizations and arranged for assassination attempts against South Korean leaders. Attacks against South Korea continued through the 1980s. In October 1983, North Korean terrorists led a bombing attack against South Korean officials. In May 1984, United Nations personnel in charge of the demilitarized zone discovered tunnels under the boundary between North and South Korea. The tunnels were designed to allow spies and assassins to infiltrate to the south. North Korea was suspected in the bombing of a South Korean airliner in November 1987 that killed 115 people.

A Closed Communist Society

In the early twenty-first century, North Korea remained one of the world's most isolated nations in terms of international relations. The North Korean communist government exerted almost complete control over its citizens' lives, and individual liberties continued to be severely restricted.

North Korea's sole political party, called the Korean Workers' Party, runs the government. In 1996, only about 11 percent of the twenty-six million people in North Korea belonged to this party. Nonetheless, the party makes all the nation's laws and decides who the candidates for office should be. The most powerful governmental body is the Central People's Committee, headed by the president of the nation. The committee is usually composed of forty-five members. The legislative body, the Supreme People's Assembly, has 687 members; the assembly elects people to the Central People's Committee but otherwise has little power.

North Korea is divided into nine provinces governed by local communist committees. North Korea maintains one of the largest militaries in the world, composed of seven hundred thousand in 1990. All North Korean men must serve in the military for five years, between ages twenty and twenty-five. Children are required to attend school for eleven years. The only university in North Korea is Kim Il Sung University.

Kim's last years

By the 1970s, North Korea's military spending reached 25 percent of the national budget and was undermining the nation's economy. Much of the budget also went to constructing grand monuments to honor Kim. Statues of Kim sprang up everywhere. The focus on heavy industry and high military expenditures led to severe shortages in domestic goods. The standard of living declined rapidly as harvests and industrial productivity decreased. The North Korean population tripled between 1954 and 1994, putting a further strain on national resources.

Relations between North and South Korea began to improve by 1990. For the first time since the Korean War (1950–53), the prime ministers from North and South Korea met. In 1991, both Korean governments were recognized in the United Nations. However, in 1993, it was discovered that Kim was developing North Korean nuclear capabilities, in violation of the international Nuclear Nonproliferation Treaty. Kim threatened to withdraw from the treaty. In August 1994, former U.S. president **Jimmy Carter** (1924–; served 1977–81; see entry) traveled to North Korea to strike a deal and ease tensions. The controversial agreement he reached with Kim's representatives promised U.S. aid to North Korea.

Kim had groomed his son Kim Jong Il (1942–) to take over North Korea's leadership. By the late 1980s, Kim Jong Il assumed control over most daily operations. Kim Il Sung died of a heart attack on July 8, 1994. Informants provided striking information on the extreme efforts used to try to sustain Kim's life. Apparently, a clinic of two thousand specialists had been created by Kim simply for himself and his son. The clinic experimented with drugs and diets to keep the elder Kim alive through his later years. Kim Jong Il became the de facto leader upon his father's death and officially took leadership of the country in 1997.

For More Information

Books

Armstrong, Charles K. *The North Korean Revolution, 1945–1950*. Ithaca, NY: Cornell University Press, 2003.

Bridges, Brian. *Korea and the West*. New York: Routledge, 1986.

Buzo, Adrian. *The Making of Modern Korea*. New York: Routledge, 2002.

Mazarr, Michael J. *North Korea and the Bomb: A Case Study in Nonproliferation*. New York: St. Martin's Press, 1995.

Oberdorfer, Don. *The Two Koreas: A Contemporary History*. Reading, MA: Addison-Wesley, 1997.

Suh, Dae-sook. *Kim Il Sung: The North Korean Leader*. New York: Columbia University Press, 1988.

Tennant, Roger. *A History of Korea*. New York: Columbia University Press, 1996.

Jeane Kirkpatrick

Born November 19, 1926
Duncan, Oklahoma

U.S. diplomat

J eane Kirkpatrick was the first American woman to be named a permanent representative to the United Nations (UN). The UN is an international organization that was established at the conclusion of World War II (1939–45); its purpose is to peacefully resolve conflicts before they lead to war. Kirkpatrick held this post from 1981 to 1985. She exercised greater influence over the formulation of U.S. foreign policy than any other representative before her. Respected for the strength and conviction of her views, she remained active in American political life long after leaving office. In 1985, Congress awarded Kirkpatrick its highest civilian honor, the Presidential Medal of Freedom.

"We have war when at least one of the parties to a conflict wants something more than it wants peace."

Political beginnings

Born Jeane Duane Jordan on November 19, 1926, Jeane Kirkpatrick was the daughter of Leona Kile Jordan and Welcher F. Jordan, an oil-drilling contractor in the town of Duncan, Oklahoma. Both parents took politics seriously and instilled in Jeane a sense of civic duty.

Jeane Kirkpatrick. *Courtesy of the Library of Congress.*

Jeane finished her undergraduate work at Barnard College and went on to earn a master's degree in political science from Columbia University in New York in 1950. She then worked in an intelligence and research bureau at the U.S. State Department. The bureau was headed by Evron "Kirk" Kirkpatrick, a former political science professor. After a year of study at the Institute of Political Science in Paris, France, Jeane returned to the United States and married Kirkpatrick in 1955. They honeymooned at a political science conference at Northwestern University. Jeane's marriage to Evron Kirkpatrick led her from a scholarly interest in politics to active participation in the Democratic Party. The couple raised three sons while Jeane was working on her doctorate and beginning her career as a college professor. She received her Ph.D. (doctoral degree) in 1968 from Columbia University.

Jeane Kirkpatrick concentrated on furthering her career as an academic, first as an assistant professor of political science at Trinity College in Washington, D.C., and later as associate professor and then full professor at Georgetown University, also in Washington, D.C. During the 1970s, she was a political activist and held several important positions in the Democratic Party while writing political articles. In 1974, Kirkpatrick published *Political Woman,* a work dealing with women in state legislatures.

In 1979, one of Kirkpatrick's articles appeared in the November issue of *Commentary.* Kirkpatrick laid out her criticism of U.S. foreign policy in the article, titled "Dictatorships and Double Standards." The foundation of her argument was the importance of weaving a careful course between support for authoritarian political regimes and opposition to totalitarian governments. Authoritarian governments are headed by a single leader or a small group of people who are not constitutionally answerable for their actions and who demand total obedience from all citizens. Authoritarian governments are often military dictatorships. Totalitarian governments, such as communist governments, exert almost complete control over citizens' lives. A communist government controls the economy by controlling production and prices; it controls political opposition by restricting individual liberties and banning all political parties other than the Communist Party.

Early U.S. policy during the Cold War (1945–91), a prolonged conflict for world dominance between the democratic

United States and the communist Soviet Union, was to support oppressive authoritarian regimes, primarily military dictatorships in Latin America, because of their strong anticommunist positions. Totalitarian regimes, Kirkpatrick argued, could not be expected to change. In her view, authoritarian regimes held more potential for reform and thus were proper recipients of U.S. support. Despite her Democratic standing, Kirkpatrick's argument fit the views of hard-line conservatives of the time, such as Republican presidential hopeful **Ronald Reagan** (1911–; served 1981–89; see entry), the former governor of California. Reagan invited Kirkpatrick to join his group of advisors; she accepted the offer and participated in Reagan's successful 1980 campaign for the presidency.

At the United Nations

President Reagan appointed Kirkpatrick as permanent representative to the United Nations in 1981. She was a Democrat and the top woman in his administration. Kirkpatrick was also a member of the National Security Council, the part of the executive branch of the U.S. government that advises the president on matters of foreign policy and defense. Kirkpatrick spoke fluent French and Spanish, but she had no experience in directing foreign affairs or in managing a diplomatic post. The two institutions where she was supposed to fulfill her responsibilities—the State Department in Washington, D.C., and the United Nations in New York—at first viewed her as a complete outsider.

Kirkpatrick shared President Reagan's anti-Soviet views and could be counted on to be a tough, articulate spokesperson at the United Nations. Reagan and Kilpatrick's admiration for each other and their shared beliefs on foreign policy gave Kirkpatrick a strong position in the administration. She is considered one of the chief architects of Reagan's hard-nosed anticommunist policies. Communism is a system of government in which a single political party, the Communist Party, controls nearly all aspects of society. In a communist economy, goods produced and wealth accumulated are, in theory, shared equally by all. Communist nations such as the Soviet Union are incompatible with capitalist democracies such as the United States. A democratic system of government allows multiple political parties. Capitalism is an economic system in which

Jeane Kirkpatrick, U.S. ambassador to the United Nations, looks on as U.S. president Ronald Reagan (left) greets Soviet foreign minister Andrey Gromyko at a meeting of the UN General Assembly, September 23, 1984.
Reproduced by permission of the Corbis Corporation.

property and businesses can be privately owned. Production, distribution, and prices of goods are determined by competition in a market relatively free of government intervention.

Relations between the United States and the Soviet Union had reached their lowest point in the years following the Soviet invasion of Afghanistan in late 1979. The United States responded by strengthening its military systems and bolstering the strength of its allies in Western Europe. Kirkpatrick's stance in the UN reflected the Reagan administration's confrontational attitude in world affairs. Although her straightforward style was often criticized, Kirkpatrick was credited with giving strong, effective responses to Soviet attacks. However, as her four years at the UN progressed, the U.S. position toward the Soviets became less confrontational and leaned more toward a posture of negotiation with the Soviets. This set the tone for future discussions on disarmament (reduction or removal of nuclear weapons) and the end of the Cold War in 1991.

Books and Honors of Jeane Kirkpatrick

Honors:

Jeane Kirkpatrick has been awarded medals by President Václav Havel (1936–) of the Czech Republic, for promoting democracy, human rights, and the enlargement of the North Atlantic Treaty Organization (NATO), a peacetime alliance of the United States and eleven other nations, and a key factor in the attempt to contain communism; and President H. E. Arpad Goncz (1922–) of Hungary, for contributions to NATO enlargement and a democratic Europe. She twice received the Fiftieth Anniversary Friend of Zion Award from the prime minister of Israel and the Casey Medal of Honor from the Center for Security Studies. She also received America's highest civilian honor, the Presidential Medal of Freedom (1985).

Books:

Leader and Vanguard in Mass Society (1971)

Political Woman (1974)

The New Presidential Elite (1976)

The Withering Away of the Totalitarian State (1990)

Good Intentions (1996)

Going home

In 1985, Kirkpatrick resigned from her position and officially joined the Republican Party. She returned to Georgetown University to teach, write, and speak. Kirkpatrick became a fellow at the American Enterprise Institute, a conservative research group in Washington, D.C. In 1993, she cofounded Empower America, a conservative public policy organization. Heads of state and foreign ministers continued to seek her advice on world affairs. In 2003, President George W. Bush (1946–; served 2001–) appointed Kirkpatrick to the Human Rights Commission of the Economic and Social Council of the United Nations.

For More Information

Books

Finger, Seymour Maxwell. *American Ambassadors at the UN: People, Politics, and Bureaucracy in Making Foreign Policy.* New York: UNITAR, 1990.

Gerson, Allan. *The Kirkpatrick Mission: Diplomacy without Apology: America at the United Nations, 1981–1985.* New York: The Free Press, 1991.

Kirkpatrick, Jeane J. *Dictatorships and Double Standards: Rationalism and Reason in Politics.* New York: Simon and Schuster, 1982.

LeVeness, Frank P., and Jane P. Sweeney, eds. *Women Leaders in Contemporary U.S. Politics.* Boulder, CO: L. Rienner, 1987.

Shultz, George P. *Turmoil and Triumph: Diplomacy, Power, and the Victory of the American Ideal.* New York: Charles Scribner's Sons, 1993.

Winik, Jay. *On the Brink: The Dramatic, Behind-the-Scenes Saga of the Reagan Era and the Men and Women Who Won the Cold War.* New York: Simon and Schuster, 1996.

Web Sites

"Dr. Jeane Kirkpatrick." *Harry Walker Agency.* http://www.harrywalker. com/speakers_template_printer.cfm?Spea_ID=143 (accessed on September 10, 2003).

"Jeane Kirkpatrick to speak at KU." *The University of Kansas: Office of University Relations.* http://www.ur.ku.edu/News/00N/AprNews/Apr18/ jeane.html (accessed on September 10, 2003).

Henry Kissinger

Born May 27, 1923
Fürth, Germany

U.S. secretary of state and
national security advisor

German-born Henry Kissinger was a major influence on U.S. foreign policy through most of the Cold War. He worked as an author and as a consultant to various federal agencies and later became national security advisor and secretary of state. He was the architect of détente, the policy of easing tensions between the United States and the Soviet Union. He led the effort to reestablish formal relations with communist China, and he was a key negotiator of the peace settlement in the Vietnam War (1954–75). He was awarded the 1973 Nobel Peace Prize for facilitating the peace agreement. Kissinger also negotiated the first strategic arms limitation treaty (SALT I) with the Soviet Union, which was signed in 1972.

"There cannot be a crisis next week. My schedule is already full."

An international beginning

Henry Kissinger was born in Fürth, Germany, in 1923 to an Orthodox Jewish family. In 1938, the family emigrated from Germany to escape persecution of Jews by the Nazi Party (known primarily for its brutal policies of racism). The Kissingers first went to England and then to New York City.

Henry Kissinger. *Photograph by Wally McNamee. Reproduced by permission of the Corbis Corporation.*

Kissinger attended City College in New York and worked in a shaving brush factory to support himself. In 1943, during World War II (1939–45), Kissinger became a naturalized U.S. citizen and was drafted into the U.S. Army. He was assigned to an intelligence, or information-gathering, unit. After the war, he was briefly assigned to a district administrator position in occupied Germany.

Upon returning to the United States, Kissinger entered Harvard University in 1946, where he earned an undergraduate degree with honors in 1950. He went on to earn a Ph.D. in international relations in 1954. In his dissertation, or graduate essay, he analyzed political strategies that had historically been used in Europe and began forming his own ideas on how foreign policy should be conducted. In 1954, Kissinger joined the Harvard staff as an instructor and worked with the Council on Foreign Relations. The council explored alternative foreign policy strategies—that is, strategies that would not involve the massive nuclear retaliation promoted by then–U.S. secretary of state **John Foster Dulles** (1888–1959; see entry). The council proposed a strategy that included limited use of nuclear weapons and increased spending for conventional forces; this strategy was designed to give the United States more flexibility in responding to crises. In 1957, Kissinger published a book on this subject. Titled *Nuclear Weapons and Foreign Policy,* the book established Kissinger as a leading authority on U.S. strategic foreign policy.

Foreign affairs consultant

During the 1950s, Kissinger was a consultant on foreign issues for New York governor Nelson A. Rockefeller (1908–1979) during Rockefeller's unsuccessful bids for the Republican presidential nomination. In 1961, Kissinger published another book, *The Necessity for Choice.* In this work, he further spelled out his concepts of a flexible response, which emphasized a more balanced development of military capabilities with sufficient conventional forces and smaller nuclear weapons in response to more limited hostilities. President **John F. Kennedy** (1917–1963; served 1961–63; see entry) adopted Kissinger's ideas in forming his Cold War strategies in early 1961. Around this time, Kissinger became a full professor at Harvard.

At Harvard, Kissinger was involved in various foreign policy development groups, and he acted as a consultant for several federal agencies from 1955 to 1968. From 1959 to 1969, he directed Harvard's Defense Studies Program. From 1961 to 1967, he was a consultant for the Arms Control and Disarmament Agency. For the Kennedy administration, he was also advisor to the National Security Council (NSC). Under the administration of President **Lyndon B. Johnson** (1908–1973; served 1963–69; see entry), Kissinger was a consultant to the State Department. During that period, he traveled to South Vietnam to assess the war and determine whether any new strategies could be employed. He returned convinced that the war was necessary to contain communism; he believed that any hasty withdrawal of U.S. forces would lead to a loss of U.S. credibility in the world.

After Republican **Richard M. Nixon** (1913–1994; served 1969–74; see entry) won the presidential race in November 1968, he recruited Kissinger to be his national security advisor. Over the next few years, Kissinger and Nixon would work very closely together and discover that they shared many of the same perspectives on foreign policy. Nixon required that all information from his secretary of defense and secretary of state come through Kissinger. As a result, Kissinger became the most powerful person in the administration other than the president himself.

Ending the Vietnam War

A top priority for Nixon and Kissinger was to end U.S. involvement in the Vietnam War. Vietnam had been one of several French colonies in an Asian peninsula called Indochina, which extends from the southeastern border of China into the South China Sea. Following World War II, **Ho Chi Minh** (1890–1969; see entry) led communist rebel forces in ongoing battles to end French domination in Vietnam. By 1954, the French forces were defeated. As a result of a meeting in Geneva, which included the United States, China, and the Soviet Union, Vietnam was partitioned temporarily into North Vietnam and South Vietnam. Ho Chi Minh's forces controlled North Vietnam, with support from the Soviet Union and communist China. South Vietnam was under Western control.

The Geneva agreement called for national elections to be held in 1956 to establish a single unified government for Vietnam, as well as the other Indochina countries of Laos and Cambodia. The agreement also prohibited any of the three countries from joining military alliances or allowing foreign military bases within their borders. However, the United States objected to communist control of the north and refused to observe the ban on military assistance to South Vietnam. A separate South Vietnamese government was established in 1955, and the United States offered its support.

In response, North Vietnam, along with South Vietnamese rebel forces known as the Vietcong, conducted a civil war to try to gain control of South Vietnam; North Vietnam wanted to unify the country under communist rule. U.S. military assistance to South Vietnam escalated dramatically through the 1960s. By 1967, the United States had over five hundred thousand troops in Vietnam, and U.S. casualties averaged five hundred per week. The war had become highly unpopular among American citizens; peace protesters and staunch supporters of the war clashed in large, nationwide demonstrations. By 1968, it was obvious that the war was not winnable for the United States. Hoping to avoid a humiliation for the United States, Kissinger sought to negotiate a settlement with North Vietnam. However, the North Vietnamese would not accept Kissinger's terms, which included formal recognition of South Vietnam's government. Instead, North Vietnam chose to continue with the war, still hoping to reunify the country.

After the peace talks failed, Kissinger introduced a strategy called Vietnamization. Under this plan, the United States began withdrawing troops and turned the ground war over to the South Vietnamese army. The United States continued to provide training supplies and air power. To give the South Vietnamese forces a boost, Kissinger approved secret bombings of North Vietnamese supply camps in Cambodia. Then, U.S. and South Vietnamese troops entered Cambodia to destroy enemy sanctuaries, or safe places normally protected from attack. Almost all of Kissinger's aides resigned in protest; they were appalled by this congressionally unauthorized invasion. Kissinger's aggressive military tactics damaged his relationships with academic colleagues and members of Congress. He gained a reputation for being arrogant and became a target of antiwar protests.

By 1972, most U.S. troops had been withdrawn from Vietnam. But with the presidential election approaching in November, Nixon insisted that Kissinger achieve a settlement in the war. Nixon hoped that ending the war would increase his chances for reelection. While intense bombing continued, Kissinger reached an apparent agreement in late October. Kissinger made the surprise announcement only days before the election, and Nixon won the election handily. However, the South Vietnamese leaders rejected the agreement, and further talks with North Vietnam broke down in December. Nixon ordered renewed intensive bombing of North Vietnamese cities for eleven days through late December; these are known as the "Christmas Bombings."

By early January, North Vietnam renewed the peace talks, and a cease-fire settlement, very similar to the earlier agreement, was reached. This time, Nixon put pressure on South Vietnam to agree as well. The last U.S. combat troops left Vietnam in late March 1973. Later that year, in October,

U.S. national security advisor Henry Kissinger (far left) speaks with North Vietnamese negotiator Le Duc Tho; a translator is between them. *Courtesy of the National Archives and Records Administration.*

Kissinger and North Vietnamese negotiator Le Duc Tho (1911–1990) were awarded the Nobel Peace Prize. However, Le Duc Tho refused to accept the award on principle because it was offered by a Western country. Despite the settlement, fighting soon resumed between the North Vietnam and South Vietnam forces, which led to the victory in the North in 1975 and reunification of Vietnam under communist rule.

Renewed relations with China

During the first year of Nixon's presidency, the United States and the Communist People's Republic of China (PRC) agreed to pursue improved relations. In July 1971, Kissinger secretly traveled to China to arrange a visit by Nixon. Kissinger was the first U.S. official to visit the Chinese communists since the PRC government was formed in October 1949. At the time of the communist victory, the overthrown noncommunist Chinese leaders fled to the island of Taiwan and formed a new government called the Republic of China (ROC). For the next few decades, the United States recognized the noncommunist ROC, not the PRC, as the official government of China. During his visit to China, Kissinger indicated that the United States was willing to recognize the noncommunist ROC government as part of one China. The recognition meant the United States did not consider the ROC as a truly independent nation but only part of the greater China that was governed by the PRC; this was a major shift in U.S. perspective and a major victory for the PRC. President Nixon journeyed to the PRC seven months later, in February 1972, to begin the process of renewing official relations.

Détente with the Soviets

Kissinger believed that the United States and the Soviet Union should begin working more closely together. After establishing better U.S. relations with the PRC in 1972, he was determined to ease tensions even further by achieving a balance of power between the two superpowers. Kissinger wanted the United States to move away from its policy of massive retaliation in case of conflict. He preferred Mutual Assured Destruction (MAD), a military strategy in which the

threat of catastrophic damages by a nuclear counterstrike would deter any launch of a first-strike attack. This strategy recognized that both superpowers had sufficient nuclear weapons to destroy each other. The effectiveness of MAD hinged on the superpowers agreeing to hold the same number of nuclear weapons. The balance would deter nuclear war, because any nuclear aggression by either side would be, in effect, assured suicide. Kissinger had begun negotiating a strategic arms limitation agreement in November 1969, hoping to maintain nuclear balance.

Kissinger secretly traveled to Moscow in 1972 with the goal of scheduling a summit meeting between President Nixon and Soviet leader **Leonid Brezhnev** (1906–1982; see entry) that May. When Nixon arrived in May, he signed several agreements with the Soviets, including SALT I, the Strategic Arms Limitation Treaty that Kissinger had initiated in 1969. The other agreements involved cultural and scientific exchanges. Kissinger indicated that if the Soviets could help

Members of the Nixon administration (left to right): CIA director Richard M. Helms, national security advisor Henry Kissinger, Secretary of State William P. Rogers, President Richard Nixon, Secretary of Defense Melvin R. Laird, chairman of U.S. Joint Chiefs of Staff Thomas H. Moorer, and Alexander M. Haig, Kissinger's chief military assistant. *Reproduced by permission of the Richard Nixon Library.*

persuade the North Vietnamese to negotiate for peace, the United States would sign a trade agreement to provide the Soviets much-needed grain. After the Soviets traveled to North Vietnam, Kissinger negotiated a grain sale agreement in September. In October, Nixon and Brezhnev signed another arms control agreement, the ABM Treaty, which restricted defensive antiballistic missile systems. In 1973, Brezhnev journeyed to the United States to further the improved relations between the two superpowers.

While Kissinger was busy improving relations with the PRC and the Soviet Union, U.S. relations with Western European allies were deteriorating. The Western European countries felt left out of the negotiations between the United States and the Soviet Union and feared their security was being threatened. They were concerned that discussions would lead to reductions in U.S. forces as well as support for Western Europe, potentially leaving them vulnerable to future Soviet attack if the Soviets reneged on their deals with the United States.

Cold War elsewhere

In 1973, Nixon appointed Kissinger as secretary of state. Kissinger maintained his position as national security advisor as well. Kissinger had firm control over foreign affairs while Nixon was becoming increasingly consumed with the growing domestic Watergate situation. This was a scandal that began on June 17, 1972, when five men were caught burglarizing the offices of the Democratic National Committee in the Watergate complex in Washington, D.C. This led to a cover-up, political convictions, and, eventually, Nixon' s resignation.

In October 1973, Kissinger convinced Nixon to provide support to Israel during its war with Egypt despite protests from Secretary of Defense James Schlesinger (1929–). Meanwhile, Kissinger and Brezhnev tried to negotiate a cease-fire between the two countries. The United States and the Soviet Union were involved because the United States had supported Israel since it declared formation of the Jewish state and the Soviets strongly courted Egypt's friendship. They both had desires to hold control of the Middle East and the oil-rich areas there. Despite U.S. and Soviet intervention, negotiations broke down as Israel gained the advantage on the battlefield. In reaction, Nixon threatened a nuclear attack. To ease the situation, the United Nations obtained a cease-fire resolution and placed a peacekeeping force in the region.

Kissinger soon began what was called "shuttle diplomacy," flying back and forth between Israel and Egypt to work out a peace settlement. As a result, the United States and Egypt reestablished formal relations, which had been broken off in 1967. These events formed the foundation for a historic treaty between Israel and Egypt in 1978, while **Jimmy Carter** (1924–; served 1977–81; see entry) was president. However, U.S. support of Israel during the conflict led to an oil embargo, or legal restriction of trade, by other Arab nations. They refused to ship oil for several months (December 1973–March 1974), causing high oil prices, inflation, and increased trade deficits, and making Kissinger very unpopular with many on the home front.

In Latin America, Kissinger secretly supported a military coup, or government overthrow, of Chile's elected leader, **Salvador Allende** (1908–1973; see entry). Allende embraced socialism, a system in which the government owns or controls all means of production and all citizens share in the work and products. Allende was nationalizing industries and introducing land reform to restructure the Chilean economy and ease the nation's poverty. Nationalism refers to the strong loyalty of a person or group to its own country. Previous U.S. owners of these nationalized companies were not compensated for their losses. The United States did not want Allende to be Chile's president because neither Nixon nor Kissinger believed that Chile should have a socialist government. They worried that Chile could be the first of many South American governments to fall to communism.

In 1973, Allende was overthrown and replaced with a military dictator named Augusto Pinochet (1915–). Pinochet would proceed to establish a brutal regime over Chile's citizens, leading to much criticism of Kissinger's efforts. The United States worked with harsh and dictatorial regimes such as Pinochet's because these regimes shared the U.S. government's anticommunist views. The United States preferred to support strong central governments, even brutal ones, rather than let communist influences take hold in struggling Latin American countries.

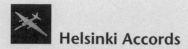

Helsinki Accords

While Henry Kissinger was serving as national security advisor for President Richard Nixon, one of his main foreign policy goals was to reduce political and military tensions between the United States and the Soviet Union. This goal was achieved—even exceeded—at a meeting of thirty-five nations in Helsinki, Finland, in August 1975. Kissinger was no longer serving as national security advisor at that time, but his earlier efforts—and several years of discussions between the United States and the Soviet Union—had led up to the event, which was called the Conference on Security and Cooperation in Europe (CSCE). The participating countries included the Soviet Union and the rest of the Western and Eastern European nations, the United States, and Canada. On August 1, these nations signed what became known as the Helsinki Accords. By signing the accords, each nation agreed to:

- Continue pursuing the policies of détente
- Recognize the rights of independent nations to choose their political systems
- Denounce the use of threat of force and support of terrorism
- Respect the fundamental individual freedoms of thought and religious belief
- Work toward increased international trade

Kissinger's role in the secret bombing of Cambodia and the coup of Allende raised questions about the legality of his actions and the extent of his power. Nonetheless, Kissinger persevered and was spared formal challenges by Congress. Meanwhile, as Nixon became increasingly entangled in the Watergate scandal, his future as president was in doubt. Noting these developments, the Soviets became less interested in discussions with the faltering administration, and détente suffered by late 1973. Nixon resigned as president on August 9, 1974.

The Ford administration

New president Gerald R. Ford (1913–; served 1974–77) kept Kissinger as national security advisor and secretary of state. However, conservative critics attacked détente policies, charging that Kissinger was selling out to the Soviets. In addi-

- Encourage a freer flow of ideas

The Helsinki Accords did not have the force of law or the same obligation as a more formal treaty. Instead, the agreement represented a mutual moral commitment to seek these common goals. Most important, from the Soviet perspective, the accords provided official recognition of European postwar boundaries by allowing communist Eastern European nations to sign the treaty as well. The Soviet-controlled Eastern European nations now had a much higher level of international recognition.

In the following years, the United States, particularly under President Jimmy Carter's administration, would stress the human rights elements of the accords. This would cause increased friction with Eastern European governments and the Soviet Union. The Soviets believed that the United States was interfering in the domestic affairs of the Soviet Union and Eastern European nations. A second CSCE summit was held in Paris in November 1990 to formally mark the end of the Cold War. At that session, participating nations, which included the Soviet Union, represented by **Mikhail Gorbachev** (1931–; see entry), signed a sweeping arms reduction treaty for Europe and made a formal commitment to support democracies based on human rights and fundamental freedoms.

tion, liberals complained about Kissinger's disregard for human rights issues—certain economic and political freedoms that all people, simply by being human, deserve—which he had neglected to consider when establishing pro-U.S. military dictatorships in Latin America. President Ford removed Kissinger as national security advisor in November 1975 in an effort to satisfy the critics.

The high point of détente came in 1975 with the Helsinki Accords, an agreement signed by thirty-five nations including the United States and the Soviet Union. The historic international agreement addressed many topics, including the recognition of post–World War II national boundaries and the promotion of human rights. For thirty years, the Soviets had sought official recognition of the postwar boundaries of Eastern European countries under their influence. With the Helsinki Accords, they finally achieved that goal (see box).

But the Helsinki Accords provided another target for conservative critics of Kissinger's détente policies. During his 1976 campaign for the Republican presidential nomination, former California governor **Ronald Reagan** (1911–; see entry) charged that Kissinger and the Ford administration had caved in to Soviet demands. In addition, Reagan attacked U.S. acceptance of the PRC. During the national election that fall, Democratic presidential candidate Jimmy Carter attacked the policies of Kissinger as well.

Life after public office

When Carter took office as president in January 1977, Kissinger left his post as secretary of state and went back to work as a consultant; he also continued writing books and presenting lectures. His later books include several memoirs: *The White House Years* (1979), *For the Record* (1981), and *Diplomacy* (1994). Kissinger's stature as an elder statesman and an expert on U.S. foreign policy enabled him to form his own foreign policy consulting firm in Washington, D.C., called Kissinger Associates, Inc. Many of his clients were international corporations.

In 1983, President Reagan appointed Kissinger to lead the Central American Policy Committee. In 1987, Kissinger traveled to Moscow to consult with Soviet leader Gorbachev. In 1988, Kissinger advised Vice President **George Bush** (1924–; see entry) on foreign matters during Bush's successful campaign to succeed Reagan as president. During Bush's presidency, Kissinger encouraged the president to work more closely with Gorbachev and support new Soviet reforms. In later years, Kissinger remained a respected though still controversial foreign affairs expert sought at times by both public officials and the news media for his perspectives on national security issues.

For More Information

Books

Bell, Coral. *The Diplomacy of Detente: The Kissinger Era*. New York: St. Martin's Press, 1977.

Isaacson, Walter. *Kissinger: A Biography*. New York: Simon and Schuster, 1992.

Kissinger, Henry. *Diplomacy.* New York: Simon and Schuster, 1996.

Kissinger, Henry. *The White House Years.* Boston: Little, Brown, 1979.

Szulc, Tad. *The Illusion of Peace: Foreign Policy in the Nixon-Kissinger Years.* New York: Viking, 1979.

Thornton, Richard C. *The Nixon-Kissinger Years: Reshaping America's Foreign Policy.* New York: Paragon Books, 1989.

Web Sites

Gerald R. Ford Library and Museum. http://www.ford.utexas.edu (accessed on September 8, 2003).

The Richard Nixon Library and Birthplace. http://www.nixonfoundation.org (accessed on September 8, 2003).

Helmut Kohl

Born April 3, 1930
Ludwigshafen, Germany

German chancellor

"I have been underestimated for decades. I have done very well that way."

Helmut Kohl. *Photograph by Hermann J. Kippertz. Reproduced by permission of AP/Wide World Photos.*

Helmut Kohl became the chancellor of West Germany in the early 1980s. After West Germany and East Germany reunited on October 3, 1990, he became chancellor of the entire country, winning Germany's first nationwide elections since World War II (1939–45). At the end of the war, Germany had been divided along zones of Allied occupation. The Soviet zone was called East Germany; like the Soviet Union, East Germany had a communist government. The three other occupied zones, controlled jointly by the British, the French, and the Americans, were called West Germany. Like the occupying Western countries, West Germany had a democratic government and a capitalist economy.

Kohl engineered the reunification of his country and then oversaw its rise to economic dominance in Europe. He was the longest-serving German leader since 1945, acting as chancellor for a total of sixteen years. Kohl saw three U.S. presidents, five Soviet leaders, and nine Japanese prime ministers come and go during his time in office.

Faithful beginnings

Helmut Michael Kohl was born April 3, 1930, the third child of Hans and Cacilie Kohl. The Kohls were conservative and felt great pride in their country. Both parents were Roman Catholic; they took their faith seriously, and family was very important to them. They voted, as long as it was possible to cast a free vote, for the Catholic Centre Party of Germany.

Helmut Kohl's personality was shaped by the Palatinate, the German region where he grew up. His heartfelt enjoyment of life and his admitted fondness for good food and drink reflect attitudes prevalent in the area. Surveys taken there indicate that the Palatines are convinced life is merrier in the Palatinate than in any other part of the world.

Helmut's father, Hans, had been an officer in World War I (1914–18). When Hans returned home, he began a civil service career and rose to the grade of senior secretary. He resigned from the Stahlhelm (the German federation of war veterans) to protest the seizure of power by Adolf Hitler (1889–1945) and the crimes being committed by Hitler's Nazi Party, which was known primarily for its brutal policies of racism. Hans was a calm, deliberate man who made a lasting impression on his son.

Kohl spent his childhood in the Ludwigshafen district of Friesenheim. Even though 1930 was a difficult economic year for Germany, the Kohls lived modestly. Massive unemployment affected many of their neighbors, but Kohl's father's job was secure. When Kohl was nine years old, World War II broke out and everything changed. Frequent bombing raids reduced extensive sections of Ludwigshafen to ash and rubble. Eighty percent of the city was destroyed. Working as a member of the fire brigade when he was twelve years old, Helmut experienced the horror of seeing burned corpses.

At the end of 1944, Kohl was sent to a pre-military training camp, where he was trained to be an antiaircraft gunner's helper. He also served as a messenger in Bavaria, an area in southern Germany. About this time, his brother Walter was killed in the war. When the war ended, Kohl walked home across a devastated Germany. He arrived back home in June 1945.

Growing up in the Palatinate also shaped Kohl's worldview. The region lies along the western border of Germany and had historically been subject to occupation by various ruling powers. In 1948, at the age of eighteen, Kohl was present when young people pulled up boundary posts near an Alsatian village and demonstrated for a free, boundless Europe. (Alsace is a region in northeast France that borders southwestern Germany. Long under dispute by France and Germany, the area was taken and held by the Germans during World War II, from 1940 to 1944.) For Kohl, the quest for European integration, an economic and political alliance much like the later European Union of the twenty-first century, had a strong emotional element. Early in his life, he had been drawn to the idea of eliminating barriers to stronger alliances between nations, which seemed to him unnecessary and divisive.

Return to normal

Helmut Kohl returned to school when his city returned to some normalcy in the summer of 1946. He was student body president, participated in many extracurricular activities, and became a member of a political party called the Christian Democratic Union (CDU). Graduating from high school in 1950, Kohl went on to the University of Frankfurt and then changed to the University of Heidelberg. Having started out in law, Kohl switched his major to history with an emphasis in both constitutional law and political science. He was awarded a doctorate with honors from the University of Heidelberg in 1958. Kohl's dissertation, or graduation essay, focused on the reemergence of political parties in West Germany after the fall of Nazism in 1945.

The following year, Kohl was hired as an executive assistant in an iron foundry in Ludwigshafen. Later in 1959, he was with the Rhineland-Palatinate-Saar Chemical Industry Association as head of the department responsible for economic and fiscal policy, where he stayed until 1969. This promotion provided Kohl with the financial security he needed to marry his longtime sweetheart, Hannelore Renner. They had met at a dance class ball in Friesenheim in 1948, when she was fifteen and he was eighteen. She went on to study foreign languages and worked as a foreign correspondence clerk, using her skills in English and French. The two kept in contact by writing, and she offered to type his doctoral dissertation for him. They finally married in 1960 and had two sons: Walter was born in 1963 and Peter in 1965.

Politics

Although he was working full-time, Kohl was already very active in the CDU. After the war, the CDU was a political party with no paid positions. One could not make a living from politics, so having a professional career was important. However, political affairs fascinated Kohl, and he gave most of his energy to politics. He was elected to the state legislature in 1959. He entered national politics in 1964, when he was elected executive of the federal CDU organization. The CDU had a large Roman Catholic base of voters and included a number of Protestant leaders. Though known to be conservative, the party served to unite diverse interest groups, including women, businessmen, and farmers. The party also promoted social programs such as federal health insurance.

Kohl was minister-president of his home state of Rhineland-Palatinate from 1969 until 1976. He became a member of the lower house of Parliament and leader of the CDU in 1976. Kohl was made chancellor of West Germany in 1982, when the ruling chancellor, Helmut Schmidt (1918–), was removed from office by a no-confidence vote. Kohl was then elected as chancellor in 1983 and won every subsequent election until the reunification of Germany.

Chancellor Kohl

In his first government address as chancellor, Kohl stressed that his foreign policy would rest on Germany's alliance with the United States and cooperation with the North Atlantic Treaty Organization (NATO). NATO began as a military alliance of Western European nations and the United States and Canada; the alliance was formed in 1949 to contain communist expansion. In response, the communist-led countries of Eastern Europe formed the Warsaw Pact a few years later. The Warsaw Pact was a mutual military alliance between the Soviet Union and the Eastern European nations under Soviet influence, including East Germany. Kohl chose to ally West Germany with the United States not because it was the strongest nation, but because it was a fellow democracy. (A democracy is a government that includes several political parties whose members are elected to office by vote of the people.) Kohl would maintain cordial relations with the

Soviet Union and East Germany (also known as the German Democratic Republic, or GDR), but he openly preferred closer ties with the United States and the European community.

Immediately after taking office, Kohl began the process of improving West Germany's relations with its Western allies. He met with French prime minister François Mitterrand (1916–1996) in Paris, British prime minister **Margaret Thatcher** (1925–; see entry) in London, and U.S. president **Ronald Reagan** (1911–; served 1981–89; see entry) in Washington, D.C. Kohl pushed hard for a united Europe that would bind a united Germany in an alliance with its former enemies. However, Germany continued to labor under the cloud of its recent Nazi past. Kohl campaigned tirelessly to reassure the NATO powers and the Soviet Union that a unified Germany posed no threat. Nonetheless, neighboring countries were not yet ready to trust Germany, the nation that had started World War II. Germany would therefore take a slow road to recover its economic strength and international standing. A divided Germany meant restricted economic growth.

Under Kohl's leadership, West Germany concentrated on its economic place in the world. Kohl worked to establish a good reputation for West Germany; he wanted the new nation to be seen as independent but trustworthy. In 1947, the U.S. government had offered a massive financial aid program called the Marshall Plan to help rebuild European countries that had suffered wartime damage. The Soviet Union refused to allow its Eastern European regimes, including East Germany, to participate in this aid program. The Soviets had suffered greatly at the hands of the invading Germans, so they strongly opposed rebuilding Germany's economic base. As time passed, the United States would become increasingly concerned that the Soviets were keeping East Germany economically repressed, in preparation for long-term control of the territory. Europe therefore became a divided region, with the capitalist Western countries benefiting from U.S. aid and the Eastern bloc struggling to establish communist economic principles. Thus the Cold War competition between the United States and the Soviet Union continued, and the front line of the battle shifted to the boundary between West Germany and East Germany, the line where capitalism and communism stood toe-to-toe.

Kohl was initially a strong advocate for basing intermediate-range American missiles on West German soil. He initially argued that the threat of Soviet expansion into Western Europe could only be stopped with the American missile systems in place. However, after his first five years as chancellor, Kohl came to oppose Reagan's proposed high-tech antimissile system, known popularly as the "Star Wars" initiative. NATO's efforts to modernize its short-range nuclear weapons based in West Germany further alarmed Kohl. He believed that the presence of weapons in his country would increase the probability of a nuclear war while decreasing the likelihood that the Western allies would come to West Germany's aid. From then on, Kohl opposed NATO's plans for modernization and demanded that the West start talks with the Soviet Union on the reduction of short-range nuclear systems. He believed nuclear weapons were counterproductive to unifying Germany and Europe.

Moscow connection

Helmut Kohl's hard-line views on nuclear systems and his basic anti-Soviet position, in which he endorsed a unified and integrated Europe free of communist influence, had made him an unpopular figure in Moscow. In a *Newsweek* magazine interview, Kohl actually compared the public relations efforts of new Soviet president **Mikhail Gorbachev** (1931–; see entry) to those of former Nazi propaganda chief Joseph Goebbels (1897–1945). Goebbels was notorious for fabricating information (propaganda) about Hitler and the Nazis as Germany steadily took over one European nation after another. He was able to gain support for Hitler within Germany during the early years. Obviously, such remarks did not improve German-Soviet relations. However, Kohl continued his efforts to normalize relations with East Germany and the Soviet Union. His country was delicately balanced between economic involvement with Eastern Europe and a military alliance with Western forces that could face down the Eastern bloc if necessary.

After the fall

In 1989, rebellion against communist rule spread from one Eastern European nation to another as the populations took advantage of new reforms introduced by Gorbachev and the Soviets that allowed for greater freedoms of expression. In October 1989, public demonstrations against the East Germany communist leaders grew, which led to their resignation and the opening of the Berlin Wall on November 9. East and West Germany soon moved toward reunification. As West German chancellor, Kohl had to deal with unprecedented political and economic problems presented by this unexpected historic event.

Kohl commanded the political discussion on a new East-West relationship. He visited Moscow in January 1990 to gain Soviet consent for German unification talks. In June, he assured President **George Bush** (1924–; served 1989–93; see entry) that the reunified Germany would remain in NATO. The last external obstacle to reunification was removed in July, when Kohl received Gorbachev's agreement that a united, sovereign Germany could remain in NATO. In September, a treaty signed in Moscow made reunification official: The German Democratic Republic (GDR, or East Germany) would be formally absorbed into the Federal Republic of Germany (FRG, or West Germany) on October 3, 1990. That fall, Kohl participated in the official end of World War II when Germany signed the Treaty on the Final Settlement with Respect to Germany. (The emerging Cold War rivalry between the United States and the Soviet Union in the late 1940s had blocked final negotiations at that time.) Then on September 12, Kohl was involved in the signing of the Conventional Forces Treaty for Europe (CFE), which effectively ended the Cold War. This treaty was a nonaggression agreement between members of NATO and the Warsaw Pact. The Warsaw Pact was subsequently dissolved in 1991.

Helmut Kohl soon took a step that had been unimaginable before 1990—campaigning in East Germany against communist candidates. It was the first nationwide elections since Hitler came to power in 1933. Kohl and the Christian Democrats swept state and federal elections in January 1991, and Kohl became the first chancellor of a reunited Germany. He was reelected in 1994 and remained chancellor until his electoral defeat in 1998. A campaign finances scandal in 1999 forced Kohl to resign his honorary chairman position of the CDU in 2000.

Early political advisors urged Kohl to rid his speech of its traces of dialect, or speech pattern, so he would appear

The Berlin Wall

The world was stunned when the Berlin Wall went up on August 13, 1961. In the previous seven months, approximately two hundred thousand East Germans had abandoned most of their belongings and headed to the western sectors of Berlin. The East German economy could not afford the continued loss in population. In order to stop the flow, Soviet leader **Nikita Khrushchev** (1894–1971; see entry) decided to institute a plan he had devised years earlier: constructing a wall between East and West Berlin, to seal off the western sectors of the city from the eastern sector.

An initial barrier of barbed wire was hastily put up overnight after a secret meeting of Eastern European Warsaw Pact leaders in Moscow a week earlier. The barbed wire was connected to concrete posts. The barrier ran through the heart of Berlin. Constructed street by street, it followed the boundary between the Soviet East Berlin sector and the western sectors of the city. Soviet tanks sat poised a few blocks back. Materials for the permanent construction of the wall were then brought into Berlin and one of the ugliest symbols of the Cold War was constructed.

Construction of the wall caught the West completely off guard. East Berliners who left for their jobs in West Berlin discovered that their trains stopped at the new boundary. And families, many of whom had relatives living in all sectors of the city, suddenly found themselves split apart. U.S. president **John F. Kennedy** (1917–1963; served 1961–63; see entry) chose to do nothing, fearing any interference could ultimately lead to war. Khrushchev guessed correctly that as long as West Berlin was left unharmed and its access routes were open to West Germany, the United States would not risk war.

The Wall remained intact for twenty-eight years. On November 10, 1989, East Germany dismantled the Berlin Wall and opened access to West Germany. The United States was on the verge of achieving one of its central Cold War objectives—Germany whole and free in a Europe whole and free.

more worldly. In his political life, Kohl often used the word *Heimat* to speak of home in a dual sense: where one was born and where one feels at home. Political opponents often used Kohl's lack of sophistication as a point of ridicule. They criticized him, calling him folksy and average, yet these qualities were part of what made Kohl an appealing character to regular Germans. At 6 feet 4 inches, Kohl was an imposing figure. But his easygoing manner, combined with sharp political skills, made him the people's choice for sixteen years. Voters instinctively felt that Kohl was in control, and they had grown used to his style. Many Germans could hardly remember that there was ever a chancellor other than Kohl.

Kohl never severed his ties to his native city. The Kohl family continued to live in Oggersheim, a district of Ludwigshafen, after his retirement from public life.

For More Information

Books

Bering, Henrik. *Helmut Kohl*. Washington, DC: Regnery Publishing, 1999.

Clemens, Clay, and William Paterson. *The Kohl Chancellorship*. Portland, OR: Frank Cass, 1998.

Muchler, Gunter, and Klaus Hofmann. *Helmut Kohl, Chancellor of German Unity: A Biography*. Bonn, Germany: Press Information Office of the Federal Government, 1992.

Smyser, W. R. *From Yalta to Berlin: The Cold War Struggle over Germany*. New York: St. Martin's Press, 1999.

Sodaro, Michael J. *Moscow, Germany, and the West from Khrushchev to Gorbachev*. Ithaca, NY: Cornell University Press, 1990.

Szabo, Stephen F. *The Diplomacy of German Unification*. New York: St. Martin's Press, 1992.

Web Sites

"Newsmakers: Helmut Kohl." *ABC News*. http://abcnews.go.com/reference/bios/kohl.html (accessed on April 2, 2003).

"Newsmaker Profiles: Helmut Kohl, German Chancellor." *CNN Interactive*. http://www.cnn.com/resources/newsmakers/world/europe/kohl.html (accessed on April 2, 2003).

Aleksey Kosygin

Born February 20, 1904
St. Petersburg, Russia
Died December 18, 1980
Moscow, Russia, Soviet Union

Soviet chairman of the
Council of Ministers

For many years, Aleksey Kosygin played an important role in government administration and economic planning for the Soviet Union. At the peak of his power, he served sixteen years as chairman of the Council of Ministers, a top leadership position in the Soviet Union. He attempted to reform the failing Soviet economic system, but because of strong resistance from other Soviet leaders, he had little success in this effort. He was also involved in several key foreign affairs issues, including the Vietnam War (1954–75) and the Cuban Missile Crisis (1962). Unlike many other Soviet leaders, Kosygin's overall philosophy regarding government policy involved using pragmatism, or common sense, rather than communist ideology as the basis for his decision making.

"Where there are mutual concessions, there is sensible compromise."

Early years and education

Aleksey Nikolayevich Kosygin was born to a working-class family in St. Petersburg, Russia, a city later known as Leningrad. His father was a lathe operator in a local factory. Young Aleksey became caught up in the revolutionary fervor

Aleksey Kosygin.
Reproduced by permission of the United Nations.

of the 1917 Bolshevik Revolution, when Vladimir I. Lenin (1870–1924) and his communist followers took control of the Russian government. Communism is a system of government in which a single political party, the Communist Party, controls nearly all aspects of people's lives. In a communist economy, private ownership of property and businesses is prohibited so that goods produced and wealth accumulated can be shared equally by all.

In 1919, at age fifteen, Kosygin volunteered for the Red Army, which was defending the Bolsheviks' newly established communist government against forces who were trying to retake control of the government. The Red Army and the Bolsheviks prevailed, and in 1921 Kosygin joined the Komsomol, a government youth organization. Along with many other Soviet youths, he entered the recently established Communist Party technical education system in Leningrad, which taught basic education and political doctrine. At the Leningrad Cooperative Technicum trade school, Kosygin learned how to organize and manage cooperatives. Cooperatives are farmlands owned by the government but managed by farmers; the farmers share in the production and profits.

Following graduation in 1924, Kosygin moved to Siberia, in the eastern Soviet Union, to help create a cooperative work system within the state-controlled economy. Kosygin became head of the Siberian Association cooperatives, and he formally joined the Communist Party in 1927. While in Siberia, he married; he and his wife would have two children. In 1930, after six years in Siberia, Kosygin returned to Leningrad and entered the Leningrad Textile Institute. Completing his education there in 1935, he worked his way up in the Leningrad textile plants from shop foreman to factory manager.

Early political career and war years

By the late 1930s, Soviet premier **Joseph Stalin** (1879–1953; see entry) had completed a series of murderous purges of top Communist Party leaders. As a result, the party had many job openings for the new generation of educated young men in the Soviet Union. Promotion in the Communist Party could be very rapid for any young party member who impressed Stalin. Kosygin was fortunate enough to do just that, and by 1938, he began serving in various party positions.

He was first appointed head of Leningrad's Industrial Transport Department. He was also appointed mayor of Leningrad and elected to the Supreme Soviet, the Soviet legislative body. By January 1939, at age thirty-four, he was appointed to a top position in the textile industry of the Soviet Union and elected as a member of the Communist Party's Central Committee. (The Central Committee in the Communist Party was an important administrative body that oversaw day-to-day party activities.)

Kosygin quickly gained national prominence. In 1940, he was named deputy chairman of Sovnarkom, renamed the Council of Ministers in 1946. The council was responsible for the economic planning of Soviet industry. In this position, Kosygin became known for his sensible management style and conservative workmanlike approach. Though he was an impeccable dresser in his leadership roles, Kosygin was comfortable among factory workers. He was serious, knowledgeable, tough-minded, and skillful.

Kosygin played a critical role for the Soviets throughout World War II (1939–45). He directed the Soviet war economy and evacuated industries and workers eastward, away from the advancing German army. For example, in January 1942, he heroically helped five hundred thousand inhabitants of Leningrad elude a massive German blockade of the city by leading them across a frozen lake to safety. The city had been under siege for six months.

Khrushchev and Brezhnev years

After the war, Kosygin continued to direct Soviet economic planning as deputy chairman of the Council of Ministers. In March 1946, he became a candidate for the Politburo, the last official step before gaining full voting membership. The Politburo was the executive body of the Central Committee; its members were responsible for making important national policy decisions. In 1948, Kosygin served as Soviet minister of finance in addition to his other roles. Kosygin worked to help the Soviet economy recover from the ravages of war; this included rebuilding the defense industry. Perhaps because he focused on administration rather than party politics and ideology, Kosygin was able to barely escape one of Stalin's Communist Party purges in 1948. Having survived the purge,

Kosygin moved up to full membership in the Politburo. In 1949, he was named minister of food and light industry.

Following the death of Stalin in March 1953, Kosygin lost his Politburo position because the group was reduced from twenty-five to ten members. Under the new Soviet leader, **Nikita Khrushchev** (1894–1971; see entry), he continued to hold important economic positions, including his role as minister of food and light industry. In 1957, when Khrushchev strengthened his party leadership position, Kosygin regained his earlier position as deputy chairman of the Council of Ministers. He also rejoined the Politburo. Kosygin had hopes of moving up to chairman of the council; however, in 1958 Khrushchev took the position for himself. The relationship between the two was never particularly friendly, but Khrushchev did name Kosygin head of the Soviet economic planning commission, called Gosplan, in 1959 and 1960.

As the Soviet economy declined, Khrushchev lost political support. He was finally ousted from power in late 1964. Kosygin reportedly played a role in Khrushchev's ouster. In place of Khrushchev, **Leonid Brezhnev** (1906–1982; see entry) took over party leadership, and Kosygin finally became chairman of the Council of Ministers. They were now the top two officials in the Soviet Union. Kosygin was fully in charge of economic policies and essentially ran the nation's government while Brezhnev tended to party matters. The two worked smoothly together, even as Brezhnev steadily took over most of the decision making for the country. Kosygin became more and more involved in foreign affairs as a troubleshooter. He traveled to Beijing, China, in September 1969 to negotiate a border settlement that would ease tensions between the two communist countries.

Kosygin was very concerned about the continued decline of the Soviet economy. He believed that the Soviet central economic planning system needed basic reform, so he proposed to decentralize production, particularly in agriculture. As early as 1965, he attempted to introduce the basics of a free market economy, or economic conditions dictated by open competition, into the communist system. He favored monetary rewards for factory managers and workers, believing that higher pay would increase industrial production efficiency. He also pushed for acquisition of Western technology to modernize the Soviet economy.

Glassboro Summit

Even though Aleksey Kosygin's primary role in the Soviet government was to head economic planning, he also tackled several key foreign issues. One was the Vietnam War (1954–75). The war involved U.S. efforts to protect noncommunist South Vietnam from takeover by communist-ruled North Vietnam. As U.S. casualties mounted in the escalating war, President **Lyndon B. Johnson** (1908–1973; served 1963–69; see entry) was increasingly anxious to negotiate for peace with North Vietnam; he hoped the Soviets would assist by bringing their fellow communist country to the negotiating table. However, while a Soviet delegation including Kosygin was visiting North Vietnam, the United States began intensive bombing of the region. Despite Johnson's urgent invitations to the Soviets, Kosygin, irate over the U.S. bombing campaign, would not speak to U.S. officials for two years. Finally, in 1967, even as the war raged on, Kosygin agreed to meet.

Kosygin traveled to the United States in June as part of the Soviet United Nations delegation, and he met with Johnson at Glassboro State College in Glassboro, New Jersey, over a weekend. Though the talks were friendly, the two leaders reached few agreements on the Vietnam War. Kosygin believed it was inappropriate for the United States to be militarily involved in the internal affairs of Vietnam.

Aleksey Kosygin shakes hands with U.S. president Lyndon B. Johnson at the Glassboro Summit in 1967. *Reproduced by permission of the Corbis Corporation.*

Despite Kosygin's hard-line position against U.S. involvement in Vietnam, the Glassboro talks helped improve the relationship between the two leaders. This ultimately led to the signing of the Nuclear Nonproliferation Treaty in 1968, which prohibited the spread of nuclear weapons to other countries. Kosygin and Johnson also agreed to begin strategic arms limitation talks. However, the 1968 Soviet invasion of Czechoslovakia, which both Kosygin and the United States strongly opposed, delayed arms control talks.

Many Soviet officials were highly uncomfortable with Kosygin's proposals for reform. In addition, both Kosygin and Khrushchev had earlier wanted to increase emphasis on the production of consumer goods and light industry. But Brezhnev, Khrushchev's successor, wanted to increase military spending and conduct a massive buildup of arms. When Czechoslovakia attempted to radically reform its communist system in 1968, Soviet communist leaders militarily crushed the Czech reform movement and tabled Kosygin's ideas. However, Kosygin would continue to warn of major problems as Soviet productivity fell and the economy in general deteriorated through the 1970s.

End of career

After suppressing Czechoslovakia's reform movement, Brezhnev steadily gained greater control of the Soviet government and would eventually take over Kosygin's foreign affairs responsibilities. Kosygin remained chairman of the Council of Ministers until October 1980, when he resigned because of ill health. He had suffered two heart attacks in the 1970s. Despite Kosygin's many years of service to the Soviet Union, Brezhnev gave no tribute to Kosygin upon his retirement. When Kosygin died in December at age seventy-six, no official government notice was published for two days. However, his ashes were buried at the Kremlin wall, near the ashes of other deceased Soviet leaders. Just as Kosygin had warned, the Soviet economy would continue its decline, a decline that would lead to the collapse of the Soviet Union only a decade later.

For More Information

Books

Linden, Carl A. *Khrushchev and the Soviet Leadership*. Baltimore, MD: Johns Hopkins University Press, 1990.

McNeal, Robert H. *The Bolshevik Tradition: Lenin, Stalin, Khrushchev, Brezhnev*. 2nd ed. Englewood Cliffs, NJ: Prentice-Hall, 1975.

Owen, Richard. *Crisis in the Kremlin: Soviet Succession and the Rise of Gorbachev*. London: Gollanz, 1986.

Tatu, Michel. *Power in the Kremlin: From Khrushchev to Kosygin*. New York: Viking Press, 1969.

Igor Kurchatov

**Born January 8, 1903
Simskii Zavod,
Southern Ural Mountains, Russia
Died February 1960
St. Sarov (or Arzamas-16),
Russia, Soviet Union**

**Nuclear physicist and
developer of the Soviet atomic bomb**

A brilliant nuclear physicist, Igor Kurchatov headed the development of the atomic bomb in the Soviet Union. Kurchatov's successful development of the bomb played an important role in Cold War politics. The Cold War was an intense political and economic rivalry between the United States and the Soviet Union that lasted from 1945 to 1991. When the United States discovered by way of spy planes that the Soviet Union had detonated its first atomic bomb, it felt compelled to accelerate its own nuclear weapons program. Like his American counterpart, **J. Robert Oppenheimer** (1904–1967; see entry), Kurchatov in his later years stressed that atomic energy should only be used for peaceful purposes.

"I am glad that I … have dedicated my life to Soviet atomic science. I deeply believe, and am firmly convinced, that our people and our government will use the achievements of that science solely for the good of mankind."

Early life

Igor Kurchatov was born on January 8, 1903, to Vassili and Maria Kurchatov in the southern Ural Mountains of Russia. He had an older sister, Antonina, and a younger brother, Boris. Vassili was a forester when Igor was born but soon became a highly respected land surveyor. Maria was a

Igor Kurchatov. *Reproduced by permission of AP/Wide World Photos.*

teacher. The couple settled in the Simsky Factory Township, where Vassili received state honors for his work and was designated a noble. This status allowed his three children to attend school.

When Kurchatov was nine years old, his family moved to Simferopol in Crimea, on the Black Sea. As a youngster, Kurchatov was enthralled with the beauty of both his native Urals and the mountains and sea of Crimea. He graduated with honors from the Simferopol public schools, and only three years later, in 1923, he graduated from Tavricheski (later Crimean) University. At the university, he studied mathematics and physics. Upon graduation, Kurchatov went to Petrograd for a short time to study shipbuilding, for he had once dreamed of a naval career. There, he wrote his first scientific paper; the subject was the radioactivity found in snow. Kurchatov then took a job at Pavlovsk Observatory and published his paper.

Career begins in Leningrad

In 1925, a renowned physicist, Abram Ioffe (1880–1960), invited Kurchatov to join his institute in Leningrad. The institute was the main Soviet center for nuclear physics, and Kurchatov quickly gained a reputation as a brilliant young scientist. There, he became reacquainted with Marina Sinelnikov, whom he had met before in Simferopol. They married on February 3, 1927.

By 1932, Kurchatov and several other Soviet scientists had decided to devote themselves to the study of nuclear physics. It was a new, fascinating field but not expected to yield any practical applications for decades. Kurchatov's Leningrad team built a cyclotron for studying the nucleus of an atom. (A cyclotron is a particle accelerator, or atom smasher, in which small particles are made to travel very fast and then collide with atoms, causing the atoms to break apart.) The scientists eagerly kept up with published nuclear physics research from Cavendish Laboratory in England, part of Cambridge University and long a gathering area for the world's top physicists. They also followed the work of Italian-born American physicist Enrico Fermi (1901–1954) and his team at the University of Rome in Italy. In 1938, German scientists successfully split the nucleus of the element uranium. This reaction, called nuclear fission, released tremendous amounts of energy and was the first step in developing an atomic bomb.

World War II (1939–45) began in Europe in 1939. When the Germans invaded the Soviet Union in 1941, Kurchatov and his Soviet research team halted their work. Kurchatov was assigned to Crimea to help protect the Soviet Black Sea Fleet from mines planted by the Germans. Within the next couple of years, Kurchatov and other Soviet scientists astutely noticed that the previously abundant publication of nuclear research in scientific journals had ceased. They soon presumed that this silence could mean only one thing: Other nuclear physicists must be secretly working on a bomb.

In fact, the United States had brought together a grouping of the world's best physicists, including American, English, and Canadian physicists and German physicists who had fled Nazi rule. In 1943, these scientists converged on the New Mexico desert at a newly established location known as Los Alamos. They were there to work on the top-secret Manhattan Project, the code name for America's atomic bomb development program. U.S. leaders feared that Germany would hold the world hostage if it developed the first atomic bomb. To prevent this, the U.S. government asked the scientists at Los Alamos to create an atomic bomb before the Germans could. At the time, no one realized that the world war had halted the Germans' bomb research.

All research at Los Alamos was done under a veil of secrecy. Nevertheless, Soviet leader **Joseph Stalin** (1879–1953; see entry) soon had reports about the Manhattan Project from Soviet spies. In late 1943, Stalin chose Kurchatov to lead the Soviet Union's own secret atomic bomb effort. A year and a half later, on July 16, 1945, the United States successfully tested an atomic bomb. On August 6 and August 9, the United States dropped atomic bombs on Hiroshima and Nagasaki, Japan, to finally end World War II.

Stalin ordered Kurchatov to push the Soviet atomic bomb "catch-up" project into high gear. He made clear the urgency of the project and demanded that Kurchatov develop a Soviet atomic bomb by 1948. The Soviets feared that if the Americans remained the only ones with an atomic bomb, they would force U.S. interests further into other countries—

Russian Research Centre Kurchatov Institute

The Russian Research Centre Kurchatov Institute was founded by Igor Kurchatov in December 1943 at Arzamas-16, several hundred miles east of Moscow. Originally called Laboratory No. 2 of the USSR Academy of Science, the research center underwent several name changes during the Cold War: In 1949, it was called the Laboratory of Measuring Instruments of the USSR Academy of Science; in 1956, it became the Institute of Atomic Energy; and in 1960, it was renamed the I. V. Kurchatov Institute of Atomic Energy. The center took its present name in 1991.

Originally, in the early 1940s, about one hundred scientists worked at the laboratory on the top-secret Soviet atomic bomb project. In January 2002, approximately fifty-three hundred workers were actively pursuing scientific research at the Kurchatov Institute. International scientific meetings are routinely held at the

The Kurchatov Institute in Moscow. *Photograph by Ivan Sekretarev. Reproduced by permission of AP/Wide World Photos.*

institute. Igor Kurchatov's home at Arzamas-16, known as the "Forester's Cabin," is preserved as a museum in the institute's gardens.

even the Soviet Union—and eventually dominate the world. Although Kurchatov was the scientific team leader, Stalin appointed Lavrenty Beria (1899–1953), leader of the dreaded Soviet secret police, the KGB, to organize and manage the Soviet bomb project. Beria further pressured Kurchatov to quickly develop and build the atomic bomb. With the brutal Stalin as his ultimate boss, Kurchatov was already under considerable pressure; Beria would hint to him that failure on the bomb project could mean a death sentence.

Kurchatov set about his task with great enthusiasm, a bit out of fear but also out of a sense of patriotic duty to the Soviet Union, which had been devastated by German attacks in World War II. Both Kurchatov and Beria had exceptional organizational skills. While Kurchatov planned the design and construction of the bomb, Beria mobilized thousands of workers. Most of the workers were prisoners from the vast system of Soviet labor prison camps known as the Gulag. They would mine uranium (one of the raw materials needed for atomic bomb manufacture), build a nuclear reactor, and build facilities for bomb production.

A supersecret atomic weapons laboratory, where the Soviets' first plutonium bomb would take shape, was developed in the spring of 1946 in the small town of Sarov, about 250 miles (402 kilometers) east of Moscow. Together, the laboratory and the new community it spawned were named Arzamas-16. Thanks to Kurchatov's sense of humor, Arzamas-16 soon got the nickname "Los Arzamas," a pun on Los Alamos, the U.S. atomic bomb laboratory. The original town name, Sarov, dropped off the map, and the Soviet scientists went about their work in total secrecy. They were paid well, and Stalin put no budget restraints on the project.

Kurchatov and his team benefited from information about the U.S. Manhattan Project. Spies such as Klaus Fuchs (1911–1988), David Greenglass (1922–), and Theodore Hall (1925–1999), all of whom worked at Los Alamos, funneled detailed plans to Beria's KGB between 1943 and 1945. Fuchs, a physicist, was a refugee from Germany who also happened to be a communist. He first worked on the bomb in England, then ended up on the Los Alamos team. The United States tested its plutonium-type atomic bomb in July 1945; only weeks before that, Fuchs had sent detailed descriptions of the bomb to the Soviets. Beria turned the U.S. secrets over to Kurchatov. Historians agree that this information helped speed up the successful development of the Soviet atomic bomb by one to two years. Nevertheless, Kurchatov still had to recheck all the information and re-create the bomb with Soviet minds and hands.

By November 1946, Kurchatov was building a full-scale plutonium reactor, and on December 25 he and his fellow scientists produced a nuclear chain reaction, the first step to building an atomic bomb. It was also the first nuclear chain reaction produced in Europe or Asia. Two and a half years later, after more intensive work and a series of technical delays, Kurchatov and his team were ready to test a plutonium atomic bomb. They gathered in the early-morning light on August 29, 1949, at the Semipalatinsk Test Site by the Irtysh River in northeastern Kazakhstan. The trial test was dubbed "First Lightning." Beria was present for the test; he was highly skeptical that it would be a success. Kurchatov and his team knew that failure might mean they would be shot. But the team delivered. At precisely 7 A.M., the 100-foot (30.5-meter) tower holding the bomb exploded in an awesome fireball. Those watching erupted in relief and celebration.

A few days later, a U.S. Air Force B-29 on a weather mission over the North Pacific detected a very high radioactivity count in the atmosphere. From this information, U.S. scientists realized that the Soviets had detonated a plutonium atomic bomb. U.S. president **Harry S. Truman** (1884–1972; served 1945–53; see entry) delivered the news to a shocked America on September 23, 1949. The United States had thought it was ahead in the Cold War weapons race; now it was clear that the Soviets had caught up.

Kurchatov, the man

Kurchatov was an individual who had a broad range of interests and an enthusiasm that was contagious. From the early 1940s on, he sported a long shaggy beard. He and his wife, Marina, were a devoted couple who lived together happily for thirty-three years. For the last fourteen years of Kurchatov's life, they lived in a two-story house built for them in a piney woods area close to the main laboratory at Arzamas-16. To reach the lab from his house, Kurchatov followed a zigzag path through the woods. His home was called the "Forester's Cabin." It had eight spacious rooms, including a large library with over thirty-five hundred books, a second library-billiards room, Kurchatov's personal study, and a hothouse where Marina grew exotic plants of many types.

Many paintings, showing a fine appreciation of art, adorned the walls of the Forester's Cabin. Some favorites were watercolors of Crimea in different seasons. (The Kurchatovs had both grown up in Crimea, and they vacationed there as often as they could. There, Igor loved to climb to the top of Mount Ai-Nikola to watch the sunrise and hear the birds sing.) The Kurchatovs loved to entertain in their home, inviting Igor's scientific team, as well as other friends and guests, to visit them. Among their many friends were scientists from around the world. In 1947, on New Year's Eve, the Kurchatovs opened their home to Igor's entire laboratory staff for a night of laughing and dancing. Even on ordinary days, music was often heard coming from the Kurchatov home. Marina played the piano, and Igor played the balalaika (a triangular Eastern European stringed instrument) and mandolin. The Kurchatovs had a large collection of recordings by many artists, including Rachmaninoff, Tchaikovsky, Beethoven, Brahms, and Mozart.

Kurchatov enjoyed the gardens around his home. He often met with his team of scientists at an outdoor table surrounded by jasmine and lilac bushes. There, they worked over problems, and Kurchatov would give them their work instructions for the next month. Only a few hours after they had returned to work, he would walk through the woods to the laboratory to see how much they had accomplished.

Kurchatov had great energy, and his thought processes were exceptionally clear, organized, and focused on the task at hand. He taught students and colleagues to ignore clutter and irrelevant details and go straight to the main point. As noted on the Russian Research Centre Kurchatov Institute's Web site, a former colleague recalls him saying: "Always do the main thing both in your life and in your work. Otherwise the irrelevant, no matter how important it might be, will easily fill up your entire life, consume all your energy and prevent you from getting to the roots." Always kind and helpful, Kurchatov enjoyed developing strong bonds with students and fellow scientists. They in turn displayed a great deal of loyalty toward him. Kurchatov remained humane and natural and had a great sense of humor. He was also highly patriotic and devoted to his Soviet homeland.

Post-1949

After his success in developing the Soviet atomic bomb, Kurchatov gained great status and respect within the Soviet Union. But realizing the bomb's enormous destructive power, Kurchatov constantly stressed that atomic energy should be used for peaceful purposes, to benefit humans.

Nuclear physicist Igor Kurchatov (with hat raised) waves to crowds aboard a Russian cruiser in April 1956, as he travels with (left to right) Soviet leader Nikita Khrushchev, Soviet premier Nikolai Bulganin, and Soviet airplane designer A. N. Tupolev. *Reproduced by permission of the Corbis Corporation.*

However, the nuclear arms race between the Soviet Union and the United States only accelerated. Scientists in both countries began work on a thermonuclear bomb, also known as the hydrogen bomb or H-bomb, which was far more powerful than the atomic bomb (A-bomb). The United States tested its first H-bomb on November 1, 1952; the Soviets tested their H-bomb on August 12, 1953. The Soviets had again evened the race with the United States, and Kurchatov acknowledged that **Andrey Sakharov** (1921–1989; see entry), the chief Soviet H-bomb designer, had enormously helped Russia. Nevertheless, the overwhelming power of the nuclear bombs caused Kurchatov to question the ongoing expansion of nuclear weapons. He withdrew from supervising nuclear testing in 1956.

Meanwhile, Stalin had died in March 1953, and **Nikita Khrushchev** (1894–1971; see entry) had risen to the top leadership position in the Soviet Union. In February 1956, Khrushchev invited Kurchatov to speak before the Twentieth

Party Congress, otherwise noted for when Khrushchev gave his famous "Crimes of Stalin" speech, in which he denounced the behavior of his predecessor. At the meeting, Kurchatov strongly urged scientists worldwide to work together for civilian uses of nuclear energy. He specifically included American scientists but said that the United States must accept an offer that the Soviets made to ban all nuclear weapons.

In April 1956, Kurchatov traveled with Khrushchev to Great Britain. Khrushchev had so much confidence that Kurchatov would not divulge secrets or attempt to defect that he allowed Kurchatov to go by himself to Britain's laboratories and visit with British physicists. As noted on *The American Experience: Race for the Superbomb* Web site, Khrushchev commented, "It should go without saying that so remarkable a man, so great a scientist, and so devoted a patriot would deserve our complete trust and respect."

In Britain, Kurchatov spoke before an audience of international scientists at the Harwell nuclear center. For the first time in history, the world heard a description of Soviet nuclear research. Kurchatov called for international cooperation, asking all nations to declassify their nuclear projects, build confidence and understanding of each other, and use nuclear energy in the service of peace. For his dedication to the peace effort, the World Peace Council awarded him the Joliot-Curie Medal in 1959, an award that made Kurchatov extremely proud.

Health problems would soon end Kurchatov's life. In 1958, Kurchatov had a growth removed near his collarbone. He died in February 1960.

For More Information

Books

Glynn, Patrick. *Closing Pandora's Box: Arms Races, Arms Control, and the History of the Cold War*. New York: Basic Books, 1992.

Herken, Gregg. *The Winning Weapon: The Atomic Bomb and the Cold War, 1945–1950*. New York: Knopf, 1980.

Isaacs, Jeremy, and Taylor Downing. *Cold War: An Illustrated History, 1945–1991*. Boston: Little, Brown, 1998.

Morris, Charles R. *Iron Destinies, Lost Opportunities: The Arms Race between the USA and the USSR, 1945–1987*. New York: Harper and Row, 1988.

Web Sites

Oregon Public Broadcasting. "Citizen Kurchatov: Stalin's Bomb Maker." *Cold War I.* http://www.opb.org/lmd/coldwar/citizenk (accessed on September 9, 2003).

Public Broadcasting Service. "Race for the Superbomb." *American Experience.* http://www.pbs.org/wgbh/amex/bomb/peopleevents/pande AMEX59.html (accessed on September 9, 2003).

Russian Research Centre Kurchatov Institute. http://www.kiae.ru/index. html (accessed on September 9, 2003).

Douglas MacArthur

Born January 26, 1880
Little Rock, Arkansas
Died April 5, 1964
Washington, D.C.

U.S. general

Considered a war hero in World War II (1939–45) as commander of the U.S. Army and Air Forces in the Pacific campaign against Japan, Douglas MacArthur played a crucial role in rebuilding Japan during the early years of the Cold War. The Cold War was an intense political and economic rivalry from 1945 to 1991 between the United States, the Soviet Union, and China with limited military conflict. MacArthur later led U.S. forces during the first year of the Korean War (1950–53). Holding very strong anticommunist views, he became the most controversial U.S. military figure of the Cold War. Promoting a military conquest of communist China and reunification of Korea, he was a major critic of U.S. foreign policy toward the Far East.

A military family

MacArthur was born in Little Rock, Arkansas, on January 26, 1880, to Arthur MacArthur, a soldier and decorated Civil War veteran, and Mary Hardy, daughter of a wealthy family in Norfolk, Virginia. He was raised on various army posts in Texas and the American Southwest, as his father became one of

"Old soldiers never die, they just fade away."

Douglas MacArthur.
Reproduced by permission of Getty Images.

the highest-ranking officers in the army. MacArthur's mother was an ambitious woman and strongly influenced his drive for high achievement. His brother would become a naval captain.

MacArthur received his secondary education at the West Texas Military Academy in San Antonio from 1883 to 1897. He then attended the military academy at West Point and graduated first in his class in 1903. He then served as a junior engineering officer for the U.S. Army Corps of Engineers at several army posts in the United States, the Philippines, and Panama. In 1913, MacArthur joined the general staff of the War Department and was often sent on field assignments. In World War I (1914–18), MacArthur switched to combat infantry units from the engineers and fought in France. Promoted to colonel, he held several field commands and showed unusual bravery and flair. He received a number of decorations and rose to the rank of brigadier general by 1918. He served as part of the occupation forces in Germany before returning to the United States in April 1919.

Following the war, MacArthur was appointed superintendent of West Point. He introduced major new reforms during his three years there from 1919 to 1922, including raising the school's academic standards. In 1922, he married a wealthy socialite widow, Louise Brooks. They would have no children and divorce after seven years of marriage. From 1922 to 1930, MacArthur held several positions that included two tours in the Philippines, and he eventually rose to a major general. During this period, he became very interested in Far Eastern international issues.

MacArthur was recognized for his high intelligence and extraordinary command abilities. However, he would be also considered egotistical and aloof except by his closest friends and associates. He worked hard to cultivate a strong public image of his military accomplishments. During his career, he would repeatedly question the civilian authority over the military as established in the U.S. Constitution. This trait would bring him into great controversy.

Leader of the army

In 1930, President Herbert Hoover (1874–1964; served 1929–33) appointed MacArthur U.S. Army chief of staff, the youngest to hold that position in U.S. history. MacArthur would serve in that position for five years, primarily attempting to maintain an effective military force during the economic hard times of the Great Depression (1929–41), the worst financial crisis in American history. In the summer of 1932, however, his image was strongly tarnished when he led a charge of army troops to remove several thousand World War I veterans from Washington, D.C. The veterans had been peacefully protesting to Congress for advanced pay of their promised benefits, owing to the high unemployment brought by the Depression. They had refused to leave when Congress turned them down. MacArthur was also unpopular for his fight against the prevailing pacifist mood of the nation. His stance was that the country needed to maintain a high level of military preparedness.

On a more constructive note, MacArthur played a key role in establishing the Civilian Conservation Corps (CCC) for President Franklin D. Roosevelt (1882–1945; served 1933–45). The CCC was a federal program for providing work for more than 250,000 unemployed young men. It proved to be one of the most successful economic relief programs during the Depression of the 1930s.

In 1935, MacArthur resigned the chief of staff position to become a military advisor to the newly established Philippine government. During his six years there, he strove to build a Filipino force capable of combating Japanese military expansion in the region. This experience would prepare him for the upcoming World War II campaign against Japan, as well as carrying out U.S. Cold War policies aimed at containing the spread of communism in the Far East. Communism is a system of government in which the nation's leaders are selected by a single political party that controls almost all aspects of society. Private ownership of property is eliminated and government directs all economic production. The goods produced and accumulated wealth are, in theory, shared relatively equally by all.

In April 1937, MacArthur married Jean Faircloth. They would have one son. In December 1937, MacArthur retired from the U.S. Army and assumed the role of private military advisor to the Filipino leadership.

World War II in the Pacific

With the decline in relations between Japan and the United States in early 1941, MacArthur was reinstated in the

General Douglas MacArthur wades ashore during the United States' landing in the Philippines in October 1944.
Courtesy of the National Archives and Records Administration.

U.S. military as a lieutenant general with command of U.S. Army forces in the Far East. For the first several months, optimism ran high that the Japanese advances in the region could be turned back before long. However, the surprise Japanese attack on the U.S. military fleet at Pearl Harbor, Hawaii, on December 7, 1941, quickly dashed optimistic hopes. Only hours after the Pearl Harbor attack, Japanese forces landed in the Philippines. The Japanese forces continually advanced, as MacArthur's troops used a series of delaying actions while in steady retreat. By March 1942, the U.S. troops were under siege, and Roosevelt ordered MacArthur to Australia to rebuild a larger force of American and Australian forces. MacArthur became commander of the Southwest Pacific Area Theater.

Shortly after MacArthur left for Australia, the U.S. forces on the Philippines surrendered to Japanese troops. Nonetheless, under public pressure, Roosevelt awarded MacArthur the Congressional Medal of Honor for his delaying tactics and promoted him to full general. The U.S. media reported MacArthur's techniques as a courageous defense against superior forces that bought time for the United States to begin regrouping for war. Roosevelt, though, privately believed MacArthur mishandled the logistical support badly, but gave in to the continuing public and congressional adoration of MacArthur.

For the next thirty months, MacArthur mounted a counteroffensive against the Japanese with the goal of eventually recapturing the Philippines. He began with an attack on New Guinea and then hopped from island to island. In the fall of 1944, MacArthur led a major invasion of the Philippines. However, progress proved much slower than expected, dragging into 1945 with high casualties. During this period in April 1945, MacArthur became commander of all U.S. forces in the Pacific. The battle for the Philippines became largely irrelevant in August 1945, when the United States dropped atomic bombs on two Japanese cities. The Japanese soon surrendered. As supreme commander of Allied forces in the Pacific, MacArthur formally accepted the surrender onboard the battleship USS *Missouri* on September 2.

Rebuilding Japan

Following the surrender, President **Harry S. Truman** (1884–1972; served 1945–53; see entry) appointed MacArthur the occupation commander of Japan. MacArthur would prove a very positive influence on the successful rebuilding of Japan's economy and society, and in containing the expansion of communism in the region. MacArthur brought major change in dismantling the Japanese military and war industry, and introducing democratic reforms. A new constitution was written under MacArthur's direct leadership, which guaranteed certain human rights, such as freedom of the press, freedom of speech, and greater rights for women. MacArthur also introduced a new educational system and sweeping economic reforms.

MacArthur was responsible as well for establishing a prowestern government in South Korea. Korea had been divided into Soviet and U.S. occupation zones at the conclusion of World War II, much like the division of Germany in Europe. MacArthur selected Syngman Rhee (1875–1965) as the

Japan and the Cold War

Though Japan was stripped of all its military capability following its defeat in World War II, it still played a vital role in Cold War developments in the Far East. Following Japan's surrender in September 1945, the United States appointed General Douglas MacArthur as the supreme commander of Allied occupation forces.

Though appointed to simply carry out policies made by the Allies, MacArthur, through his strong-willed manner, operated relatively independently in setting the course of change in Japan. MacArthur was so dominant a figure that he became the sole symbol of postwar reconstruction to the Japanese public. His dignified manner, dramatic flair, dedication, firmness, and clear sympathy for the war-torn country won great esteem from the population and brought Japan under U.S. influence during the Cold War. MacArthur introduced democratic concepts, education reforms, and economic change. He broke up the major landholdings held by a few landlords and distributed the land into numerous peasant farms. He also broke up industries owned by a few wealthy families. In addition, MacArthur was responsible for attracting over two billion dollars' worth of relief goods for the Japanese people between 1945 and 1951. Through his efforts, Japan became a West-aligned nation, representing a first line of defense in containing communist expansion in the Far East.

new South Korean leader. However, Rhee imposed a harsh rule that quickly grew unpopular with U.S. political leaders in Washington. MacArthur's role ended in 1948, when the new South Korean government, known as the Republic of Korea, was formed.

By 1948, as communist victory in the civil war in China was growing more obvious, MacArthur switched his emphasis to the rebuilding of industry rather than social reform. He also became a leading critic of President Truman's decision to reduce foreign aid to the Chinese Nationalist government. Nationalism refers to the strong loyalty of a person or group to its own country. The Chinese Nationalists wanted to once again raise the world prominence of China. Truman believed there was little chance for the government to survive much longer against the communist revolutionary forces of **Mao Zedong** (1893–1976; see entry). In October 1949, Mao's forces finally gained control of the Chinese government, and **Chiang Kai-shek** (1887–1975; see entry) fled to the island of Taiwan, where he established a new government. MacArthur immediately proposed to use Taiwan as a military base to retake Mainland China. He also strove to restrict the growth of any communist political activities in Japan, even creating a special police force of seventy-five thousand men to guard against any efforts to sabotage the newly forming Japanese economy.

Korean War

Focus shifted quickly to Korea in June 1950, however, when the communist-controlled North Korea invaded U.S.-supported South Korea. The United States responded within hours, gaining a United Nations (UN) resolution to condemn and repel the invasion. The UN is an international organization, composed of most of the nations of the world, created to preserve world peace and security. MacArthur was named commander of the UN forces dominated by U.S. forces. In 1951, the United States would sign a peace treaty with Japan, ending U.S. military occupation.

On September 15, 1950, MacArthur led a daring invasion on the coast of Korea behind enemy lines, splitting overextended North Korean forces. With the North Koreans in full retreat, MacArthur and Truman decided to pursue them through North Korea with thoughts of reunifying Korea. The UN forces met little resistance, eventually reaching the border of Chinese-controlled Manchuria. MacArthur basically ignored threats from communist China that they would commit troops to the war if U.S. forces approached the border. MacArthur even called for attacks on China itself that included an invasion from Taiwan. However, Truman wanted no part in expanding the war.

Nevertheless, Chinese communist leader Mao was becoming very nervous about U.S. intentions, given MacArthur's call for attack. Finally in late November 1950, communist China launched a massive offensive involving almost three hundred thousand Chinese troops. The UN forces hastily retreated back into South Korea. MacArthur blamed Truman for not attacking China first. By March 1951, the battlefront stabilized back to the original prewar boundary between North and South Korea at the thirty-eighth parallel. MacArthur persisted in his attacks on Truman, giving life to charges made by

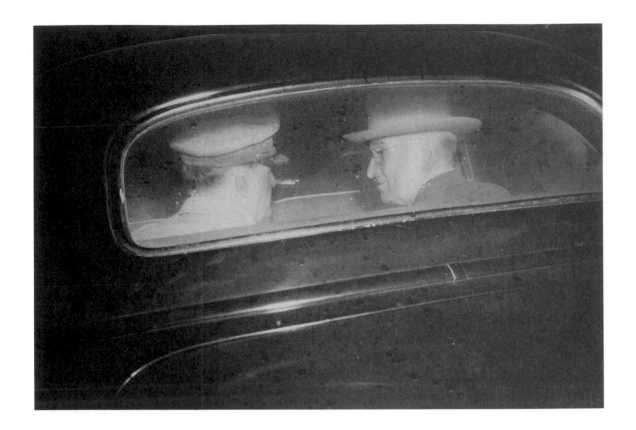

General Douglas MacArthur (left) listens to U.S. president Harry S. Truman as they are driven away in Wake Island in October 1950, months before Truman relieved MacArthur of his military commands.
Reproduced by permission of the Corbis Corporation.

U.S. senator **Joseph R. McCarthy** (1909–1957; see entry) of Wisconsin of communist subversion in the U.S. government. His aggressive position also undermined the president's efforts at seeking a cease-fire. Finally on April 11, 1951, Truman angrily relieved MacArthur of all his military commands.

A return to the United States

MacArthur returned to the United States and was welcomed by the public as a war hero, perhaps owing more to his World War II exploits than his Korean controversies. It was his first return to the United States since before World War II. MacArthur made a dramatic speech to a joint session of Congress on April 19, 1951, again harshly criticizing Truman's foreign policies. It was this speech in which MacArthur uttered the famous line, "Old soldiers never die, they just fade away." Though he was warmly received during his speech, congressional hearings that followed countered many

of MacArthur's charges. The public quickly began to lose interest in the general's perspectives. Other senior military leaders did not share his opinions, and his later speeches gained less public attention.

MacArthur also held political interests in running for president as the Republican candidate and began to focus on the 1952 presidential elections. He and his supporters had

Douglas MacArthur addresses a joint session of the U.S. Congress on April 19, 1951. *Courtesy of the National Archives and Records Administration.*

previously shown some interest in 1944 and 1948 as well, but little came from it. Although he delivered the keynote speech at the Republican National Convention in 1952, another popular military commander won the nomination instead, World War II general **Dwight D. Eisenhower** (1890–1969; served 1953–61; see entry). MacArthur was simply too controversial. Greatly disappointed, MacArthur left public life.

In 1952, MacArthur took the largely honorary position of board chairman of the Remington Rand Corporation, a computer company. He lived in New York City, making only occasional public speeches. He made one last farewell trip to the Philippines in 1961. During his later years, he wrote his autobiography, titled *Reminiscences,* which was published in 1964. He also advised President **Lyndon B. Johnson** (1908–1973; served 1963–69; see entry) to avoid a war in Vietnam, predicting it would be costly and highly unpopular with the American public. His prediction would come true. MacArthur died in Washington, D.C., in April 1964, and was buried in Norfolk, Virginia. His military career was one of the longest in U.S. history, as well as the most controversial.

For More Information

Books

Blair, Clay. *The Forgotten War: America in Korea, 1950–1953.* New York: Time Books, 1987.

James, D. Clayton. *The Years of MacArthur.* 3 vols. Boston: Houghton Mifflin, 1970–1985.

MacArthur, Douglas. *Reminiscences.* New York: McGraw-Hill, 1964. Reprint, New York: Da Capo Press, 1985.

Manchester, William. *American Caesar: Douglas MacArthur, 1880–1964.* Boston: Little, Brown, 1978.

McCullough, David. *Truman.* New York: Simon and Schuster, 1992.

Peret, Geoffrey. *Old Soldiers Never Die: The Life of Douglas MacArthur.* New York: Random House, 1996.

Schaller, Michael. *Douglas MacArthur: The Far Eastern General.* New York: Oxford University Press, 1989.

Web Site

"Conflict and Consequence: The Korean War and its Unsettled Legacy." *Truman Presidential Museum and Library.* http://www.trumanlibrary. org (accessed on September 10, 2003).

Harold Macmillan

Born February 10, 1894
London, England
Died December 29, 1986
Birch Grove, Sussex, England

British prime minister

arold Macmillan served in the British government from 1924 to 1963. During that period, he was one of the first in British government to oppose German aggression in Europe, established later useful relations with other Allied leaders during World War II (1939–45), and then guided Britain through some difficult years of the Cold War (1945–91). The Cold War was an intense political and economic rivalry from 1945 to 1991 between the United States and the Soviet Union falling just short of military conflict. During his period of leadership, it became clear that Britain had lost much world influence that it had wielded for centuries before. The two new superpowers of the United States and the Soviet Union clearly held domination in world events.

"A man who trusts nobody is apt to be the kind of man nobody trusts."

Born into British privilege

Harold Macmillan was born to an upper-middle-class family in London, England. His grandfather had founded Macmillan Publishing Company, and his father assumed head of the company. His American-born mother dominated

Harold Macmillan. *Courtesy of the Library of Congress.*

303

his early life in driving him to succeed. Macmillan was educated at Eton, a noted public school in England, and then Oxford University. At Oxford, he became active in student politics, showing off his already exceptional speaking style.

Macmillan's education was disrupted by World War I (1914–18). Joining the British army, he saw considerable combat action. Macmillan was wounded on several occasions, finally sustaining a shattered pelvis in 1916. He returned to Britain for extended recovery lasting until 1920. It left him with a permanent limp. Upon recovery, Macmillan married Lady Dorothy Evelyn Cavendish, the daughter of an English duke. Through her family, he became exposed to the upper class. The couple would have a son and three daughters.

Beginning a political career

With the British Liberal Party in decline, Macmillan joined the Conservative Party, though having liberal attitudes toward economic policy. He and a few others in the party formed a very small liberal wing. Macmillan entered politics in 1923 but lost in his election bid to gain a seat in the House of Commons. He did win the following year and would hold the seat until 1929 and then regain it later, from 1931 to 1964. Macmillan promoted his liberal economic policies, calling for some government control.

By the late 1930s, Macmillan was becoming concerned about the expansion of Germany's Nazi Party, known primarily for its brutal policies of racism. He provided fierce opposition to the tolerance of Nazi Germany by British leaders, including Prime Minister Neville Chamberlain (1869–1940). Macmillan's position on Germany was at first unpopular in Parliament. However, with Germany overrunning first Poland and then France by the spring of 1940, Chamberlain resigned under pressure of those opposing his weak policies toward Germany.

Taking Chamberlain's place was **Winston Churchill** (1874–1965; see entry), also of the Conservative Party. Churchill, seeking political unity in the war effort, created a coalition government of members from different parties. He appointed Macmillan as parliamentary secretary to the minister of supply. By June 1942, Macmillan rose to undersecretary of state and, in November, Churchill assigned him to the British minister post in Algiers, North Africa. His role was to coordinate with American, British, and French forces who were conducting a military offensive against German forces across North Africa. They followed their success in North Africa with invasions of Sicily and Italy, where Macmillan remained involved. During this time, he developed close relations with U.S. general **Dwight D. Eisenhower** (1890–1969; see entry) and testy relations with France's General Charles de Gaulle (1890–1970).

Post–World War II

Following the surrender of Germany in May 1945, new general elections were held in Britain in July to select a government to replace the special wartime coalition government. Macmillan's Conservative Party lost, and he would temporarily lose his seat in the House of Commons. A special election in November, however, brought him back. He was assigned to a committee as an expert on industrial policy. With the return of the Conservative Party in the 1951 general election, Churchill resumed his role as prime minister. In October 1951, Macmillan was appointed minister of housing and local government; he was in charge of replacing bombed-out homes, a continuing massive rebuilding program resulting from damage inflicted by German bombing in World War II. Achieving great success in a difficult post over a three-year period, Macmillan moved up to minister of defense in October 1954. However, with Churchill's heavy direct involvement in military matters, he found his role fairly limited. In addition, Britain's poor economy called for reductions in the armed forces at the time.

Churchill retired in April 1955 and was replaced by his foreign secretary, Anthony Eden (1897–1977). Macmillan replaced Eden in his former position. Once again, however, Eden, who had been a highly successful foreign secretary, continued to run foreign affairs as Churchill had done earlier. Macmillan was left with little involvement. Later in 1955, Macmillan moved to the treasury department and remained there until 1957. At the time, Britain was suffering through an economic crisis. Macmillan increased taxes and reduced

Anthony Eden, British
prime minister from 1955 to
1957. *Courtesy of the Library
of Congress.*

government spending, which successfully corrected the economic picture of the nation. Macmillan received much praise for his monetary actions.

Prime minister

An international crisis arrived in 1956 that would end up placing Macmillan in the prime minister position. After a period of deteriorating relations with the United States and other Western nations, on July 26, 1956, Egypt and its leader Gamal Abdul Nasser (1918–1970) nationalized, or took control of, the Suez Canal. The canal had been under the control of Britain and France and served as a vital waterway for oil shipments from the Middle East to Western Europe. In November, Britain, France, and Israel launched a surprise military invasion of Egypt to regain control of the canal without first advising U.S. president Eisenhower. Eden and Macmillan expected Eisenhower to support the action. Eisenhower, however, was greatly concerned that their military response might result in pushing Egypt more toward a Soviet Union alliance. Eisenhower demanded an immediate cease-fire and withdrawal of British and French forces. With Britain suffering economic problems, they could not afford to jeopardize future U.S. aid and could definitely not afford a war with Egypt. As a result, Macmillan, who in his treasury position fully understood Britain's economic situation, advised Eden to accept the cease-fire. It was a humiliating experience for both Britain and France. It also underscored that British foreign policy was subject to U.S. control. Eden resigned as prime minister shortly afterwards, claiming health problems.

Macmillan was selected the new British prime minister in Eden's place on January 10, 1957. He was selected leader of the Conservative Party twelve days later. An obvious high priority at first was to repair relations with the United

States after the Suez crisis. Fortunately, Macmillan was able to build on the friendship he had already established with Eisenhower in North Africa during World War II. The two leaders would meet on several occasions beginning in March 1957, when Eisenhower agreed to sell American missiles to Great Britain for the first time. Macmillan made sure Britain was consistently a strong supporter of U.S. actions in the Cold War. This included sending troops along with U.S. forces to Jordan and Lebanon in July 1958 to protect the Lebanese government from rebels. The British also supported the U.S. defense of the noncommunist government of the Republic of China on the island of Taiwan from possible invasion of the mainland communist government, the People's Republic of China (PRC) through the late 1950s.

At home, Macmillan sought to increase Britain's standing as a world nuclear power by pressing onward with the testing of a newly developed hydrogen bomb. However, the surprise launching of the first man-made satellite, *Sputnik,* by the Soviet Union in October 1957 showed that Britain was well behind the Soviets in missile development. Macmillan met with Eisenhower in Washington, D.C., immediately afterwards to discuss pooling their scientific resources. As a result, Macmillan turned to a stronger alliance with the United States. In addition, efforts to build its own nuclear missiles failed, so Britain became increasingly dependent on U.S. missile development. In another agreement between Macmillan and Eisenhower, Britain would assist in U.S. missile development in exchange for the United States basing its *Polaris* submarines in Britain. The meetings between Macmillan and Eisenhower would continue, including sessions in Washington in June 1958, Paris in December 1959, and Camp David, Maryland, in March 1960. Macmillan also visited Soviet leader **Nikita Khrushchev** (1894–1971; see entry) in Moscow in February 1959. He was the first British prime minister to visit the Soviet Union since World War II.

Britain as Cold War intermediary

Though a strong anticommunist himself, Macmillan disagreed with the hard-line policies of Eisenhower and his secretary of state, **John Foster Dulles** (1888–1959; see entry), toward the Soviet Union. As a result, Macmillan wanted Britain to play the role of intermediary in trying to bring the two superpowers together. He believed Britain could play the crucial role in resolving various issues, including nuclear arms control and the long-term postwar status of Germany.

Macmillan particularly looked forward to a summit meeting in Paris he had arranged between Eisenhower and Khrushchev for May 1960. However, only ten days before the summit was to begin, the Soviets shot down a U.S. spy plane over Soviet territory. When Eisenhower refused to apologize for the flight, Khrushchev angrily refused to participate in the summit. It was a major blow to Macmillan's foreign strategy for Britain.

During his first years as prime minister, Macmillan strongly supported the social programs the Liberal Party had established in Britain after the world war. With the British economy in good shape, Macmillan easily won reelection in October 1959. Macmillan proceeded to establish a very close relationship with new U.S. president **John F. Kennedy** (1919–1963; served 1961–63; see entry) after Kennedy's election in November 1960. Despite their personal closeness, Kennedy preferred not using Macmillan as an intermediary when dealing with Khrushchev. Kennedy wanted to be more personally active in U.S. foreign affairs. Macmillan felt particularly left out during the Cuban Missile Crisis in October 1962. For security reasons, Kennedy failed to inform Macmillan of the discovery of Soviet nuclear missiles secretly placed in Cuba until just before the rapidly growing crisis became public.

As a result, Macmillan turned more toward developing relations with Western Europe. However, West German chancellor **Konrad Adenauer** (1876–1967; see entry) distrusted Macmillan's efforts to work with the Soviets, and French president Charles de Gaulle thought Macmillan was too close to the United States. De Gaulle believed Macmillan had abandoned France in the 1956 Suez crisis, when he and Prime Minister Eden had so readily accepted the U.S. cease-fire. De Gaulle wanted to limit U.S. influence in Europe. Adenauer and de Gaulle teamed up to block Macmillan's efforts to establish new trade relations in Europe. They even blocked Macmillan's attempt to gain British membership in the European Common Market.

In December 1962, while seeking Common Market membership, Macmillan met with Kennedy. Kennedy agreed

to sell *Polaris* missiles to Macmillan for British nuclear submarines. The following month, in January 1963, de Gaulle announced France would veto any British membership into the Common Market. The result was that Britain was blocked from joining the increasingly independent Western Europe during the Cold War. On the other hand, some believed joining the European trade alliance would have cost some of Britain's independence by having to conform to European policies.

The British felt increasingly vulnerable to nuclear attack as the arms race between the United States and the Soviet Union was escalating through the 1950s. To ease those fears, Macmillan sought an agreement for nuclear disarmament with the two superpowers. Though he was unable to achieve actual disarmament, Macmillan was finally able to gain agreement on limiting nuclear testing. On July 25, the three nations signed the Limited Nuclear Test Ban Treaty of 1963.

Declining political support

In a major foreign affairs achievement, Macmillan guided Britain through a period in which the nation granted

The Cold War Memoirs of Harold Macmillan

Following his departure as prime minister of Great Britain in October 1963, Harold Macmillan enjoyed a long retirement. One of his key activities until his death in December 1986 was writing a six-volume set of memoirs with personal observations of British government. The volumes include excellent insights into British foreign policy strategies during the Cold War and his interactions with other world leaders. They were all published by the prestigious family publishing company, Macmillan. The volumes addressing Cold War issues include: *Tides of Fortune, 1945–1955* (1969); *Riding the Storm, 1956–1959* (1971); *Pointing the Way, 1959–1961* (1972); and *At the End of the Day, 1961–1963* (1973).

independence to most of its last remaining colonies, including South Africa, without major incident. He announced the new British policy in the famous "winds of change" speech in February 1960 in Capetown, South Africa. In the speech, Macmillan announced the new British policy of supporting African nationalist movements and opposed the South African policies of racial segregation called apartheid.

Macmillan began losing popular support through the early 1960s, as the British economy faltered. With unemployment rising, Macmillan had to impose wage freezes and other unpopular measures beginning in 1961. Then a scandal in his government involving one of his cabinet members, British war minister John Profumo (1915–), led to much criticism. Profumo was forced to resign after it was revealed that he had had an affair with a woman who was also involved with a man presumed to be a Soviet spy. In October 1963, Macmillan resigned after undergoing surgery. He retired from the House of Commons in September 1964.

In retirement, Macmillan continued as chancellor of Oxford University, a position he had held since 1960. He also served as chairman of Macmillan Publishing Co. for awhile. Much of his time, however, was spent writing a number of memoirs and other books. Macmillan wrote six volumes of memoirs. In 1984, Macmillan was granted the title of Earl of Stockton. In December 1986, he died on the family estate in East Sussex, England.

For More Information

Books

Aldous, Richard, and Lee Sabine, eds. *Harold Macmillan and Britain's World Role.* New York: St. Martin's Press, 1996.

Fisher, Nigel. *Harold Macmillan: A Biography.* New York: St. Martin's Press, 1982.

Horne, Alistair. *Harold Macmillan.* 2 vols. New York: Viking, 1989–1991.

Scott, Leonard V. *Macmillan, Kennedy, and the Cuban Missile Crisis: Political, Military, and Intelligence Aspects.* New York: St. Martin's Press, 1999.

Turner, John. *Macmillan.* New York: Longman, 1994.

Mao Zedong

Born December 26, 1893
Shaoshan, Hunan Province of China
Died September 9, 1976
Beijing, China

Chairman of the People's Republic of China

"In a very short time, in China's central, southern and northern provinces, several hundred million peasants will rise like a mighty storm, like a hurricane, a force so swift and violent that no power, however great, will be able to hold it back."

Mao Zedong. *Reproduced by permission of the Corbis Corporation.*

Mao Zedong imposed an ideology upon an entire society and created a regime that eliminated opposition. He led the long struggle that made China a communist nation in 1949. Communism is a system of government in which a single party, the Communist Party, controls all aspects of people's lives. In economic theory, it prohibits private ownership of property and business, so that goods produced and wealth accumulated are shared relatively equally by all. Communism was adapted from the theories of German philosopher Karl Marx (1818–1883) and Russian revolutionary Vladimir I. Lenin (1870–1924). Mao's interpretation of Marxism for colonial and peasant-based economies became known as Maoism.

Maoism was a model and an inspiration for many Third World national liberation movements. Third World refers to poor, underdeveloped or economically developing nations in Africa, Asia, and Latin America. Many were seeking independence from political control of Western European nations. Mao developed his theory around the revolutionary potential of the rural peasantry, rather than the city-based, industrial workers of Marxist/Leninist ideology. Third World communist leaders used modifications of the three devices prescribed by Maoist doctrines in conducting a revolution. These included the party (whose role is to provide leadership for the revolution), the army (a tool to seize state power), and the united front (a means to win the support of the people).

Mao was an ardent opponent of international capitalism but turned to the United States when looking for allies against a possible Soviet attack. Capitalism is an economic system where property and businesses are privately owned. Prices, production, and distribution of goods are determined by competition in a market relatively free of government intervention. Mao invited U.S. president **Richard M. Nixon** (1913–1994; served 1969–74; see entry) to visit China in 1972. This meeting in Beijing exemplified Mao's standing as a world statesman and his achievement in securing America's recognition of communist China as a world power. Mao was chairman of the Chinese Communist Party from October 1949 until 1976. It was not until 1971 that the United Nations recognized the Communist Party as the sole legitimate government of China. Known popularly as "Chairman Mao," Mao Zedong ruled Mainland China until his death in 1976.

Early life

Mao Zedong, also spelled Mao Tse-tung, was born on December 26, 1893, into a Chinese homeland that appeared to be falling apart. The fading Qin dynasty was both hated and feared, but it could not contain the spiraling social and economic unrest. Foreign powers consumed most of China's natural resources in their centralized state, and the country seemed ripe for change.

Mao was the son of a peasant who had become a wealthy farmer in Hunan Province. He received a traditional education in the classics at a primary school in the village of Shaoshan. Forced by his father to work in the fields, Mao ran away from the family farm at the age of thirteen to continue his education in the city of Changsha. There, he was introduced to Western ideas and became involved in the revolution against the Manchu Dynasty. He was still a student when the revolution of 1911–12 overthrew the Manchu government and made China a republic. At the age of eighteen, Mao joined the revolutionary army as a common soldier.

Tiananmen Square

For seven weeks in the late spring of 1989, Chinese citizens occupied a public square in the heart of Beijing. It was called Tiananmen Square. More than a million people assembled there in mass, pro-democracy demonstrations. A democratic system of government allows multiple political parties. Their members are elected to various government offices by popular vote of the people. Over three thousand hunger strikers gathered at the central Monument to the People's Heroes in the square. They gathered in the shadows of Mao's mausoleum, which occupies a southern section of the square. On June 4, the government struck back, sending tanks from all directions into the square, killing hundreds of workers and students and imposing a martial law that would last for fourteen months.

A stunning moment occurred when a young man stood before the line of tanks in Tiananmen Square that June day, halting their progress with his mere presence. The youth, or "tank man" as he was called, received worldwide attention in the media. He stood in defiance on what was called, ironically, the Avenue of Eternal Peace. Although he risked his life by standing in front of the tanks, it has been noted that the first tank driver also rose to the challenge by allowing the moment of rebellion.

Tiananmen Square is the place where Mao had proclaimed a "People's Republic" in 1949 on behalf of the Chinese people who had "stood up." In an earlier time, Mao would have embraced "tank man" as a vital part of his people's war, because he stood up against the government. In 1989, Mao's domination of China was complete and all-inclusive. Mao's legacy was a regime that did not allow for individual thinking or action. Opposition was not tolerated—it was erased.

After resuming his education in Changsha, Mao became involved in student politics and founded the New People's Study Society. The society encouraged students to participate in public affairs. Many of its early members later became prominent members of the Chinese Communist Party. After graduating from the Changsha teachers' training college in 1918, Mao went to Peking (Beijing) University and in 1919 took a leading part in the May Fourth Movement, which involved student protests against the Paris Peace Conference's decision to hand over German gains in Shandong Province, formerly Chinese, to Japan. Mao's involvement in this movement pushed him away from Western liberalism to Marxism. He became attracted to the ideas of communism,

became a Marxist, and in 1921 was a founding member of the Chinese Communist Party in Shanghai.

During his Changsha studies, Mao was greatly influenced by one of his professors, Xu Teli, and in 1920 married Xu's daughter, Yang Kaihui. Together, Mao Zedong and Yang Kaihui had three children.

A view of Tiananmen Square, with a portrait of Mao Zedong in the center. *Photography by Susan D. Rock. Reproduced by permission.*

Revolution

The communists joined forces with Sun Yat-sen's Kuomintang (Nationalist Party) in 1923 in an effort to unite China. Mao concentrated on political work among the peasants of his native province and advocated a rural revolution. **Chiang Kai-shek** (1887–1975; see entry) succeeded Sun when Sun died in 1925. Chiang conducted a bloody purge of the Chinese communists, and they were driven from the cities. Mao escaped the 1927 uprising and established a base in the southern province of Kiangsi. His wife, Yang Kaihui, was executed by the Kuomintang in Changsha in 1930.

While in Kiangsi, Mao put into practice his theory of a peasant-based revolution. With the help of General Zhu De, he joined military doctrine to his political thinking to create the guerrilla tactics of the "people's war" and build the Red Army. His activities were so successful that in 1931 he was able to declare the founding of the new Chinese Soviet Republic in Kiangsi, with himself as the first chairman. Chiang's Nationalist forces gradually encircled the communist forces and were about to take control in 1934. In order to escape, Mao led his Red Army on a year-long, 6,000-mile (9,654-kilometer) march to reach Shaanxi in northwest China and set up a new base. The Long March, as it was called, began with about 90,000 people but ended with only about 8,000 survivors on the dangerous trek. The survivors emerged as a tightly knit band under the leadership of Mao.

For a brief time in 1936, the Nationalists renewed their alliance with the communists in order to ward off the increasing threat of Japanese invaders. The ensuing war sapped the Nationalist government's strength, while the Communist Party's political and military power was restored. By 1945, the communists controlled areas populated by nearly one hundred million Chinese. On October 1, 1949, Mao was proclaimed president of the newly established People's Republic of China.

Sino-Soviet treaty

Mao took his first trip abroad in December 1949. He traveled to the Soviet Union to negotiate the Sino-Soviet Treaty of Friendship, Alliance, and Mutual Assistance. (*Sino* means Chinese.) The treaty pledged the two countries to come to each other's defense in case of attack. It also included extensive Soviet financial and military aid.

In 1949, the Cold War (1945–91) in Europe had become a war of position. The Cold War was fought over ideologies—communism versus democracy. It was a war of mutual fear and distrust primarily between the two superpowers, the United States and the Soviet Union. The European continent

was clearly divided in two. In Asia, the situation was much more fluid and dynamic. It was a war of maneuver. The Soviet Union was aware that communist success in China would be a strategic shift of major proportions. Soviet leader **Joseph Stalin** (1879–1953; see entry) was eager to secure a firm alliance for the Soviet Union and to ensure China did not ally with the United States. China could then be counted on to tie down British and French forces and slow the buildup of North Atlantic Treaty Organization (NATO) forces in Europe. The Sino-Soviet alliance was a victory for socialism in the world.

After signing the treaty, Mao retired to a largely ceremonial role in China as chairman of both the Communist Party and the People's Republic. Day-to-day administration was left to party bureaucrats, who eventually fell under the influence of technical and military advisors from the Soviet Union.

In 1957, Mao initiated the Great Leap Forward Movement. It was an attempt to break with the Russian model of communism. Mao proposed to decentralize the economy by

Mao Zedong (center) greets a group of communist army officers in September 1949.
Reproduced by permission of AP/Wide World Photos.

Staying Afloat

Mao Zedong was an avid swimmer. When he was in his early sixties, and at the height of his political power as leader of the Chinese People's Republic, swimming was a central part of his life. He swam with top party leaders in a large pool that was constructed for them at their compound in Beijing. Party business was conducted in the pool much the same way it had been in his youth, swimming in local streams with close friends and debating the challenges their nation faced.

Mao advocated swimming as a way of strengthening the bodies of Chinese citizens. He swam in the heavily polluted rivers of south China as well as the stormy ocean off the north China coast, where the Communist Party leadership gathered for its annual conferences. One of Mao's earliest poems celebrated the joys of being in the water.

establishing independent local communes, while at the same time hoping to renew revolutionary vigor. It was a monumental failure with disastrous results. By 1959, over twenty million people had died, mostly of starvation, and Mao was forced to retire as chief of state. He was, however, able to retain his title of chairman of the Communist Party and his control of the country.

By the 1960s, disputes between China and the Soviet Union had grown into a struggle for leadership of the communist world. Mao considered himself to be the true interpreter of the principles of communism. The Sino-Soviet split widened when Mao ordered nuclear research that led to Chinese nuclear weapons testing. The final break came after the failure of the Great Leap Forward. The Soviet Union cut off all aid.

The Cultural Revolution

In a weakened position, Mao fought back by instituting the Cultural Revolution. It was a mass mobilization of urban Chinese youth that took place from 1966 through 1976. Mao initiated the movement in order to prevent further development of a Soviet-style communism. Schools were closed, and students were presented with copies of the "Quotations of Chairman Mao." Organized into battalions of "Red Guards," the students were sent throughout the countryside in order to create local rebellions. Many people died in the ensuing purges, including scores of senior leaders who had been colleagues of Mao for more than three decades.

The cult of Mao was one of the results of the Cultural Revolution in China. Mao's ideas were popularized in *The Little Red Book,* or *Mao Zedong on People's War.* His book of quotations was given almost scriptural authority by the masses.

Young and old learned his slogans and studied his writings. Mao also wrote poetry. Giant portraits of Mao were displayed on billboards all around China. His face became familiar throughout the world. Mao would later argue that the creation of the personality cult had been necessary to counter entrenched party interests. He wanted to keep a radical edge to the Chinese communist movement and not let it get too conservative and bureaucratic. Mao thought too many communist leaders in China were getting too comfortable in their long-held positions and letting the communist movement drift away from his hard-core philosophy. He did not want Chinese communists to become too friendly with noncommunists elsewhere.

Chinese youth cheer for their hero, Chairman Mao Zedong, in 1968. *Reproduced by permission of Getty Images.*

Final days

By the early 1970s, illness plagued Mao, and the running of the country was left largely to his third wife. In 1939,

Mao had married actress Jiang Qing (two years after divorcing his second wife). They had two daughters together. During the Cultural Revolution, she was appointed deputy director and became leader of the "Gang of Four." They restricted the arts and enforced ideology, with many people dying in purges. Her radical domestic policies ensured that many of the basic precepts of the Cultural Revolution continued in force until Mao died in 1976. Following Mao's death, Jiang Qing made an unsuccessful attempt to seize power and was arrested and sentenced to life imprisonment for her part in the Cultural Revolution. She committed suicide in 1991.

During his lifetime, Mao Zedong controlled artistic, intellectual, military, industrial, and agricultural planning and policies in the most populated nation on earth. After his death, Chinese leaders reversed many of his policies and ended the emphasis on his personality. They looked to Japan, the United States, and European countries for help in modernizing China's industry, agriculture, science, and armed forces. These goals were called the Four Modernizations.

For More Information

Books

Chou, Eric. *Mao Tse-tung, the Man and the Myth*. New York: Stein and Day, 1982.

Schram, Stewart R. *Mao Tse-tung*. New York: Simon and Schuster, 1967.

Short, Philip. *Mao: A Life*. New York: Henry Holt, 2000.

Spence, Jonathan D. *Mao Zedong*. New York: Viking, 1999.

George C. Marshall

Born December 31, 1880
Uniontown, Pennsylvania
Died October 16, 1959
Washington, D.C.

U.S. secretary of state, army general, and
U.S. Army chief of staff

George Marshall was a highly respected U.S. military leader and U.S. official. He served as an army general, secretary of state, and secretary of defense. He was the first military person to be awarded the Nobel Peace Prize for his role in the European economic recovery following World War II (1939–45). Most importantly, the Cold War (1945–91) took shape during his time as secretary of state. The policies he developed would influence the next forty years of rivalry with the Soviet Union.

The young officer

George Catlett Marshall Jr. was born on New Year's Eve in 1880 in Uniontown, Pennsylvania, son of Laura Bradford and George C. Marshall Sr., a coal merchant. Marshall was a direct descendent of John Marshall (1755–1835), the first chief justice of the U.S. Supreme Court. Marshall attended the Virginia Military Institute, where his leadership abilities began to show as he moved up in rank to a captain of the cadets. Upon graduating in 1901, Marshall received a com-

"Our policy is directed not against any country or doctrine, but against hunger, poverty, desperation and chaos. Its purpose should be the revival of a working economy in the world so as to permit the emergence of political and social conditions in which free institutions can exist."

George C. Marshall.

mission in the army as a second lieutenant. Only days after receiving his commission in February 1902, he married Elizabeth Coles. They would have no children.

For the next fourteen years, Marshall served at several posts around the country in addition to two stints in the Philippines. In 1906, he was appointed to the Infantry-Cavalry School at Fort Leavenworth in Kansas. He graduated first in his class and showed exceptional skills for staff work. In 1908, he was appointed instructor at the school. Despite the skills he showed, including serving as an aide to two generals between 1913 and 1916, there was little room for advancement, given the small size of the U.S. Army at that time. In 1916, he finally made the rank of captain.

Early in his career, Marshall showed a quiet self-confidence and a strong self-discipline, as he kept a strong temper under control. The soft-spoken Marshall seemed cool and aloof in manner to those who did not know him well, but very warm and open to those close to him. He also had great communication skills, both in military situations and with civilians.

Rising in the ranks

During World War I (1914–18), Marshall was assigned to the staff of the First Infantry Division. He was one of the first U.S. soldiers to arrive in France in 1917. However, due to his staff skills, he would not have a field command. Instead, he played a key role in training newly arriving U.S. troops and planning battle strategies. During the war, Marshall caught the attention of General John J. Pershing (1860–1948), head of the U.S. Army in Europe. In 1918, Marshall was assigned to the operations staff of Pershing's general headquarters, where he was involved in the planning of major U.S. offenses. By November 1918, at war's end, he was chief of operations for the U.S. First Army. He was one of Pershing's top tactical experts. Pershing recommended Marshall for promotion to brigadier general. Following the war, however, Marshall returned to the rank of major in the smaller postwar army. Through the early 1920s, Marshall served as a key aide to Pershing, who was the army chief of staff. Through Pershing, Marshall became well acquainted with military affairs at the highest levels in Washington, D.C. In 1923, Marshall was promoted to lieutenant colonel.

In 1924, Marshall was assigned to command a U.S. infantry regiment in China for three years before returning to Washington, D.C. There, he became instructor at the National War College. Upon returning to the United States, tragedy struck. His wife died suddenly from a heart condition, putting him into deep depression. Marshall became more absorbed in his career. He became head of the Infantry School at Fort Benning, Georgia, and revamped the program. Two hundred future generals came from the school while he was there from 1927 to 1933. While at Fort Benning, he married Tupper Brown, a widow with three children.

During the early 1930s, Marshall became a colonel and commanded army posts in Georgia and South Carolina, and organized the Civilian Conservation Corps (CCC) camps in several states. The CCC was a federal program that provided jobs to unemployed young men during the Great Depression (1929–41), the worst financial crisis in American history. In 1936, he finally achieved the rank of brigadier general, serving as commander at Fort Vancouver in the state of Washington.

A World War II leader

In 1938, Marshall was recalled to Washington, D.C., to become head of the army's War Plans Division. By April 1939, President Franklin D. Roosevelt (1882–1945; served 1933–45) appointed Marshall deputy army chief of staff. He would soon be promoted to chief of staff and was sworn in on September 1, 1939, the same day Germany invaded Poland, starting World War II. Marshall strongly lobbied Congress to enlarge the armed forces in preparation for war. Following the German conquest of France in early 1940, Congress became much more responsive to Marshall's requests. By 1943, the army had grown from 175,000 to 8.3 million.

Following the entrance of the United States into World War II in 1941, Marshall held a crucial role in military planning, the training of troops, and the development of new weapons. He reorganized the War Department in early 1942 and was the leading person in the newly established U.S. joint chiefs of staff. He became Roosevelt's key military advisor, accompanying the president at all war summit conferences.

In 1944, Marshall became general of the army. *Time* magazine selected Marshall "Man of the Year." After successfully attaining victory in World War II and becoming an American hero, Marshall resigned as chief of staff in November 1945 at the mandatory military retirement age of sixty-five.

Soldier turned statesman

One week after Marshall's resignation, President **Harry S. Truman** (1884–1972; served 1945–53; see entry) appointed Marshall as U.S. special emissary to China. His job was to resolve the civil war between the Chinese communist forces led by **Mao Zedong** (1893–1976; see entry) and the Chinese Nationalist government headed by **Chiang Kai-shek** (1887–1975; see entry). Though temporarily achieving some success in early 1946, the two sides soon resumed fighting. Marshall declared the situation hopeless. Upon returning to the United States in January 1947, Marshall influenced Truman to reduce foreign aid to Chiang's government. Marshall believed communist victory was inevitable, given the lack of popularity for the Nationalist government among the general population. The Nationalist government did fall in October 1949. This resulted in Marshall becoming the target of U.S. senator **Joseph R. McCarthy** (1909–1957; see entry) of Wisconsin during congressional hearings. McCarthy accused Marshall of not providing greater support to Chiang and "allowing" the communists to win.

Upon his return to the United States, Marshall was appointed secretary of state. Marshall was so highly respected in 1947 that he was unanimously approved by the Senate with no hearings or opposition. He was the first military leader to become secretary of state. Convinced the Soviets posed a major risk to Europe, Marshall took a hard-line approach against the Soviets. To create a State Department most responsive to this new threat, Marshall undertook a major reorganization of the department. The department would be ready to tackle its new increased role as a superpower in world affairs. He also influenced the creation of the National Security Council in 1947 to better coordinate foreign and military policy.

A brief trip to Europe pointed out to Marshall how severe Europe's economic problems were. He and other admin-

The Marshall Plan

In a speech at Harvard University on June 5, 1947, U.S. secretary of state George C. Marshall unveiled a new major U.S. economic aid program for Western Europe. Marshall feared the high poverty and unemployment rates in the region following the devastating effects of World War II created an unstable political climate ripe for the spread of communism. Seventeen nations in Western Europe applied for aid under the program—commonly known as the Marshall Plan—between April 1949 and December 1951.

The United States created the Economic Cooperation Administration (ECA) to distribute thirteen billion dollars over a four-year period. The European nations receiving the assistance formed the Organisation for European Economic Cooperation (OEEC) to coordinate their participation. The program was highly successful, restoring industry, increasing agricultural production, expanding trade, and stabilizing monetary systems. It solved much hunger and despair. The eco-nomic productivity of some nations rose by as much as 25 percent.

Marshall offered the plan to the Soviet Union and Eastern European countries as well. However, the Soviets rejected participation and forced those Eastern European countries under its control to not participate as well, even though Czechoslovakia and Poland had already expressed interest. The Soviets claimed conditions of the program posed too much of a Western intrusion in domestic economies. They would offer a separate, far less effective plan to the Eastern European countries.

The Marshall Plan was successful in the rapid economic revival of Western Europe, but it also contributed to the growing split between East and West in Europe, setting the stage for future hostile confrontations between the two superpowers, the Soviet Union and the United States. Nonetheless, for his role in developing the program and for the positive benefits, Marshall received the Nobel Peace Prize in 1953.

istration officials believed the hardships made a ripe situation for the spread of communism beyond Eastern Europe into Western Europe. The communist parties were already making gains in Italy and France. Marshall was convinced the most effective way to contain the further spread of communism in Europe was to substantially improve Western European economic conditions. Marshall pulled together a group to devise a plan. By June 1947, Marshall announced the Economic Recovery Program, more commonly known as the Marshall Plan (see box).

U.S. president Harry S.
Truman (far left) discusses
the Marshall Plan with (left
to right) George Marshall,
Paul G. Hoffman, and W.
Averell Harriman.
Photograph by Abbie Rowe.
Reproduced by permission of
the Harry S. Truman Library
and the Corbis Corporation.

Marshall played an influential role in shaping many early Cold War events. With Soviet communist pressure applied to Greece and Turkey in early 1947, Marshall successfully pressed Truman and Congress for four hundred million dollars in U.S. aid to those countries. (The Soviet Union had naval stations in Turkey, and nearby Greece was fighting a civil war with communist-dominated rebels.) Marshall opposed creation of the state of Israel and advised Truman not to react too quickly in 1948, when the state of Israel was created. Marshall believed such rapid recognition would harm relations with Arab nations in the region. However, in a rare occasion of Truman going against Marshall's advice, the president, under pressure from conservative Republicans and the Jewish population in the United States during an election year, extended formal recognition within hours of Israel's formation. Marshall was also key in creating a Western European and U.S. defense alliance known as the North Atlantic Treaty Organization (NATO), a key factor in the attempt to contain communism. Similarly, he developed defense and economic alliances with Latin American countries, known as the Rio Pact and the Organization of American States.

In June 1948, the Soviets also blockaded access to the Western-controlled sections of Berlin. Truman followed Marshall's advice to combat the blockade by using a massive airlift of supplies to West Berlin, rather than resorting to a more direct military confrontation, as advised by others in the administration. The blockade ended peacefully in May 1949.

The last assignment

After a very busy two years as secretary of state, Marshall resigned due to health problems. However, duty would call again soon. With the beginning of the Korean War (1950–53) in June 1950, Truman asked Marshall to serve as secretary of defense, though he was seventy years of age. As he had done earlier in World War II, Marshall oversaw the rebuilding of the U.S. armed forces and production of weapons. Marshall would also support Truman in the removal of the controversial General **Douglas MacArthur** (1880–1964; see entry), after MacArthur became a leading critic of Truman's and Marshall's war strategies.

Once more, Marshall retired in September 1951, after he had completed his tasks and the war against communist North Korea had come to a stalemate. He remained a high-ranking advisor to the U.S. government. Marshall died at Walter Reed General Hospital in Washington, D.C., in 1959 after suffering a series of strokes. He was buried in Arlington National Cemetery. In 1964, the George C. Marshall Research Library was dedicated in Lexington, Virginia.

For More Information

Books

Cray, Ed. *General of the Army: George C. Marshall, Soldier and Statesman.* New York: Norton, 1990.

Donovan, Robert J. *The Second Victory: The Marshall Plan and the Postwar Revival of Europe.* New York: Madison Books, 1987.

Hogan, Michael J. *The Marshall Plan: America, Britain, and the Reconstruction of Western Europe, 1947–1952.* New York: Cambridge University Press, 1987.

Pogue, Forrest C. *George C. Marshall.* 4 vols. Colorado Springs, CO: U.S. Air Force Academy, 1963–87.

Stoler, Mark A. *George C. Marshall: Soldier-Statesman of the American Century.* Boston: Twayne Publishers, 1989.

Joseph R. McCarthy

Born November 14, 1908
Appleton, Wisconsin
Died May 2, 1957
Bethesda, Maryland

U.S. senator

Joseph McCarthy, an infamous and highly controversial U.S. senator from Wisconsin, became America's leading anti-communist figure. His influence peaked between 1950 and 1953. McCarthy gained national attention by asserting that communists had infiltrated the U.S. government at its highest levels. Some called McCarthy a patriot; others accused him of making vicious, untrue charges against innocent Americans, ruining their careers. McCarthy's sensationalized committee investigations greatly contributed to the anticommunist hysteria sweeping the country. The United States' diplomatic efforts toward the communist countries of the Soviet Union, Eastern Europe, and Asia were adversely affected for several decades.

"Have you no sense of decency, sir? At long last, have you left no sense of decency?" — *U.S. Army attorney Joseph N. Welch, speaking to Joseph McCarthy at the Army-McCarthy hearings*

Pre-Senate years

Joseph Raymond McCarthy was the fifth of seven children born to Timothy and Bridget McCarthy. The Mc-Carthys, of Irish descent and faithful Roman Catholics, worked long, hard hours on their isolated rural 142-acre Wis-

Joseph R. McCarthy.
Reproduced by permission of Getty Images.

consin farm. McCarthy's father, a strict disciplinarian, expected his son to take on many farm responsibilities. McCarthy's mother, realizing her son possessed a strength of character and deciding at least one of her children had to rise above the family's simple rural life, urged her son to become "somebody." However, at fourteen, McCarthy dropped out of school to work in the family's potato and cabbage fields. Uncomfortable working under his father's supervision, he soon began raising poultry on an acre of land rented from his father. He was an amazingly successful poultry entrepreneur until a cold spell killed his flock.

At nineteen, McCarthy moved to the nearby town of Manawa, worked as a store manager, and talked and argued ceaselessly about community issues with his customers. Realizing his gift of oratory and perhaps even then thinking in terms of running for a town office, McCarthy decided he must have a formal education. He returned to high school at age twenty. After completing high school in one year, he entered Marquette University. After two years of engineering studies, he switched to the field of law, which accommodated his love of debate and drama. McCarthy also was a member of the university boxing team where, even when clearly outclassed, he was known for boxing with fierce aggression until thoroughly bloodied. McCarthy graduated from Marquette in 1935.

McCarthy opened his first law practice in the Wisconsin town of Waupaca and joined a number of civic organizations. As a Republican in 1939, he made his first successful run for office, a circuit judgeship in Wisconsin's tenth district. World War II (1939–45) interrupted McCarthy's budding political career. He joined the Marine Corps and served in the Pacific primarily at a desk assignment as an intelligence officer. Riding in the tail gunner section of an aircraft, McCarthy apparently flew several times on noncombat missions. Always keenly aware of appearances for political purposes, however, he made sure he was photographed sitting in the tail gunner (back) section. Suggesting he served as a tail gunner of a dive bomber, the pictures would be widely used in his later Senate campaigns in Wisconsin.

In 1944, McCarthy returned to Wisconsin on a thirty-day leave and ran against incumbent (currently serving) U.S. senator Alexander Wiley (1884–1967) in the Republican primary. "Tail-Gunner Joe," as McCarthy referred to himself, lost but won a great deal of name recognition. Following the war, in 1946, he ran for the Senate again, this time taking on popular incumbent senator Robert M. La Follette Jr. (1895–1953), who had served for twenty-one years. With a surprise victory over La Follette, McCarthy took his place as the new U.S. senator from Wisconsin in January 1947. Soon, McCarthy would play a major role in the second "Red Scare" that was sweeping over America (see box).

Troublemaker in the Senate

By the end of 1949, McCarthy's Senate career had been ineffective. His only accomplishment had been to team with Pepsi-Cola Company to lift controls on sugar rationing. He had developed a reputation in the Senate as a troublemaker. With arrogant, rude, and inconsistent behavior, he had made many enemies. He knew he had little support in Wisconsin for reelection in 1952. McCarthy needed control of a powerful issue to draw attention and support his way. Friends suggested that a forceful anticommunism campaign, a subject he had never expressed any interest in before, might just resonate with voters. Communism is a governmental system in which a single party controls all aspects of society. In economic theory, it bans private ownership of property and businesses, so that goods produced and wealth accumulated are shared equally by all.

With little knowledge or preparation, McCarthy latched onto the anticommunism idea and launched his campaign on February 7, 1950, in a speech before the Ohio County Women's Republican Club in Wheeling, West Virginia. McCarthy would dub himself the exposer of communists, and the American people and press listened intently. McCarthy played on Cold War (1945–91) and Red Scare fears by maintaining that the communist world, particularly the Soviet Union, was in a showdown with the democratic nations led by the United States. The Cold War was an intense political and economic rivalry between the United States and the Soviet Union, falling just short of military conflict. In the Wheeling speech, McCarthy held up a list he claimed contained 205 names of U.S. State Department employees who

Second Red Scare

Red Scares occurred during a time when Americans were especially fearful that communists would edge closer to the United States and eventually take over. The term "red" was used to refer to communists. The first Red Scare occurred after World War I between 1918 and 1920. The second Red Scare peaked after World War II between 1947 and 1953. This time period paralleled the first years of the Cold War, an intense ideological battle between the democratic United States and the communist Soviet Union.

Americans became obsessed with the fear and hatred of communism and subversive elements, real and imagined, within their homeland. By the end of 1948,

Americans believed if they were not constantly vigilant the Cold War could be lost right on U.S. soil. Contributing to this viewpoint were the investigations of the House Un-American Activities Committee (HUAC). Reinstated in 1945, the HUAC, charged with investigation of subversive activities that posed a threat to the U.S. government, labeled roughly forty organizations as communist "front" groups. Front groups had patriotic names but, according to the HUAC, really were organizations intent on promoting communist ideas.

Richard M. Nixon (1913–1994; see entry), then a young Republican congressman from California, was an aggressive

supposedly were known members of the Communist Party. McCarthy refused to reveal his sources or give all but a few names on the list. Sometime later, it was discovered that the list he held up was his laundry list. But he had caught Americans' attention and became an instant celebrity as the nation's leading anticommunist, appearing on the covers of *Time* and *Newsweek* magazines.

McCarthyism

McCarthy's strategy was attack then avoidance. He attacked by casting doubt on an individual's political loyalties, forcing the individual to defend himself publicly. He then avoided producing any real evidence, saying that his job was not to provide all the evidence but to make the charges. However reckless and irresponsible the charges, they were nevertheless unnerving. By early 1951, many Americans did not care if the charges were true or not—they were mesmerized member of the HUAC. In late 1947, the HUAC investigated ten members of the Hollywood film industry for communist leanings. In 1948, the strange case of former U.S. State Department official Alger Hiss (1904–1996) went before the HUAC. Eventually, in early 1950, Hiss was found guilty of supplying State Department documents to the Soviets. The HUAC also charged that civil rights groups were filled with communists.

Other occurrences leading to heightened apprehensions were repeated public statements by **J. Edgar Hoover** (1895–1972; see entry), director of the Federal Bureau of Investigation (FBI), that communism could spread like a disease across America. The most chilling news to reach Americans came in the fall of 1949, when President Harry S. Truman revealed that the Soviet Union had successfully tested an atomic bomb. Within a few years, several spies who had funneled U.S. atomic secrets to the Soviet Union were unmasked, tried, and convicted. Meanwhile, Chinese communist rebels had overtaken Mainland China in October 1949. By 1950, loyal Americans, to protect their country, were on the lookout for communists even in the smallest village. Americans were highly sensitive and receptive to the dramatic and aggressive communist charges that Senator Joseph McCarthy began to level in February 1950.

by McCarthyism. The term McCarthyism entered the U.S. vocabulary permanently and came to mean challenging a person's individual freedoms and character with lies and mean-spirited suggestions.

Simply being named by McCarthy as a possible subversive was career ending. (A subversive is a person who attempts to overthrow or undermine an established political system.) Many innocent Americans were devastated. Republican leadership knew the outrageousness of McCarthy's charges but also knew it was political suicide to try and reel him in. McCarthy stayed on the offensive, suggesting anyone who criticized his tactics must also be a communist. The House Un-American Activities Committee (HUAC) energetically investigated all those on whom McCarthy cast suspicion. Not only did he attack many lower-level government officials, but knowing no bounds, he attacked at the highest levels. McCarthy went after celebrated former army general and current secretary of defense **George C. Marshall** (1880–1959; see entry), eventually contributing to his resignation. He attacked Secretary of State **Dean G. Acheson** (1893–1971; see entry) as the "Red Dean," and proceeded right to personal attacks on President **Harry S. Truman** (1884–1972; served 1945–53; see entry). McCarthy's talent lay in just the right timing and drama to grab headlines. He became the center of the Red Scare hysteria. He was reelected to his Senate seat in 1952. In 1953, McCarthy, a bachelor, showed a human side by marrying his political assistant, Jean Kerr. Together, they adopted a baby daughter in January 1957.

Senate Permanent Investigations Subcommittee

In 1952, Republican candidate **Dwight D. Eisenhower** (1890–1969; served 1953–1961; see entry) was elected president. McCarthy was assigned to a seemingly unimportant committee called the Government Operations Committee in an effort to take him largely out of public view. However, McCarthy figured out a way to regain headlines once again. He created and made himself chairman of the Permanent Subcommittee on Investigations. With the assistance of a bright young lawyer, Roy Cohn (1927–1986), McCarthy again attacked the State Department. The committee became known as the "McCarthy Committee."

Among other things on the committee, McCarthy charged that communists within the State Department were subverting the radio programming of Voice of America. Voice of America routinely broadcast democratic messages to over eighty foreign countries. The program barely survived the assault. The McCarthy Committee also targeted public libraries, demanding the removal of any book that appeared to support communism. Even President Eisenhower was constantly under attack. Angered over McCarthy's antics, the president nevertheless wanted to avoid any public confrontations with him. However, McCarthy's plans to investigate the CIA were stopped.

By early 1954, public criticism of McCarthy began to rise. In March, noted television journalist Edward R. Murrow (1908–1965) contended in his television program that McCarthy was exploiting America's fears for personal gain and was intimidating honest Americans. Finally, McCarthy pushed too far when he attacked the U.S. Army. McCarthy

COMMUNIST PARTY ORGANIZATION U.S.A-FEB. 9, 1950

had declared that the U.S. Army's base at Fort Monmouth, New Jersey, harbored a communist spy ring. In hearings, no evidence was uncovered to back McCarthy's charges. Ultimately, in the spring of 1954, the army's lawyer, Joseph N. Welch (1890–1960), was able to bring McCarthy's long stream of unjustified attacks to an end with the famous utterance: "Have you no sense of decency, sir? At long last, have you left no sense of decency?" During the hearings, known as the Army-McCarthy hearings, McCarthy's bullying tactics had been thoroughly exposed to the public.

The Senate voted to censure, or officially reprimand, McCarthy, meaning his behavior from 1950 to 1954 had been highly dishonorable. Though he remained in the Senate, he was ostracized, or ignored, by his colleagues. McCarthy, who sometimes drank heavily, died on May 2, 1957, of an inflamed liver at the age of forty-eight.

Through the following decades, Americans struggled to comprehend how a person in a place of authority could

Senator Joseph R. McCarthy points to a map of the United States labeled "Communist Party Organization" at a House Un-American Activities Committee hearing in June 1954. U.S. Army attorney Joseph N. Welch is seated at the table in front of McCarthy.

use fear to discredit innocent lives and so thoroughly trample their constitutionally protected rights. Many Americans would consider McCarthy's tactics not much different in spirit than the terror orchestrated by harsh communist rulers in the Soviet Union on Soviet citizens. The Red Scare and McCarthyism shook the foundation of individual liberties in America during the early Cold War years.

For More Information

Books

Cohn, Roy. *McCarthy.* New York: The New American Library, 1968.

Herman, Arthur. *Joseph McCarthy: Reexamining the Life and Legacy of America's Most Hated Senator.* New York: Free Press, 2000.

Kutler, Stanley I. *The American Inquisition: Justice and Injustice in the Cold War.* New York: Hill and Wang, 1982.

Oshinsky, David M. *A Conspiracy So Immense: The World of Joe McCarthy.* New York: Free Press, 1983.

Reeves, Thomas C. *The Life and Times of Joe McCarthy: A Biography.* New York: Stein & Day, 1982.

Schrecker, Ellen. *Many Are the Crimes: McCarthyism in America.* Boston: Little, Brown, 1998.

Sherrow, Victoria. *Joseph McCarthy and the Cold War.* Woodbridge, CT: Blackbirch Press, 1999.

Robert S. McNamara

Born June 9, 1916
San Francisco, California

U.S. secretary of defense

Robert S. McNamara played an important role in U.S. foreign policy during the Cold War period of the 1960s. The Cold War was an intense political and economic rivalry from 1945 to 1991 between the United States and the Soviet Union, falling just short of direct military conflict. Smart and ambitious, McNamara came from the business world to serve as U.S. secretary of defense under Presidents **John F. Kennedy** (1919–1963; served 1961–63; see entry) and **Lyndon B. Johnson** (1908–1973; served 1963–69; see entry).

McNamara was one of a group of superior managers emerging from World War II (1939–45)—smart, arrogant, and seemingly capable of tackling anything. He was young and vigorous and seemed—along with the rest of young President Kennedy's advisors—to be the new face of the new superpower, the United States. McNamara became famous for applying his sharp, mathematical mind to the problems of troop deployment and arms requirements during the peak of the U.S. involvement in the Vietnam War (1954–75). As the military engagement in Vietnam grew, he became a lightning rod for criticism of U.S. war policy. He was seen as cold and harsh, as

"Coercion ... merely captures man. Freedom captivates him."

Robert S. McNamara.
Courtesy of the Library of Congress.

the war continued, and the number of lives lost rose. McNamara came to represent all that was good and bad about the United States during the Vietnam War.

A business scholar

Robert Strange McNamara was born on June 9, 1916, to Robert J. and Claranell Strange McNamara in San Francisco, California. The man who would later be considered one of the smartest men of his generation was raised by parents who never went to college. In fact, his father did not attend school past the eighth grade. Robert J. McNamara was from a family of Irish immigrants. Raised in poverty and sick throughout much of his childhood, through hard work McNamara's father created a middle-class life for his family.

McNamara graduated from the University of California at Berkeley in 1937. He went on to earn a master's degree in business administration at the Harvard School of Business in 1939. His strength as a mathematician and his expertise in statistical analysis were emerging. Following an impressive performance at Harvard, he was asked to come back and teach. He became a junior faculty member. He also married Margaret McKinstry Craig in 1940; the couple would have two daughters and a son.

At this time, Europe was disintegrating into what would become World War II, and some of the power brokers in the United States were beginning to prepare for the United States' entrance into the war. One of these people was U.S. War Department official Robert A. Lovett (1895–1986). Lovett believed that the Air Force would play a key role in the coming conflict, and that the United States was woefully unprepared. He needed men who could calculate how many planes were needed, and how many inductees would be needed to fly them. Also, he needed to know how many trainers would be required to train the inductees—and then get the planes and the inductees and the trainers all to the right place at the right time.

Lovett asked Harvard Business School to train the men he needed. McNamara was one of the teachers. He was so good that, in 1943, he was commissioned as a captain in the Air Force and sent to help Lovett plan the continuing conflict. For his work during the war, McNamara was presented with the Legion of Merit Medal.

A manager for Ford Motor Company

As the war ended, the team that had managed the U.S. Air Force was noted as being, perhaps, the best group of young managers around. The group, including McNamara, had experienced twenty years of organizational challenges in just a few short years. Recognizing their strengths as a team, a group of the Air Force managers decided to market themselves to corporate America as a group. They were smart, hard working, and could make an impact on a business. In 1946, McNamara and the group, which later became known as the "Whiz Kids," joined Ford Motor Company in Dearborn, Michigan.

In the mid-1940s, Ford was losing more than nine million dollars a year. McNamara was initially part of the Finance Division of Ford. He quickly established a reputation for using numbers to show how to add value to the company's automobiles without adding manufacturing costs, so that Ford could better compete in the marketplace. Over the years, McNamara rose through the company ranks and was elected to director of Ford in 1957. In 1960, he was elected president of Ford. He had just taken office, however, when he received a call from President-elect John F. Kennedy.

Secretary of defense

President Kennedy was about to take office and was looking to fill key positions within his government. On the advice of Lovett, Kennedy asked McNamara to meet with him. Impressed with McNamara, Kennedy offered him a choice of positions, either the secretary of treasury or the secretary of defense. McNamara was not interested in becoming secretary of treasury. He felt he had more impact on the national economy as president of Ford. But he was interested in secretary of defense, seeing it as a good platform for a commitment to national service.

Prior to accepting the position, McNamara expressed to Kennedy his concern that he was not qualified for the po-

Defense Secretary Robert S. McNamara (center) consults with President John F. Kennedy at a Cabinet meeting. *Courtesy of the John F. Kennedy Library.*

sition. Kennedy, impressed with McNamara's intellect, was not concerned. After all, he reasoned, there were no schools for being president either. McNamara served as secretary of defense from 1961 to 1968, first under President Kennedy and later under President Johnson.

Early in the Kennedy administration, a number of foreign events occurred that challenged the new administration. In particular, the failed invasion of Cuba by U.S.-supported Cuban exiles at the Bay of Pigs left the impression that President Kennedy did not know how to handle communist expansion backed by the Soviets. Communism is a system of government in which a single party, the Communist Party, controls all aspects of people's lives. In economic theory, it prohibits private ownership of property and business, so that goods produced and wealth accumulated are shared relatively equally by all. McNamara's statistical analysis prior to the invasion turned out to be flawed, when the administration later learned the estimated number of Cubans who were being counted on to rise up against Cuban leader **Fidel Castro** (1926–; see entry) proved far too high. The smaller-than-expected force experienced immediate defeat by Castro's army. Later, McNamara learned the information given to him for his analysis was inaccurate.

In 1961, many in the White House and Congress were debating what to do about the U.S. arms race with the Soviet Union. McNamara was no exception. The United States had 450 missiles. The joint chiefs of staff, the key military advisory group to the president, was advising Kennedy to increase the number to 3,000. However, McNamara recommended 950. In terms of military effectiveness, the military experts concluded that 450 missiles were just as effective as 950. Though McNamara agreed from a military standpoint, for political reasons, McNamara asserted the United States needed at least 950.

In the Kennedy White House and later during the early Johnson days, McNamara was considered a man of action: always in control, always rational, always organizing. He could read faster than people could talk and demanded that briefings be written rather than orally presented to save him time. He always supported his reasons with statistics. As a result, as the country became mired in the Vietnam War, statistics became the focus of anger and derision.

The Vietnam War

For many people in the 1960s, the Vietnam War was "McNamara's War." The Vietnam War primarily involved U.S. efforts to protect noncommunist South Vietnam from takeover by communist-ruled North Vietnam. U.S. aid to South Vietnam began as early as January 1955. Steadily, U.S. military support escalated until hundreds of thousands of U.S. troops were in Vietnam by 1967. As the war evolved, McNamara was often the face of the war, explaining victories and defeats in numbers and body counts. The costs in human lives aside, progress was often measured in the cost of air power used compared to the dollars of resulting damage. As the war continued and took more lives, McNamara's approach seemed cold and harsh. It seemed to ignore some key questions, such as why Vietnam was important to the United

From Cultured Businessman to Cold Warrior

While Robert McNamara worked at Ford Motor Company, he was known as a driven and exacting man. But he also had another side. He removed himself from the world of the automotive executives, choosing to live in Ann Arbor, Michigan, a cultured college town. There, he attended art openings and concerts with his wife, and belonged to a book club. He prided himself on having broad interests.

Years later, when friends of his from Ann Arbor would see McNamara on television, talking about body counts and kill ratios and tramping around with troops fighting Cold War communist expansion in the jungles of far-off Vietnam, they would wonder what had happened to the man they had known.

States, and just how committed the North Vietnamese were to their cause.

Initially a strong supporter of the war, McNamara became known as the architect of early U.S. policy in Vietnam. By the mid-1960s, however, he was becoming disillusioned. He no longer believed what the generals were telling him, and he was increasingly vocal about his concerns. At the end of 1965, U.S. general William Westmoreland (1914–) in Vietnam requested 200,000 more troops—bringing the total number in Vietnam to 410,000. McNamara was skeptical. He went to Vietnam himself to review the situation and did not like what he saw. He was not sure the United States could win—or that if it did, the price would be worth it.

McNamara voiced his concerns within the Johnson administration, but not to the public. While his son was protesting the war, McNamara still publicly supported President Johnson and the generals. But his challenges to the generals within White House walls were not received well, and he gradually became distant from the joint chiefs of staff and other Johnson advisors. In 1967, McNamara wrote a memo to Johnson stating that the war could not be won, largely due to the weakness of the South Vietnamese government. He recommended a political compromise. The generals were furious at McNamara's memo. In 1968, Johnson removed him from the White House by appointing him head of the World Bank, an international organization created by the United Nations for financing projects in developing nations.

McNamara came to represent to the American public both the strengths and the weaknesses of American intervention in Vietnam. He appeared consistently rational, full of good intentions, and sure he was doing the right thing. However, he seemed blind to indications that perhaps he was not doing the right thing. After the war ended, McNamara publicly admitted some of the doubts and debates of the U.S. leadership during the Vietnam War.

After the war

In 1981, McNamara retired from public service, but not from controversy. He authored several books, including *The Essence of Security; One Hundred Countries, Two Billion People;* and *Out of the Cold.* The book that revived debate on the Vietnam War, however, was *In Retrospect: The Tragedy and Lessons of Vietnam.* In the book, McNamara discussed the tensions within the White House during the Vietnam War.

While McNamara confessed his growing doubts about the war at the time more soldiers were being sent to Vietnam and the bombing of North Vietnam was increasing, the admission pleased no one. Supporters of the war felt he had betrayed the soldiers' sacrifice. Opponents of the war felt he should have spoken out much earlier. The aging McNamara weathered the controversy, as he had the social unrest spurred by massive antiwar protests during the 1960s.

Over the years, McNamara—the scholar, the mathematician, the Whiz Kid—has received numerous awards and recognition. He was honored with the Presidential Medal of Freedom (with Distinction), the Albert Einstein Peace Prize, the Franklin Delano Roosevelt Freedom from Want Medal, and the Dag Hammarskjöld Honorary Medal.

For More Information

Books

Draper, Theodore. "McNamara's Peace." *New York Review of Books,* May 11, 1995.

Halberstam, David. *The Best and the Brightest.* New York: Ballantine Books, 1969.

Hendrickson, Paul. *The Living and the Dead: Robert McNamara and Five Lives of a Lost War.* New York: Random House, 1997.

McNamara, Robert S. *The Essence of Security: Reflections in Office.* New York: Harper & Row, 1968.

McNamara, Robert S. *Out of the Cold: New Thinking for American Foreign and Defense Policy in the 21st Century.* New York: Simon and Schuster, 1989.

McNamara, Robert S., and Brian VanDeMark. *In Retrospect: The Tragedy and Lessons of Vietnam.* New York: Times Books, 1995.

McNamara, Robert S., James G. Blight, and Robert R. Brigham. *Argument Without End: In Search of Answers to the Vietnam Tragedy.* New York: Public Affairs, 2000.

Vyacheslav Molotov

Born February 25, 1890
Kukarka, Nolinsk region,
Vyatka province, Russia
Died November 8, 1986
Moscow, Russia, Soviet Union

Soviet revolutionary,
politician, and statesman

V yacheslav Molotov was the closest friend and loyal aide of
Joseph Stalin (1879–1953; see entry) throughout Stalin's
reign as leader of the Soviet Union. Won over to communism
as a teenager, Molotov never strayed from the strict party line
and always viewed Stalin's policies, however terror-filled, as
correct. Molotov's talks with Western powers in the years following World War II (1939–45) helped fuel the Cold War
(1945–91). The Cold War was an intense political and economic rivalry from 1945 to 1991 between the United States
and the Soviet Union, falling just short of military conflict.

"Stalin's henchman
Molotov, 96, died old
and in bed, a privilege he
helped to deny to
millions." — *U.S.*
commentator George F. Will

Young revolutionary

Vyacheslav Mikhaylovich Scriabin was born to middle-class parents in the small central Russian town of Kukarka.
Around 1912, he adopted his revolutionary surname "Molotov," which means hammer. Molotov was related to Russian
composer Aleksandr Nikolaevich Scriabin and as a youngster
studied the violin. During this time, the tsars, Russia's monarchy, ruled the country harshly, decreasing local rule and ap-

Vyacheslav Molotov.
Courtesy of the Library
of Congress.

pointing aristocrats to administer over the industrial workers and peasants. This led to poor working conditions, greater poverty and hunger, and growing discontent among the citizens. As Molotov's family became more interested and involved in the peasant and worker unrest in the early and mid-1900s, he decided to forgo study in music for a more practical education. He attended high school in the nearby city of Kazan. There, Molotov was introduced to the ideas of German philosopher Karl Marx (1818–1883), considered the father of communism. Communism is a system of government, where a single party, the Communist Party, controls all aspects of people's lives. In economic theory, it prohibits private ownership of property and business, so that goods produced and wealth accumulated are shared relatively equally by all.

Revolutionary ideas had reached into the Nolinsk region by 1905. The young, impressionable Molotov and his friends listened to speeches and heard of the general railroad strikes, the workers' rebellion in Saint Petersburg, and landowners' estates burning in several Russian provinces. Molotov joined student Marxist groups and began learning about the Bolsheviks (communists) when a close friend's father began financially supporting them. Molotov joined the Social Democratic Party in 1906 at the age of sixteen and leaned toward the Bolshevik faction.

Molotov soon learned revolutionary tactics such as agitation, which involved getting workers riled up about injustices they were being subjected to and inciting them to take action, and getting the communist message to everyday Russians. Arrested and exiled for two years for radical politics in opposition to the tsar, he ended up in Vologda near the city of Saint Petersburg. Even in exile, Molotov continued to hone his revolutionary skills, as he worked among railroad workers. After his release from exile, he studied at Saint Petersburg Polytechnic. Molotov met Joseph Stalin in 1912 through his aunt who rented a room to Stalin. Stalin was already constantly sought after by police for spreading revolutionary communist propaganda, but Molotov and Stalin struck up a life-long friendship. Also that year, Molotov became associated with the new Communist Party newspaper, *Pravda,* which means "truth."

Through the next five years, Molotov was exiled several more times for revolutionary activities but maintained his work for *Pravda*. Back in Saint Petersburg by 1916, he worked closely with Bolshevik leader Vladimir I. Lenin (1870–1924) and Stalin in opposition to the Provisional Government. Molotov helped organize workers' strikes, which preceded the February Revolution in 1917. Molotov was a member of the Military Revolutionary Committee that planned the successful Bolshevik coup, known as the "October Revolution," that same year. The October Revolution marked the beginning of the communist state in Russia.

Continuing to gain Stalin's trust and holding several party posts in the provinces, Molotov rose through the Communist Party ranks, establishing himself as a strict party line administrator. In November 1920, he was appointed secretary, or chief official, of the Central Committee of the Ukrainian Bolshevik Party. On a trip to the Ukraine, Molotov met a young Jewish female party worker, Polina Zhemchuzhina, on a sugar beet farm where she labored. They were soon married. Stalin was the best man.

Communist Party ascent

In March 1921, Molotov was elected to full membership in the Central Committee of the entire Communist Party, a membership he would retain until 1957. In 1921, he was briefly the secretary (head) of the Central Committee before being replaced by Stalin in 1922. Molotov, now Stalin's most trusted and faithful aide, remained second in command of the Central Committee. Upon Lenin's death in 1924, Stalin, with Molotov's help, continued to concentrate power in his hands, fighting off all opponents. Stalin arranged for Molotov to gain full membership in the Politburo on January 1, 1926, a membership he retained until 1952. The Central Committee was the administrative body of the Communist Party that ruled the Soviet Union. The secretary of the Central Committee was the top power in the party, therefore the top power in the country. The Politburo, known as the Presidium between 1953 and 1966, was contained in the Central Committee and directed party policy.

Stalin loyalist

Molotov and Stalin worked together constantly, as Stalin managed to take full control of the Soviet government by the late 1920s. Molotov took the lead in Stalin's plan of collectivization of agriculture, in which private ownership of land was abolished and all farmers on state farms were grouped together. It was Molotov who "dealt" with the wealthier peasants resisting collectivization, murdering many or sending them to labor camps in Siberia. Molotov also wholeheartedly went along with Stalin's political purges of the 1930s. Many of those purged were Stalin's and Molotov's old Bolshevik friends and colleagues. Without hesitation, Molotov signed their death warrants or approved their removal to the labor camp system. Even his own wife, who was a Jew, was sent to the labor camps without Molotov's protest. Molotov was able to work with Stalin without challenging his authority, so he was able to avoid being purged himself. On December 19, 1930, Stalin made Molotov chairman of the Council of Peoples' Commissars of the Soviet Union. This title was much like the prime minister or head of government in other countries. Of course, Stalin was the real head of power, but Molotov, in name, was head of the Soviet government.

World War II

In 1939, with Europe headed for war, while still chairman of the Council of Peoples' Commissars, Molotov also became Commissar of Foreign Affairs. Molotov opened talks with such Western powers as England and France but also began secret talks with Germany's Adolf Hitler (1889–1945) and his Nazi Party, known primarily for its brutal policies of racism. Dismayed at the rise of Nazi Germany, Stalin and Molotov secretly decided to try and deal with Hitler. Shocking the United States and Western Europe, on August 23, 1939, Molotov and Stalin concluded a treaty of nonaggression with German foreign minister Joachim von Ribbentrop (1893–1946). The Ribbentrop-Molotov Pact, also called the Soviet-German Nonaggression Treaty, divided Europe into Nazi and Soviet spheres. Despite the treaty, Hitler surprised Stalin by invading the Soviet Union on June 21, 1941.

Talks with Western countries took on a great deal of urgency. In May 1942, Molotov worked out a treaty with England for mutual economic and military aid. He proceeded on to the United States and worked out further military agree-

ments. To stop the advance of Hitler's Nazi army that was over-running Europe, the Soviets became uneasy allies of Britain and the United States. In October 1943 Molotov met with Allied leaders to plan a conference in November in Tehran, Iran. British prime minister **Winston Churchill** (1874–1965; see entry), U.S. president Franklin D. Roosevelt (1882–1945; served 1933–45), and Stalin, with Molotov by his side, attended. Churchill, Roosevelt, and Stalin were dubbed the "Big Three." Molotov would attend all postwar conferences.

The Big Three met again in February 1945 in Yalta in the Crimea region (a peninsula that juts out into the Black Sea) of the Soviet Union to decide defeated Germany's post-war fate. Always sullen and serious, Molotov was even less willing than Stalin to come to agreement with Churchill and Roosevelt. Eventually the latter two gave in to many of the Soviets' demands. Roosevelt, realizing the great devastation the Nazis had caused the Soviet Union, wanted to go along with the Soviets as much as possible. It was Molotov who was

Vyacheslav Molotov signs a document in 1939.
Reproduced by permission of Bildarchiv Preussischer Kulturbesitz.

The Molotov Cocktail

Soviet foreign minister Vyacheslav Molotov had the privilege of having a weapon named after him during World War II. As the Nazi Germany army was launching a massive offensive against the Soviet Union in 1941, the retreating Soviet Army was desperate to try to repel the attack any way they could. A key element of the German attack was large numbers of armored tanks. An effective, but simple, weapon against tanks was a crude bomb made of a bottle filled with a flammable fluid, usually gasoline, and fitted with a wick at the neck, often a rag soaked in gasoline. A Soviet soldier would ignite the wick and hurl it at a German tank, aiming for the engine compartment and trying to set the engine on fire, or aiming it at the space between the turret, or gun enclosure, and the main tank shell. The soldiers began calling these antitank weapons Molotov Cocktails after the foreign minister.

Though simple in construction, it took daring to use the Molotov Cocktails, as the thrower had to be within a throwing

A soldier prepares to throw a Molotov Cocktail, named after Vyacheslav Molotov. *Reproduced by permission of AP/Wide World Photos.*

distance of the often-advancing tank with enemy foot soldiers shortly behind. The association of his name with a crude but deadly weapon added to Molotov's communist hard-line public image through the Cold War.

largely responsible for beginning the division of Europe into the Eastern (Soviet) European sphere of influence and the Western (United States, Britain, and France) European sphere.

Cold War tensions

Roosevelt died suddenly on April 12, 1945, and Vice President **Harry S. Truman** (1884–1972; served 1945–53; see entry) took over the U.S. presidency. Within two weeks, Truman called Molotov to the White House and thoroughly berated him for the way the communists were taking over Eastern Europe. Molotov was enraged. Molotov and Stalin realized that the wartime Allied cooperation was at an end. The Cold War was at hand. At the next postwar conference in July 1945 in Potsdam, Germany, President Truman took Stalin and Molotov aside and told them the United States had a new powerful weapon. Truman did not think they realized he was speaking of an atomic weapon. However, the Soviets had had spies deep within the U.S. atomic weapon development program, the Manhattan Project, for some time and already knew of the successful U.S. detonation of the world's first atomic bomb. The Soviets were already pursuing their own atomic program, of which Molotov was initially in charge.

In February 1946, Stalin made a speech in Moscow that seemed to declare another war, this time on all capitalist countries. At the Council of Foreign Ministers Conference in Paris in April, Molotov inflamed Cold War tensions more by speaking as though all countries must come under communism sooner or later. It was in Paris that Molotov became known as Comrade Nyet (the Russian word for "no"). The Sovicts, defensive about their own weakened condition after the war, wanted desperately to build a buffer zone around the Soviet Union to protect it from future Western aggression. They refused to budge on their occupations of Eastern European countries that were forming the buffer zone. Molotov also stressed his country wanted to keep Germany in a weakened state and divided. But on this point the United States wanted to strengthen and reunite Germany to resist what it saw as a real possibility of Soviet expansion farther west. Because of these unbending opposite viewpoints, the Paris Peace Conference from the end of July into October 1946 was a failure.

Meanwhile, the United States detonated two atomic bombs in the Pacific to remind the Soviets of its nuclear monopoly. But the Soviet atomic project was progressing rapidly. By that time, Stalin had taken the busy Molotov off the atomic development project and replaced him with Lavrenty Beria (1899–1953), head of the KGB, the dreaded Soviet secret police. Also inside the Soviet Union, Stalin had resumed his purge of all individuals he deemed anti-Stalin in any way. The loyal Molotov, however, continued to hold Stalin's trust.

What to do with the divided Germany continued to be a point of debate between the Soviets and the United States,

Britain, and France. In March 1948, Molotov, still Soviet foreign minister, charged the Western powers with using the Germany issue to annoy Soviet leadership. With Molotov's approval in June 1948, the Soviets began a total land blockade of the Western sectors of the city of Berlin that had been divided after World War II among the Allies, just as the whole of Germany had been divided. Inflaming Cold War tension even more, the blockade lasted until May 1949. The Allies, through a massive airlift of goods, supplied the blockaded city.

Fall from power

About March 1949, Molotov seemed to have possibly landed at last on Stalin's purge list. Unexplainably, he disappeared from Soviet politics. Then sometime in midsummer, he was relieved of his foreign minister position. However, Molotov remained a member of the Politburo. Nevertheless, by late 1952, the ever more paranoid Stalin was clearly suspicious of Molotov, even thinking he may have been spying for the United States.

Only Stalin's death in March 1953 saved Molotov from being another purge victim. Even so, Molotov was the only Soviet official to show emotion at Stalin's funeral in 1953. Upon Stalin's death, Molotov was returned to his post as Soviet foreign minister, and he retained that position until June 1956, when disagreements grew with innovative **Nikita Khrushchev** (1894–1971; see entry), the Soviet Union's new leader. Molotov's hard-line stance against the United States and Western European nations did not correlate with Khrushchev's idea of peaceful coexistence. Molotov also denounced Khrushchev's speeches against Stalin. Molotov firmly held to the correctness of Stalin's policies.

In early 1957, Molotov joined with the so-called Anti-Party group of party conservatives to remove Khrushchev from power at a Presidium (formerly the Politburo) meeting in June. The attempt failed. Molotov refused to admit he had been wrong. Molotov was stripped of all his posts and practically exiled when sent to Mongolia as ambassador between 1957 and 1960.

Between 1960 and 1962, Molotov managed to head the Soviet delegation to the International Atomic Energy

Agency in Vienna, Austria. His consistent criticism of Khrushchev, however, cost him that post. He began a long retirement in 1962. During Khrushchev's last months as secretary general in 1964, he had Molotov expelled from the Communist Party. Molotov continued to live in Moscow in obscurity with his wife, who had returned from the labor camps. In 1984, he was readmitted to the party due to the influence of **Andrey Gromyko** (1909–1989; see entry), Soviet foreign minister from 1957 to 1985. Gromyko had once worked under Molotov. Molotov wrote his memoirs, but they remained unpublished at his death in 1986.

For More Information

Books

Bromage, Bernard. *Molotov: The Story of an Era.* London: Peter Owen, Ltd., 1956.

Chuev, Feliks. *Molotov Remembers: Inside Kremlin Politics.* Chicago: I. R. Dee, 1993.

Conquest, Robert. *The Great Terror: Stalin's Purge of the Thirties.* New York: Macmillan, 1968.

Diljus, Milovan. *Conversations with Stalin.* New York: Harcourt, Brace & World, 1962.

Isaacs, Jeremy, and Taylor Downing. *Cold War: An Illustrated History, 1945–1991.* Boston: Little, Brown, 1998.

Kennedy-Pipe, Caroline. *Stalin's Cold War: Soviet Strategies in Europe, 1943 to 1956.* Manchester, Eng.: Manchester University Press, 1995.

Resis, Albert. *Stalin, the Politburo, and the Onset of the Cold War, 1945–1946.* Pittsburgh: University of Pittsburgh Center for Russian and East European Studies, 1988.

Taubman, William. *Stalin's American Policy: From Entente to Detente to Cold War.* New York: Columbia University Press, 1982.

Zubok, Vladislav M., and Constantine Pleshakov. *Inside the Kremlin's Cold War: From Stalin to Khrushchev.* Cambridge, MA: Harvard University Press, 1996.

Richard M. Nixon

Born January 9, 1913
Yorba Linda, California
Died April 22, 1994
New York, New York

U.S. president, vice president,
senator, and congressman

"The Cold War isn't thawing; it is burning with a deadly heat. Communism isn't sleeping; it is, as always, plotting, scheming, working, fighting."

Richard Nixon was the thirty-seventh president of the United States. He also served as vice president for both terms of U.S. president **Dwight D. Eisenhower** (1890–1969; served 1953–61; see entry) through the 1950s and before that was a member of the U.S. Congress from 1947 to 1953. As a result, his public career spanned over half of the forty-six years of the Cold War (1945–91). Politically benefiting from a strong public anticommunist position in the 1940s and 1950s, Nixon would open the door to formal relations with communist China and pursue détente, or the easing of tensions, with the Soviet Union in the early 1970s. He would also become the first U.S. president to resign from office after facing almost certain impeachment over a domestic scandal.

From debate team to the navy

Richard Milhous Nixon was born on January 9, 1913, in Yorba Linda, California, near Los Angeles. He was the second of five sons. His father, Frank, ran a service station and grocery store in nearby Whittier. His mother, Hannah Mil-

Richard M. Nixon. *Courtesy of the Library of Congress.*

hous, was from a Quaker background. Nixon's father was combative and volatile, but his mother was much more restrained. Nixon would show traits of both in his later life, though his mother was his main lasting influence.

Nixon was also a hard worker, which led him to be an excellent student. At Whittier High School, Nixon was particularly good in debate, wining many debate contests. Graduating as an honors student, Nixon received a scholarship to Harvard University, but his family could not afford to send him there. He attended Whittier College instead. Graduating second in his class at Whittier, Nixon earned a scholarship to Duke University Law School in Durham, North Carolina, in 1934. He graduated third in his class in 1937. Moving back home to Whittier, Nixon practiced law from 1937 to 1942. As a young successful lawyer, he met Thelma "Pat" Ryan, a schoolteacher, in 1937, while they both were participating in an amateur play. They would marry in 1940 and have two daughters.

With the entrance of the United States in World War II (1939–45) in December 1941, Nixon moved his family to Washington, D.C., where he worked for several months in the Office of Price Administration. Unhappy with the administrative process, he joined the Navy in August 1942 and served in the South Pacific from 1942 to 1946. He attained the rank of lieutenant commander.

Young politician in Congress

Upon returning to California after the war, Nixon entered politics at the encouragement of a group of influential Whittier businessmen. In 1946, he surprisingly defeated popular five-term Democrat Jerry Voorhis (1901–1984) for a seat in the U.S. Congress. During the campaign, Nixon suggested that his opponent had communist leanings. He would use this strategy again in 1950, when he defeated another popular Democrat, Helen Gahagan Douglas (1900–1980), for a U.S. Senate seat. Nixon found he could use Cold War issues to his benefit and gained both a reputation for his campaign methods and the nickname "Tricky Dick."

While in Congress, Nixon continued to pursue anticommunist issues to gain notoriety. He introduced a bill in

1948 that would require individual Communist Party members and organizations with connections to the Communist Party to register with the government. The Senate killed the bill. He also served from 1948 to 1950 on the House Un-American Activities Committee (HUAC), a congressional group established to investigate and root out any communist influences within the United States. He gained much public attention in his pursuit of former State Department employee Alger Hiss (1904–1996), who had also been a foreign policy advisor to President Franklin D. Roosevelt (1882–1945; served 1933–45). Nixon charged that Hiss was a spy for the Soviet Union in the late 1930s. Though Hiss forever denied the charges and no hard evidence was found, Nixon did obtain an indictment for perjury that led to a later conviction.

Vice president

In 1952, World War II hero Dwight D. Eisenhower won the Republican presidential nomination. He selected Nixon as his running mate. Eisenhower believed Nixon would satisfy the more conservative elements of the Republican Party plus attract votes from the western United States. While Eisenhower took a more positive approach to the campaign, Nixon tended to raise more personal issues concerning the Democrats and their candidates. He even delved into personal issues about himself and his family to help his campaign. During the campaign, for example, Nixon was accused of accepting money from wealthy businessmen for his personal use. To save his place on the Republican ticket, Nixon provided a detailed explanation to a national television audience in what became known as the "Checkers Speech," for his reference to the family dog named Checkers. The speech worked: the public came to strongly support him. He remained Eisenhower's running mate and the two won the election handily.

Nixon was Eisenhower's vice president for eight years. During that time, he was never fully accepted into the administration's inner circle of advisors. However, he did campaign vigorously for Republican candidates, and many believe he redefined the vice president's position into a more active role. Known more for his hard-hitting campaign tactics, Nixon did

make gains in working educational reform and a civil rights bill through Congress.

Through his years as vice president, Nixon also began redefining his personal political position to more of a moderate in politics to attract broader support for a possible presidential nomination in 1960. Through a series of illnesses suffered by Eisenhower from 1955 to 1957, Nixon gained much experience and public visibility while presiding over numerous Cabinet (a president's closest set of advisors) and National Security Council meetings in Eisenhower's temporary absences. He also made several foreign trips. One trip to Moscow led to a famous impromptu confrontation with Soviet leader **Nikita Khrushchev** (1894–1971; see entry) at an international trade fair. Known as the "kitchen debate," because the dialogue took place in front of an exhibit that highlighted an American kitchen, they had a spirited discussion of the merits of communism and capitalism. This episode further increased Nixon's popularity in the United States.

U.S. vice president Richard Nixon makes a dramatic point with Soviet premier Nikita Khrushchev in 1959. *Reproduced by permission of the Corbis Corporation.*

A successful return to politics

Nixon won the Republican nomination for president in 1960 but lost a very close race to his Democratic opponent, U.S. senator **John F. Kennedy** (1919–1963; served 1961–63; see entry) of Massachusetts. A major factor in the race was a series of four televised debates between the two candidates. Though Nixon appeared to do well on the debate issues, Kennedy portrayed an image of youthful energy and poise. Many, including Eisenhower, urged Nixon to challenge the election results, but he chose not to and gained much public respect for not doing so.

Returning to private life, Nixon wrote a best-selling book, *Six Crises,* in 1961 (published a year later). In 1962, he reluctantly agreed to run for governor of California and lost his second straight election. Discouraged with politics, Nixon moved to New York to join a prestigious law firm. For the next five years, Nixon worked to build a strong political base for future campaigns. Following the Republicans' landslide loss in the 1964 presidential election behind U.S. senator Barry Goldwater (1909–1998) of Arizona, interest in Nixon rose again as a party moderate. Politics even entered other parts of Nixon's family life as his daughter Julie married Eisenhower's grandson, David Eisenhower, in 1967. Nixon gained the Republican nomination once again in 1968, reflecting a remarkable political comeback.

This time, the Democrats were greatly divided over the Vietnam War (1954–75). President **Lyndon B. Johnson** (1908–1973; served 1963–69; see entry), beleaguered by antiwar protests, had announced he would not seek reelection. The leading Democratic candidate, U.S. senator Robert F. Kennedy (1925–1968) of New York, was assassinated while campaigning in Los Angeles. Nixon ended up winning in another very close race over Democrat Hubert Humphrey (1911–1978), who had served as vice president in Johnson's administration.

White House years

As president, Nixon proved to be aggressive on both domestic and foreign issues. He introduced environmental legislation as well as welfare and health care reform. He also addressed civil rights needs by introducing the nation's first affirmative action programs to require government contractors to hire minorities. It was the most active domestic legislative agenda since Roosevelt's of the 1930s.

Nixon's Cold War accomplishments included obtaining a cease-fire in the Vietnam War, normalizing relations with communist China, and easing tensions between the United States and the Soviet Union, including the signing of arms control treaties. To assist in foreign matters, Nixon appointed Harvard professor **Henry Kissinger** (1926–; see entry) first as national security advisor and later as secretary of state.

During his 1968 presidential campaign, Nixon claimed to be the "peace candidate." He promised to bring an honorable end to U.S. involvement in the Vietnam War. He did begin withdrawing ground troops from the region, but in turn escalated bombing campaigns. He adopted the policy that South Vietnam would assume greater responsibility for the ground war with support from the United States in the form of supplies and air support. The policy was called Vietnamization of the war. Meanwhile, negotiations with North Vietnam proved very slow. At first, Kissinger conducted them in secret, but in 1972 they became more public. Nixon expanded the ground war into the neighboring countries of Laos and Cambodia with U.S. and South Vietnamese troops to destroy enemy staging areas.

During the three years of negotiation under Kissinger, over twenty thousand more U.S. soldiers died. Throughout his time in office Nixon, like President Johnson before him, was the target of major antiwar protests. Nixon countered that he was supported by what he called the "silent majority," which Nixon believed were most Americans who simply were not politically vocal. On May 4, 1970, Ohio National Guard troops fired on a crowd of two thousand war protesters on the campus of Kent State University, killing four and wounding nine. The incident became a further rallying point for protesters. With negotiations continuing to falter, Nixon ordered intense bombing of North Vietnam cities in late December 1972, known as the "Christmas bombings." Finally, a cease-fire agreement was reached in January 1973.

The agreement succeeded in getting the United States out of Vietnam, but it did not save South Vietnam. In April 1975, the last few Americans were evacuated from the U.S.

embassy, as South Vietnam fell to the North. The collapse of South Vietnam led to the fall of noncommunist governments in Laos and Cambodia, and massive numbers of deaths.

Improving relations with China and the Soviet Union

The United States had refused to recognize the Chinese government, known as the People's Republic of China (PRC), since it was established in October 1949. This had occurred for two reasons: An influential group of Chinese Americans known as the China Lobby and other Americans who were pro-Chinese had strongly lobbied to recognize only the Taiwanese government of the Republic of China (ROC) and keep the PRC out of the United Nations (UN); also, there was a strong anticommunist mood in the United States as well as a fear that a unified global communist movement led by China and the Soviets was underway.

Upon taking office, Nixon sought to establish discussions with the PRC through low-level contacts. After Nixon lifted travel and trade restrictions on the PRC in 1971, China officials responded that they were interested in increased talks. Nixon sent Kissinger to the PRC that year to lay plans for Nixon to visit. Nixon journeyed to China the following year for ten days in February 1972. Since the communist takeover, he was the first U.S. president to visit China while in office. The talks progressed well, resulting in the Shanghai Communiqué, a statement in which Nixon accepted only one China. Nixon agreed that the Taiwanese government of the Republic of China (ROC) was part of the PRC, not a separate nation. Later in 1979 (after Nixon's presidency), the United States would establish formal relations with the PRC.

Nixon next also sought improved relations with the Soviets. Fearing the new U.S. relations with the PRC and struggling with their own growing economic problems, the Soviets were ready to talk as well. In May 1972, Nixon traveled to Moscow to meet with Soviet leader **Leonid Brezhnev** (1906–1982; see entry). There, they signed two arms control treaties, including the Strategic Arms Limitation Treaty (SALT I), and several other agreements focusing on such topics as cultural exchanges, space exploration, and health research. The treaties strictly limited de-

fensive antiballistic missile systems (ABMs) and froze offensive intercontinental ballistic missiles (ICBMs) at certain levels. Later in 1972, Nixon established a trade agreement providing the Soviets with grain and some new Western technologies. This period of détente, or the easing of tensions, however, would be short-lived and end not long after Nixon left office.

In Latin America, Nixon continued past U.S. policies of seeking to overthrow governments suspected of being pro-

U.S. president Richard Nixon is surrounded by American and Chinese officials as he walks along the Great Wall of China in February 1972. *Courtesy of the National Archives and Records Administration.*

U.S. president Richard Nixon (left) exchanges signed copies of the Strategic Arms Limitation Treaty with Soviet leader Leonid Brezhnev in May 1972. *Reproduced by permission of the Corbis Corporation.*

communist. After President **Salvador Allende** (1908–1973; see entry) nationalized, or took control and ownership of, U.S. mining interests in Chile as part of economic reform measures, Nixon imposed economic restrictions on Chile from 1971 to 1973. These included restrictions on foreign financial assistance and private investments from the United States. In addition, millions of dollars were secretly given to opposition groups in Chile, leading to Allende's eventual overthrow and death in September 1973. Chilean army commander-in-chief Augusto Pinochet (1915–1999) took over leadership of the country.

A controversial second term

In 1972, Nixon ran for reelection. He won in one of the largest landslides in U.S. history over the still badly divided Democrats and their candidate, U.S. senator George Mc-Govern (1922–) of South Dakota. After securing the Vietnam cease-fire agreement in January 1973, Nixon's main foreign policy involvement following reelection was an attempt to settle the Middle East dispute between the Arab nations and Israel. The October War of 1973 proved a major hurdle, as Israel, with limited support from the United States, badly defeated Arab forces. Following the brief war, in what became known as "shuttle diplomacy," Kissinger journeyed back and forth between the two sides, trying to create a breakthrough in resolving longstanding problems. However, in retaliation for U.S. support of Israel during the war, the oil-producing Arab nations through the Organization of Petroleum Exporting Countries (OPEC) limited oil exports to the United States. The fuel shortages led to higher gas prices and long lines at U.S. service stations as well as much less support for U.S. negotiation with the Arab nations.

Much of Nixon's second term of office was consumed with a scandal that eventually led to his resignation. What became known as Watergate involved employees of the Republican Party's Committee to Re-elect the President. They were caught burglarizing and wiretapping the national headquarters of the Democratic National Committee in June 1972 at the Watergate hotel and office complex in Washington, D.C. The burglars included former CIA and FBI agents hired by the Republicans with party campaign funds to conduct political espionage. Many Republican Party officials—as well as some of Nixon's closest advisors—received criminal convictions.

Eventually, astonishing connections to the White House were uncovered, including attempts at a cover-up and bribery of indicted defendants. Much evidence came from recorded White House conversations: it was revealed, for instance, that Nixon participated in the cover-up by directing the CIA to interfere with the FBI investigation and by giving "silence" money to the defendants. Spectacular televised Senate hearings extended into the summer of 1974. During Nixon's last eighteen months in office, he was consumed by the Watergate scandal, leaving Kissinger to run foreign affairs.

Facing certain impeachment by the House and conviction by the Senate, Nixon announced his resignation from the presidency on national television the evening of August 8, 1974. As Nixon and his family departed the White House grounds by helicopter the following day, millions watched on

The Final Comeback

Richard Nixon resigned as U.S. president on August 8, 1974, and left the following day in disgrace. Many would have disappeared from public view the remainder of their lives after what he experienced. His actions relating to the Watergate burglary had been subjected to lengthy public hearings televised to the nation. Evidence mounted concerning his alleged cover-up of domestic political espionage activities. However, Nixon had been a fighter all his life, and he did not simply fade away once having left office.

Instead, in an effort to set his place in history, he wrote a series of books, including his memoirs, *The Memoirs of Richard Nixon* (1978). These books set his place in history, and he regained recognition as an expert in foreign relations by 1985. Several of the books were best-sellers. Nixon would serve as advisor at times to presidents **Ronald Reagan** (1911–; served 1981–89; see entry), **George Bush** (1924–; served 1989–93; see entry), and Bill Clinton (1946–; served 1993–2001).

Richard Nixon wrote the following books after 1978:

Leaders. New York: Warner Books, 1982.

Real Peace. Boston: Little, Brown, 1984.

No More Vietnams. New York: Arbor House, 1985.

1999: Victory without War. New York: Simon and Schuster, 1988.

In the Arena: A Memoir of Victory, Defeat, and Renewal. New York: Simon and Schuster, 1990.

Beyond Peace. New York: Random House, 1994.

television. One month later, on September 8, his successor in the White House, Gerald R. Ford (1913–; served 1974–77), pardoned Nixon of all charges.

Life after resignation

Nixon led an active private life after leaving office, despite the controversies leading to his downfall. Nixon retired first to his secluded estate in San Clemente, California, for six years and then moved to New York City, then New Jersey. Through a series of widely read books he authored, Nixon salvaged his career and enjoyed the status of an elder statesman in his last years. He remained active in various issues. For example, after the collapse of the Soviet Union in 1991, Nixon campaigned for political support and economic aid for Russia and the other former Soviet republics. In 1994, Nixon announced the creation of the Nixon Center for Peace and Freedom, which focused on foreign policy issues. Later that year, he died of a massive stroke. He was buried next to his wife, who had died in 1993, on the grounds of the Nixon presidential library in Yorba Linda.

For More Information

Books

Aitken, Jonathan. *Nixon: A Life.* London: Weidenfeld and Nicolson, 1993.

Ambrose, Stephen E. *Nixon.* 3 vols. New York: Simon and Schuster, 1987–91.

Emery, Fred. *Watergate: The Corruption of American Politics and the Fall of Richard Nixon.* New York: Times Books, 1994.

Hoff, Joan. *Nixon Reconsidered.* New York: Basic Books, 1994.

Morris, Roger. *Richard Milhous Nixon: The Rise of an American Politician.* New York: Henry Holt, 1990.

Nixon, Richard M. *The Memoirs of Richard Nixon.* New York: Grosset and Dunlap, 1978.

Nixon, Richard M. *Six Crises.* Garden City, NY: Doubleday, 1962. Reprint, New York: Simon & Schuster, 1990.

Reeves, Richard. *President Nixon: Alone in the White House.* New York: Simon and Schuster, 2001.

Thornton, Richard C. *The Nixon-Kissinger Years: Reshaping America's Foreign Policy.* New York: Paragon House, 1989.

Web Site

The Richard Nixon Library and Birthplace. http://www.nixonfoundation. org (accessed on September 12, 2003).

J. Robert Oppenheimer

Born August 22, 1904
New York, New York
Died February 18, 1967
Princeton, New Jersey

Physicist and developer of the
U.S. atomic bomb

"We knew the world could not be the same. A few people laughed, a few people cried. Most people were silent. I remembered the line from the Hindu scripture, the Bhagavad Gita: 'I am become Death, the destroyer of worlds.' I suppose we all thought that, one way or another."

J. Robert Oppenheimer.
Reproduced by permission of Getty Images.

At 5:30 A.M. on July 16, 1945, the United States successfully detonated the world's first atomic bomb. The scientist in charge of the U.S. project to develop the bomb was J. Robert Oppenheimer. A brilliant physicist, Oppenheimer watched in amazement as the New Mexico sky and landscape lit up brighter than a hundred sunrises. That moment marked the dawning of the nuclear age. Nuclear weapons developed and manufactured for decades thereafter influenced Cold War (1945–91) politics more than any other single issue after 1945. Oppenheimer's part in the Cold War would be a push for arms control and turning nuclear power into a benefit for mankind.

The Cold War was a prolonged conflict for world dominance between the two superpowers, the democratic, capitalist United States and the communist Soviet Union. Communism was a political and economic system, in which the Communist Party controlled all aspects of citizens' lives, as well as all economic policies. Private ownership of property was banned. Communism was not compatible with America's democratic way of life. The Cold War was a war of mutual fear and distrust. The scorecard was kept by the number of nuclear weapons each superpower possessed and had pointed at the other.

Young Oppenheimer

On August 22, 1904, J. Robert Oppenheimer was born to Julius and Ella Oppenheimer at their home on West Ninety-fourth Street in New York City. Many surmised the "J" in Oppenheimer's name stood for Julius, but apparently it was simply a "J," tying him to his father without making him a "junior." A partner in a fabric importing business, Oppenheimer's father immigrated to America from Germany in 1888 at the age of seventeen. He reportedly thrived on intellectual challenges concerning many topics, such as philosophy, religious freedom, and the art world. Oppenheimer's mother, an artist with German heritage from Baltimore, Maryland, gave her son her enthusiasm and her time—reading with him and listening to his thoughts.

Just before Oppenheimer's brother Frank was born in 1912, the family moved to a spacious upscale apartment overlooking the city and the Hudson River. The family lived comfortably, had a summer house on Long Island, took trips to Europe, and sent the boys to the private Ethical Culture School through high school. The Oppenheimers were of Jewish descent but were not members of a temple. Instead, they belonged to the Society for Ethical Culture, which was based on ethics, not religion, and undertook social reform campaigns.

As a child, Oppenheimer received from his grandfather in Germany a small mineral collection. Young Robert was fascinated with the rocks, their crystalline structure, and avidly added to the collection throughout his teen years. He became the youngest member ever of the New York Mineralogical Club, where he delivered a paper at the age of twelve. Oppenheimer, shy and awkward among his peers, was clearly brilliant in the classroom. Before long, his parents suspected he was a genius. He could easily identify obscure pieces of classical music, had a keen interest in scientific subjects, and could learn foreign languages with ease. Both parents created a home environment where the young Oppenheimer's independence and intellectual talent was nurtured.

Two teachers at his Ethical Culture High School had a lifelong influence on Oppenheimer. The first was Herbert

Smith, who had just completed a master's degree in English at Harvard when he came to the school. Oppenheimer was in Smith's homeroom all four years, and they developed a lasting friendship. The second was Augustus Klock, a highly skilled physics and chemistry teacher. In the book *Robert Oppenheimer, Letters and Reflections,* Oppenheimer explained that he first took physics and the next year chemistry from Klock, and he felt "a great sense of indebtedness to him ... he was a remarkably good teacher." Francis Ferguson, a student from New Mexico, entered Smith's homeroom his senior year and also became another lifelong friend of Oppenheimer's.

Graduating from Ethical Culture in 1921, both Oppenheimer and Ferguson expected to attend Harvard University that fall. However, Oppenheimer, on a family trip to Europe, became very ill and had to spend the 1921–22 school year recuperating. Doctors advised that Oppenheimer be removed from the cold, damp winter in New York. His parents asked Smith to accompany Oppenheimer on a trip to New Mexico—to the Page Dude ranch near Cowles, and to visit with Ferguson and his family in Albuquerque.

The New Mexico high country of western mountains and plateaus enthralled Oppenheimer. He became an expert horseman, exploring the Sangre de Cristo Mountains region northeast of Santa Fe. During these explorations, Oppenheimer first came upon the Pajarito Plateau and the boys school, Los Alamos Ranch School. Twenty years later, this would be the site recommended by Oppenheimer for the laboratory of the Manhattan Project, the U.S. wartime project to build an atomic bomb.

Harvard, September 1922 to June 1925

In September 1922, Oppenheimer entered Harvard, where he thrived. Years later, he looked back to say how exciting his Harvard years were, how much he loved the unlimited opportunity to learn. Having taken advanced studies at Ethical Culture High School, he entered Harvard as a sophomore. During his second year, he took seven required classes, several electives, and still found spare time to read classics and literature from around the world. He also developed a sense of humor and a bit of a social life. He majored in chemistry, but his passion soon became physics, figuring out concepts and equations before professors finished presenting problems. Oppenheimer graduated summa cum laude (with highest honors) in June 1925 at the age of twenty-one.

Cambridge and Göttingen

In September 1925, Oppenheimer entered Cambridge University to study at the prominent Cavendish Laboratory, where many of the world's most forward-thinking physicists researched. There, Oppenheimer was immersed in the "new" physics—the theory of relativity from Albert Einstein (1879–1955) and the quantum theory, to which Oppenheimer would make significant contributions. In September 1927, Oppenheimer continued his graduate study in Germany at the University of Göttingen. On May 11, 1927, Oppenheimer took and passed all his oral exams for his doctorate degree. Oppenheimer had completed his Ph.D. only two years after leaving Harvard.

Oppenheimer returned to the United States near the end of the summer of 1927. Due to his outstanding reputation in Europe, he was soon offered teaching positions at about ten of America's finest universities. He spent part of the 1927–28 school year at Harvard and part at the California Institute of Technology, known as Cal Tech, in Pasadena. Then, in the fall of 1928, he returned for one more time to study and work with physicists in Europe, first at the University of Leiden in the Netherlands, then in Zurich, Switzerland. Between 1926 and 1929, Oppenheimer authored sixteen papers on quantum theory.

Research, teaching, and marriage

From fall 1929 to 1942, Oppenheimer's days were spent teaching and researching at both the University of California at Berkeley and Cal Tech in Pasadena. For Oppenheimer, the social upheavals of the 1930s—involving the stock market crash and the Great Depression (1929–41), the worst financial crisis in American history—had little meaning. He remained immersed in his research and teaching, conveying to his students the new physics and the beauty of its patterns. However, a sad time for Oppenheimer came in 1931, when his mother died, then his father in 1937.

By 1937, Oppenheimer finally awakened to the social hardships and unrest caused by the economic woes of the Depression. Some of his students had no money to continue in school. Others could find no work upon graduation. Oppenheimer became interested in communism, as did many American intellectuals of the time. To many young intellectuals, it seemed to be a perfectly logical way to organize society and solve social problems. However, Oppenheimer had nagging suspicions that were confirmed in 1938, when he met three physicists who had just returned from Russia. They all reported a suffering society that endured murder and terror at the hands of Soviet dictator **Joseph Stalin** (1879–1953; see entry). As a result, Oppenheimer completely turned his back on communist thought.

In 1938, word came that German scientists had successfully carried out nuclear fission, the splitting of an atom. Oppenheimer's mind began to race even faster than usual. The lab at Berkeley, where Oppenheimer headed up the staff, was known as the University of California Radiation Laboratory. Immediately, tests were set up to check the validity of the German experiments. Fears abounded that Germany would use the knowledge to build an atomic bomb, enabling them to hold the rest of the world hostage under threat of its use.

Meanwhile, Oppenheimer's brother Frank had married in 1937 and was scheduled to receive his doctorate in physics in the summer of 1939 at Cal Tech. Oppenheimer went to Pasadena for the occasion. There, he met Katherine (Kitty) Puening Harrison. The two were married in late 1940 and had their first child, Peter, on May 12, 1941. In August 1941, the Oppenheimers bought a home in Berkeley and settled there. They would have a daughter, Katherine (called Toni), in 1944 and would be married for twenty-seven years until Oppenheimer's death.

The Manhattan Project

On December 7, 1941, the Japanese bombed Pearl Harbor in Hawaii, and the United States entered World War II

(1939–45). Earlier in 1941, the National Academy of Sciences had proposed an all-out effort to build an atomic bomb before the Germans did. No one realized that the Germans, wrapped up in the war in Europe, had halted all work toward the bomb. U.S. efforts centered at the University of Chicago's Metallurgical Laboratory with Enrico Fermi (1901–1954) as principal investigator; at the University of California at Berkeley's Radiation Laboratory, where Oppenheimer researched; and at Columbia University's physics department. Fermi, a Nobel Prize–winning Italian physicist, had fled his native country a few years earlier.

Beginning in 1942, General Leslie R. Groves (1896–1970), who was in charge of carrying out the atomic bomb project, established two large engineering production centers at remote sites for manufacture of material needed to make atomic bombs: the Clinton Engineer Works in Oak Ridge, Tennessee (site Z), and the Hanford Engineer Works in eastern Washington State (site W), near the town of Richland. By mid-1942, research on the bomb project occurred at several universities across the country. Oppenheimer realized that one central site was needed to bring scientists together to design a bomb using material being manufactured at Oak Ridge and Hanford. Oppenheimer suggested to Groves that a site might be located in a remote area of New Mexico. They chose a site 100 miles (160 kilometers) north of Albuquerque that was once the Los Alamos Ranch School that Oppenheimer had visited on horseback as a teenager.

In November 1942, Groves selected Oppenheimer to be scientific director of the Manhattan Project at the new Los Alamos laboratory. Oppenheimer would lead his team of physicists to success in only two-and-a-half years. On Monday, July 16, 1945, the world's first atomic bomb was successfully detonated. The test's code name was Trinity (see box). One atomic bomb was dropped on Hiroshima, Japan, on August 6, and another on Nagasaki, Japan, on August 9. The Japanese surrendered, and World War II came to an end.

Oppenheimer became known as the "father of the atom bomb." It was a title he continually tried to correct by saying he was not the "father" but the director of the laboratory where the bomb was developed. In the book *The Story of J. Robert Oppenheimer,* Denise Royal reported that Oppenheimer had some misgivings about the accomplishment, stating, "I'm a little scared of what we built ... [but] a scientist

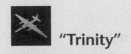

"Trinity"

The location of the actual test site of the United States' first atomic bomb detonation was near the northwest corner of the Alamogordo Air Base in New Mexico. J. Robert Oppenheimer, scientific head of the bomb project, gave the code name "Trinity" to the test. The name came from one of his favorite poems by John Donne (1572–1631).

On Saturday, July 14, 1945, the "gadget," as the bomb was called, was placed at the top of a 100-foot (30.5-meter) steel tower, where it would be detonated. The test was set for 4:00 A.M. Monday morning, July 16. Thunder rumbled, and rain poured down Sunday night and in the early hours of Monday morning. Oppenheimer and General Leslie R. Groves, military head of the project, popped out of their dugout every few minutes to check the weather. The tension during those early hours was high. The weather finally began clearing by 4:00 A.M., and Trinity was a go for 5:30 A.M.

The moment before detonation, no one breathed. As noted on the Los Alamos National Laboratory Web site, Groves remembered he could only think what he would do if the count went to zero and nothing hap-

pened. But at exactly 5:29:45 A.M., the gadget exploded. The tension in Oppenheimer's face relaxed immediately. General Thomas Farrell, deputy to Groves, later wrote that the force of the gadget, equivalent to 21,000 tons (19,000 metric tons) of TNT, lit up the country "with the intensity many times that of midday sun.... It lighted every peak, crevasse, and ridge of the nearby mountain range with a clarity and beauty that cannot be described but must be imagined. Seconds after the explosion came first the air blast pressing hard against the people, to be followed almost immediately by the strong, sustained awesome roar that warned of doomsday and made us feel we puny things were blasphemous to dare tamper with the forces heretofore reserved for the Almighty." Oppenheimer quoted a line from the Bhagavad Gita, an ancient Hindu sacred text: "I am become Death, the destroyer of worlds."

World War II would be over in a few weeks. On August 6, 1945, the first atomic bomb, named "Little Boy," was dropped on Hiroshima, Japan. On August 9, 1945, the second atomic bomb, "Fat Man," was dropped on Nagasaki. Japan surrendered unconditionally on August 14, 1945.

cannot hold back progress because he fears what the world will do with his discoveries."

A national figure

Oppenheimer resigned as director of the Los Alamos Laboratory in October 1945 and returned to university life at

Cal Tech. A year later he resumed teaching at Berkeley. Oppenheimer soon realized he had become a national figure, and a quiet life of university teaching would not be possible. On January 12, 1946, President **Harry S. Truman** (1884–1972; served 1945–53; see entry) awarded Oppenheimer the "United States of America Medal of Merit" for his leadership on the Manhattan Project. Oppenheimer graciously accepted, but he had by that time devoted himself to seeing that atomic energy became an instrument of peace, for mankind's benefit. Correctly predicting that international control of the new atomic weapons technology would prove difficult, he dedicated the rest of his life to that goal.

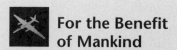

For the Benefit of Mankind

Igor Kurchatov (1903–1960; see entry) successfully directed the Soviet atomic bomb project, holding the same position in the Soviet project as Oppenheimer had in the Manhattan Project. However, following detonation of the Soviet atomic bomb, Kurchatov, just like Oppenheimer, devoted the rest of his life to stressing the peaceful uses of the atom for the benefit of human society.

In 1946, Oppenheimer played an active role developing the U.S. congressional report, the Acheson-Lilienthal Report, calling for an international authority to control all atomic energy research. Bernard Baruch (1870–1965), the U.S. representative to the United Nations (UN), delivered the report to the UN. The Soviets completely rejected the suggestions in the report because they were deeply involved in the development of their own atomic bomb. They feared that the United States would use its monopoly in atomic weapons to attempt to gain influence over the Soviet Union and the communist countries of Eastern Europe under Soviet control. The Soviets were not about to turn over their atomic research to international control before they caught up with the United States.

On August 29, 1949, the Soviets succeeded in detonating an atomic bomb. Atomic weapons became a focal point of the Cold War. The United States and the Soviet Union would continuously attempt to one-up the other in nuclear weaponry.

The H-bomb debate

Becoming a familiar person in Washington, D.C., from 1947 to 1953 Oppenheimer served on many govern-

J. Robert Oppenheimer (far left) points to a picture of the atomic bomb blast in Hiroshima, Japan. American Chemical Society official H. D. Smythe, Manhattan Project engineer K. D. Nichols, and chemist Glenn Seaborg look on. *Reproduced by permission of the Corbis Corporation.*

ment committees, traveling to meeting after meeting. Most importantly, he began a six-year term on the General Advisory Committee (GAC) within the U.S. Atomic Energy Commission (AEC). AEC was the governmental agency in charge of the nation's nuclear program (the terms atomic and nuclear were used interchangeably, but nuclear soon became the more updated term). GAC was composed of prestigious scientists who had been with Oppenheimer at the Manhattan Project. Those scientists included Fermi, James B. Conant (1893–1978), and I. I. Rabi (1898–1998).

From the time Moscow tested its first atomic bomb in 1949, the national debate over arms control turned almost exclusively to whether or not to develop the thermonuclear or hydrogen bomb (H-bomb). The H-bomb was many times more powerful than the atomic bombs dropped on Japan. Its development had been considered at the start of the Manhattan Project, but too many technical problems pushed it to the background. The H-bomb was the special interest of physicist Edward Teller (1908–2003).

The highly influential GAC was asked to report on H-bomb debate. The report was delivered on October 30, 1949. Oppenheimer at that time was chairman of the GAC. Recognizing there was no nuclear arms control treaty on the horizon between the United States and the Soviet Union, the GAC called for intensified efforts to develop nuclear weapons for defensive purposes. They also recommended conducting further research in the thermonuclear process that involved nuclear fusion (combining nuclei of atoms), as opposed to nuclear fission (splitting nuclei) that had been used in the already developed atomic weapons. However, most importantly, the report opposed using the fusion process to develop a very powerful and destructive bomb. The GAC objected on moral grounds that its only use would be to exterminate civilians. Oppenheimer's stand against the H-bomb would not be forgotten.

Three of the five AEC commissioners agreed with the GAC report. Nevertheless, President Truman authorized development of the H-bomb in January 1950. Teller became the lead scientist. Technical problems were overcome, and the United States successfully tested its first H-bomb on November 1, 1952. A year later, not to be left behind, the Soviets tested an H-bomb on August 12, 1953. **Andrey Sakharov** (1921–1989; see entry) was the chief developer of the Soviet H-bomb.

Oppenheimer caught in Red Scare

Oppenheimer had moved, in 1947, from California to Princeton, New Jersey, and become director of the Institute for Advanced Study. During Oppenheimer's service on the GAC and at the Institute, a communist scare, called the "Red Scare," was sweeping America. Influenced greatly by U.S. senator **Joseph R. McCarthy** (1908–1957; see entry) of Wisconsin, the government and American public began to see "red" every-where. ("Red" was another word for communist.) Hundreds of innocent Americans were accused of being involved in communist plots to overthrow the U.S. democratic way of life.

Suddenly in early 1953, Lewis Strauss (1896–1974), chairman of the AEC, ordered the removal of classified documents from Oppenheimer's safe. Apparently, Strauss had been greatly angered by Oppenheimer's opposition to development of the H-bomb. Nothing more came of it until November, when **J. Edgar Hoover** (1895–1972; see entry), director of the Federal Bureau of Investigation (FBI), received a letter from William L. Borden, who had been secretary of the Joint Congressional Committee on Atomic Energy. In the letter, after pointing out the access Oppenheimer had to national security issues, Borden accused Oppenheimer of being a Soviet spy. Hoover drew up a report on Oppenheimer. Strauss then met with President **Dwight D. Eisenhower** (1890–1969; served 1953–61; see entry), who decided to withdraw Oppenheimer's security clear-ance. Oppenheimer met with Strauss on December 21, 1953, and looked over the twenty-four points against him. Amazing-ly, twenty-two dealt with his left-wing political associations back in the 1930s, one with his association with French physi-cist and friend Haakon Chevalier (1901–1985), and the twenty-fourth with his opposition to the H-bomb development.

The Red Scare, or communist witch-hunt, had reached all the way to the developer of America's atomic bomb. Hearings on the accusations against Oppenheimer were held in April and May 1954 before the AEC's Personnel Security Board. On June 29, 1954, Oppenheimer's security clearance was not renewed. Oppenheimer emerged from the hearings a changed man. His energy seemed drained, and as noted by former students and fellow scientists who visited him back at the Institute, he appeared old and frail, even though he was just fifty years old.

Oppenheimer was strongly backed by the scientific community and reappointed as director of the Institute. Strauss, who was on the Institute's board of directors, ap-proved, saying security was not a problem in the job. However, in the minds of the American public, Oppenheimer appeared to have been a communist or a subversive, one who attempts to overthrow or undermine an established political system.

Honors

While maintaining his position at the Institute, Oppenheimer devoted the rest of his life to the advancement of physics, traveling, lecturing, and writing. In 1958, the French government awarded him the Legion d'honneur (Legion of Honor). He was invited to participate in the Organization of American States (OAS) Professorship Program and traveled to Mexico and South America in 1961. The OAS was an organization of Central and South American countries that sought to maintain political stability in the region by providing a means to resolve disputes. Oppenheimer continued to travel and lecture throughout the world. He spent the last thirteen years of his life speaking on the need for the people of the world to communicate and understand one another.

In the early 1960s, President **John F. Kennedy** (1917–1963; served 1961–63; see entry) invited Oppenheimer to the White House for a dinner honoring Nobel Prize winners. Some Americans saw this as a step toward an apology for the government's wrongdoing against Oppenheimer in 1954. Before Kennedy's assassination in November 1963, the president approved Oppenheimer for the AEC's Enrico Fermi Award, in honor of the late Italian-born physicist who had initiated the atomic age with his first controlled nuclear chain reaction at the University of Chicago in 1942. Oppenheimer and Fermi had worked together on the Manhattan Project. The award included a citation, gold medal, and $50,000. President **Lyndon B. Johnson** (1908–1973; served 1963–69; see entry) presented the award to the fifty-nine-year-old Oppenheimer on December 2, 1963, in the White House Cabinet Room. Oppenheimer grasped his wife's hand as Johnson made the presentation, and in a thank you he acknowledged that it must have taken some courage for the president to make the award.

In 1964, Oppenheimer and his wife made a nostalgic trip back to Los Alamos. Returning to the Institute, Oppenheimer focused on the building and the development of a new library. A lifelong chain smoker, Oppenheimer was diagnosed with cancer of the larynx in March 1966. He retired from the directorship of the Institute in mid-1966 but in the fall served as senior professor of physics, a position Albert Einstein once held. He continued going to his office until just before he died on February 18, 1967.

For More Information

Books

Isaacs, Jeremy, and Taylor Downing. *Cold War: An Illustrated History, 1945–1991*. Boston: Little, Brown and Company, 1998.

Michelmore, Peter. *The Swift Years: The Robert Oppenheimer Story*. New York: Dodd, Mead & Company, 1969.

Rabi, I. I., Robert Serber, Victor F. Weisskopf, Abraham Pais, and Glenn T. Seaborg. *Oppenheimer*. New York: Charles Scribner's Sons, 1969.

Royal, Denise. *The Story of J. Robert Oppenheimer*. New York: St. Martin's Press, 1969.

Smith, Alice K., and Charles Weiner, eds. *Robert Oppenheimer: Letters and Recollections*. Cambridge, MA: Harvard University Press, 1980.

Web Sites

Los Alamos National Laboratory. http://www.lanl.gov/worldview/ (accessed on July 18, 2003).

U.S. Department of Energy, Office of Scientific and Technical Information. "Historical Records of the Atomic Energy Commission." *Open-Net*. http://www.osti.gov/opennet/nsi_desc.html (accessed on September 13, 2003).

Ayn Rand

**Born February 2, 1905
St. Petersburg, Russia
Died March 6, 1982
New York, New York**

Novelist and philosopher

In describing her beliefs, Ayn Rand stated, as noted on the Ayn Rand Institute Web site, "My philosophy, in essence, is the concept of man as a heroic being, with his own happiness as the moral purpose of his life, with productive achievements as his noblest activity, and reason ... his only absolute [most important quality]." Rand's early experiences while growing up in Russia, coupled with the philosophy of objectivism (which says a person's own life and happiness is the ultimate good; see box), made her a vocal opponent of communism. Her position as an internationally published author and widely read philosopher made her a prominent and highly respected figure during the Cold War (1945–91).

"The smallest minority on earth is the individual. Those who deny individual rights cannot claim to be defenders of minorities."

Ayn Rand. *Reproduced by permission of AP/Wide World Photos.*

Earliest years

Alissa (Alice) Zinovievna Rosenbaum, later known as Ayn Rand, was the first of three daughters born to Zinovy Zacharovich ("Fronz") and Anna Borisovna (Alice) Rosenbaum. Her younger sisters were Natasha and Elena. The Rosenbaum family lived in a large, comfortable apartment overlooking one of the great squares of the Russian city of Saint Petersburg. They lived above the pharmacy owned by Rand's father. She respected her father, but he was distant. In addition, Rand did not get along well with her mother, seeing her in a negative light as a very social person who was fundamentally indifferent to the world of ideas. Rand's mother would often show her off at parties when she was very young because she was so bright and intelligent. The young Alissa learned she was admired by adults for the qualities of her mind.

Winds of change

In the 1910s, Russia was at war with Germany and Austria. Times were difficult under the leadership of the tsar, the emperor of Russia. People stood in long bread lines in the cold Russian winter. Mass strikes by workers kept production of goods at a very low level. To make matters worse, over one million Russian army deserters from the front lines began looting shops and homes as they retreated back into Russia. Unrest gripped the entire country.

It was on Rand's birthday in 1917 at the age of twelve that she witnessed the first shots of the Russian Revolution from her balcony in Saint Petersburg. Huge angry crowds gathered, protesting the current regime. A unit of the National Guard appeared and ordered the crowd to break up. When they screamed in defiance, the soldiers began shooting and the crowd scattered. But the next day, they returned and were joined by the very soldiers who had shot at them. By the end of February, the tsar had abdicated, or given up the throne, and political power passed to the citizens of Russia.

The euphoria over the downfall of the tsar and new freedom did not last long. By the end of October, the Bolshevik revolutionaries saw their opportunity and conducted a bloody coup. The Bolsheviks made up a revolutionary political party of Russian workers and peasants that became the Communist Party after the Russian Revolution of 1917; the terms Bolshevik and communist became interchangeable, with communist eventually becoming more common.

A communist gang nationalized Rand's father's shop. Nationalization refers to a government taking ownership of a business. She watched her father stand helpless and frustrated at the loss of the business he had built by himself. The communists demanded her family give up everything they had worked for; this horrible injustice came to signify what communism was all about in young Alissa's mind.

Communism, which was promoted everywhere, was based on the principle that one must live for the state and not for oneself. To Rand, communism was the horror at the root of all the other horrors taking place around her. This was the source of the bloodshed, the confiscation of property, the night arrests, and the fear gripping her beautiful city. She viewed communism as an unspeakable evil, the destroyer of individual freedom and initiative. This viewpoint was to become the basis for her new philosophy and would define her life thereafter.

Moving on

After communism was instituted, there was little money in the Rosenbaum household. Food and fuel were scarce in the city and crime was rampant. In 1918, the family was able to obtain travel permits and left for Crimea, by the Black Sea in southwestern Russia, where the family had spent many summers. In 1921, Rand graduated from high school and then Crimea also fell to the Bolsheviks. As the family prepared to return to Saint Petersburg, which was now called Petrograd, Rand burned her diary. She had written down her philosophical ideas and plans for stories, but she knew those would be considered heretical, or against the established views, if discovered by the communists in Petrograd.

Rand began studies at the University of Petrograd, majoring in history with a minor in philosophy. It was here that she watched her first American movies and was fascinated by the bright world projected there. It was in sharp contrast to the dark, brooding atmosphere of Russia. Rand graduated with highest honors in 1924 from the newly renamed University of Leningrad. The city had once again been renamed, to Leningrad, in 1924 when Vladimir I. Lenin (1870–1924), considered the father of communism, died. While in her undergraduate program, Rand took a class from Professor Nicolas O. Lossky (1870–1965), a distinguished in-

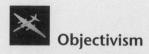

Objectivism

According to objectivism, a person's own life and happiness is the ultimate good. To achieve happiness requires a morality of rational selfishness, one that does not give undeserved rewards to others or ask them for oneself.

Objectivism was made for the era of industrial capitalism. It teaches that a harmony of interests exists among rational individuals, so that no one's benefit need come at the price of another's suffering. Because the human mode of living is production, we are all creators, making new goods through our productive work. Because reason is our means of survival, we stand to benefit from every discovery others make, every image or story they share, and every dollar they earn by production and trade.

Objectivism honors achievement and celebrates greatness because civilization rests on the shoulders of the industrious. It holds that humans live best as rational traders, dealing with others by exchanging value for value. It teaches integrity because rational beings are honest—they love truth more than deception. Objectivism values reasonable action, purposeful living, and self worth. Its major element of individualism operates in a capitalist economy, leaving no room for collectivism or communism.

ternational authority on Plato. Through his course, she found further definition for her emerging philosophical system, which she termed objectivism.

New beginnings

Rand gathered together the necessary paperwork to visit relatives in Chicago, Illinois, and was able to leave Russia in January 1926. She never returned. She left France by ship February 10 and arrived in New York City on February 18 with fifty dollars in her pocket. During her six-month stay in Chicago, she adopted the pen name Ayn Rand. Ayn was the name of a Finnish writer whose work she had not read but whose name she liked and took as her own. Following her time in Chicago, she left for Hollywood, California.

The very day Ayn arrived in Hollywood, she found a job as a movie extra with director Cecil B. DeMille (1881–1959). It was on the set of his film *King of Kings* that she met actor

Frank O'Connor (1897–1979). They were married on April 15, 1929, and remained married until he died in 1979. They never had any children as Rand considered writing her priority in life. She became a naturalized U.S. citizen on March 13, 1931.

Writing for life

As a young child, Rand had begun to invent her own stories and movie scenarios. It was while on a summer family trip to Austria, Switzerland, and England in 1914 that she had decided to become a writer. She read *The Mysterious Valley* by French writer Maurice Champagne (1868–1951) and fell in love with its hero, Cyrus. This character became the model for the heroine in her first novel, *We the Living,* which she completed in 1933. In her novel, the heroine's name is Kira, the feminine form of Cyrus.

In 1918, the works of French writer Victor Hugo (1802–1885) influenced her. His was a world of unprecedented scope and imaginative plots, and man was seen as a hero. At this time, Rand became conscious of style in writing. Her belief in the heroic character of man would be the underlying theme of all her writings and indeed of her philosophy of objectivism.

Rand spent several years in Hollywood until she and O'Connor moved to New York City in 1934. Her days were spent writing screenplays, short stories, and a novel, and also working odd jobs and mastering English. Her talent paid off with two Broadway plays and publication of *We the Living* in the United States and England in 1936.

The book that made Rand famous was *The Fountain-head.* Published in 1943 after a dozen rejections, this novel presented her mature portrait of "man as hero." Rand had become a significant influence on American culture and history. The novel was later to become a film starring Gary Cooper (1901–1961) and Patricia Neal (1926–). Rand moved back to Los Angeles with O'Connor in 1943 to write the screenplay.

The Fountainhead created controversy with its very strongly conservative tone in which the individual is praised above the common good of society, but her epic novel *Atlas Shrugged* was the literary and philosophical high of Rand's career. It combined her philosophy of strong individualism (anticollectivism) with a science fiction setting. By 1957, the

Writer Ayn Rand testifies before the House Un-American Activities Committee (HUAC) on October 20, 1947.
Reproduced by permission of the Corbis Corporation.

Cold War was well entrenched and the American economy was strong, so the theme of individualism over collectivism had a stronger appeal. After the publication of *Atlas Shrugged* in 1957, she turned to nonfiction. She wrote many essays and columns and made numerous public appearances as a lecturer.

Rand was an active and vocal opponent of communism and collectivism, a theory that promotes group control. In 1947, Rand was called as a "friendly witness" by the U.S. House Committee on Un-American Activities (HUAC). The committee was charged with investigating activities by organizations and individuals posing a threat to the U.S. government. Rand testified about the communist penetration of the film industry in Hollywood. She primarily discussed the movie *Song of Russia*, which she felt totally misrepresented life in the communist Soviet Union as being better than it actually was. She claimed that "anticapitalist" themes were often included in Hollywood productions. HUAC drew deep divisions in the country as it led to blacklisting, or refusing to employ, some workers in a system that claimed to honor freedom.

Creating an institute

Rand met future associates Barbara Branden (1929–) and Nathaniel Branden (1930–) in 1950. With Nathaniel, she prepared a course entitled "The Basic Principles of Objectivism," to be presented at the Nathaniel Branden Institute to promote her philosophy. This institute, formed in 1958, promoted lectures, courses, and publications in philosophy. It was the first formal organization to promote objectivist ideas.

The world was in the grips of an intense political and economic rivalry between the United States and the Soviet

Union from 1945 to 1991. This showdown of capitalism versus communism was a fight for freedom called the Cold War. It was being played out on the world stage, and it touched the heart of Rand's philosophy. The Cold War was a battle of philosophies, or ideas on how to live life, between the communist Soviet Union and the democratic, capitalist United States. From Rand's early years, communism had evolved into a system of government in which a single party, the Communist Party, controlled all aspects of people's lives. In economic theory, it prohibited the private ownership of property and business so that all goods produced and wealth accumulated were supposedly shared by all. In reality, the Soviet people lived in poverty and had no individual liberties. Communism also banned all religious practices.

Democracy, on the other hand, is a system of government consisting of several political parties whose members are elected to leadership roles by the general population. Citizens enjoy individual liberties such as freedom of speech, press, and religion. Capitalism promotes and encourages private ownership of property and businesses. Prices, production, and distribution of goods are determined by competition in a market relatively free of government intervention. Communism and capitalism are completely incompatible.

To further promote her cause of capitalism and objectivism, Rand began publishing a newsletter known in 1962 as the *Objectivist Newsletter*. It became the *Objectivist* in 1966 and the *Ayn Rand Letter* in 1971. In 1963, Rand received an honorary doctor of humane letters degree from Lewis and Clark College in Oregon.

In October 1951, Rand and O'Connor moved back to New York City on a permanent basis. O'Connor died in 1979; Rand died in her New York apartment on March 6, 1982. At the funeral, Rand's body was laid next to the symbol she had adopted as her own—a 6-foot dollar sign. In the years since her death, interest in her ideas has only increased and many of her writings have been published posthumously.

For More Information

Books

Branden, Barbara. *The Passion of Ayn Rand*. New York: Anchor Books, 1986.

Hull, Gary, and Leonard Peikoff, eds. *The Ayn Rand Reader.* New York: Plume, 1999.

Web Sites

All About Ayn Rand. http://ayn-rand.com (accessed on September 14, 2003).

Ayn Rand Institute: The Center for the Advancement of Objectivism. http://www.aynrand.org (accessed on September 14, 2003).

Ayn Rand Society. http://aynrandsociety.org (accessed on September 14, 2003).

Ronald Reagan

Born February 6, 1911
Tampico, Illinois

U.S. president, governor, and actor

Ronald Reagan was the fortieth president of the United States. Previously a radio sportscaster and Hollywood actor, his exceptional skills as an orator brought him the label "the Great Communicator" during his political career. Appearing easygoing with a folksy charm, he brought a hardline anticommunist direction to the White House. Reagan has been credited as one of the key individuals responsible for ending the Cold War (1945–91). The Cold War was a prolonged conflict for world dominance between the two superpowers, the democratic, capitalist United States and the communist Soviet Union. The weapons of conflict were commonly words of propaganda and threats.

Sportscaster and movie actor

Ronald Wilson Reagan was born in Tampico, Illinois, in February 1911. He was the second child born to Jack Reagan and Nelle Wilson. Reagan acquired the nickname "Dutch" from his father while an infant. Reagan's father was a struggling shoe salesman who had periodic bouts with alco-

"Freedom is a fragile thing and is never more than one generation away from extinction. It is not ours by inheritance; it must be fought for and defended constantly by each generation, for it comes only once to a people. Those who have known freedom, and then lost it, have never known it again."

Ronald Reagan. *Courtesy of the Library of Congress.*

387

holism. For several years, the family moved from town to town as Jack Reagan held various jobs. In 1920, the family settled in Dixon, Illinois. Despite poor finances, Reagan was able to attend Eureka College in Eureka, Illinois. He played football and participated in the drama society. Though not earning exceptional grades, he was very popular and elected class president his senior year.

Reagan graduated in 1932 with a degree in economics and sociology. He decided to enter the new and growing field of radio broadcasting. His first broadcasting job was with WOC in Davenport, Iowa. He provided play-by-play descriptions of Eureka College football games, entirely from memory when he would return to the radio station. He next moved to WHO in Des Moines, where he broadcast Chicago Cubs baseball games. Because the station could not afford for him to broadcast directly from the games, his accounts came from ticker tape summaries arriving in the station.

In the early spring of 1937, Reagan attended Cubs spring training camp in Southern California. While there, he took a screen test with Warner Brothers studio in Hollywood. The studio signed him to a five-year acting contract. Though he appeared mostly in low-budget "B" movies (as opposed to big-budget blockbusters), he commonly played the role of an easy-going, All-American "good guy." Many claimed he was essentially playing himself. Reagan appeared in more than fifty movies over a twenty-seven-year period. His most notable films were *Knute Rockne—All American* (1940) and *Kings Row* (1942). While filming a movie in 1938, he met actress Jane Wyman (1914–). They married in 1940, had one daughter, Maureen, and adopted a son, Michael. The couple divorced in 1948.

During World War II (1939–45), Reagan was commissioned as a cavalry officer and assigned to the army film unit in Los Angeles, where he made training films. To the public, however, he was portrayed as a combat field soldier.

From liberal Democrat to conservative Republican

Following the war, Reagan was voted president of the actors' union, called the Screen Actors Guild, from 1947 to

1952 and again in 1959. To the dismay of many of its members, Reagan testified as a "friendly witness" before the House Un-American Activities Committee (HUAC). With the Cold War rivalry between the United States and the Soviet Union taking shape, the committee was created to search for communist influences within the nation. Communism is a system of government in which the nation's leaders are selected by a single political party that controls all aspects of society. Private ownership of property is eliminated and government directs all economic production. The goods produced and accumulated wealth are, in theory, shared relatively equally by all. All religious practices are banned. Reagan helped rid the Hollywood film industry of supposed communist sympathizers. As a result, actors, directors, and writers suspected of communist ties were blacklisted, meaning they could not be hired without fear of the employer being accused of aiding the communist cause. Many of the union members were disgusted with his committee appearance.

During this early postwar period, Reagan maintained a Democratic Party allegiance. He had been influenced by his father, who had landed a federal administrative role in the New Deal programs of President Franklin D. Roosevelt (1882–1945; served 1933–45). The programs were designed to combat economic hardships brought on by the Great Depression (1929–41), the worst financial crisis in American history. Reagan supported Roosevelt's Democratic successor, President **Harry S. Truman** (1884–1972; served 1945–53; see entry), in the 1948 presidential elections. Reagan's views, however, were becoming increasingly conservative and influenced by his future wife, Nancy Davis (1923–), whom he met in 1949 (and married in 1952).

By 1950, Reagan began supporting Republican candidates, including the successful presidential campaigns in 1952 and 1956 of **Dwight D. Eisenhower** (1890–1969; served 1953–61; see entry) Through the 1950s, Reagan's movie acting career declined. He became host of the popular television drama series *General Electric Theater*. Reagan also became a spokesman for General Electric, touring company offices across the nation giving inspirational speeches. Yet his increasingly conservative views led General Electric to fire Reagan as its spokesman and television program host when his speeches became more ultraconservative, which alienated some middle-of-the-road viewers.

Reagan's political visibility was steadily growing. In 1960, he delivered over two hundred campaign speeches in support of Republican candidate **Richard Nixon** (1913–1994; served 1969–74; see entry), who lost to Democratic challenger **John F. Kennedy** (1919–1963; served 1961–63; see entry). By 1962, Reagan formally changed his political party affiliation to the Republican Party. He also actively campaigned for Nixon's unsuccessful bid for the California governorship that year. He next campaigned on behalf of the 1964 Republican presidential candidate, U.S. senator Barry Goldwater (1909–1998) of Arizona. In the last week before election day, Reagan gave a thirty-minute nationally televised speech. The speech brought him to national prominence in politics and made him a key spokesman for the Republican right, or most conservative members.

Governor Reagan goes to the White House

With his newfound prominence, Reagan ran for governor of California in 1966 and upset Democrat incumbent Pat Brown (1905–1996). Reagan pledged to crack down on campus antiwar protesters opposing the Vietnam War (1954–75). He served two terms until 1974. During that time, he erased a large state budget deficit through large tax increases and reductions in state education and welfare programs.

While governor, Reagan became the most recognized national spokesman for conservative causes. He made a belated run at the Republican presidential nomination in 1968 and then supported Nixon again in 1972. In 1976, Reagan made his first hard run for the party's nomination in a harsh attack on a fellow Republican, President Gerald Ford (1913–; served 1974–77). Reagan was critical of SALT I (a strategic arms agreement with the Soviet Union) and the détente policies of U.S. secretary of state **Henry Kissinger** (1923–; see entry). (Détente was a mutual agreement to relax or ease tensions between the United States and the Soviet Union.) Ford barely managed to win the Republican nomination but lost to his Democratic opponent, Georgia governor **Jimmy Carter** (1924–; served 1977–81; see entry) in the national election.

By 1980, Reagan was in a good position for a strong showing in the presidential race. He easily won the party's

nomination for president and chose longtime politician **George Bush** (1924–; served 1989–93; see entry) as his running mate. Reagan proposed major tax cuts and increased defense spending while balancing the budget.

Reagan's opponent, President Carter, running for re-election, was facing serious problems at home and abroad. The U.S. economy was struggling with high inflation, or rising price of goods, and unemployment rates, and Carter had been unable to resolve the ongoing Iran hostage crisis. A group of militant Iranian students had stormed the U.S. embassy in Tehran in November 1979, taking the American staff hostage. The Iranians demanded that Carter return the former unpopular leader of Iran, the shah, Mohammad Reza Pahlavi (1919–1980), who had been given permission by Carter to come to the United States for cancer treatment. Negotiations between the United States and Iran led nowhere, and a military rescue operation to free the hostages ended in disaster, when eight U.S. soldiers died in a helicopter crash. Carter was seen as weak and ineffective on international issues.

U.S. president Jimmy Carter (left), the Democratic nominee, shakes hands with his Republican challenger, former California governor Ronald Reagan, during a 1980 presidential debate in Cleveland, Ohio. *Photograph by Ron Kuntz. Reproduced by permission of the Corbis Corporation.*

Reagan campaigned to bring America back to international respectability and charged that Carter had underfunded the military, allowing the Soviets to gain a military advantage. He also claimed the strategic arms agreement SALT II that Carter had signed in 1979 gave the Soviets an advantage. Reagan handily defeated Carter and became president at sixty-eight years of age. On the very day of Reagan's inauguration in January 1981, the hostages were freed from Iran. Questions were later raised if secret deals had been made to ensure the release came after Reagan had won the election, since an earlier release might have benefited Carter's reelection chances.

Only weeks after Reagan took office, a mentally disturbed individual named John Hinckley (1955–) fired six shots at the president and his entourage as they were leaving a Washington, D.C., building. Reagan was wounded in the chest with a bullet lodged only one inch from his heart. His press secretary, James Brady (1940–), was critically wounded in the head. Though out of the hospital soon, Reagan was physically weakened for several months.

Reagan began pressing a major economic program that became known as "Reaganomics." He and his advisors believed major tax cuts would stimulate business activity, produce more jobs, and reduce the need for welfare programs. Reagan managed to get major income tax reductions through Congress in addition to sizable increases in military spending and cuts in social service programs. When a severe recession struck the U.S. economy in 1982, the unemployment rate reached its highest level, 11 percent, since the Depression. Bankruptcies, farm foreclosures, and the trade deficit soared. A modest tax increase was passed in 1982, and by 1983, the economy had begun to improve. For the remainder of Reagan's time in office, the economy steadily grew. The huge increase in military spending, however, when combined with the tax cuts, tripled the national debt to over $3 trillion by 1988.

Cold War tensions rise

A pressing Cold War issue for Reagan was the war between the Soviet Union and Afghanistan. The Soviets had invaded Afghanistan in December 1979 to support an unpopular pro-Soviet leader against rebel forces trying to take over the government. With the fall of a pro-U.S. government in Iran at about the same time as the Soviet invasion, U.S. officials feared the Soviets would seek control of the Persian Gulf oil fields. Carter had responded by cutting U.S. grain sales to the Soviets and increasing U.S. naval presence in the region. Reagan restored the grain sales, claiming it hurt American farmers more than the Soviets, and began secret support of the Afghan rebels. For example, in 1985, the United States provided $300 million to help finance the war effort. The Afghan war became an unpopular, costly guerrilla, or irregular and independent, war for the Soviets through the 1980s.

The increases in military spending were designed to expand and modernize the armed forces and increase respect for the United States in the world. The military budget rose from $126 billion in 1979 to $312 billion in 1988. More specifically, Reagan denounced the policies of détente, which called for equality between the two superpowers in terms of nuclear weapons strength. Instead, Reagan wanted to build a clear military superiority over the Soviets. The tough actions were accompanied with tough talk as well. Reagan publicly referred to the Soviet Union as the "evil empire" in a Florida speech. He also referred to the Soviet leaders as "godless" monsters. Defense spending included monies for the MX missile defense system, an expanded naval fleet, new army tanks, and the B-1 bomber. He also assembled new intermediate-range nuclear missiles in Western Europe in the face of large antinuclear public protests.

In March 1983, Reagan proposed a massive new missile defense system called the Strategic Defense Initiative (SDI). More popularly known as "Star Wars" after the popular science fiction movie, SDI was envisioned as a space-based network of satellites armed with lasers and other complex technologies to destroy Soviet missiles fired at U.S. targets. The initial cost estimates of developing the system were staggering, and critics questioned the technical feasibility. The Soviets were alarmed and claimed it violated existing arms control agreements. The science community, though skeptical of the proposal, enjoyed the additional funding for research. The Soviets were further troubled by what it would cost them to keep up with the new technologies. SDI became the biggest issue between the United States and the Soviet Union.

U.S. president Ronald Reagan addresses the nation on March 23, 1983, to talk about the development of the new Strategic Defense Initiative (SDI) missile defense system, also known as "Star Wars." *Photograph by Larry Rubenstein. Reproduced by permission of the Corbis Corporation.*

During this period, U.S. officials began publicly talking of a winnable nuclear war and developing measures for a quick recovery. Public fear of nuclear war rose to levels not seen since the Cuban Missile Crisis in October 1962, when the Soviet Union and the United States came close to war over the existence of Soviet nuclear missiles in Cuba. The Soviets responded with a tough stance in maintaining their rule in the communist world.

In December 1981, the communist government of Poland, under pressure from the Soviets, imposed martial law, or military rule over civilians, to break a strike by a labor union that became known as the Solidarity Movement. With tensions peaking over Reagan's aggressive style, the Soviets shot down a Korean commercial airliner in September 1983 that strayed into Soviet airspace, killing 269 people onboard. The Soviets, on heightened alert probably because of the escalation in U.S. Cold War rhetoric, suspected the airplane was a U.S. spy plane testing Soviet defenses in a sensitive area. Reagan called the downing a barbaric act.

As with previous presidents, Reagan moved decisively to combat the possible spread of communism in Latin America. In the Caribbean island nation of Grenada, Reagan seized on the occurrence of domestic strife between two procommunist factions to launch an invasion by U.S. troops in late October 1983 to supposedly protect U.S. medical students and restore order. After U.S. forces gained control of the country, a new democratic pro-U.S. government was established. Reagan came under much international criticism for becoming involved in an internal political struggle without United Nations (UN) support. The Grenada invasion, however, was the first successful military operation since before the Vietnam War and helped reestablish confidence in U.S. military capability. With the U.S. economy growing, Reagan easily won reelection in 1984. Reagan won the most electoral votes, 525, in history.

Relations with Soviets

During the early 1980s, the Soviets experienced a series of aging leaders including the last years of **Leonid Brezhnev** (1906–1982; see entry), then the brief tenures of Yuri Andropov (1914–1984) and Konstantin Chernenko (1911–1985). The Communist Party and the Soviet Union were run by aging hard-liners, but the death of Chernenko in March 1985 made way for the younger, college-educated **Mikhail Gorbachev** (1931–; see entry) to take over.

Recognizing the looming economic crisis of the Soviet Union, Gorbachev introduced major changes under the policies of *perestroika* (reform) and *glasnost* (openness). Gorbachev appointed **Eduard Shevardnadze** (1928–; see entry) as Soviet foreign minister to seek an end to the Cold War rivalry with the West. U.S.-Soviet relations began to improve significantly. Reagan began to back off from his tough language towards the Soviets. The Soviets cut back on their foreign commitments, including withdrawing troops from Afghanistan and cutting aid to Cuba.

Reagan met with Gorbachev in a series of summit meetings through the next few years. At the Reykjavik, Iceland, summit in October 1986, despite the two leaders laying a foundation for later meetings, Gorbachev and Reagan came away strongly disappointed that no agreement could be reached, with Reagan resolved to pursue the SDI initiative and

Did Reagan End the Cold War?

Following the collapse of the Soviet Union at the end of 1991, debate focused on President Ronald Reagan's role in ending the Cold War. Some historians and Reagan supporters have claimed Reagan was the primary figure leading to the downfall of communist governments in Eastern Europe in 1989 and the Soviet Union. His aggressive Cold War policies in fueling an expensive arms race in the 1980s, they have argued, caused an economic collapse in the Soviet Union. Other historians and critics of Reagan's hard-line policies have asserted that the Soviet economy was already struggling by the late 1970s. In addition, they reasoned, Soviet social problems were mounting under the leadership of aging communist leaders in the early 1980s.

When Mikhail Gorbachev assumed the Soviet leadership in 1985, corruption and economic problems were so severe major reforms were obviously needed. Because the Soviet Union was already progressing toward internal collapse, critics have claimed Reagan's hard-line policies needlessly endangered the world with nuclear destruction. They believed that the buildup of weapons not only hastened collapse of the Soviet economy but crippled the U.S. economy as well with massive national debt.

Perhaps the more reasonable assessment of Reagan's role came from long-time U.S. foreign policy expert **George Kennan** (1904–; see entry). In the 1990s, Kennan contended that the two individuals most responsible for ending the Cold War were Gorbachev with his reforms, and Reagan, despite whether Reagan knew what the implications of his policies would be.

Gorbachev insisting the United States stop it as a basis for beginning more detailed negotiations. Gorbachev would later back off from his demand in order to rejuvenate discussions.

By December 1987, new arms control treaties were signed. These included a treaty eliminating intermediate-range nuclear forces (INF) from Europe. The INF treaty was the first to actually reduce the level of nuclear arsenals, or collections of weapons, rather than simply freeze them at certain levels. Reagan's willingness to negotiate arms control agreements and support Gorbachev's reform efforts within the Soviet Union was key to the eventual fall of communist governments, first across Eastern Europe in 1989, and soon after in the Soviet Union in 1991. The foundation for ending the Cold War had been laid.

Controversy in Latin America

In 1985, Reagan had introduced the Reagan Doctrine to guide U.S. Cold War policy in Third World countries. Under the doctrine, the United States would provide military and economic support to various military dictatorships in Third World countries to resist possible revolutionary movements. He also supported oppositional forces rising up against potentially pro-Soviet governments such as cases in Angola, Afghanistan, and Nicaragua.

U.S. president Ronald Reagan (left) says goodbye to Soviet leader Mikhail Gorbachev (far right) following a tense summit in Reykjavik, Iceland, in October 1986. *Reproduced by permission of AP/Wide World Photos.*

The one country that attracted perhaps the most interest from the Reagan administration was Nicaragua. The pro-Soviet Sandinista government led by Daniel Ortega (1945–) had overthrown a U.S.-supported military dictatorship in July 1979. U.S. officials believed Ortega was building a pro-Soviet government.

In 1981, Reagan cut off U.S. and international aid and provided $10 million and another $19 million a year later to recruit and train a guerrilla army known as the contras. Congress was not supportive of the administration's efforts and passed a law in 1982 restricting assistance to overthrow the government. In response, the administration switched to more covert, or secret, operations. In 1984, the Central Intelligence Agency (CIA) mined Nicaraguan harbors (placed military explosives at or near the surface of the water), essentially constituting an act of war under international law. Congress passed a second law cutting off all funds for U.S. operations in Nicaragua.

The Reagan administration, however, remained persistent. In November 1985, a new covert plan was approved to sell arms to Iran in exchange for the release of American hostages being held by terrorists in Lebanon and to funnel some of the money gained from the sales to the contras in Nicaragua for weapons and supplies. The illegal arms-for-hostages deal was publicly revealed in November 1986. A few weeks later came the revelation that some of the $48 million funds had gone to Nicaragua, breaking more laws.

Following the investigations of special commissions and an independent investigator, two in the Reagan administration were convicted of obstructing justice and other offenses. They were the head of the National Security Council (NSC), Rear Admiral John Poindexter (1936–), and NSC aide Marine Lieutenant Colonel Oliver North (1943–). Both Reagan and Vice President Bush persistently denied knowledge of the covert operation. A later investigation released in late 1992—long after Reagan was out of office and just before Bush had lost his presidential reelection bid—suggested otherwise. Though Reagan's popularity declined during the early months of the scandal revelations, it soon rebounded.

During Reagan's second term of office other skirmishes broke out in various parts of the world. Libya caught Reagan's attention as a promoter of international terrorism in the early 1980s. In 1986, Reagan ordered air attacks against Libyan targets on the North African coast after a reported Libyan missile attack on U.S. aircraft. The Soviets condemned U.S. actions and terrorist attacks increased. U.S. naval ships also began escorting Kuwaiti oil tankers through the Persian Gulf region as the Iran-Iraq War expanded in the region. Several military encounters resulted and became increasingly deadly. In July 1988, the U.S. Navy shot down an Iran Air commercial airliner with over 100 people onboard, mistaking it for an attacking jet fighter. Not long afterwards, a Pan Am airliner containing 270 people was sabotaged and crashed in Lockerbie, Scotland, as a reprisal by terrorists supported by Iran, Libya, and Syria.

Declining health

In 1989, Bush succeeded Reagan in the White House and Reagan retired to his Los Angeles home. He published an autobiography, *An American Life,* in 1990. In 1994, Reagan publicly acknowledged that he was suffering from Alzheimer's disease, a degenerative brain condition. Though Reagan would make few public appearances through the 1990s, his popularity among conservative Republicans remained high. In February 1998, Congress renamed National Airport in Washington, D.C., to Ronald Reagan Washington National Airport.

For More Information

Books

Fischer, Beth A. *The Reagan Reversal: Foreign Policy and the End of the Cold War.* Columbia: University of Missouri Press, 1997.

FitzGerald, Frances. *Way Out There in the Blue: Reagan, Stars Wars, and the End of the Cold War.* New York: Simon & Schuster, 2000.

Mandelbaum, Michael, and Strobe Talbott. *Reagan and Gorbachev.* New York: Vintage Books, 1987.

Morris, Edmund. *Dutch: A Memoir of Ronald Reagan.* New York: Random House, 1999.

Pemberton, William E. *Exit with Honor: The Life and Presidency of Ronald Reagan.* Armonk, NY: M. E. Sharpe, 1997.

Reagan, Nancy. *My Turn: The Memoirs of Nancy Reagan.* New York: Random House, 1989.

Reagan, Ronald. *An American Life.* New York: Simon & Schuster, 1990.

Wallison, Peter J. *Ronald Reagan: The Power of Conviction and the Success of His Presidency.* Boulder, CO: Westview Press, 2003.

Condoleezza Rice

Born November 14, 1954
Birmingham, Alabama

U.S. national security advisor

C ondoleezza Rice was America's top advisor on the Soviet Union during the administration of President **George Bush** (1924–; served 1989–93; see entry), helping to write U.S. policy regarding the unification of Germany at the end of the Cold War in November 1990. The Cold War was an intense political and economic rivalry from 1945 to 1991 between the United States and the Soviet Union, falling just short of military conflict. For her part, Rice said she felt fortunate to have been given the chance to help shape America's response to these extraordinary events.

Rice was front and center at one of the most historic scenes in modern political history—the end of the Cold War era: In 1991, the Soviet Union broke apart and relations between the United States and the Soviets normalized. Returning to Washington, D.C., in January 2000 as part of the administration of President George W. Bush (1946–; served 2001–), Rice took on the role of national security advisor, the chief foreign policy advisor to the president.

"It is a dangerous thing to ask why someone else has been given more. It is humbling—and indeed healthy—to ask why you have been given so much."

Condoleezza Rice.
Photograph by Linda A. Cicero. Reproduced by permission of AP/Wide World Photos.

Early life

An only child born to John Wesley Rice and Angelena Ray Rice, Condoleezza Rice was surrounded by love from the very beginning. Her father called her his "little star" and worked very hard to give her every advantage. An ordained Presbyterian minister, he also worked as a teacher, coach, and guidance counselor. Her mother was a teacher and a pianist. She named her daughter after an Italian musical term, *con dolcezza*—"to play with sweetness." Condi, as she is called, was the delight of her parents and they were the driving force in her life.

Her education began in her hometown of Birmingham, Alabama. It was evident early on that she was a high achiever, and she rose to any challenge. She excelled both in academics and in the arts. Under the guidance of her educator parents, she skipped first and seventh grades. After her father moved the family to Denver, Colorado, Rice decided to take college courses while still in high school. She enrolled at the University of Denver at the age of fifteen. She graduated with a bachelor's degree in political science cum laude (with honors) in 1974 when she was nineteen. Rice earned a master's degree at the University of Notre Dame in 1975 and a doctorate from the University of Denver's Graduate School of International Studies in 1981. Both of her advanced degrees were also in political science.

After graduation, Rice went to work at Stanford University as a Soviet expert on the political science faculty. She was twenty-six years old at the time.

Influences

Condoleezza Rice was born at a time when her country was dealing with civil rights on a national level and the Cold War on an international level. Civil rights are personal liberties that belong to an individual such as freedom of speech and freedom from discrimination. A descendent of black Americans from the South, Rice was raised in Titusville, a middle-class suburb of black professionals in Birmingham, Alabama. In the 1950s and 1960s, Birmingham was the most racially segregated city in the South and was a focal point of the civil rights movement. Efforts to achieve civil rights often resulted in violence.

On September 15, 1963, a bomb killed four young girls while they were attending church at the 16th Street Baptist Church. Eleven-year-old Denise McNair was the youngest who died. She had attended kindergarten with young Condoleezza. A group called "nightriders" came out at night to start fires or hide bombs in the segregated black neighborhoods. Rice's father was one of the men who took to the neighborhood streets with a shotgun to protect their families.

Even though her parents could not sit down to eat at the local Woolworth's counter, they wanted their daughter to believe she could one day be U.S. president. In 1965, when Rice was eleven, her father took her to Washington, D.C., where she stood in front of the White House. Even though at the time most blacks were not allowed to vote, according to Antonia Felix's *Condi: The Condoleezza Rice Story*, she told her father, "One day, I'll be in that house."

Rice's parents were devoted to education and achievement, which they felt would enable Rice to be a success in whatever profession she chose. She was also often reminded that she would have to be "twice as good," but never to think of herself as a victim. Her ancestors had taken every opportunity to learn and had passed that appreciation of learning to their children. In the end, it was Rice's own family legacy of dedication to the educational process and not the civil rights struggle that defined her story.

The Cold War

While a junior at the University of Denver, Rice attended a lecture given by Professor Josef Korbel (1909–1977) that would change her life. He was a former central European diplomat and a Soviet specialist. His daughter, Madeleine Albright (1937–), later became secretary of state for President Bill Clinton (1946–; served 1993–2001). Rice spent time in the Korbel home and decided she wanted to study the Soviet Union. She had recently given up on her dream of becoming a concert pianist, and Russia became her new passion. Her attraction for Soviet studies came into focus at Notre Dame. She also had an interest in military strategy. She wrote about the problems of arms control and U.S.-Soviet relations in a research paper, which, in turn, led to her doctoral dissertation. Rice visited Russia several times over a five-year period in the late 1970s and early 1980s while doing research for her dissertation. When she arrived at Stanford University, she was a member of the Center for International Security and Arms Control.

As noted in Antonia Felix's book *Condi: The Condoleezza Rice Story*, *George* magazine's Ann Reilly Dowd wrote a profile on Rice that summarized her position: "Condi came to see the Cold War not as a war of ideas between communism and democracy but as something more primordial [basic or elemental]—a raw contest between two great competing national interests." Communism is a system of government in which a single party controls all aspects of society. In economic theory, it bans private ownership of property and businesses so that all goods produced and wealth accumulated are supposedly shared equally by all. Democracy is a political system consisting of several political parties whose members are elected to various government offices by vote of the people. Its economic system is called capitalism, where property and business are privately owned and competition in the marketplace establishes financial success or failure.

A call to Washington, D.C.

In 1989, while Rice was teaching at Stanford, she received a call. It was from Brent Scowcroft (1925–), the national security advisor to President George Bush. He wanted Rice to come to Washington. They got along well; both spoke fluent Russian and were academically oriented. Both had taught Soviet history. Bush asked Rice to serve on the National Security Council (NSC), an advisory group in the executive branch of government consisting of the president; the secretaries of state, defense, army, navy, and air force; and the national security advisor and staff. She took a leave of absence from Stanford and put her Soviet expertise into practice.

Rice joined the forty-member team as director of Soviet and East European affairs. Four months later, she was senior director for Soviet affairs. She was also named special assistant to the president for national security affairs. She served as an aide to Scowcroft and helped coordinate the U.S. foreign policy-making process by gathering information and writing briefing papers.

Events climaxed in December 1989 at the Malta Summit. (Malta is an island nation in the Mediterranean Sea 60 miles [97 kilometers] south of Sicily, Italy.) Rice accompanied Scowcroft as part of the U.S. delegation when President Bush met with Soviet leader **Mikhail Gorbachev** (1931–; see entry). They met on the Soviet cruiser *Maxim Gorky* to discuss the reunification of Germany. At Malta, the two leaders opened up a new age of cooperation between the superpowers—and Rice was there. With the collapse of the communist government in East Germany as well as other Eastern European countries in 1989, the Soviet Union soon broke apart in the next two years. Rice was at the center of American-Soviet policy during the breakup until she left her post in March 1991. The Soviet Union would cease to exist on December 31, 1991.

Publications and Awards

Condoleezza Rice's books include:

The Soviet Union and the Czechoslovak Army, 1948–1983: Uncertain Allegiance. Princeton, NJ: Princeton University Press, 1984.

The Gorbachev Era (edited with Alexander Dallin). Stanford, CA: Stanford Alumni Association, 1986.

Germany Unified and Europe Transformed (with Philip Zelikow). Cambridge, MA: Harvard University Press, 1995.

She also wrote numerous articles on Soviet and Eastern European foreign and defense policy.

Rice was a Fellow of the American Academy of Arts and Sciences and was awarded honorary doctorates from Morehouse College in 1991, the University of Alabama in 1994, and the University of Notre Dame in 1995.

The professor

Returning to Stanford, Rice was again an educator. In 1993, she was appointed provost (a university's chief budget and academic officer). It was a bumpy ride, as the university was facing several financial problems. She was also criticized for not doing enough to promote diversity.

Rice's professional activities were not limited to the university. She volunteered her time as cofounder of the Center for a New Generation. The center was an after-school

U.S. national security advisor Condoleezza Rice meets with Secretary of State Colin Powell (far left) and President George W. Bush. *Photograph by J. Scott Applewhite. Reproduced by permission of AP/Wide World Photos.*

academy in East Palo Alto, California, that helped children from underfunded public school districts. She also served as a corporate board member for several corporations, including Chevron, a giant in the U.S. oil industry. Chevron named a supertanker after her. She also resumed her writing career.

Back to Washington, D.C.

In 1999, Rice left Stanford to join the presidential campaign of then–Texas governor George W. Bush. Upon Bush's election in 2000, the president-elect named her as his national security advisor. She filled the crucial role of presidential sounding board. Her combination of charm, intelligence, and charisma served her well as the chief referee between the often powerfully divided opinions within a presidential administration. She was said to deliver her considered wisdom in whispers, not shouts. Her role as national security advisor within the Bush administration brought her into the forefront on the declared war on terrorism following the September 11, 2001, terrorist attacks on New York City and Washington, D.C., and in the war against Iraq in 2003.

Rice claimed her dream job would be to one day become the National Football League commissioner. A huge sports fan, she also worked out regularly. It was reported that more business was conducted on the tennis court at Camp David, the presidential retreat in Maryland, than sitting on the porch. Despite giving up her early ambitions of becoming a concert pianist, she continued to play regularly on the Steinway her parents had given her when she was fifteen. She was accomplished enough to have performed with cellist Yo-Yo Ma (1955–) at Constitution Hall in Washington, D.C., in 2002.

Rice has described herself as a deeply religious person. Like her parents before her, she wanted to make a difference in the lives of young people. As noted in Antonia Felix's *Condi: The Condoleezza Rice Story,* while speaking to a group of graduates at Stanford University in 1985, she urged them to make a difference in their world. She talked to them about tackling the problems of the Cold War. "All you have to do with the large, huge, and very frightening problems that we face is to make a contribution," she said. "If you focus too much on solving that problem, rather than just making a contribution to its solution ... you will become paralyzed at the enormity of the task and be unable to do anything at all."

For More Information

Books

Felix, Antonia. *Condi: The Condoleezza Rice Story.* New York: Newmarket Press, 2002.

The International Who's Who, 2003. London and New York: Europa Publications Ltd., 2002.

Thomas, Evan. "The Quiet Power of Condi Rice." *Newsweek* (December 16, 2002): pp. 24–35.

Web Site

Biography of Dr. Condoleezza Rice, National Security Advisor. The White House, http/www.whitehouse.gov/nsc/ricebio.html (accessed on February 7, 2003).

Andrey Sakharov

Born May 21, 1921
Moscow, Russia
Died December 14, 1989
Moscow, Russia

Physicist and Soviet dissident

"Intellectual freedom is essential to human society. Freedom of thought is the only guarantee against an infection of people by mass myths, which, in the hands of treacherous hypocrites and demagogues, can be transformed into bloody dictatorships."

Andrey Sakharov.
Photograph by Bruno Mosconi.
Reproduced by permission of AP/Wide World Photos.

Andrey Sakharov, one of the greatest theoretical physicists of the twentieth century, was often called the father of the Soviet Union's hydrogen bomb. He also spoke out internationally against the oppressive Soviet system of government. His wife, Yelena Bonner (1923–), was also greatly involved in protecting the human rights of Soviet citizens. Together, they were among the leading advocates of democracy, economic reform, and intellectual freedom in their country. A democratic system of government allows multiple political parties whose members are elected to various government offices by popular vote of the people. Sakharov and Bonner's principled dissent and compassion would be acknowledged the world over when he won the Nobel Peace Prize in 1975 for his courageous efforts.

Early years

Andrey Dmitrievich Sakharov was born into a solid, middle-class family of professionals in Moscow. His mother was Ekaterina (Katya) Sofiano and his father was Dmitri

Sakharov, a physics teacher. A brilliant student, young Sakharov was considered a science prodigy, or highly talented child, and attended Moscow State University. He graduated with a physics degree in 1942, then worked as an engineer in a military factory.

In 1945, Sakharov entered the Lebedev Physics Institute in Moscow. Shy and thoughtful, he spent the genius and energy of his young adult years developing thermonuclear weapons, so called because of the incredible heat associated with their reaction. During his time at the Institute, he published numerous articles on fusion thermonuclear reactions. Fusion involves the joining together of atomic nuclei with other elements such as hydrogen. Bombs based on fusion are referred to as hydrogen bombs (H-bombs). They are vastly more powerful than the atomic bombs the United States dropped on the Japanese cities of Hiroshima and Nagasaki near the end of World War II (1939–45).

In 1948, Soviet authorities, fearing the United States was developing an H-bomb, commanded Sakharov to work on the Soviet hydrogen bomb project. He was sent to the newly established super secret weapons laboratory, Arzamas-16. Located about 250 miles (400 kilometers) east of Moscow, Arzamas-16 was nicknamed Los Arzamas after Los Alamos, New Mexico, site of the Manhattan Project, the secret U.S. nuclear weapons development project. All of the Soviets' great physicists would live and work there for periods of time.

In 1949, Sakharov married his first wife, Klavdia (Klava) Vikhiveva. They would have two daughters, Tanya and Lyuba, and one son, Dmitri (Dima).

Dangerous thoughts and the father of the H-bomb

Back in 1948, Sakharov had thoughtfully considered the Soviet policy of collectivism. Collectivism is when a business such as a farm is jointly owned and operated by those farming the land. Farmers share equally in the production and profits. In collectivism, private ownership of property is not allowed. In Sakharov's opinion, collectivism had been carried to excess by Soviet leaders. He was also dismayed at the arrests and murder of citizens who dared to speak against the policies of Soviet leader **Joseph Stalin** (1879–1953; see entry). Sakharov turned down an offer to join the Communist Party. This party existed within communism, a system of government in which a single party, the Communist Party, controls all aspects of people's lives. In economics theory, communism prohibits private ownership of property and business so that all goods produced and wealth accumulated are supposedly shared equally by all. Because of Sakharov's standing among the elite community of Soviet scientists, his boldness was not punished. Stalin desperately needed Sakharov to apply his brilliance to the development of the H-bomb.

On November 1, 1952, the United States detonated its first hydrogen bomb. On August 12, 1953, the Soviet Union successfully detonated "Joe-1." Although much smaller and not a true H-bomb, "Joe-1's" detonation meant the Soviets were in the Cold War race with the United States for weapon superiority. The Cold War was an intense political and economic rivalry from 1945 to 1991 between the United States and the Soviet Union, falling just short of military conflict.

Sakharov and his staff continued to work on the development of a true hydrogen bomb. On November 22, 1955, at the Semipalatinsk Test Site, the Soviets detonated their first real hydrogen bomb. Sakharov was credited with working out its theoretical basis. For his efforts, he was awarded several of the Soviet Union's highest honors. He received the Order of Stalin, the Order of Lenin, and was made a Hero of Socialist Labor three times. He had been elected a member of the prestigious Soviet Academy of Sciences in 1953.

Budding dissident

Sakharov was profoundly affected by the destructive power of what he had developed. During the late 1950s, his concern grew over the dangerous effects of nuclear testing. He considered the testing unnecessary and contrary to humanity and international law. Interestingly, **J. Robert Oppenheimer** (1904–1967; see entry), developer of America's first atomic bomb in 1945, and **Igor Kurchatov** (1903–1960; see entry), also at Arzamas-16 and developer of the Soviet's first atomic bomb in 1949, came to similar conclusions. The atomic bombs developed by Oppenheimer and Kurchatov, the type dropped on Japan in August 1945, were much less powerful than the new H-bombs.

Sakharov asked questions about nuclear responsibility and the rights of human beings in the same manner he asked questions about the physical world—formulating hypotheses and searching for reliable evidence to support his hypotheses. He quickly found that his thinking and the openness with which he discussed his ideas automatically made him a dissident, an individual who disagrees with the ideas of those in power. He soon came to sympathize with other dissidents. Sakharov's moral awakening prompted him to risk both life and reputation in a prolonged confrontation with his government over issues of nuclear responsibility and human rights.

Outspoken

Sakharov first collided with authority in 1961 in his opposition to further nuclear testing. Soviet prime minister **Nikita Khrushchev** (1894–1971; see entry) rejected all of Sakharov's arguments for containing nuclear weaponry. The more Sakharov attempted to express his opinions about cutting back on nuclear testing, the more he was threatened by Soviet authorities. At a time when few others dared, Sakharov readily assumed grave personal risks for his views.

In an international publication in 1968, Sakharov called for an end to the arms race and asked for cooperation between the United States and Soviet Union on world problems. He was pulled off secret projects and dismissed as head consultant of the State Committee for Atomic Energy. Stripped of his security clearance and dismissed from weapons research, Sakharov returned to research in fundamental science at the Lebedev Institute. Shortly after this, his wife died and left him a widower after twenty years of marriage.

In the late 1960s, Sakharov began an open campaign to make Soviet society more humane. He attended trials of political prisoners and publicized the plight of persecuted religious believers and oppressed populations within the Soviet Union as well as the countries under Soviet control such as Poland and Czechoslovakia. He called on the government to

Human rights activist Yelena Bonner, wife of Andrey Sakharov. *Photograph by Ivan Sekretarev. Reproduced by permission of AP/Wide World Photos.*

allow citizens to exercise freedoms guaranteed by the Soviet Constitution but denied in practice. Sakharov was perceived as the salvation of the dissident movement. Political dissidents were a disorganized and repressed group. The Soviet official propaganda presented them as minor figures who were victims of foreign influence. When the famous physicist joined them, he gave the human rights groups in Moscow a needed jolt of respect.

Yelena Bonner

It was while attending a human rights trial in 1970 that Sakharov met Yelena Georgyevna Bonner. She was born in Merv, Turkmenistan, on February 15, 1923, the daughter of a prominent Armenian communist and Comintern secretary. The Comintern was a political body formed to guide the expansion of communism in the world by the Soviet Union. Her father was arrested at the height of the Stalinist purges when she was fourteen. Stalin directed purges that killed millions and sent many more millions to isolated, harsh labor camps. Most of the people were killed for reasons no one but Stalin understood. Bonner's father was shot, and her mother was exiled to the labor camps. Bonner was wounded twice while serving as a nurse in World War II. After the war, the determined young woman earned a degree in pediatrics from the First Leningrad Medical Institute.

Sakharov and Bonner were married in 1972. She spurred Sakharov on, expanding his network of contacts and giving international dimension to their common cause of human rights. In 1975, Sakharov received the Nobel Peace Prize. The citation called him "the conscience of mankind." With acts of courage and moral conviction, he held the Soviet Union accountable to the world for the treatment of its citizens. It was Bonner who read his statement of acceptance and received the Nobel Peace Prize on his behalf since he was forbid-

The Helsinki Accords

One of Andrey Sakharov's most powerful alliances was with prizewinning novelist Aleksandr Solzhenitsyn (1918–), another internationally known dissident. Helsinki, the capital of Finland, became the location for important international conferences. One such conference, held in 1975, produced the Helsinki Accords. It was attended by thirty-three European nations and the United States and Canada. European security and cooperation in economic, technological, and humanitarian concerns dominated discussions. The Western world saw this agreement among European countries as a significant contribution to détente, or easing of tensions between countries.

Soviet leader **Leonid Brezhnev** (1906–1982; see entry) was among those who signed the agreement. He was greatly enthused about most parts of the agreement but was very displeased with the section addressing human rights. He and other Soviet leaders decided to ignore that part.

After the agreement was signed, Solzhenitsyn and Sakharov, along with Yelena Bonner and a group of prominent civil rights activists, organized the Moscow Helsinki Group. This group monitored human rights violations within the Soviet Union and proved very unpopular with the Soviet government. Many of those who participated in the group were imprisoned or exiled. Nevertheless, the group managed to alert the rest of the world to the oppression of Soviet citizens by their government.

den to travel to Oslo, Norway. He was denied a visa on the grounds that he knew too many state and military secrets of the Cold War. Yuri Andropov (1914–1984), head of the Soviet secret police (KGB), placed Sakharov under constant surveillance.

Gorky

Sakharov helped organize the Committee on Human Rights and openly protested the Soviet military intervention in Afghanistan in December 1979. This enraged Soviet leaders, and in January 1980 Sakharov was stripped of all his state titles, seized by the secret police, sentenced, and removed to internal exile in Nizhny Novgorod, then known as the closed city of Gorky. Bonner was allowed to freely come and go from Gorky. She served as Sakharov's connection to the outside world until 1984, when she was no longer allowed to leave Gorky as well.

Andrey Sakharov reads his Nobel Peace Prize citation in 1975. *Reproduced by permission of the Corbis Corporation.*

Gorky, a port city 250 miles (about 400 kilometers) from Moscow, was not open to Western journalists and foreigners. Sakharov lived there in forced residence until December 1986. Although Sakharov and Bonner were constantly insulted in the Soviet press, they remained somewhat protected by Sakharov's status as a nuclear scientist. In 1986, a work crew arrived at their apartment and installed a telephone. Sakharov soon received a phone call from Soviet president **Mikhail Gorbachev** (1931–; see entry), who lifted the sentence of exile, calling Sakharov and Bonner back to Moscow. Gorbachev had inherited an immensely depressing economic situation in the Soviet Union. Sakharov's official return became a symbol of Gorbachev's *perestroika* (reform) and *glasnost* (openness) as he strove to build a socialist democracy.

Politics

Sakharov emerged from exile to become leader of the new opposition in the Congress of People's Deputies. He was elected in 1989 and appointed as a member of the commission responsible for drafting a new Soviet constitution. On the day he died in December 1989, he had made a plea before the Soviet Congress for multiple political parties and an open market economy. Bonner found him dead of a heart attack in his study later that evening. He did not live to see the crumbling of the Soviet state that came in 1991. Bonner continued to campaign for democracy and human rights in Russia into the twenty-first century and worked tirelessly for the defense and self-determination of all the peoples of the former Soviet Union.

For More Information

Books

Bonner, Elena. *Alone Together*. New York: Knopf, 1986.

Lourie, Richard. *Sakharov: A Biography*. Hanover, MA: Brandeis University Press, 2002.

O'Balance, Edgar. *Tracks of the Bear*. Novato, CA: Presidio Press, 1982.

Sakharov, Andrei. *Sakharov Speaks*. New York: Alfred A. Knopf, 1974.

Time/CBS. *People of the Century*. New York: Simon & Schuster, 1999.

Web Sites

"Andrei Sakharov (1921–1989)." *The American Experience: Race for the Superbomb*. http://www.pbs.org/wgbh/amex/bomb/peopleevents/pande AMEX67.html (accessed on September 14, 2003).

"Yelena Bonner: Human Rights Activist." *Radio Free Europe: Radio Liberty*. http://www.rferl.org/50Years/celebrating/BonnerBiography.html (accessed on September 14, 2003).

Eduard Shevardnadze

Born January 25, 1928
Mamati, Georgia, Soviet Union

Soviet foreign minister and president of Georgia

"Only the policy that is morally right is victorious; only the political idea which takes human freedom as the measure of all things will be invincible."

Eduard Shevardnadze.
Reproduced by permission of the Embassy of Georgia.

Eduard Shevardnadze, foreign minister of the Soviet Union from 1985 to 1990, helped reform and transform the internal structure and international relations of his country. Led by Soviet president **Mikhail Gorbachev** (1931–; see entry), their overall policies were known as *glasnost* (openness) and *perestroika* (restructuring).

Shevardnadze encouraged cooperation and compromise with the United States. He and Gorbachev became the much-heralded architects who brought about the end of the Cold War (1945–91). The Cold War was an intense political and economic rivalry from 1945 to 1991 between the United States and the Soviet Union, falling just short of military conflict. Following the breakup of the Soviet Union in 1991, Shevardnadze returned to his native Georgia to head its government.

Reformist

Eduard Amvros'evich Shevardnadze, the son of a teacher, was born in the village of Mamati in western Georgia. Georgia was then a republic in the Soviet Union. As a youth, he joined the Komsomol, the Communist Youth League, and rose to leadership positions within the organization. He graduated from K'ut'aisi State Pedagogical Institute, where he majored in history.

Shevardnadze joined the Communist Party in 1948 and diligently worked his way through the ranks. Between 1964 and 1968, he served in the Georgian Soviet Socialist Republic (SSR) as the minister of public order maintenance. Between 1968 and 1972, he was the minister of foreign affairs for the Georgia republic. During these years, when corruption was rampant in all levels of the Georgia government, Shevardnadze began his campaign of reform. Ultimately, Shevardnadze removed roughly 75 percent of local Georgian leadership. In 1972, Vassily Mzhevandze, Georgian Communist Party chief, was brought down by Shevardnadze, who then replaced him.

Between 1972 and July 1985, Shevardnadze was the first secretary of the Central Committee of the Communist Party of Georgia. Not only was he successful in his fight against corruption, but he also developed Georgia's economy and culture. His work in these areas greatly exceeded the progress made in the Soviet Union as a whole. His accomplishments did not go unnoticed in Moscow.

Foreign minister

Soviet general secretary **Leonid Brezhnev** (1906–1982; see entry) died in November 1982. Yuri Andropov (1914–1984) replaced Brezhnev as general secretary but died in February 1984. During his short time as the most powerful Soviet, Andropov began to reform government and improve the inefficiency of Soviet industry. In government, his efforts were aimed at the corruption permeating the massive Soviet bureaucracy. In industry, he tried to put more planning and decision making into the hands of local managers. Most importantly, Andropov elevated a younger generation of Communist Party members, including Gorbachev and Shevardnadze, to positions where they could aid his reform efforts.

At Andropov's death, Konstantin Chernenko (1911–1985) took over and allowed the Party's old guard to hang on to power a bit longer. But Chernenko died on March 10,

1985. By 11:00 P.M. that day, the Politburo decided the fifty-four-year-old Gorbachev would be the new leader of the Soviet Union. The next day, Gorbachev called for a reformed Soviet government with more openness *(glasnost)* and a more democratic approach. He called for restructuring of the Soviet bureaucracy *(perestroika)* and wanted to stop the nuclear arms race. An overwhelming majority of the Soviet Communist Party gave enthusiastic support to their leader's new thinking. Although Gorbachev expected to breathe new life into the existing Soviet system, he also believed the Soviet Union would remain communist.

Gorbachev appointed Shevardnadze as his foreign minister. A Georgia native, Shevardnadze was the first foreign minister not from Russia itself. Gorbachev and Shevardnadze both supported economic and democratic experiments in the Eastern European countries that had long been under communist control. Gorbachev also brought Boris Yeltsin (1931–; see box) to Moscow as the first secretary of the Central Committee of the Moscow Communist Party. This position was similar to that of a mayor of a large U.S. city. Yeltsin, wide open to reform, set about revitalizing Moscow's government administration. Yeltsin eventually followed Gorbachev as head of Russia.

Gorbachev and Shevardnadze knew defense spending was hurting the Soviet Union's economy. Shevardnadze found that the money needed for the arms race with the United States left many other problems within the Soviet Union unattended. The two leaders intended to replace antagonism toward the United States with cooperation.

Within a week after Shevardnadze became foreign minister, he announced a summit meeting between the leaders of the Soviet Union and the United States, set for November 1985 in Geneva. Shevardnadze met with U.S. secretary of state George Shultz (1920–) in September to pave the way for the summit meeting. By the end of the November summit, U.S. president **Ronald Reagan** (1911–; served 1981–89; see entry) and Gorbachev had reached a comfortable rapport. Although no decisions on arms reduction were agreed to, the two leaders agreed talks would continue toward scaling down nuclear weapon arsenals.

After more arms reduction talks between the two leaders at Reykjavik, Iceland, in October 1986, Shevardnadze and

Boris Yeltsin

Boris Yeltsin was born in 1931 in Sverdlovsk, Soviet Union. Possessing the soul of a radical reformer, Yeltsin did not join the Communist Party until he was thirty years old, probably because he was impressed with attempts by Soviet leader **Nikita Khrushchev** (1894–1971) to repair the crimes of former Soviet leader Joseph Stalin. Yeltsin rose rapidly within the Communist Party structure. From 1976 to 1985, he served in the Presidium, the important policy-making body of the party. He acquired a reputation as bright, open to new ideas, and willing to act on those ideas.

In 1985, the newly appointed leader of the Soviet Union and Communist Party, Mikhail Gorbachev, brought Yeltsin to Moscow. Within six months, Yeltsin was first secretary of the Moscow Communist Party Central Committee. He brought sweeping reform to the Moscow administration.

Between 1985 and 1990, Gorbachev allowed a new thinking to dominate the Soviet Union and Eastern European nations. By mid-1990, Gorbachev, who never intended for the Communist Party to be brought down, decided he must turn more conservative and go back to hard-line communist rule in order for him to survive politically. Yet in mid-1991, when Gorbachev left Moscow for a holiday, the conservatives who were still disgruntled about Gorbachev's changes attempted a coup to oust Gorbachev completely from rule. Yeltsin stepped in as leader of the reform democratic forces that opposed the

Boris Yeltsin. *Reproduced by permission of Getty Images.*

conservative communists and brought Gorbachev safely back to Moscow. The coup failed, but it was the radical democratic Yeltsin who took power.

Yeltsin became the first president of the Russian Republic. He moved Russia toward a market-based economy. Despite difficulties with Muslim separatists in the region of Chechnya and two heart attacks, Yeltsin was again elected president in 1996. He underwent quintuple heart bypass surgery performed by famed U.S. heart surgeon Michael DeBakey (1908–) and was able to continue running the Russian government. He remained president until 2000 when Vladimir Putin (1953–), Yeltsin's preferred successor, was elected. Yeltsin authored *Against the Grain* (1990) and *The Struggle for Russia* (1994).

Shultz continued to meet regularly for talks and to set the agenda for yet another summit meeting. Meanwhile, Gorbachev was withdrawing Soviet forces from a civil war situation in Afghanistan. Shevardnadze strongly supported this action.

Ending the Cold War

In December 1987, the summit meeting in Washington, D.C., led to the signing of the historic Intermediate-Range Nuclear Force (INF) treaty. For the first time, the United States and Soviet Union agreed to actually eliminate certain nuclear weapons. At the signing on December 8 in the East Room of the White House, Shevardnadze sat in the front row along with other dignitaries.

When Reagan's vice president, **George Bush** (1924– ; served 1989–93; see entry), was inaugurated as the next U.S. president in January 1989, his administration took a much more cautious approach to the Soviets than had Reagan in his last years in office. New secretary of state James A. Baker (1930–), however, made his first visit to Moscow in May 1989 and quickly developed a respectful and trusting relationship with his Soviet counterpart, Shevardnadze. Baker realized Gorbachev and Shevardnadze clearly needed international support to carry out continued reform in the Soviet Union and Eastern Europe, but it was slow in coming from Washington.

In September, Shevardnadze traveled to Moscow to garner support from Washington for the reforms. He and Gorbachev were under increasing pressure from conservative old-line communists to halt reform. In the United States, Shevardnadze flew with Baker to his ranch in Jackson Hole, Wyoming. While there, Shevardnadze discussed the pullback of communist influence and control of Eastern European nations, as well as the difficult ethnic problems arising within the republics of the Soviet Union. The terror campaigns of former Soviet leader **Joseph Stalin** (1879–1953; see entry) were still remembered in various republics and continued to generate the hatred and mistrust of those in Moscow. Shevardnadze said Gorbachev was struggling with keeping those republics, such as the Baltic states and his own Georgia, within the Soviet Union yet give them some sense of reform and local rule. The Baltic states of Lithuania, Latvia, and Estonia had been brought into the Soviet Union by force in 1940, under Stalin, and sought freedom.

In Wyoming, Shevardnadze and Baker also discussed arms control. Shevardnadze informed Baker that the Soviet Union would no longer insist on limiting the so-called "Star Wars" program, a plan to devise a shield of satellites armed with laser weapons over the United States for protection against incoming missiles. Shevardnadze also agreed to dismantle the Soviet early warning system at Krasnoyarsk in Siberia. Baker made no similar concessions, which disappointed both Shevardnadze and Gorbachev. Nevertheless, for the first time, Baker knew the Soviets were genuinely attempting reform and urged the still-reluctant President Bush to support Moscow in its undertakings.

By the fall of 1989, Hungary, Poland, and East Germany had abandoned communism without Moscow intervention. In November, the Berlin Wall, symbol of the Cold War, came down. Many people believed this symbolically and fully ended the Cold War. Gorbachev was awarded the Nobel Peace Prize in June 1990 for his efforts. In spite of Iraqi ties to the Soviet Union, Gorbachev and Shevardnadze fully backed the United States in its intentions to free the Middle Eastern country of Kuwait from the army of Iraqi dictator Saddam Hussein (1937–) in 1990. The Persian Gulf War ensued in 1991, and the United States successfully freed Kuwait.

Despite the easing of international tensions, Gorbachev and Shevardnadze were under continued pressure at home. Conservative communist critics and the Soviet military wanted a much stronger old-line communist rule. Critics bitterly opposed the concessions in Eastern Europe and Germany, and Gorbachev's siding with the United States in the Persian Gulf War. In contrast, the various nationalist forces within many areas of the Soviet Union demanded a lessening

U.S. secretary of state James A. Baker, who worked closely with Soviet foreign minister Eduard Shevardnadze during the Bush years. *Reproduced by permission of AP/Wide World Photos.*

of communist rule. Demonstrations and bloody confrontations had ensued. By the end of 1990, Gorbachev and Shevardnadze were fighting for their political lives.

Gorbachev, while letting Eastern European countries go their own way, always intended to keep the Soviet Union intact and communist. He turned to the conservative faction and vowed to control the nationalistic uprisings. On December 20, Shevardnadze, fearing a return to a hard-line communist dictatorship and the planned use of military force to put down unrest in the Soviet Union, resigned from his foreign minister position.

Conservative Soviet communists attempted a coup in August 1991 against Gorbachev while he and his family vacationed at their villa on the Black Sea. In Moscow, Yeltsin opposed the coup and Shevardnadze immediately supported Yeltsin. Gorbachev was brought back to Moscow, but Yeltsin was now clearly in charge. By the end of August, the Communist Party no longer existed. Shevardnadze would be briefly appointed foreign minister in November 1991, but he served only until the dissolution of the Soviet Union at the end of December. By December 25, 1991, the Union of Soviet Socialist Republics ceased to exist. The Baltic states and at least eight other republics—Armenia, Azerbaijan, Belarus, Kirghizia, Moldavia, Tadzhikistan, Ukraine, and Uzbekistan—had declared independence.

Return to Georgia

Unrest continued in Georgia throughout 1991 and a bloody civil war resulted in the ousting of the old regime president Zviad Gamsakhurdia (1939–1994). The office of president was dissolved. Shevardnadze became the chairman of the State Council of Georgia in 1992, heading the now independent republic of Georgia. In a direct referendum, he was elected to the post with approximately 90 percent of the popular vote.

In his personal life, Shevardnadze was christened in the Georgian Orthodox Church and was given his Christian name, George. Previously, all religious activities had been banned in communist regimes. Also in 1992, he founded the

Eduard Shevardnadze Foundation for Democracy and Revival. As head of Georgia, Shevardnadze first had to deal with separatists in Abkhazia, located in the northwest portion of the region. After considerable military engagements, Abkhazia declared itself an independent state in November 1994. Shevardnadze enrolled Georgia in the Commonwealth of Independent States (CIS), a group of former Soviet republics, in October 1993.

Amidst political criticism in Georgia, Shevardnadze formed a new political party in November, the Citizens' Union of Georgia. In early 1994, he signed a military cooperation treaty with Russia that allowed Russia to operate three military bases in Georgia. This move also angered his critics. Pushing forward, Shevardnadze proposed the office of president be reinstated in Georgia. The Georgia legislature approved this reinstatement in August 1995. In November elections, Shevardnadze was elected president with over 70 percent of the vote and was subsequently reelected on April 9, 2000. He also survived two attempts on his life by reactionary forces, one in August 1995 and the other in February 1998. Shevardnadze continued to focus on developing the economic and political independence of Georgia as well as taking an active role in regional and international activities. He also authored a book of his memoirs, *My Choice,* that became very popular and was translated into a number of languages.

Mrs. Shevardnadze

Nanuli Shevardnadze, like her husband and also like Gorbachev's wife Raisa, was very active publicly. She was president of the international society Georgian Women For Peace and Life, honorary president of the international society "Fetri Mandili" (White Scarf), and editor-in-chief of the newspaper *Mshvidoba Kovelta* (Peace to All). The Shevardnadzes have a son and a daughter.

For More Information

Books

Ekedahl, Carolyn M. *The Wars of Eduard Shevardnadze.* University Park: Pennsylvania State University Press, 1997.

Isaacs, Jeremy, and Taylor Downing. *Cold War: An Illustrated History, 1945–1991*. Boston: Little, Brown and Company, 1998.

Kaiser, Robert G. *Why Gorbachev Happened: Triumphs and Failure*. New York: Simon & Schuster, 1991.

Shevardnadze, Eduard. *The Future Belongs to Freedom*. New York: Free Press, 1991.

Solovyov, Vladimir, and Elena Klepikova. *Yuri Andropov: A Secret Passage into the Kremlin*. New York: Macmillan, 1983.

Web Sites

"Eduard Shevardnadze." *The Georgia Foundation*. http://www.osgf.ge/all/ika/eduard_shevardnadze.htm (accessed on September 14, 2003).

"President of Georgia: Eduard Shevardnadze." *Parliament of Georgia*. http://www.parliament.ge/gov/bio_shevardnadze.html (accessed on September 14, 2003).

Joseph Stalin

Born December 21, 1879
Gori, Georgia, Russia
Died March 5, 1953
Kuntsevo, Russia, Soviet Union

Premier of the Soviet Union

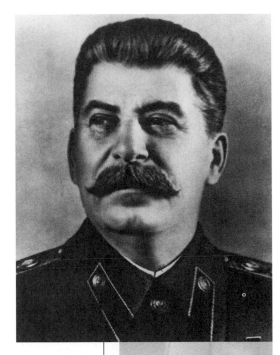

"A single death is a tragedy; a million deaths is a statistic."

Joseph Stalin was the brutal and absolute leader of the communist Soviet Union from 1929 until his death in 1953. By the late 1930s, Stalin staunchly opposed the growth across Europe of the Nazi Party of Germany's Adolf Hitler (1889–1945). When cutting deals with Hitler failed to halt the Nazi army, Stalin allied with the United States, Great Britain, and France during World War II (1939–45).

At the end of the war, Stalin immediately imposed communist rule over the countries of Eastern Europe, giving government positions to men who adhered to the strict Communist Party line and answered directly to him. Yet soon the Soviets became locked in the Cold War (1945–91). The Cold War was an intense political and economic rivalry between the United States and the Soviet Union, falling just short of military conflict. Stalin was the dominant figure in the Soviet Union for twenty-four years, a larger-than-life personality, a hero to many, and yet a ruthless and feared ruler.

Joseph Stalin. *Reproduced by permission of the Corbis Corporation.*

Early years

Stalin was born Iosif Vissarionovich Dzhugashvili in Gori, Georgia, in the Tiflis province of southwestern Russia, to an alcoholic shoemaker and a devoutly religious peasant woman of the Orthodox church. As a young adult, Iosif changed his name to Stalin, which meant "man of steel." Stalin owed his education to his mother, who planned for him to become a priest. His father died when he was about ten years old, but his industrious mother saw that he attended Orthodox elementary school in Gori. Although small in stature, Stalin excelled in school and was generally the brightest student in his classes.

In 1894, he entered the Tbilisi Orthodox Seminary in the Georgian city of Tbilisi. There he was introduced to a wide range of literature and exposed to new philosophical and social ideas. He studied the teachings of English scientist Charles Darwin (1809–1892); the revolutionary social ideology of German philosopher Karl Marx (1818–1883), considered the "father" of communism; and Russian Vladimir Lenin (1870–1924).

Marxism had just reached Georgia and its ideas captivated young Stalin, who had come from the poorest of peasant backgrounds. The communist movement opposed the longtime rule of the Russian tsarist, or royal, government, whose members lived lavishly while all other Russians lived in poverty. Communism represented a new ideal, one where government consisted of a single party, the Communist Party, which controlled all aspects of people's lives. In economics, communism prohibited private ownership of property and business so all goods produced and wealth accumulated were supposed to be shared equally by all. In contrast, a democratic system of government, such as that of the United States, allowed multiple political parties whose members were elected to various government offices by popular vote of the people. Private property is allowed and encouraged, while prices of goods are determined by competition in the marketplace.

Communist revolutionary

By the late 1890s, Stalin dedicated his life to communist revolutionary ideas and joined the Social Democratic Party in 1898. He was expelled from the seminary in 1899 for revolutionary activities, including spreading communist propaganda to Georgian railroad workers. Between 1900 and 1917, Stalin, by then a communist underground organizer and agitator, was arrested, released, arrested, exiled, and released over twelve times. The early Social Democratic movement split in the early 1900s into the Bolshevik (communist) faction and the Mensheviks (the more democratic minority party). Stalin sided with the Bolsheviks as the party organized in about 1903. Stalin's activities in Georgia actually caught Lenin's attention, but the two had little contact before 1912.

Stalin, as a Bolshevik and a disciple of Lenin, was in conflict with many of the Social Democrats in Georgia who were Mensheviks. He moved to Saint Petersburg in 1912, where he first adopted the name Stalin, and became a member of the Bolshevik Party's Central Committee, its primary leadership committee. For a time, he served as editor of *Pravda*, the Bolshevik or communist (the terms came to be used interchangeably) newspaper.

A young Joseph Stalin (here, in 1899) joined the Social Democratic Party in 1898.
Reproduced by permission of The Granger Collection Ltd.

Life as an underground revolutionary was not stable and Stalin was in exile in Siberia by early February 1917. He managed to return to Petrograd (later called Leningrad during the Cold War and then Saint Petersburg after the Cold War) in March 1917. The Bolshevik Revolution toppled the tsarist government in October 1917. In the new Soviet government, Stalin relocated to Moscow and served as the people's commissar of Nationality Affairs between 1917 and 1922. He held on to the position during this period of instability and civil war, which ended with the communists firmly in power. As people's commissar, Stalin took the responsibility of holding together the vast ethnic minorities within the Russian Empire.

Stalin gained a reputation as an efficient organizer for the communists fighting during the civil war. He also served

on various defense commissions and as political advisor to
fighters and to local communities. For the first time, Stalin
condoned brutal killings and torture to advance communist
political ideas. It was at this time that Stalin developed a hatred of the Western powers such as the United States, Great
Britain, and France, who were helping supply those opposed
to communism. Years later, after World War II, this hatred
played a part in Stalin's foreign policy during the Cold War.

General secretary

From 1921 onward, Lenin's and Stalin's ideas began to
conflict. Lenin did not entirely approve of Stalin's fiercely nationalist approach. Nationalism refers to the strong loyalty of
a person or group to its own country. Stalin increasingly expected all factions and parts of the Russian Empire to march
in unison with him and his ideals. Lenin was crippled by a
stroke in late 1922, and before his death in 1924 he all but

called for Stalin's removal, saying Stalin employed crude tactics and would not properly use caution. Lenin's concerns and subsequent warnings, however, came too late.

In 1922, Stalin was appointed general secretary of the Communist Party's Central Committee. At the time, the position was an unheralded administrative post. However, Stalin, with his crafty political instinct, managed in a short time to turn the post into the dominant authority of the Soviet Union. In doing so, he pulled all control into his camp and away from his chief rival, Leon Trotsky (1879–1940). Stalin held the general secretary post until his death in 1953. For decades after Stalin's death, it remained the key position of central leadership in the Soviet Union. Stalin used the office to brilliantly outmaneuver various political alliances that might have drained power from him. Outwitting and defaming all rivals, he was firmly in control of the Communist Party and country by 1927.

Collectivization and industrialization

In 1928 and 1929, Stalin tossed out Lenin's economic policies and launched into a government campaign to reform Soviet agriculture and focus industry on building large industrial complexes for heavy construction. In agriculture, Stalin destroyed the prosperous peasant farmers and ordered rapid collectivization of all agriculture. Private ownership of land was banned, and farmers were collected, or grouped together, to work the land. Much of what they produced was turned over to the government, with approximately twenty-five million farmers being regrouped on state farms.

Although many farmers resisted and tried to hold on to their land, most resisters were shot or sent to a system of labor camps known as the Gulag. Because of the displacement and disruption of farming, approximately ten million people died from famine. Those sent to the Gulag became the slave labor for Stalin's heavy industry construction programs. By the late 1930s, Soviet agriculture patterns under collectivization were set and would last for most of the twentieth century. The Soviet Union soon became second only to the United States in heavy industrial output. Light industry, however, such as the production of consumer goods, was ignored.

Personality cult and purges of terror

By the early 1930s, Stalin ruled over the Communist Party in such totality that all party members and military elite answered only to him. Reaching into all aspects of Soviet culture, Stalin even fancied himself the ultimate expert and judge of the arts, such as literature, poetry, theater, and music. He controlled the education of Soviet youth and the daily press. Many Soviets followed Stalin in a cult-like fashion. The term "adulation," meaning excessive flattering or admiration, was often used in praise of Stalin.

In 1934, Stalin decided to rid any lingering opposition to his rule by the use of terror, torture, and execution. Stalin began a ferocious campaign that by 1939 successfully eliminated almost all individuals of the old Bolshevik party, and upwards of 70 percent of leaders in the Communist Party and military. Many of the best-known persons in the country unexplainably disappeared.

Stalin also ordered showy trials of many leaders to make a public example of them and encourage them to confess to false charges. Stalin's purges struck not only the top party leadership, but the local levels and even the arts community. He introduced the phrase "enemy of the people," which automatically made proof of any guilt unnecessary. Brutal acts were carried out against "enemies," frequently without any grounds, and millions of Soviets were murdered. During this period, however, most Soviets thought of the hostilities as what must happen in a class struggle or during class warfare. Stalin hid his ruthlessness behind the idea that many must die before the common people could rise up.

World War II

Although Stalin's domestic agendas had occupied most of his time in the 1930s, on the foreign front he was a practical politician. He strengthened the Soviet economy and his own lock on power by broadening trade and diplomatic relationships through Europe and even with the United States. While praising U.S. president Franklin D. Roosevelt (1882–1945; served 1933–45), Stalin at the same time kept his distance, saying Roosevelt was "captain of the modern bourgeois [middle or upper class] world." Stalin also impressed upon Western nations that the Soviet Union was an enemy of the menacing Nazi German leader Hitler. Stalin tried to make alliances with France and Great Britain against the growing threat of Hitler's Nazi army. Unsuccessful, Stalin decided to try and deal with Hitler himself. In August 1939, to the surprise and shock of Western leaders, Stalin signed a treaty with Hitler that in turn led to the Nazi invasion of Poland and the start of World War II.

When the Nazi army later invaded the Soviet Union in June 1941, Stalin was stunned. Quickly regaining his composure, Stalin stayed in Moscow, assumed the chairmanship of the State Committee of Defense, and declared himself the Supreme Commander of the armed forces. Although never visiting front lines, he gathered a highly competent group of generals and was able to understand complex military strategies. By 1942, Stalin directed successful counterattacks at the battles of Stalingrad and Kursk.

In 1943, Stalin met with British prime minister **Winston Churchill** (1874–1965; see entry) and U.S. president Roosevelt in Tehran, Iran. The three became known as the "Big Three." The first postwar planning took place with Stalin largely having his way. Stalin successfully argued that the Soviet army and people were bearing the brunt of the ground fighting. By war's end, millions would have died. He stressed that the Soviet Union must protect itself by ensuring a strong influence in Eastern European countries such as Poland, Romania, Hungary, Czechoslovakia, Albania, and Bulgaria. These countries would then serve as a barrier between the Soviets and Western Europe.

Throughout its history, Russia had periodically been invaded by groups from Western Europe, and Stalin felt he must protect his country from future attacks. Stalin, Churchill, and Roosevelt met again in the Soviet town of Yalta in 1945, and later that year Stalin met in Potsdam, Germany, with U.S. president **Harry S. Truman** (1884–1972; served 1945–53; see entry), who had replaced Roosevelt upon his death; Churchill; and **Clement R. Attlee** (1883–1967; see entry), who would replace Churchill. At that time, the "Red" (Soviet) Army occupied all of Eastern Europe and half of Germany. Poland was a major point of contention, but Stalin was able to satisfy Western leaders by promising to quickly hold open elections in Poland. In actuality, those elections would never be held.

Also during the Yalta meeting, Roosevelt and Stalin negotiated that the Soviets would enter the Pacific front in the war against Japan for Roosevelt, allowing the Soviets to occupy northern Korea and the islands north of Japan. These agreements assured Stalin a "sphere of influence," or leadership, over vast regions, including Eastern Europe and Asia. When the United States dropped atomic bombs on Hiroshima and Nagasaki, Japan, in August 1945, the war with Japan ended before the Soviets became highly involved. The United States was, at the time, the only nation possessing atomic weapons.

Cold War begins

At the end of World War II, the United States and the Soviet Union emerged as the two superpowers of the world. Stalin established communist leaders at the head of governments of Eastern Europe. Wary of future East-West relations, Stalin realized the United States must not be allowed to maintain an atomic weapon monopoly. In mid-1945, Stalin placed Lavrenty Beria (1899–1953; see box) in charge of organizing the Soviet atomic bomb project. The arms race soon became the primary way America and the Soviets kept score as to who was winning the Cold War.

Stalin worked to control gains made by the Soviets. Western leaders soon realized that any negotiations with Stalin had to be resolved under his terms or not at all. At first, knowing the tremendous sacrifices the Soviet people had made during the war, sentiment among Western leaders was, in general, to back off from demands conflicting with those of Stalin. What to do with postwar Germany was the first challenge; it had been divided into four occupied sectors—Soviet, American, British, and French. Stalin was intent on dismantling German industrial equipment and carting it off to the Soviet Union to be reassembled. He was determined to so weaken Germany that it could never be a threat to the Soviet Union again. Conversely, the three Western powers began to view a rebuilt, revitalized, and reunified Germany as a block to the spread of communism to the West. Eventually, these basic differences resulted in a permanently divided Germany—the closed Soviet-supported German Democratic Republic, or East Germany, and the open democratic U.S.- and British-supported Federal Republic of Germany, or West Germany.

Lavrenty Beria

Born in southern Russia in Georgia on March 29, 1899, Lavrenty Pavlovich Beria would become head of the KGB, the dreaded Soviet secret police, and the organizational chief of the Soviet atomic bomb project. Svetlana Alliluyeva, Stalin's daughter, often referred to Beria as "my father's evil genius."

Young Beria, much as Stalin had been, was caught up in the communist movement sweeping over Russia and joined the Communist Party in 1917, the same year the revolutionary Bolsheviks triumphed over Russia's tsarist government. Committed to the cause and not averse to brutal tactics, Beria quickly rose by 1921 to the leadership of Cheka, the forerunner of the KGB. Between 1921 and 1931, he "eliminated" anyone who deviated from communist ideals or orders. Stalin appointed Beria head of the Soviet People's Commissariat for Internal Affairs (NKVD). NKVD was another early name for the KGB. Beria specialized in terror, torture, executions, and for the lucky ones, facilitating banishment to the Gulag, the harsh Soviet prison system. Beria destroyed tens of thousands of lives.

Beria was also put in charge of efforts to build a Soviet bomb, with **Igor**

Lavrenty Beria. *Courtesy of the Library of Congress.*

Kurchatov (1903–1960; see entry) as the organization's top scientist. Beria constantly bellowed to Kurchatov, "You will be camp dust," if the scientist was unsuccessful in developing the bomb. Upon Stalin's death in March 1953, Beria was one of a handful of leaders assuming they might take over from Stalin. Yet others, including Nikita Khrushchev, saw to it that Beria was falsely accused of being an agent for the West and was shot in late 1953. The announcement of his death was made in December 1953.

Stalin not only strengthened his hold on Eastern European countries but also supported communist uprisings in Greece, Turkey, and Iran. At Britain's urging, the United States intervened to stop communist takeovers in those countries. The Cold War rivalry was becoming increasingly defined. Stalin was convinced communism would eventually spread to a worldwide movement and overcome the democratic, capitalist countries of the West. The North Atlantic Treaty Organization (NATO) was established in 1949 for mutual protection of Western countries, and Stalin formed Cominform to direct communist activities around the world.

In September 1949, the Soviets successfully detonated an atomic bomb, eliminating the U.S. monopoly on atomic weapons. About the same time, Chinese communists successfully took power in China. Then in 1950, the Korean War (1950–53) started between the communist North Korea and the democratic U.S.-supported South Korea. At this point, Stalin and the spread of communism were greatly feared in the United States and Western Europe, still trying to recover from World War II. Yet unknown to Western leaders, by the early 1950s, Stalin would slip into a paranoia so severe his mind would become completely occupied by internal matters.

Great terror continued

In Eastern European countries after World War II, tensions were high at the local levels between Stalin's communists, the local communists, and anticommunists. One of the countries, Yugoslavia, under leader **Josip Broz Tito** (1892–1980; see entry) was able to maintain some independence apart from Stalin's influence. Partly due to Tito's rebellion, Stalin began an intense Sovietization of Eastern Europe in 1948. The central Communist Party in Moscow had men in place in Eastern Europe, who ruled the countries with absolute iron control. Repression of any independent thought and total conformity to party line were demanded. Any dissent was punished brutally. The countries were forced, between 1948 and 1953, to adhere to Stalin's Soviet plan of agricultural collectivization and to turn all manufacturing into heavy industry. Stalin demanded that his instructions be carried out without question throughout Eastern Europe.

To be sure both local Communist Party officials and the general public adhered to his rule, Stalin used his "show trials." False accusations were made against various leaders. Under torture, they would usually confess and then be executed. Two of the most famous show trials involved Foreign Minister Laszlo Rajk (1909–1949) in Hungary and Rudolf

Slansky (1901–1952), general secretary of the Communist Party in Czechoslovakia. Eventually, one in four Czech party members disappeared during Stalin's reign of terror.

Inside the Soviet Union, Stalin obsessed over total party loyalty. He saw an enemy or conspiracy around every corner. Just as in the 1930s when he called on the Soviets to uncover "enemies of the people," Stalin now ordered the addition of more and more labor camps for the Gulag system. One of the most concentrated, brutal purges occurred against the citizens of Leningrad in 1949. Upwards of one thousand party leaders from Leningrad were executed. Stalin's top "henchman" or ally was chief of the KGB (the secret police) Lavrenty Beria, who was also in charge of the Soviet atomic bomb project.

Paranoid end

According to Stalin's daughter, Svetlana Alliluyeva, her father increasingly and steadily lost touch with reality the last three years of his life. He completely isolated himself at the Kremlin in Moscow or at his nearby country home in Kuntsevo. Stalin was suspicious of everyone, and at the Nineteenth Party Congress in October 1952, he so feared everyone in the room that he sat alone at the end of a long table. At this time, he was also conjuring up an anti-Semitic (Jewish) campaign.

Those around Stalin continued to be terrorized by him and KGB chief Beria. Stalin constantly made up stories that his closest staff and even his family were in conspiracies against him. In his last months in early 1953, he was preparing to possibly purge the people, including the doctors, of whom he was suspicious. Stalin suffered a stroke sometime during the night of February 28, 1953. He was not discovered until late the next afternoon, for his staff had feared entering his room without his permission. Stalin died on March 5, 1953.

Stalin left behind a Soviet Union ruled by a huge government bureaucracy of ministries, party-ruled legislative bodies, and secret police. For many common Soviet citizens, Stalin had been the extremely popular "father" of the Soviet Union. Thousands paid their respects in Moscow, and his body was put on display in the Lenin Mausoleum. His ultimate successor, however, **Nikita Khrushchev** (1894–1971; see entry), was bold enough to reveal the "crimes of Stalin" in a secret speech to the Twentieth Party Congress in October 1956. Partly as a result of this speech, Stalin's body was removed from the mausoleum and buried at the Kremlin Wall.

For More Information

Books

Antonov-Ovseyenko, Anton. *The Time of Stalin: Portrait of a Tyranny.* New York: Harper and Row, 1980.

Conquest, Robert. *Stalin: Breaker of Nations.* New York: Viking, 1991.

Isaacs, Jeremy, and Taylor Downing. *Cold War: An Illustrated History, 1945–1991.* Boston: Little, Brown and Company, 1998.

Lewis, Jonathan, and Phillip Whitehead. *Stalin: A Time for Judgement.* New York: Pantheon Books, 1990.

Tucker, Robert C. *Stalin in Power: The Revolution from Above, 1928–1941.* New York: W. W. Norton & Company, 1990.

Ulam, Adam B. *Stalin: The Man and His Era.* New York: Viking Press, 1973.

Margaret Thatcher

Born October 13, 1925
Grantham, Lincolnshire, England

British prime minister

It was in May 1979 that Margaret Thatcher became Britain's first female prime minister. She would be reelected in 1983 and again in 1987 to become the first British prime minister of the twentieth century to win three consecutive general elections. Thatcher served for eleven-and-a-half years until her resignation in November 1990. Her Conservative Party victory in 1979 was a major triumph over the Labor Party, which had held power for much of the previous fifty years.

The perceived threat of the communist Soviet Union had come to be a dominant concern of the Western world at the time. The North Atlantic Treaty Organization (NATO), an alliance of Western-styled democracies, was founded in 1949 at the key instigation of Great Britain. It was a response to the growing efforts by the Soviets to control Eastern European countries. This international cooperation between the United States and Western European countries proved far more effective in responding to the Soviet threat than the United Nations, which also included the Soviets and other nations under Soviet control.

"We want a society where people are free to make choices, to make mistakes, to be generous and compassionate. This is what we mean by a moral society; not a society where the state is responsible for everything, and no one is responsible for the state."

Margaret Thatcher.

437

By December 1979, six months after Thatcher took office, NATO agreed to deploy medium-range nuclear weapons in Western Europe. This put the Soviet Union on the defensive and forced it to decide how to react to NATO's move. The Soviets could no longer be confident of overcoming NATO at one level of weaponry without triggering a response at a higher level that could lead to a full-scale nuclear war. Thatcher was immediately thrust into a situation of rapidly declining relations between the Soviets and the West.

Modest beginnings

Born Margaret Hilda Roberts, Thatcher was was the second daughter born to Alfred Roberts and Beatrice Ethel Stephenson. Her sister, Muriel, was born four years before Margaret, in May 1921. Their father was a grocer who became active in local politics. He ultimately became mayor of Grantham. Margaret was especially close to her father and spoke of him as a major influence in her life.

Like most everyone at the time, Thatcher's life was transformed by World War II (1939–45). It overshadowed her entire adolescence from the ages of fourteen to nineteen. A life of thriftiness was the rule, as food and goods were strictly rationed. Thatcher was an excellent student with a competitive nature. She knew education was the key to escape life in the small town where she had grown up. Her social life in Grantham was centered around church, school, and her home life.

Young Margaret came to political awareness just as an international crisis began to dominate the news. There were twenty-one German air raids on the town of Grantham alone, and many bombs fell close to her home and school. She worked as a volunteer during the war and carried a gas mask with her to school. The war influenced Thatcher's political development and specifically her approach to international relations.

Education

Thatcher was educated at Kesteven and Grantham's all-girls high school, winning a scholarship to Somerville College, Oxford. This was a major accomplishment for a woman in the early 1940s from a small town. She received a degree in chemistry and another in law. She also received a master's degree from Oxford. While an undergraduate, she served as president of the Oxford University Conservative Association.

Upon graduation, Thatcher went to work as a research chemist for an industrial firm for four years, from 1947 to 1951. She continued her interest in politics by running in two parliamentary elections in 1950 and 1951. She lost both races. In 1951, she married Denis Thatcher, whom she had met through their common interest in politics. They became parents in 1953 with the birth of their twins, Carol and Mark.

 "Feminine Factor"

The British media loved to dwell on the "feminine factor" during Margaret Thatcher's time in office. They often reported on supposed clashes between the prime minister and the queen of England. Thatcher tried to handle it all with a sense of humor. "I would always be asked how it felt to be a woman prime minister. I would reply: I don't know: I've never experienced the alternative."

Politics

In 1959, Thatcher was elected to one of the best Conservative Party seats in the country as a member of Parliament for Finchley, in north London. Thatcher had achieved her goal of becoming a member of the House of Commons. She was to retain this position for twenty years, through six parliaments, until she became prime minister.

Thatcher's first ministerial appointment (administrative head of a department) came in 1961, and she rose quickly through the ranks to the position of education minister in 1970. In 1974, she also worked on environmental issues and then treasury matters as part of the British Cabinet. In 1975, Thatcher was elected leader of the Conservative Party. This made her leader of the opposition (the party not in power) and the first woman to head a political party in Great Britain. She remained head of the Conservative Party for fifteen years until her retirement in 1990.

At the top

When she won her first general election in 1979, Thatcher inherited two primary challenges as the new prime minister. The first issue was the long-term economic decline in Great Britain, largely owing to over thirty years of socialism (government control of industry and extensive social welfare programs) in her country. The other issue was the growing Soviet threat to Europe and the world.

Regarding the Soviet threat, Thatcher repeatedly tried to resolve five different objectives during her time in office. First, there were only limited resources available for defense, particularly with the British economy growing slowly or not at all. This meant that if the defense expenditure was increased, it was vital that a more efficient use of government funds on domestic programs be achieved. Second, Britain needed to maintain its own interests in the world on a regular basis. Third, Britain had to help ensure that NATO responded effectively to the steadily increasing Soviet military threat. Fourth, as part of her third objective, it was vital to maintain Western unity behind American leadership. Britain, among European countries, and Thatcher, among European leaders, were uniquely placed to do that. Britain had always maintained a close relationship with the United States. Lastly, nowhere more than in defense and foreign policy did her own "Thatcher's Law" apply—that in politics, the unexpected always happens. Thatcher believed one must always be prepared and able to face whatever happened to come one's way.

The Soviet Union

When Thatcher came to power, the Cold War was at its height and she inherited Britain's "dual track" agreement with NATO in dealing with it. The Cold War was not so much a fighting war, but primarily a battle of ideologies (ideas or opinions) between the communist Soviet Union and the democratic, capitalist United States. The agreement relied on modernizing NATO's medium-range weapons while at the same time engaging in talks with the Soviet Union on arms control. The question in Western Europe was always about which should come first.

Thatcher felt the Soviet Union could not be trusted to stop seeking an expanded influence in Europe, as they had in the Third World throughout the 1970s. (Third World refers to poor underdeveloped or economically developing nations in Africa, Asia, and Latin America.) By 1980, nuclear weapons were seen as a deterrent, or obstacle, to war, not a means of waging war. Thatcher knew that the essence of deterrence was

U.S. president Ronald Reagan (far left) and British prime minister Margaret Thatcher (next to him) developed a close partnership during the 1980s. Here, the two leaders and their spouses, Nancy Reagan and Denis Thatcher, attend a function at the White House in 1988.
Reproduced by permission of the Corbis Corporation.

its ability to pose a serious threat of retaliation to the Soviets. The Soviets had nuclear weapons targeted on every major European and British city. Britons were vulnerable to a Soviet first strike. If the Soviets doubted America's willingness to launch strategic nuclear weapons in defense of Britain, they would never doubt that the Conservative Party-led British government would do so.

Britain, however, was far behind its industrial competitors in maintaining a suitable defense. Needing modern nuclear weapons in place immediately, Thatcher formed a renewed partnership with America under U.S. president **Ronald Reagan** (1911–; served 1981–89; see entry) to acquire them as part of the Trident project. Meanwhile, the Soviets wanted to split the alliance of NATO. They used propaganda (giving out information to support an idea) to achieve this end. As a result, Thatcher's main emphasis came to be on keeping the alliance together, united behind America's leadership. It was very important that American public opinion remain committed to Western Europe. Britain's security and the free

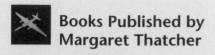

Books Published by Margaret Thatcher

In Defence of Freedom. Buffalo: Prometheus Books, 1987.

The Downing Street Years. New York: HarperCollins, 1993.

The Path to Power. New York: Harper-Collins, 1995.

The Collected Speeches of Margaret Thatcher. Edited by Robin Harris. New York: HarperCollins, 1997.

Statecraft: Strategies for a Changing World. New York: HarperCollins, 2002.

West's interests depended on the continued long-term relationship between the United States and Britain. Thatcher's foreign policy was centered on dealing with the Soviet Union.

Setting the world right

By the early 1980s, the Soviets were at the limit in their expenditure on defense. Internal economic difficulties were increasingly evident, and they could not keep up with the United States in a nuclear arms race much longer. If they could not keep up in weaponry, then the other primary option for remaining equal in world prominence was through arms control and economic trade negotiations.

Thatcher made an effort to establish a realistic relationship with the Soviet Union. The Soviets had reason to do business with her because it had been clearly demonstrated Thatcher had influence with Reagan. She had become Reagan's chief ally in NATO. Invited to visit the Soviet Union, Thatcher visited and returned to the Soviet Union on several occasions. It was there she met new Soviet leader **Mikhail Gorbachev** (1931–; see entry) in 1985.

Gorbachev's steady rise to power and the effects of his economic and political reforms were what ultimately unleashed the forces that swept away the Soviet communist system, and as a result, the Soviet Union itself. The Soviets could not control the public demand for major social reform within the Soviet Union's fifteen republics and in Eastern Europe. A cascade of events beginning in 1989 led to the breakup of the Soviet Union in 1991.

Thatcher's legacy

Margaret Thatcher played a unique role in the world changes leading up to the twenty-first century. She sparked the triumph of capitalism and the collapse of Soviet communism in promoting free economic markets and freedom of thought and speech. Thatcher resigned as prime minister of Great Britain in 1990, however, after losing support of the Conservative Party over differences concerning post–Cold War European policy. Thatcher left public life in 2002.

For More Information

Books

Campbell, John. *Margaret Thatcher*. London: Jonathan Cape, 2000.

Thatcher, Margaret. *The Downing Street Years*. New York: HarperCollins Publishers, 1993.

Thatcher, Margaret. *The Path to Power*. New York: HarperCollins Publishers, 1995.

Time/CBS News. *People of the Century*. New York: Simon & Schuster, 1999.

Zilboorg, Caroline, ed. *Women's Firsts*. Detroit: Gale, 1997.

Josip Broz Tito

Born May 7, 1892
Kumrovec, Croatia, Austria-Hungary
Died May 4, 1980
Ljubljana, Yugoslavia

President of Yugoslavia and revolutionary

Josip Broz Tito established a communist government in the country then known as Yugoslavia. Fiercely independent, Tito managed to successfully distance himself and his country from Soviet leader **Joseph Stalin** (1879–1953; see entry) and Soviet control. During the entire Cold War period, Tito took his country down a liberalized path in agriculture, management of workers, trade with Western nations, art, education, and travel between Western nations and Yugoslavia. The Cold War was an intense political and economic rivalry from 1945 to 1991 between the United States and the Soviet Union falling just short of military conflict. Tito stressed nonalignment, the right of nations to be neutral and not align with either superpower, the United States or the Soviet Union.

Early years

Josip Broz was born the seventh child in a large peasant family of fifteen children (he acquired the name Tito in 1934). His hometown of Kumrovec was located northwest of Zagreb, the capital of the province of Croatia. Broz attended

Josip Broz Tito.

school for five years from ages seven to twelve, then was apprenticed to a locksmith. He completed his training in 1910 and joined the Social Democratic Party (Communist Party) of Croatia-Slavonia the same year.

After traveling and working around the region, Broz was drafted into the Austro-Hungarian Imperial Army. He was assigned to fight on the Russian front in 1914 when World War I (1914–18) broke out. Seriously wounded and captured by the Russians in 1915, he was treated at a Russian hospital then detained at a prisoner of war camp. Broz became fluent in the Russian language and also studied the Marxist ideas of the Bolshevik, or communist, revolutionaries. Marxist philosophy was based on the teachings of German philosopher Karl Marx (1818–1883), considered the father of communism. Communism is a system of government in which a single party, the Communist Party, controls all aspects of people's lives. In economic theory, it prohibits private ownership of property and business so that all goods produced and wealth accumulated are shared relatively equally by all. The term "Bolshevik" was later replaced with the term communist.

Broz decided to join the Bolshevik cause and headed for Petrograd, formerly Saint Petersburg, to demonstrate in the streets. He was arrested and imprisoned for a short time until the October Revolution of 1917. In the October Revolution, Bolsheviks overthrew the tsar, or royalty, and put themselves in power in Russia. The Russian Civil War followed, and Broz joined a Red Guard unit. "Red" is a term that often refers to communists, and the Red Army was indeed communist. In 1920, Broz married a Russian woman, Pelege ja Beloussaowa, and they returned to Croatia.

Rise in the Communist Party

A confirmed communist revolutionary, Broz joined the Communist Party of Yugoslavia (CPY). He steadily rose through the ranks, holding several leadership positions and organizing trade unions. In 1928, Broz's revolutionary activities again led to his arrest and imprisonment, this time for five years. Upon his release in 1934, Broz adopted the pseudonym "Tito." He would use the name Tito to work underground in the CPY, since it was banned by the royal Yugoslav dictatorship in power at the time.

In 1935, Tito went back to Russia to work for the Comintern, a Soviet-sponsored organization to promote communism internationally. By 1937, Tito returned to the CPY. As a result of Stalin's purges, many CPY leaders were murdered or disappeared. Tito handpicked new leaders and rebuilt the party. Tito's CPY was ready when World War II (1939–45) started.

World War II—Partisans

In 1941, when the German army invaded the Soviet Union, Tito formed the Partisans to fight German and Italian armies as they moved into Yugoslav territories. Tito named himself military commander about this time and also became known as Marshal. For the rest of his life, he would frequently be called Marshal Tito.

The Partisans came from the well-organized underground cells of the CPY. They staunchly withstood the German army attacks in the first half of 1943 and defeated their rivals, the Serbian Chetniks. The big three Allied powers—the United States, Great Britain, and the Soviet Union—met in Tehran, Iran, in 1943 and officially recognized the Partisans. As a result, Allied aid was parachuted in to support the victorious and continuously strengthening Partisans. Tito consolidated his power at the end of World War II by purging, just as Stalin had done, those who opposed him. From his many loyalists, he formed a large army and secret police. By late 1945, the Communist Party was firmly in control of all of the Yugoslav territories. Tito proclaimed the area as the Federal People's Republic of Yugoslavia in November 1945.

Stalin versus Titoism

Immediately after World War II, the Soviets continued to occupy the countries of Eastern Europe, where communist parties had taken control of several governments. Some officials were local communists and some were appointed by Stalin. Then in 1948, a new, more centralized Sovietization of Eastern Europe began. Each nation was to be controlled by its Communist Party but subject to absolute control from Moscow. Tito immediately balked. Those in Belgrade, the cap-

ital of Yugoslavia, would not seek prior approval from Moscow for their policies and activities. Tito had ignored Stalin's suggestions on how to run the government and the economy. Stalin was enraged, and was also angry at Tito for his support of communists in the Greek Civil War, a war in which Stalin did not want to be involved. Stalin was further displeased with Tito's relations with Bulgaria and Albania.

Yugoslav leader Josip Broz Tito (far right) stands with other men in the mountains of Yugoslavia during World War II in 1944. *Reproduced by permission of Getty Images.*

For its continuing rebellious attitude, Stalin expelled Yugoslavia from the Cominform. He imposed an economic blockade that negatively impacted Yugoslavia but not its government or people's lives. Stalin even considered military action but refrained. The independent stance taken by Tito came to be known as Titoism. Titoism became the reason Stalin used to further crack down on communist parties in other Eastern European countries. Between 1948 and 1953, the year of Stalin's death, Soviet-styled communism was imposed on the Eastern Bloc. Collectivization of agriculture and development of heavy manufacturing while ignoring consumer goods became the rule. Collectivization meant elimination of all privately owned farms and grouping farmers together to work state-owned land, returning most food produced to the state.

Meanwhile, Tito used his secret police for another purge and a "reeducation" of communists who still supported Stalin. While the economy of the Soviet Union and Eastern European countries remained highly centralized, Tito began a program of decentralization. He began experimenting with allowing worker self-management in local areas. He allowed workers to form councils, and though he did not collectivize smaller farms, he did require them to supply the state with large portions of their goods. Tito also turned to the Western countries for loans and offered some cooperation with the North Atlantic Treaty Organization (NATO), a peacetime alliance of the United States and eleven other nations, and a key factor in the attempt to contain communism. He signed a trade agreement with the United States in 1949 and eventually received $150 million in aid from the United States. Tito withstood hostility from the Soviet Union and maintained his independent communist state.

Reconciliation

When Stalin died in 1953, Tito decided to explore a somewhat reconciled relationship with the new Soviet leadership. In May 1955, Soviet leader **Nikita Khrushchev** (1894–1971; see entry) surprised other communist leaders when he went to Yugoslavia and visited with Tito. Khrushchev said it was time to "bury the hatchet" and reestablish the Soviet Union's relationship with Tito and Yugoslavia.

Nevertheless, Tito's and the Soviet Union's relationship would run hot and cold. It was particularly cold one year
later with the Soviet intervention in Hungary to suppress unrest among the population. The Soviets blamed the Yugoslavs
for encouraging and supporting Hungarian rebels. Again,
twelve years later in 1968, Tito was infuriated with and opposed to the Soviet intervention in Czechoslovakia. He had
supported Czech leader Alexander Dubcek (1921–1992) as he
attempted to reform and modernize communist policies.

Nonalignment and symmetrical federalism

The independent-minded Tito came to think of his
foreign policy as "actively neutral"—neither favoring the
communist Eastern Bloc countries nor the democratic Western countries, but occupying a position in between. (A democratic system of government allows multiple political parties;
their members are elected to various government offices by
popular vote of the people.) Tito was particularly close to

Yugoslavia after Tito

The nation of Yugoslavia changed at least three times through the twentieth century. During Josip Broz Tito's reign as president, Yugoslavia was a federation of six republics and two autonomous provinces he held tightly together. The republics included Serbia, Slovenia, Croatia, Montenegro, Macedonia, and Bosnia and Herzegovina. The provinces were Kosovo and Vojvodina.

Following the death of Tito in May 1980 and the failure of the communist economy, the political federation fell apart. Most of the former republics and provinces wanted independence from the historically dominant Serbia and wished to establish independent nations such as the Republic of Bosnia and Herzegovina. By the beginning of the twenty-first century, only Serbia and Montenegro were left as members of Yugoslavia, officially called the Federation Republic of Yugoslavia.

Prime Minister Jawaharlal Nehru (1889–1964) of India and President Gamal Abdel Nasser (1918–1970) of Egypt and tried to develop common policies for a group of nations he hoped would form a nonaligned bloc, neither favoring the East nor the West. In 1956, he called together a meeting of twenty-five neutral countries to his island in the Adriatic Sea. There, he proposed a neutral bloc or his policy of "nonalignment." In the 1960s and 1970s, Tito traveled to many countries to promote nonalignment.

Between 1945 and 1953, Tito's title in Yugoslavia was premier. Beginning in 1953, he was known as president, which remained his title until 1980, the year of his death. Tito was repeatedly elected president after 1953 and eventually his term was made unlimited—or president for life. In 1971, Tito established a system, "symmetrical federalism," that he hoped would lead to a systematic succession of power after his death. Symmetrical means having dissimilar or different parts in a balanced fashion, while federalism means forming a political unity of different states under a central power.

The United States, for example, operates under federalism with its fifty states and central government. Tito's federalism consisted of six Yugoslav republics (Bosnia and Herzegovina, Croatia, Macedonia, Montenegro, Serbia, and Slovenia) and two autonomous provinces (Kosovo and Vojvodina). He established a twenty-two member collective presidency of the eight presidents from the republics and provinces and fourteen members chosen from the assemblies in each of the eight regions. Tito, of course, was chairman of the collective presidency, and he purged any leaders who did not go along with his ideals or political agenda.

Federation breakup

Throughout the decades after World War II, Tito had relied on his strength of character, charisma, and continuing popularity to hold power and to push Yugoslavia down its own independent path. He encouraged relatively broad liberties in culture and education. He allowed Yugoslavs to work and travel in Western Europe. Likewise, the Adriatic coast of Yugoslavia became a popular tourist destination for Westerners. He maintained a strong army, but as the years passed, he lessened the powers of the secret police.

During the 1970s, the economy began to weaken under high inflation (rising cost of goods), inefficient industry, and a heavy foreign debt. Despite his Yugoslav federation, nationalist issues between the republics and provinces continued to surface in ever more radical tones. Croatians called for secession from the federation; Serbia also agitated, or stirred up public debate on the issue, and pressed the federation leaders to give it a greater voice. Croatia and Serbia, the two larger regions, were unhappy that smaller regions had almost as much representation as they did. Tito tightened control, but after a four-month health decline, he died in May 1980. After his death, tensions between the republics and provinces reared up with a vengeance, eventually leading to civil wars and a violent federation breakup in the 1990s.

For More Information

Books

Auty, Phyllis. *Tito: A Biography*. New York: McGraw-Hill, 1970.

Djilas, Milovan. *Tito: The Story from Inside*. New York: Harcourt Brace Jovanovich, 1980.

Maclean, Fitzroy. *Josip Broz Tito: A Pictorial Biography*. New York: McGraw-Hill, 1980.

Pavlowitch, Stevan K. *Tito: Yugoslavia's Great Dictator, A Reassessment*. Columbus: Ohio State University Press, 1992.

Ridley, Jasper G. *Tito*. London: Constable, 1994.

West, Richard. *Tito and the Rise and Fall of Yugoslavia*. London: Sinclair-Stevenson, 1994.

Web Site

"Josip Broz Tito." *CNN Cold War*. http://www.cnn.com/SPECIALS/cold.war/kbank/profiles/tito (accessed on September 14, 2003).

Harry S. Truman

Born May 8, 1884
Lamar, Missouri
Died December 26, 1972
Kansas City, Missouri

U.S. president, vice president, senator

"All the President is, is a glorified public relations man who spends his time flattering, kissing and kicking people to get them to do what they are supposed to do anyway."

Harry S. Truman. *Reproduced by permission of AP/Wide World Photos.*

"I felt like the moon, the stars, and all the planets had fallen on me." Harry S. Truman spoke these words to a reporter on April 13, 1945, the day after being sworn in as U.S. president. President Franklin D. Roosevelt (1882–1945; served 1933–45) had died suddenly of a brain hemorrhage, and Truman was faced with leading the American people through mounting international crises.

Harry S. Truman, the thirty-third president of the United States, would be cast as a central player in the quickly developing Cold War (1945–91). The Cold War was an intense political, ideological, economic, and military global rivalry between the United States and the Soviet Union and their allies, involving hostility and conflict but not direct warfare between the two superpowers. Many historians argue that the tensest and most dramatic years of the Cold War were during Truman's presidency, which coincided with the last eight years of power for Soviet leader **Joseph Stalin** (1879–1953; see entry).

Modest beginnings

Harry S. Truman, the oldest of three children, was born on May 8, 1884 to Martha and John A. Truman, a farmer and livestock trader in Lamar, Missouri. Young Harry had very poor vision. His nearsightedness made childhood awkward since he was unable to participate in sports and games with other boys. He settled for more intellectual activities, becoming an avid reader and a good pianist. The family moved several times before settling in Independence, Missouri, in 1890, where the educational opportunities would be best for young Harry. Though not an outstanding student, Truman graduated from high school in 1901 at a time when many boys did not complete their high school education.

Truman's family did not have money for college. Rejected by the West Point military academy because of his eyesight, Truman took some business classes and found work in nearby Kansas City. At first, he was a timekeeper for a railroad construction company, then a bank clerk. In 1906, he moved back to a family farm owned by his grandmother near Grandview, Missouri, to help his father with the farm work. John Truman died in November 1914, leaving Harry with increased farm responsibilities.

While farming in Missouri, Truman broadened his world significantly. The shy, quiet boy matured into an active member of his community. Truman joined various fraternal organizations including the Masons, the oldest and largest organization for men in the world. Not associated with any particular religious beliefs or political opinions, it seeks to provide assistance to others by raising millions of dollars to assist hospitals, orphans, and the elderly, and to provide scholarships for students. Truman also signed up with the Missouri National Guard, where he served in an artillery unit from 1905 to 1911. Along with his expanding associations came a

 Is There a Period after S?

A debate has existed as to whether the middle initial of President Harry S. Truman should have a period after it. As revealed by Truman in 1962, the "S" does not stand for any specific name. When Truman was born, his parents compromised on a middle name by simply selecting an S. The letter represented both of his grandfathers, Anderson Shipp Truman and Solomon Young. Technically, then, no period should have followed the S, since it did not stand for an actual word or name. Yet researchers found that Truman himself had put a period after the S on many of his signatures while president, so the period after the S became the accepted practice among historians and others.

growing interest in local politics. Also, testing his financial skills, Truman invested in Oklahoma mines and oil exploration, but found little reward in these ventures. He was more successful in the romantic sphere, when he began dating a childhood friend, Elizabeth "Bess" Wallace, in 1910.

When the United States entered World War I (1914–18) in 1917, the thirty-three-year-old Truman reentered the Missouri National Guard. By July 1918, he had moved up to the rank of captain in charge of field artillery Battery D and served on the battlefield in France. The war experience further sharpened his leadership skills. Following the war, Truman joined the reserves, eventually rising to the rank of colonel.

Upon returning home in 1919, Truman married Wallace. They had one daughter, Mary Margaret, born in February 1924. No longer interested in farming, Truman and a former Army friend opened a men's clothing shop in downtown Kansas City. Truman again took a strong interest in civic matters, joining the American Legion, the Reserve Officers Association, and a downtown merchants group aimed at improving commerce. Unfortunately for Truman, the national economy of the early 1920s slid into a postwar slump. With mounting debt, Truman closed his store in September 1922.

A turn to politics

Though not an economic success, owning a business and participating in various organizations gained Truman recognition in the region. Through his store, Truman had also met Thomas Pendergast (1872–1945), the Democratic Party boss for Kansas City, a predominately Democratic area. Truman decided to enter politics and, with the Democratic political machine's backing, won election to a county administrative post in 1922. Truman quickly demonstrated exceptional administrative skills, tackling difficult rural road issues.

Despite his successes, Truman lost reelection in 1924 and found work with the Automobile Club of Kansas City. Two years later, he won a local election again and served two four-year terms as presiding judge of Jackson County, the top administrative job in the county. He efficiently supervised public building projects and a road program. In this very public position, Truman built a reputation for honesty, an uncommon trait for some members of the Pendergast political machine. He also exhibited a talent for bringing together diverse groups, including minorities, in support of certain causes. Truman modernized the county road system, improved public buildings, and balanced the county budget.

Senator Truman

By 1934, Truman was looking for a higher public office. He considered running for governor or for the U.S. House of Representatives, but in each case the Pendergast political group backed other candidates. Then an opportunity came in the U.S. Senate race, and Truman jumped at the chance. Running a surprisingly hard campaign, Truman narrowly won the Democratic primary and went on to easily win the general election.

Senator Truman first worked without great fanfare. Though not nationally well known, he readily won the respect of fellow senators for his hard work, friendliness, and honesty. He distrusted big business and was a steady supporter of President Roosevelt's New Deal programs, created to guide the nation's economic recovery from the Great Depression (1929–41), the worst financial crisis in American history.

Pursuing his transportation interests, Truman focused on national transportation issues and became a member of the Interstate Commerce Committee. He gained recognition for passage of the Civil Aeronautics Act in 1938, which established government regulation of the young aviation industry. He was also instrumental in the passage of the Wheeler-Truman Transportation Act of 1940. The act provided federal oversight of the railroad industry's reorganization efforts. Truman built close ties with labor organizations such as railway unions and with African Americans through his public support of civil rights issues.

In the 1940 elections, Truman won a hard-fought Democratic primary and then a tough reelection in November. During his second term, Truman gained greater national prominence. He led a Senate committee investigating fraud and waste

U.S. vice president Harry S. Truman is sworn into office, following the death of President Franklin D. Roosevelt on April 12, 1945. With Truman are his wife, Bess, and U.S. Supreme Court justice Harlan Fiske Stone, who is administering the oath. *Photograph by Abbie Rowe. Reproduced by permission of the Corbis Corporation.*

in U.S. military services and their private contractors. Known as the Truman Committee, its fairness and effectiveness brought Truman increased respect from fellow senators and industry. It was estimated the Truman Committee saved the United States $15 billion during the early years of World War II (1939–45). Through his committee leadership, Truman was seen as an advocate for the common citizen against big business, big labor, the military, and greedy politicians.

The presidency

With the presidential elections approaching in the fall of 1944, President Roosevelt began looking for a new running mate to replace Vice President Henry A. Wallace (1888–1965). Given his popularity among both conservatives and liberals in the Democratic Party, Truman proved a good compromise choice. After Roosevelt won his fourth straight presidential election, Truman was sworn in as vice president on January 20, 1945.

Shockingly, Truman served in his position as vice president for only eighty-two days. With Roosevelt's sudden death on April 12, Truman was thrust into the presidency at sixty-one years of age. Truman had only met with the president twice, and he had little familiarity with key programs. Worst yet, having focused on domestic issues in Congress, Truman had almost no foreign policy experience. Yet World War II was still raging against Japan in the Pacific and the fate of postwar Europe needed to be decided with the imposing figures of British prime minister **Winston Churchill** (1874–1965; see entry) and Soviet premier Joseph Stalin.

Truman again relied on his strong administrative skills and extensive Washington political experience. He carefully listened to the political and technical advisors available to him. He then signed the charter for a major new international organization designed to preserve peace, called the United Nations (UN), in late April 1945; accepted Germany's surrender in early May; and by July, was meeting with Churchill and Stalin in Potsdam, Germany.

U.S. president Harry S. Truman (right) and former British prime minister Winston Churchill wave to American crowds upon Churchill's visit to the United States in March 1946. *Reproduced by permission of the Corbis Corporation.*

The bomb

Among the new revelations to Truman when he became president was the top-secret Manhattan Project, established to develop an atomic bomb. A secret test of the bomb was successfully conducted on July 16, 1945. The United States was the only country in the world with an atomic bomb.

Fearing a high number of U.S. casualties in an invasion of Japan and desiring an end to the Pacific war quickly, Truman issued an ultimatum to Japan to surrender or face destruction. No specific reference to the bomb was made. Following Japan's quick rejection of the ultimatum, Truman made one of the most controversial decisions in the history of the U.S. presidency, to drop atomic bombs on two Japanese cities. The bombs fell on Hiroshima on August 6 and Nagasaki on August 9, killing more than 150,000 men, women, and children. Japan surrendered on August 14, 1945. Truman, who relied on a committee of top advisors to drop the bombs, unhesitatingly defended his decision to use the atomic bombs, reasoning that more lives than the bomb victims would have been lost had the war continued.

Cold War

Over the next two years, a global rivalry with the Soviet Union developed. Confrontations with the Soviets in their effort to spread communism soon occurred in Poland, Germany, Iran, Greece, and Turkey. The Soviet Union had already spread its communist influence into almost all of Eastern Europe. Communism is a system of government in which the nation's leaders are selected by a single political party that controls all aspects of society. Private ownership of property is eliminated and the government directs all economic production. The goods produced and accumulated wealth are, in theory, supposed to be shared equally by all. To combat further expansion of communism, Truman introduced the Truman Doctrine in March 1947 to a joint session of Congress.

The Truman Doctrine became the foundation for U.S. Cold War foreign policy for the next half century. The doctrine proclaimed that the United States would come to the assistance of any free peoples in the world threatened by communist expansion, either externally or internally. Employing a strategy of containment in restricting Soviet influence to its present extent, Truman oversaw the creation of several major programs. He promoted a massive economic assistance program known as the Marshall Plan to help Western Europe recover economically from World War II; formed a European military alliance known as the North Atlantic Treaty Organization (NATO); oversaw a massive airlift operation when the Soviets blocked Western access to West Berlin; and established a security agreement with Latin American nations called the Rio Pact.

A stunning reelection

Truman's public popularity varied greatly during his presidency. For his first few months as president, Truman enjoyed an incredibly high public approval rating of 87 percent. Yet with increased Soviet control of Eastern Europe and a struggling U.S. postwar economy following World War II, his approval rating plummeted to 32 percent by September 1946. As a result, Republicans did very well in the November 1946 midterm elections and gained control of both houses of Congress. Truman's prospects for reelection in November 1948 were not bright; nevertheless, Truman ran an energetic, hard-hitting campaign and orchestrated a major upset over New York governor Thomas E. Dewey (1902–1971; see box).

With his stunning reelection, Truman believed he had firmer public support to put new domestic programs in place. Calling these programs the "Fair Deal," Truman patterned his domestic program after Roosevelt's New Deal. He sought to address a wide range of domestic issues important to the common citizen, including more public housing, an increase in minimum wage, price supports for farmers, national health insurance, federal aid to education, tax relief for the poor, and sweeping civil rights legislation. Though he only succeeded with the housing bill, many of the other initiatives surfaced again in later administrations.

Throughout his second term as president, the Cold War continued to dominate Truman's administration. The events seemed unending, including Chinese communists taking control of Mainland China; the successful testing of an atomic bomb by the Soviet Union; the fear of communist in-

"Give 'em Hell, Harry!"—The 1948 Election

By 1948, Democratic president Harry S. Truman had adopted aggressive foreign policies to contain communist expansion. He seemed to be politically rebounding from a low public approval rating of just 32 percent registered in late 1946. Even so, few believed he had much chance to win the November 1948 presidential election.

Truman not only had to contend with his Republican opponent, New York governor Thomas E. Dewey, but other opponents were lining up as well. Former vice president and Truman's former secretary of commerce Henry A. Wallace was running on the Progressive Party ticket. Wallace advocated a less aggressive policy toward the Soviet Union. South Carolina governor Strom Thurmond (1902–2003) led the States' Rights party, known as the Dixiecrats. The Dixiecrats were conservative Democrats from the South who had bolted from the Democratic National Convention when the party adopted a strong civil rights position. Wallace appealed to the liberal Democrats and Thurmond to the conservative Democrats.

Truman responded with a highly energetic cross-country campaign that re-

stored the diverse combination of voters President Franklin Roosevelt had attracted in the 1930s. Truman pulled together organized labor, the blue-collar or industrial working class, farmers, Catholics, Eastern European immigrants, and the Jewish population. Truman aggressively hammered away at the Republicans for blocking his domestic program proposals in Congress. To attract the African American vote, he signed an executive order racially integrating the armed forces. His decision to officially recognize the newly formed nation of Israel drew Jewish voters. Truman characteristically displayed the feisty, folksy approach that appealed to many Americans, and a popular slogan of "Give 'em Hell, Harry" soon accompanied him on the road. Dewey, in contrast, expected to win the election and ran a lackluster campaign.

When people awoke the morning after the election, they were greeted with the stunning news of Truman's victory. Both Wallace and Thurmond received only 2.4 percent of the vote each while Truman had defeated Dewey 49.5 percent to 45.1 percent. The Democrats made gains in both houses of Congress as well.

filtration within the United States (known as the Red Scare) led by U.S. senator **Joseph R. McCarthy** (1909–1957; see entry) of Wisconsin, who even asserted that there were communists within Truman's own administration; revelations of a nuclear spy ring funneling information to the Soviets; and the invasion of South Korea by communist North Korea. All of these events proved major distractions from Truman's domestic agenda. With Republicans constantly charging that Truman was soft on communism, Truman not only waged the Cold War with the Soviets but was also under constant attack by McCarthy and his supporters.

China's entry into the Korean War led Truman to fire the highly popular U.S. military leader General **Douglas MacArthur** (1880–1964; see entry) in April 1951. MacArthur had publicly opposed Truman's war strategy. As the fighting in Korea dragged on into 1952, producing an apparent stalemate, the public was clearly dissatisfied and Truman's public approval rating fell to 23 percent. On March 29, 1952, Truman announced he would not seek renomination for president that fall. Unlike Roosevelt, who at his death was in his fourth term, Truman thought two terms was long enough for any president. He also realized his chances at reelection would be slim and he was weary of being president after eight long years.

Republican **Dwight D. Eisenhower** (1890–1969; served 1953–61; see entry) won the presidential election in November 1952 in a landslide over llinois Democratic governor Adlai Stevenson (1900–1965). The following January, Truman quietly retired to his home in Independence, Missouri, where he wrote his memoirs and spoke occasionally on public issues. His health declined in the mid-1960s. Truman fell into unconsciousness on Christmas Day 1972 and died in Kansas City the following day.

"Mr. Citizen"

Truman left office with a low public approval rating of just 31 percent. As time passed, however, assessments of his presidential performance by historians rose greatly. Truman showed many sides of himself as president; on the one hand, he had a very direct and abrupt manner. For example, unlike Roosevelt, he tolerated little conflict within his administration, even firing Secretary of Commerce Henry A. Wallace when Wallace publicly challenged Truman's policies toward the Soviets. On the other hand, Truman was a good party leader for the Democrats, successfully appealing to a diverse group of people. He was an energetic campaigner and always appealed to the common person with a certain charm. He liked to refer to himself as "Mr. Citizen" after retirement.

Truman as U.S. president made very difficult and at times unpopular decisions during his White House years. These included dropping the atomic bombs, responding to Soviet hostile actions, supporting civil rights legislation, jumping to the defense of South Korea, and firing the popular General MacArthur. Additionally, between 1945 and 1953, Truman, his administration, and Congress fashioned U.S. foreign policies that would not only be long lived but balanced the United States on the Cold War tightrope.

For More Reading

Books

Collins, David R. *Harry S. Truman: People's President.* New York: Chelsea Juniors, 1991.

Donovan, Robert J. *Conflict and Crisis: The Presidency of Harry S. Truman, 1945–1948.* Columbia: University of Missouri Press, 1994.

Donovan, Robert J. *Tumultuous Years: The Presidency of Harry S. Truman, 1949–1953.* Columbia: University of Missouri Press, 1994.

Farley, Karin C. *Harry Truman: The Man from Independence.* Englewood Cliffs, NJ: Julian Messner, 1989.

Ferrell, Robert. *Harry S. Truman: A Life.* Columbia: University of Missouri Press, 1994.

Hamby, Alonzo L. *Man of the People: A Life of Harry S. Truman.* New York: Oxford University Press, 1995.

McCullough, David G. *Truman.* New York: Simon & Schuster, 1992.

Offner, Arnold A. *Another Such Victory: President Truman and the Cold War, 1945–1953.* Stanford, CA: Stanford University Press, 2002.

Truman, Harry S. *Memoirs: Year of Decisions, 1945.* London: Hodder and Stoughton, 1955.

Truman, Harry S. *Memoirs: Years of Trial and Hope, 1946–1953.* London: Hodder and Stoughton, 1956.

Web Sites

"Harry S. Truman." *The White House.* http://www.whitehouse.gov/history/presidents/ht33.html (accessed on September 15, 2003).

Truman Presidential Museum & Library. http://www.trumanlibrary.org (accessed on September 15, 2003).

Zhou Enlai

**Born March 5, 1898
Huaian, Kiangsu province, China
Died January 8, 1976
Peking, People's Republic of China**

**Premier and foreign minister of
People's Republic of China**

Z hou Enlai was a leading figure of the People's Republic of China (PRC) from its founding in 1949 to 1976. He served as premier (head of state) throughout this lengthy time period and was also the PRC's foreign minister from 1949 to 1958, but remained the country's leading foreign affairs expert for decades. As a result, Zhou was the most visible PRC official and gained great respect from other world leaders for his superb negotiating skills.

Zhou was responsible for all of communist China's foreign policy through most of the Cold War and much of the PRC's domestic policy as well. The Cold War was an intense political and economic rivalry from 1945 to 1991 between the United States and the Soviet Union, falling just short of military conflict.

Student activist

Zhou Enlai was born in March 1898 into what had been a prosperous middle-class family in Huaian, within the

"All diplomacy is a continuation of war by other means."

Zhou Enlai. *Reproduced by permission of AP/Wide World Photos.*

Kiangsu (later known as Jiangsu) province of eastern China. His father was Zhou Yinen and his mother Wan Dongei. By the time of Zhou's birth, the family was struggling financially. An aunt raised young Zhou his first ten years and then two uncles took over through his teen years. Valuing education, Zhou's relatives supported his attendance at various missionary schools around China. At Nankai Normal School, he was already showing the skills of a master negotiator by leading the school's debate team.

After completing his secondary education, Zhou traveled to Japan in 1917 to further his studies, as many Chinese youths did at the time. He also became very excited about the communist revolution in Russia that same year and eagerly explored Marxist theory. Marxist theory refers to the economic and political interpretations of German philosopher Karl Marx (1818–1883), which formed the basis of communism. Communism is a system of government in which a nation's leaders are selected by a single political party that controls all aspects of society. Under communism, private ownership of property is eliminated and the government directs all economic production; all goods produced and accumulated wealth are, in theory, supposed to be shared equally by all.

Pursuing his growing interest in political activism, Zhou joined an activist Chinese study organization in Japan. Zhou returned to China to the city of Tientsin in 1919, the third-largest city and the largest port in Northern China, to take part in student demonstrations as part of the May Fourth Movement. The movement was protesting the Treaty of Versailles, the peace treaty ending World War I (1914–18), because the treaty gave Japan certain rights to the Chinese province of Manchuria. It was the beginning of a revolution in China that would build through the years with Zhou as a central figure. He was arrested for his activism in 1920 and released that fall after being in prison for four months.

Zhou soon played an instrumental role in the beginning of the Chinese communist revolution. Zhou had great sympathy for the working class, especially Chinese peasants. Freed from prison, Zhou journeyed to Paris, France, on a work-study program. There, he joined the Chinese Socialist Youth Corps, a new communist organization, and then became an organizer of a Berlin branch in Germany. While in

Europe, he associated with other future communist revolutionaries such as **Ho Chi Minh** (1890–1969; see entry), who would later lead North Vietnam. Zhou joined the Chinese Communist Party (CCP) at this time and formed the CCP European branch. He served as an officer of the European branch and also gained a broad knowledge of various cultures and political ideas from various parts of the world. This formed a foundation for his later role as a leading foreign diplomat of the CCP.

Return to China

In 1924, Zhou returned to China, to Canton in the Guangdong province. There, he became active in a new alliance between the CCP and the Nationalist Party (Kuomintang) led by **Chiang Kai-shek** (1887–1975; see entry). They were joining forces in a national revolution against China's ruling warlords, or local military leaders. Zhou assumed leadership of the Canton Communist Party and became deputy head of the Whampoa Military Academy near Canton. Chiang was head of the academy, which taught many future military leaders of China.

While in Canton, Zhou married fellow revolutionary Deng Yingchao in 1925, whom he had met during the 1919 Tientsin demonstrations. They would have no children of their own but adopted many. Among them was Li Peng (1928–), who became prime minister of communist China in 1987. Like Zhou, Deng would become a prominent CCP member and deputy chairman of the All-China Federation of Women, a key women's organization in the CCP.

The alliance army began a military expedition in 1926. By March 27, 1927, its troops were closing in on the major city of Shanghai. To help seize the city, Zhou traveled in advance to organize the city's workers to go on strike. After successfully entering the city, however, Chiang turned his Nationalist forces on CCP members, killing five thousand of them. Barely escaping, the surprised and angered Zhou traveled to Nankow, which became the new center for the CCP. In the next two months, Zhou was elected to the CCP Central Committee, the Communist Party's main administrative body; and its Politburo, the executive body of the Central Committee, responsible for making policy decisions. Zhou was also made director of the military department of the CCP Central Committee.

In August 1927, Zhou led a communist force of thirty thousand troops to gain control of the town of Nanchang in retaliation for the Shanghai massacre. The military operation was known as the Nanchang Uprising. At first, the CCP took the city, but the Nationalists quickly retook it. Zhou retreated to Hong Kong, then to Shanghai, where the CCP began operating underground. Despite the Nanchang defeat, this event would long be celebrated as the beginning of the Chinese Red Army. By 1928, Chiang's Nationalists had united China under one government.

The Long March

Because Moscow during these early years guided CCP activities, Zhou traveled to Moscow in 1928 to be reaffirmed once again as the CCP military leader. Maintaining his leadership role, he returned to China to rebuild the organization. The CCP switched its focus from failed city uprisings with large losses to organizing rural peasants and farmers. In 1931, Zhou left Shanghai for the Kiangsi province in southwest China where **Mao Zedong** (1893–1976; see entry) and others were building the rural-based communist rebellion. In Kiangsi, they established the Chinese Soviet Republic, with Zhou serving on its Central Executive Committee and as leader of its army. They then worked to expand the communist base over the next several years.

In October 1934, Chiang launched an attack to destroy the growing communist stronghold. Chiang's army won a series of military victories over the CCP, driving the Red Army from Kiangsi and south-central China. After suffering 60,000 casualties, Zhou and Mao decided to embark on a major retreat that became known as the Long March. The Long March was an epic journey to a new base in northwestern China. They trudged some 6,000 miles (9,650 kilometers) over one year's time. Of the 90,000 or so who started the journey, only about 8,000 survived. Zhou's wife, Deng, was one of the few women to make the journey. During the Long March, in January 1935, leadership of the party and Central Committee's military department switched from Zhou to

Mao and remained this way for the rest of their lives. The march arrived at Yen-an in the northern Shensi province in October 1935.

Zhou the diplomat

From the new base in Yen-an, Zhou readily tackled his new role as chief negotiator for the CCP. A priority of Zhou's was to rebuild an alliance with the Nationalists against the growing Japanese aggression. Japan had invaded Manchuria in 1931 and was expanding its control from there. In December 1936, Chiang was arrested by one of his generals, who sought to end the civil war with the CCP and instead focus all Chinese on Japanese aggression. Seizing the opportunity, Zhou immediately traveled to argue for saving Chiang's life. After days of negotiation, he was successful and obtained agreements from Chiang to end the civil war and join forces against Japan. The communists gained much greater respect from the Chinese general public due to Zhou's diplomacy.

War broke out with Japan in July 1937. Zhou served as the CCP representative within the government for the next several years. Following Japan's surrender to the United States and allied forces in August 1945, ending World War II (1939–45), Mao and Zhou traveled to Chungking to reach a peace agreement with Chiang. They proposed a coalition government of Chinese communists and Chiang's Nationalists, yet the lack of success in negotiations led to the involvement of the United States to help reach a settlement. U.S. president **Harry S. Truman** (1884–1972; served 1945–53; see entry) sent General **George C. Marshall** (1880–1959; see entry) but still no resolution was reached. Zhou returned to Yen-an and civil war resumed in 1947 after an eleven-year pause.

Only two years later, the communists gained control of the Chinese government. They formed the People's Republic of China (PRC) on October 1, 1949. Chiang's nationalist government fled to the island of Taiwan off the south coast of Mainland China. There, Chiang established the Republic of China (ROC), with hopes of eventually retaking the mainland. Mao became chairman of the PRC's Communist Party, serving as the country's spiritual and philosophical leader. Zhou was the PRC's premier and foreign minister. As premier,

U.S. special emissary George C. Marshall (second from left) reviews the troops in Yenan, China, in March 1946, along with Chinese officials (left to right) Zhou Enlai, Chu Teh, Chang Chi-Chung, and Mao Zedong. *Reproduced by permission of AP/Wide World Photos.*

Zhou was chief administrator of the vast bureaucracy he created for the nation of one billion people. Zhou was also vice chairman of the committee drafting a constitution for the new country. As foreign minister, Zhou was in charge of establishing all foreign relations. Since Zhou already had a strong background in international issues and had many foreign contacts, he became the long-term voice of the PRC and traveled extensively. Perhaps his greatest contribution, through his many years of service, was the professionalism he brought to the new government and the respect he quickly gained for it.

The United States versus communist China

Zhou's interactions with the United States during the Cold War were numerous and varied. They involved the PRC's role in the United Nations (UN), armed conflict in Korea, confrontation over the existence of the ROC, and finally, the building of an improved relationship. In 1949, Zhou considered the United States to be the primary obstacle to world acceptance of the PRC. The China Lobby, a group of influential nationalist supporters in the United States, put substantial pressure on the U.S. government to withhold recognition of the PRC and block the PRC's inclusion in the UN. Opposed to all communist governments, the United States blocked UN acceptance of the PRC for years and for three decades recognized the ROC on Taiwan as the only legitimate Chinese government. In addition, the United States placed a trade embargo, which prohibited commerce such as ships in and out of ports, on the PRC from 1950 until 1971 and kept a sizable military force in South Korea and Japan.

In June 1950, communist North Korea invaded U.S.-supported South Korea. A UN coalition led predominantly by U.S. forces quickly responded. Zhou kept the PRC out of the conflict at first; however, he warned the United States that the PRC would become involved if U.S. forces penetrated into North Korea. Not only did U.S. forces cross the boundary between North and South Korea by the fall of 1950, but they actually pushed all the way to the Chinese border with North Korea. Feeling threatened by the U.S. aggressiveness, Zhou unleashed three hundred thousand PRC troops in November 1950 to fight directly against U.S. forces. The PRC army successfully pushed U.S. forces back across North Korea and into South Korea before reaching a stalemate at the original boundary by the spring of 1951. Peace would not come until 1953.

Zhou also felt threatened by the U.S.-backed ROC off the south coast. Twice during the 1950s, the PRC bombarded ROC-held islands off the mainland coast. These islands were heavily fortified by ROC forces, and both times the United States intervened by gaining guarantees from the ROC to not attack the PRC.

A peak in Zhou's influence came at the 1954 Geneva conference following a key communist military defeat of French forces in Vietnam at Dien Bien Phu. Zhou was able to negotiate a peace settlement including a cease-fire from the communist Vietminh forces and a partitioning of the country with the communists in control of the North. Zhou won praise for his skill even though U.S. secretary of state **John Foster Dulles** (1888–1959; see entry) refused to shake hands with Zhou and the United States refused to sign the agreement.

In 1969, **Richard M. Nixon** (1913– 1994; served 1969–74; see entry) became U.S. president. Before long, he sent indications to Zhou that he was interested in improving relations between the two nations. Zhou readily seized the opportunity and Nixon dropped the trade embargo. In July and October 1971, U.S. national security advisor **Henry Kissinger** (1923–; see entry) made two secret trips to China to begin discussions with Zhou. These meetings set the stage for Nixon's historic visit to Peking in February 1972 to meet Mao. It was the first visit by a U.S. president to the PRC. Owing to Zhou's superb negotiating skills, Nixon recognized the Chinese on Taiwan as part of the PRC, rather than the ROC being China's main government or even a separate government of its own.

Chinese premier Zhou Enlai attends the Geneva Conference in 1954.
Courtesy of the National Archives and Records Administration.

Expanding foreign relations and surviving domestic upheavals

Aside from dealing with conflicts involving the United States, Zhou explored possible expansion of PRC influence in other parts of the world. He toured Eastern Europe in 1957 seeking more direct relations outside Soviet influence. Zhou was also interested in nationalist movements (those seeking independence) and forming new ties with underdeveloped countries. From 1956 to 1964, Zhou traveled widely throughout Africa and Asia. Though he formally gave up his position as foreign minister in 1958, Zhou still kept most of the duties and responsibilities of the post. One of his more bitter relationships was with India's leader Jawaharlal Nehru (1889–1964) over a border dispute. The dispute turned into armed conflict in 1962 and was a rousing PRC victory.

Zhou also had to negotiate through internal upheavals orchestrated by Mao. The Great Leap Forward in 1955 and 1956 was an effort to transfer control of agriculture and

Sino-Soviet Relations

A longstanding challenge in Zhou Enlai's foreign policy was relations with the Soviet Union, known as Sino-Soviet relations (*Sino* means "Chinese"). Initially, the Soviets provided guidance to the young CCP through the 1920s and 1930s. Soon after the communist Red Army defeated the Nationalist Chinese government in 1949, Zhou established a defense alliance with the Soviets. Serving both as premier and foreign minister of the PRC, Zhou was the key PRC contact with the Soviets.

Examples of his contact included Zhou acting as the CCP representative at the funeral of **Joseph Stalin** (1879–1953; see entry) in March 1953. Significant differences grew between the CCP and the Soviet Communist Party, however, by the mid-1950s as Soviet leader **Nikita Khrushchev** (1894–1971; see entry) introduced reforms with which Zhou and the Chinese did not agree. In a historic February 1956 speech, Khrushchev severely criticized Stalin's past policies. Zhou disagreed with the speech, believing it would weaken Soviet communist rule. Proving him right, Eastern European countries immediately tried to break from Soviet control and Khrushchev responded with deadly military force.

In 1957, Zhou traveled to Moscow to protest the Soviet Union's aggressive actions in Eastern Europe. By 1959, relations began to improve, and Zhou returned to Moscow to obtain much-needed Soviet assistance in the construction of numerous industrial and power plants. This assistance lasted only until July 1960, when the Soviets pulled out due to growing differences. The countries formally split in 1961 when Zhou walked out of a Moscow Communist Party meeting. He laid a wreath at Stalin's tomb in defiance of Khrushchev's policies. This proved to U.S. officials that not all communists were the same, nor did they represent a monolithic (standing as one) communist threat to take over the world.

In 1964, Zhou visited Moscow to resolve differences once again; progress was slow, though, and border clashes between the two communist governments grew in frequency. Finally, in 1969, a resolution was negotiated, ending the border clashes between the two communist powers. An uneasy peace was established for the last several years of Zhou's leadership.

industry to local communes. It led to disastrous results, including famine. Zhou next survived the Cultural Revolution, which lasted from 1966 to 1976. During the Cultural Revolution, Mao sought to rejuvenate the revolutionary spirit of the CCP by purging bureaucrats, intellectuals, and others. Zhou provided a moderating influence on these events by discreetly protecting some key moderate leaders. Yet Zhou suffered a heart attack in 1967 after being harassed by the Red Guard, a special force created by Mao to carry out the Cultural Revolution. The following year, in October 1968, the Red Guard tortured to death one of Zhou's adopted daughters.

The Zhou legacy

Highly intelligent and amazingly good with details, Zhou was one of the most widely respected diplomats in the world and the most liked Chinese leader. Zhou loved to dance and watch movies and exuded personal charm. Courteous and thoughtful, he showed much tact. Despite his long dedication to the CCP since its founding, he was not known as an ideologue, or one driven by his political beliefs, but a master of practical diplomacy. Communist Party leader Mao Zedong had zeal, while Zhou was moderate. Zhou restrained extremists within the CCP and kept diplomatic doors open to foreign nations.

Zhou died of bladder cancer in January 1976 after three years of serious illness. Mao died in September. After Zhou's death, a brief power struggle followed, with Zhou supporter Deng Xiaoping (1904–1997) finally claiming leadership, which lasted until his own death in 1997. Three years after Deng's death, the United States and the PRC established direct formal relations. In keeping with his very modest lifestyle, Zhou had his ashes scattered over China with no specific monument erected. He also wrote no memoirs or autobiography.

For More Information

Books

Kai-yu, Hsu. *Chou En-Lai: China's Gray Eminence*. New York: Doubleday, 1968.

Keith, Ronald C. *The Diplomacy of Zhou Enlai*. New York: Macmillan, 1989.

Kissinger, Henry. *The White House Years*. Boston: Little, Brown, 1979.

Roots, John McCook. *Chou: An Informal Biography of China's Legendary Chou En-lai*. New York: Doubleday, 1978.

Shao, Kuo-kang. *Zhou Enlai and the Foundations of Chinese Foreign Policy*. New York: St. Martin's Press, 1996.

Suyin, Han. *Eldest Son: Zhou Enlai and the Making of Modern China, 1898–1976*. New York: Hill and Wang, 1994.

Wilson, Dick. *Zhou Enlai: A Biography*. New York: Viking Press, 1984.

Where to Learn More

Books

Barson, Michael, and Steven Heller. *Red Scared! The Commie Menace in Propaganda and Popular Culture.* San Francisco: Chronicle Books, 2001.

Brubaker, Paul E. *The Cuban Missile Crisis in American History.* Berkeley Heights, NJ: Enslow, 2001.

Ciment, James. *The Young People's History of the United States.* New York: Barnes and Noble Books, 1998.

Collier, Christopher. *The United States in the Cold War.* New York: Benchmark Books/Marshall Cavendish, 2002.

FitzGerald, Frances. *Way Out There in the Blue: Reagan, Star Wars, and the End of the Cold War.* New York: Simon & Schuster, 2000.

Gaddis, John L. *We Now Know: Rethinking Cold War History.* New York: Oxford University Press, 1997.

Gates, Robert M. *From the Shadows: The Ultimate Insider's Story of Five Presidents and How They Won the Cold War.* New York: Simon & Schuster Trade Paperback, 1997.

Glynn, Patrick. *Closing Pandora's Box: Arms Races, Arms Control, and the History of the Cold War.* New York: Basic Books, 1992.

Grant, R. G. *The Berlin Wall.* Austin, TX: Raintree Steck-Vaughn, 1999.

Herring, George C. *America's Longest War: The United States and Vietnam, 1950–1975.* 2nd ed. New York: Knopf, 1988.

Huchthausen, Peter A., and Alexander Hoyt. *October Fury*. Hoboken, NJ: Wiley, 2002.

Isaacs, Jeremy, and Taylor Downing. *Cold War: An Illustrated History, 1945–1991*. Boston: Little, Brown, 1998.

Jacobs, William Jay. *Search for Peace: The Story of the United Nations*. New York: Atheneum, 1996.

Keep, John L. H. *A History of the Soviet Union, 1945–1991: Last of the Empires*. New York: Oxford University Press, 1995.

Kelly, Nigel. *Fall of the Berlin Wall: The Cold War Ends*. Chicago: Heineman Library, 2001.

Kort, Michael G. *The Cold War*. Brookfield, CT: Millbrook Press, 1994.

LaFeber, Walter. *America, Russia, and the Cold War, 1945–1996*. 8th ed. New York: McGraw-Hill, 1997.

Parrish, Thomas. *Berlin in the Balance, 1945–1949: The Blockade, the Airlift, the First Major Battle of the Cold War*. Reading, MA: Addison-Wesley, 1998.

Parrish, Thomas. *The Cold War Encyclopedia*. New York: Henry Holt, 1996.

Pietrusza, David. *The End of the Cold War*. San Diego, CA: Lucent, 1995.

Sherrow, Victoria. *Joseph McCarthy and the Cold War*. Woodbridge, CT: Blackbirch Press, 1999.

Sibley, Katherine A. S. *The Cold War*. Westport, CT: Greenwood Press, 1998.

Smith, Joseph. *The Cold War, 1945–1991*. 2nd ed. Malden, MA: Blackwell, 1998.

Stein, Conrad. *The Korean War: "The Forgotten War."* Springfield, NJ: Enslow, 1994.

Walker, Martin. *The Cold War: A History (Owl Book)*. New York: Henry Holt, 1995.

Magazines

Hoover, J. Edgar. "How to Fight Communism." *Newsweek,* June 9, 1947.

Levine, Isaac Don. "Our First Line of Defense." *Plain Talk,* September 1949.

"X" (George F. Kennan). "The Sources of Soviet Conduct." *Foreign Affairs,* July 1947.

Novels

Brunner, Edward. *Cold War Poetry*. Urbana: University of Illinois Press, 2000.

Clancy, Tom. *The Hunt for Red October*. New York: Berkley Publishing Group, 1985.

Clancy, Tom. *Red Storm Rising*. New York: Berkley Publishing Group, 1987.

Clancy, Tom, and Martin Greenberg. *Tom Clancy's Power Plays: Cold War*. New York: Berkley Publishing Group, 2001.

George, Peter. *Dr. Strangelove, or How I Learned to Stop Worrying and Love the Bomb.* New York: Bantam Books, 1964.

Le Carre, John. *Spy Who Came in from the Cold.* New York: Coward, Mc-Cann & Geoghegan, 1978.

Littell, Robert. *The Company: A Novel of the CIA.* New York: Overlook Press, 2002.

Web Sites

The Atomic Archive. http://www.atomicarchive.com (accessed on September 26, 2003).

CNN Interactive: The Cold War Experience. http://www.CNN.com/SPECIALS/cold.war (accessed on September 26, 2003).

"Cold War History: 1949–1989." *U.S. Air Force Museum.* http://www.wpafb.af.mil/museum/history/coldwar/cw.htm (accessed on September 26, 2003).

The Dwight D. Eisenhower Library and Museum. http://www.eisenhower.utexas.edu (accessed on September 26, 2003).

George Bush Presidential Library and Museum. http://bushlibrary.tamu.edu (accessed on September 26, 2003).

Gerald R. Ford Library and Museum. http://www.ford.utexas.edu (accessed on September 26, 2003).

International Spy Museum. http://spymuseum.org (accessed on September 26, 2003).

John F. Kennedy Library and Museum. http://www.cs.umb.edu/jfklibrary/index.htm (accessed on September 26, 2003).

Lyndon B. Johnson Library and Museum. http://www.lbjlib.utexas.edu (accessed on September 26, 2003).

The Manhattan Project Heritage Preservation Association, Inc. http://www.childrenofthemanhattanproject.org (accessed on September 26, 2003).

National Atomic Museum. http://www.atomicmuseum.com (accessed on September 26, 2003).

National Security Agency. http://www.nsa.gov (accessed on September 26, 2003).

President Mikhail Sergeyevich Gorbachev. http://www.mikhailgorbachev.org (accessed on September 26, 2003).

The Richard Nixon Library and Birthplace. http://www.nixonfoundation.org (accessed on September 26, 2003).

Ronald Reagan Presidential Library. http://www.reagan.utexas.edu (accessed on September 26, 2003).

"Secrets, Lies, and Atomic Spies." *Nova Online.* http://www.pbs.org/wgbh/nova/venona (accessed on September 26, 2003).

Truman Presidential Museum & Library. http://www.trumanlibrary.org (accessed on September 26, 2003).

U.S. Central Intelligence Agency (CIA). http://www.cia.gov (accessed on September 26, 2003).

Woodrow Wilson International Center for Scholars. *The Cold War International History Project.* http://wwics.si.edu/index.cfm?fuseaction= topics.home&topic_id=1409 (accessed on September 26, 2003).

Index

A

ABM treaty, *2:* 262

Acheson, Dean G., *1:* 1 (ill.), **1–8,** 7 (ill.), 30 (ill.); *2:* 214, 334

Acheson-Lilienthal Report, *2:* 373

Adenauer, Konrad, *1:* 9 (ill.), **9–16,** 13 (ill.), 131; *2:* 308

AEC. *See* Atomic Energy Commission (AEC)

Afghanistan
Brezhnev, Leonid, and, *1:* 50
Carter, Jimmy, and, *1:* 50, 70, 78; *2:* 393
Gorbachev, Mikhail, and, *1:* 156; *2:* 420
Gromyko, Andrey, and, *1:* 164
Reagan, Ronald, and, *2:* 392–93
Sakharov, Andrey, and, *2:* 413
Shevardnadze, Eduard, and, *2:* 420
Soviet Union and, *1:* 50, 70, 78, 156, 164; *2:* 252, 392–93, 413, 420

Africa, *2:* 310, 470

African Americans
Carter, Jimmy, and, *1:* 71, 73
discrimination and, *2:* 402–3
Hoover, J. Edgar, and, *1:* 192
poverty and, *1:* 201–3
segregation and, *1:* 68, 71, 73; *2:* 221–22
Truman, Harry S., and, *2:* 460

Agriculture
in Chile, *1:* 21–22
in China, *1:* 121–22
in Cuba, *1:* 86
in Soviet Union, *1:* 44, 46; *2:* 232, 238, 239, 278, 348, 429
Stalin, Joseph, and, *2:* 429

Albert Einstein Peace Prize, *2:* 216, 343

Albright, Madeleine, *2:* 403

Alien Enemy Bureau, *1:* 187

Allende, Salvador, *1:* 17 (ill.), **17–24,** 21 (ill.); *2:* 263–64, 362

Alliluyeva, Svetlana, *2:* 433, 435

"American Relations with the Soviet Union." *See* Clifford-Elsey Report

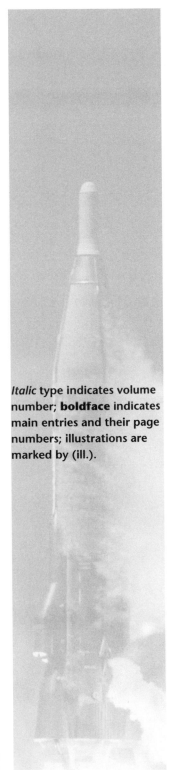

Andropov, Yuri
  Brezhnev, Leonid, and, *1:* 45
  Communist Party and, *2:* 417
  death of, *1:* 45, 152; *2:* 395, 417
  economy and, *2:* 417
  election of, *1:* 45, 152
  Gorbachev, Mikhail, and, *1:*
    152–53; *2:* 417
  Harriman, W. Averell, and, *1:*
    175
  Komsomol and, *1:* 45
  Reagan, Ronald, and, *1:* 155
  Sakharov, Andrey, and, *2:* 413
  Shevardnadze, Eduard, and, *2:*
    417
Angola, *1:* 50, 164
Antiballistic missiles, *2:* 361
ANZUS Pact, *1:* 128
Apartheid, *2:* 310
Arabs, *1:* 36–37
Argentina, *1:* 76
Arms race. *See* Nuclear weapons,
    race for
Army-McCarthy hearings, *2:* 335
Arzamas-16, *2:* 286, 287, 409
Ashurst, Henry F., *1:* 190 (ill.)
Atlas Shrugged, 2: 383–84
Atomic bombs. *See also* Nuclear
    weapons
  development of, *1:* 31, 38; *2:*
    212, 283, 285–88, 351, 366,
    371–72, 432, 433, 458
  testing of, *1:* 6, 31, 106, 108; *2:*
    285, 287–88, 333, 366, 371,
    372, 373, 434, 458
  use of, *1:* 3, 31; *2:* 285, 297,
    371, 372, 409, 432, 458
Atomic Energy Commission
    (AEC), *1:* 3; *2:* 373–75
"Atoms for Peace," *1:* 140–41
Attlee, Clement R., *1:* 25 (ill.),
    25–32, 30 (ill.)
  Bevin, Ernest, and, *1:* 31, 33, 35
  election of, *1:* 27, 33, 36, 106
  Potsdam Conference and, *1:*
    28, 35–36, 66; *2:* 431

B

Baghdad Pact, *1:* 130, 132
Baker, James, *1:* 57; *2:* 420–21,
    421 (ill.)

Ball, George, *1:* 7 (ill.)
Baltic States, *1:* 57
Baruch, Bernard, *1:* 3, 64, 126; *2:*
    373
Baruch Plan, *1:* 3
Batista y Zaldívar, Fulgencio, *1:*
    84–85
Battle of Normandy, *1:* 136
Battle of Stalingrad, *2:* 233
Battle of the Bulge, *1:* 136
Bay of Pigs, *1:* 87, 113, 144; *2:*
    223, 340–41
BCCI scandal, *1:* 114–15
Begin, Menachem, *1:* 78 (ill.), 79
Beria, Lavrenty, *2:* 286–87, 351,
    432, 433, 433 (ill.), 435
Berlin. *See also* Berlin Wall
  airlift in, *1:* 38–39; *2:* 327, 352,
    459
  blockade in, *1:* 38–39; *2:* 327,
    352
  division of, *1:* 106, 132; *2:* 224,
    235–36
  Eisenhower, Dwight D., and, *1:*
    137
  Kennedy, John F., and, *2:* 218,
    226
  Soviet Union and, *1:* 137
  Truman, Harry S., and, *2:* 459
  World War II and, *1:* 137
Berlin Wall
  Adenauer, Konrad, and, *1:*
    14–16
  Christian Democratic Union
    and, *1:* 14–15
  communism and, *2:* 226
  construction of, *1:* 14, 107; *2:*
    225–26, 237, 275
  fall of, *1:* 53, 57; *2:* 273–74,
    275, 421
  Kennedy, John F., and, *1:* 15; *2:*
    218, 225–26, 275
  Khrushchev, Nikita, and, *1:* 14;
    2: 225–26, 237, 275
Bevin, Ernest, *1:* 31, 33 (ill.),
    33–40, 39 (ill.)
Big Three
  Churchill, Winston, and, *1:*
    104–6
  definition of, *1:* 65
  Molotov, Vyacheslav, and, *2:*
    349
  Potsdam Conference and, *1:*
    65, 66

Tehran Conference and, *2:* 431
Yalta Conference and, *1:* 65,
66; *2:* 431–32
Yugoslavia and, *2:* 446
Black Panthers, *1:* 192
Blacklists, *2:* 384, 389
Blease, Coleman L., *1:* 64
BOI. *See* Bureau of Investigation
(BOI)
Bolshevik Revolution
communism and, *1:* 187; *2:*
231, 380–81
Communist Party and, *1:* 45
February Revolution, *2:* 347
Gromyko, Andrey, and, *1:*
159–60
Khrushchev, Nikita, and, *2:* 231
Kosygin, Aleksey, and, *2:* 277–78
Lenin, Vladimir I., and, *2:* 278,
347, 427
Molotov, Vyacheslav, and, *2:*
346–47
October Revolution, *2:* 347
Rand, Ayn, and, *2:* 380–81
Stalin, Joseph, and, *2:* 346, 347,
427–28
success of, *1:* 42
Tito, Josip Broz, and, *2:* 445
Bonner, Yelena, *2:* 408, 412 (ill.),
412–13, 413–14, 415
Borden, William L., *2:* 376
Brady, James, *2:* 392
Brandeis, Louis D., *1:* 2
Branden, Barbara, *2:* 384
Branden, Nathaniel, *2:* 384
Brandt, Willy, *1:* 15, 15 (ill.), 48
Brazil, *1:* 76
Bretton Woods Conference, *1:*
2–3
Brezhnev Doctrine, *1:* 47
Brezhnev, Leonid, *1:* 41 (ill.),
41–52, 48 (ill.), 49 (ill.); *2:*
240 (ill.), 362 (ill.)
ABM treaty and, *2:* 262
Afghanistan and, *1:* 50
Andropov, Yuri, and, *1:* 45
Angola and, *1:* 50
Brandt, Willy, and, *1:* 48
Brezhnev Doctrine and, *1:* 47
Carter, Jimmy, and, *1:* 49, 50,
74–75
character of, *1:* 41, 46, 47
Chernenko, Konstantin, and, *1:*
44, 45

China and, *1:* 47
Communist Party and, *1:* 41,
42, 43–46, 49–50
coup d'état and, *1:* 45–46
Czechoslovakia and, *1:* 43, 47;
2: 282
death of, *1:* 45, 51, 152; *2:* 395,
417
détente and, *1:* 48–49; *2:*
360–61
Dubcek, Alexander, and, *1:* 47
early life of, *1:* 42–43, 45
economy and, *1:* 46, 51
Egypt and, *1:* 50
election of, *1:* 41, 45
Ethiopia and, *1:* 50
on Europe, *1:* 41
as first secretary, *2:* 240
Ford, Gerald, and, *1:* 48–49
freedom and, *1:* 46, 47
Gorbachev, Mikhail, and, *1:*
152
Great Terror and, *1:* 42–43
Gromyko, Andrey, and, *1:* 164,
166
Helsinki Accords and, *2:* 413
human rights and, *1:* 75
Israel and, *1:* 50
Jews and, *1:* 75
KGB (Soviet secret police) and,
1: 46
Khrushchev, Nikita, and, *1:* 43,
44–46; *2:* 238
Kissinger, Henry, and, *2:*
261–62
Komsomol and, *1:* 42
Kosygin, Aleksey, and, *2:* 280,
282
military and, *1:* 47, 51
Moldavia and, *1:* 43–44
nation building and, *1:* 50
Nixon, Richard M., and, *1:*
48–49, 50; *2:* 261–62, 360–61
nuclear weapons and, *1:* 47,
48–49, 77–78, 166; *2:* 360–61
October War and, *1:* 50
Palestine Liberation Organiza-
tion and, *1:* 50
Poland and, *1:* 51
Reagan, Ronald, and, *1:* 51
Romania and, *1:* 43
Somalia and, *1:* 50
space programs and, *1:* 47
Stalin, Joseph, and, *1:* 44

Strategic Arms Limitation Talks
and, *1:* 49, 50, 77–78, 166; *2:*
261, 360–61
Syria and, *1:* 50
Third World and, *1:* 50
Vietnam War and, *1:* 50
Warsaw Pact and, *1:* 47–48
West Germany and, *1:* 47–48
World War II and, *1:* 43
Brinkmanship, *1:* 128–29, 130
British Commonwealth of Na-
tions, *1:* 29
British Empire, *1:* 25, 29
Brown, Pat, *2:* 390
Brown v. Board of Education, 1: 68
Brussels Pact, *1:* 38
Brzezinski, Zbigniew, *1:* 74, 75, 75
(ill.)
Bulganin, Nikolay, *2:* 233, 234,
290 (ill.)
Bullitt, William C., *2:* 209
Bureau of Investigation (BOI). *See*
Federal Bureau of Investiga-
tion
Bush, Barbara, *1:* 54, 61
Bush, George, *1:* 53 (ill.), **53–61,**
59 (ill.)
as author, *1:* 61
Baker, James, and, *2:* 421
Carter, Jimmy, and, *1:* 55, 81
Central Intelligence Agency
and, *1:* 55
China and, *1:* 55
early life of, *1:* 53–54
election of, *1:* 56; *2:* 399, 420
Ford, Gerald, and, *1:* 55
Germany and, *2:* 405
Goldwater, Barry, and, *1:* 54
Gorbachev, Mikhail, and, *1:* 57,
58, 157; *2:* 405
honors for, *1:* 54
imperialism and, *1:* 59
Iran-Contra scandal and, *1:* 56,
60; *2:* 398
Iraq and, *1:* 60
Kennan, George F., and, *2:* 217
Kissinger, Henry, and, *2:* 266
Kohl, Helmut, and, *2:* 274
military and, *1:* 54, 58
Nixon, Richard M., and, *1:* 55;
2: 364
Noriega, Manuel, and, *1:* 59
nuclear weapons and, *1:* 57, 58
oil and, *1:* 54

Organization of American
States and, *1:* 60
Panama and, *1:* 59–60
Persian Gulf War and, *1:* 60
presidency of, *1:* 56–60
Reagan, Ronald, and, *2:* 391
Republican Party and, *1:* 54, 55
retirement of, *1:* 61
Rice, Condoleezza, and, *2:* 401,
404–5
Russia and, *1:* 58–59
Somalia and, *1:* 60
Soviet Union and, *1:* 57, 58; *2:*
420, 421
Texas and, *1:* 54–55
Ukraine and, *1:* 58
United Nations and, *1:* 55, 60
on United States of America, *1:*
53
vice presidency of, *1:* 55–56
Watergate scandal and, *1:* 55
World War II and, *1:* 54
Yeltsin, Boris, and, *1:* 58–59
Bush, George W., *1:* 61; *2:* 253,
401, 406 (ill.), 406–7
Bush, Jeb, *1:* 61
Byrnes, James F., *1:* 3, 62 (ill.),
62–69, 67 (ill.), 127

C

Camp David Accords, *1:* 70, 78
(ill.), 78–79; *2:* 263
Capitalism
Cold War and, *2:* 384–85
colonialism and, *1:* 178–79
communism and, *1:* 111, 150,
181, 186; *2:* 210–11, 237,
251, 272, 351, 357, 385,
433–34
democracy and, *1:* 42
dictatorship and, *1:* 84–85, 99
economy and, *1:* 3, 26, 42, 86,
111, 119, 127, 150, 178; *2:*
211, 237, 251–52, 313, 385,
404
facism and, *1:* 186
Ho Chi Minh and, *1:* 178–79
Indochina and, *1:* 181
Kennan, George F., and, *2:* 211
Kosygin, Aleksey, and, *2:* 280–82
Mao Zedong and, *2:* 313

objectivism and, *2:* 382
property and, *1:* 3, 42, 86, 111,
  150, 178; *2:* 211, 237,
  251–52, 313, 385, 404
Rand, Ayn, and, *2:* 385
Soviet Union and, *2:* 280–82
Stalin, Joseph, and, *2:* 210–11,
  351
United States of America and,
  1: 86, 127
West Germany and, *2:* 268
Carter Center, *1:* 80
Carter, Jimmy, *1:* 70 (ill.), **70–81,**
  78 (ill.); *2:* 391 (ill.)
  Afghanistan and, *1:* 50, 70, 78;
    2: 393
  African Americans and, *1:* 71,
    73
  as author, *1:* 79–80
  Brezhnev, Leonid, and, *1:* 49,
    50, 74–75
  Brzezinski, Zbigniew, and, *1:*
    74, 75
  Bush, George, and, *1:* 55, 81
  Camp David Accords and, *1:*
    70, 78–79; *2:* 263
  China and, *1:* 39, 70, 77, 120
  Clifford, Clark M., and, *1:* 109,
    114
  Clinton, Bill, and, *1:* 81
  Conference on Security and
    Cooperation in Europe and,
    1: 75
  Democratic Party and, *1:* 73
  Deng Xiaoping and, *1:* 120
  détente and, *1:* 74–75
  dictatorship and, *1:* 76
  discrimination and, *1:* 73
  early life of, *1:* 71–72
  economy and, *1:* 76–77; *2:* 391
  election of, *1:* 55, 74; *2:* 390,
    391–92
  elections monitored by, *1:*
    80–81
  energy policy and, *1:* 76–77
  as farmer, *1:* 72, 73
  as governor, *1:* 73–74
  Great Depression and, *1:* 71–72
  Helsinki Accords and, *2:* 265
  honors for, *1:* 81
  human rights and, *1:* 70,
    71–72, 75–76, 80–81
  Iran hostage crisis and, *1:* 70,
    79; *2:* 391

Kissinger, Henry, and, *2:* 266
Latin America and, *1:* 76
"malaise speech" of, *1:* 77
as naval officer, *1:* 72–73
Nicaragua and, *1:* 81
North Korea and, *1:* 81; *2:* 248
nuclear weapons and, *1:* 49, 70,
  74–75, 77–78, 81, 166; *2:*
  248, 392
Olympics and, *1:* 70, 78
Pahlavi, Mohammed Reza, and,
  1: 79
Panama and, *1:* 77, 81, 125
presidency of, *1:* 73–79
Reagan, Ronald, and, *2:* 391–92
Rickover, Hyman G., and, *1:*
  72–73
Sakharov, Andrey, and, *1:* 75
segregation and, *1:* 73
Soviet Union and, *1:* 50, 70,
  74–75, 77–78; *2:* 393
Strategic Arms Limitation Talks
  and, *1:* 49, 70, 77–78, 166; *2:*
  392
Vance, Cyrus, and, *1:* 74
Vietnam War and, *1:* 76
Carter, Lillian Gordy, *1:* 71
Carter, Rosalynn Smith, *1:* 72, 73,
  80–81
Castro Argiz, Angel, *1:* 83
Castro, Fidel, *1:* 82 (ill.), **82–91**
  Allende, Salvador, and, *1:* 20,
    22
  as author, *1:* 91
  Bay of Pigs and, *1:* 87; *2:* 341
  Central Intelligence Agency
    and, *1:* 87, 88
  China and, *1:* 86
  communism and, *1:* 86, 88; *2:*
    223
  Cuban Missile Crisis and, *1:*
    88–89, 90
  De Rivera, José Antonio Primo,
    and, *1:* 84
  democracy and, *1:* 86
  early life of, *1:* 83–84
  Eastern Bloc and, *1:* 86
  economy and, *1:* 86–87, 88, 91
  Eisenhower, Dwight D., and, *1:*
    87; *2:* 223
  Gorbachev, Mikhail, and, *1:* 91
  imperialism and, *1:* 82–83, 87
  Khrushchev, Nikita, and, *2:* 223
  Martí, José, and, *1:* 84

nation building and, *1:* 83, 88
Operation Mongoose and, *1:*
    88; *2:* 226
presidency of, *1:* 86–91
reputation of, *1:* 87–88
revolution and, *1:* 84–85,
    143–44
Soviet Union and, *1:* 86, 87,
    88–89, 91
26th of July Movement and, *1:*
    85
Castro, Raúl, *1:* 85, 88
Casualties. *See* Death
CCC. *See* Civilian Conservation
    Corps (CCC)
CDU. *See* Christian Democratic
    Union (CDU)
Center for a New Generation, *2:*
    405–6
Center for International Security
    and Arms Control, *2:* 404
Central American Policy Commit-
    tee, *2:* 266
Central Committee
  of Communist Party, *1:* 162
  Gorbachev, Mikhail, and, *1:*
    152–53
  Khrushchev, Nikita, and, *2:* 232
  Kosygin, Aleksey, and, *2:* 279
  Molotov, Vyacheslav, and, *2:*
    347
  Shevardnadze, Eduard, and, *2:*
    417
  Stalin, Joseph, and, *2:* 429
  Yeltsin, Boris, and, *2:* 419
  Zhou Enlai and, *2:* 465
Central Intelligence Agency (CIA)
  Allende, Salvador, and, *1:* 24
  Bush, George, and, *1:* 55
  Castro, Fidel, and, *1:* 87, 88
  Cuba and, *1:* 87, 88, 113, 144;
    2: 223
  Foreign Intelligence Advisory
    Board and, *1:* 113
  formation of, *1:* 109
  Guatemala and, *1:* 141
  imperialism and, *1:* 24, 87, 88,
    141, 144; *2:* 223, 398
  Iran and, *1:* 141
  Nicaragua and, *2:* 398
  Watergate scandal and, *2:* 363
Central Party, *1:* 10
CFE. *See* Conventional Forces in
    Europe (CFE) treaty

Chamberlain, Neville, *1:* 27, 103;
    2: 304
Champagne, Maurice, *2:* 383
Chang Chi-Chung, *2:* 468 (ill.)
"Checkers Speech," *2:* 356
Chernenko, Konstantin, *1:* 44,
    45, 152; *2:* 395, 417–18
Chernobyl disaster, *1:* 153
Chiang Ching-kou, *1:* 98, 99
Chiang Kai-shek, *1:* 92 (ill.),
    92–99, 97 (ill.)
  death of, *1:* 99
  early life of, *1:* 92–93
  Ho Chi Minh and, *1:* 179
  Japan and, *1:* 94–96
  Korean War and, *1:* 98
  Nationalists and, *1:* 93–97; *2:*
    465, 466, 467
  New Life Movement of, *1:* 94
  popularity of, *1:* 39, 96
  religion and, *1:* 92, 94
  Republic of China and, *1:* 92,
    97–99, 118; *2:* 467
  revolution and, *1:* 92, 93–97,
    117; *2:* 298–99, 315–16, 324,
    465, 466, 467
  Soviet Union and, *1:* 93
  Sun Yat-sen and, *1:* 93
  Truman, Harry S., and, *1:* 96,
    98
  United Front and, *1:* 96
  World War II and, *1:* 96
  Zhou Enlai and, *1:* 94–96
Chiang Kai-shek, Madame, *1:* 94,
    95, 95 (ill.)
Chile, *1:* 17–24, 76; *2:* 263–64,
    362
China. *See also* People's Republic
    of China (PRC); Republic of
    China (ROC); Taiwan
  agriculture in, *1:* 121–22
  Bevin, Ernest, and, *1:* 39
  Brezhnev, Leonid, and, *1:* 47
  brinkmanship and, *1:* 130
  Bush, George, and, *1:* 55
  Carter, Jimmy, and, *1:* 39, 70,
    77, 120
  Castro, Fidel, and, *1:* 86
  communism in, *1:* 93–97,
    117–23; *2:* 235, 312, 314–15,
    317–18, 319, 360, 434
  Communist Party in, *2:* 313,
    315, 317, 318, 465, 465–66,
    467

Cuba and, *1:* 86
Cultural Revolution in, *1:* 119;
   2: 246, 318–20, 471–72
democracy and, *2:* 314
Dulles, John Foster, and, *1:* 130
economy of, *1:* 96, 116,
   118–19, 121–23; *2:* 313,
   317–18, 470–71
Eisenhower, Dwight D., and, *1:*
   130
Four Modernizations in, *2:* 320
Gang of Four in, *1:* 119, 120; *2:*
   320
Great Britain and, *1:* 39; *2:* 307
Great Leap Forward in, *1:*
   118–19; *2:* 317–18, 470–71
Great Wall of, *2:* 361 (ill.)
India and, *2:* 470
isolationism and, *1:* 116, 121
Japan and, *1:* 94–96, 117; *2:*
   467
Johnson, Lyndon B., and, *1:*
   201
Khrushchev, Nikita, and, *1:*
   118; *2:* 235
Kim Il Sung and, *2:* 245–46
Kissinger, Henry, and, *2:* 255,
   260, 360, 470
Korean War and, *1:* 5, 98; *2:*
   243–44, 299–300, 469
Kosygin, Aleksey, and, *2:* 280
Long March in, *1:* 94, 117; *2:*
   316, 466–67
MacArthur, Douglas, and, *2:*
   298–99, 299–300
Marshall, George C., and, *2:*
   324, 467
May Fourth Movement in, *2:*
   314
most-favored-nation trade status of, *1:* 121
names in, *1:* 180
nation building and, *2:* 470
Nationalists in, *1:* 93–97, 117;
   2: 298, 315, 324, 465, 466,
   467
New Life Movement in, *1:* 94
Nixon, Richard M., and, *1:*
   98–99; *2:* 260, 313, 354, 359,
   360, 470
North Atlantic Treaty Organization and, *2:* 317
North Korea and, *2:* 245–46
North Vietnam and, *2:* 257

nuclear weapons and, *2:* 318
perestroika and, *1:* 121
Red Army in, *2:* 316, 466
Red Guard in, *2:* 318, 472
Red Scare and, *2:* 333
revolution in, *1:* 5–6, 39, 92,
   93–97, 117; *2:* 243, 298–99,
   313, 315–16, 324, 464–67
Rusk, Dean, and, *1:* 202
Sian Incident in, *1:* 94–96
Sino-Soviet Treaty and, *2:*
   316–17
Soviet Union and, *1:* 47, 93,
   116, 118; *2:* 235, 280,
   316–18, 471
Stalin, Joseph, and, *2:* 317
Taiwan and, *1:* 98–99, 130; *2:*
   469
Tiananmen Square, *1:* 121; *2:*
   314
Truman, Harry S., and, *1:* 96,
   98, 139; *2:* 298, 324, 467
United Front in, *1:* 96
United Nations and, *1:* 98–99,
   119; *2:* 313, 360, 469
Vietnam and, *2:* 469
World War II and, *1:* 96; *2:* 316
China Lobby, *1:* 95, 98; *2:* 360,
   469
Christian Democratic Union
   (CDU), *1:* 11, 14–15; *2:* 270,
   271, 274
Christmas bombing, *2:* 259, 359
Chu Teh, *2:* 468 (ill.)
Churchill, Winston, *1:* 100 (ill.),
   100–108; *2:* 457 (ill.)
Attlee, Clement R., and, *1:*
   27–28
as author, *1:* 102, 103
Bevin, Ernest, and, *1:* 35
Big Three and, *1:* 104–6
communism and, *1:* 100, 107
death of, *1:* 108
early life of, *1:* 101–2
election of, *1:* 27, 32, 40, 107;
   2: 304, 305
Elizabeth II and, *1:* 100–101
Harriman, W. Averell, and, *1:*
   171
Hitler, Adolf, and, *1:* 102–3,
   104
honors for, *1:* 100–101, 103
Iron Curtain and, *1:* 100, 107
as journalist, *1:* 101–2

Kennedy, John F., and, *1:* 101
Macmillan, Harold, and, *2:*
304–5
military and, *1:* 101
Molotov, Vyacheslav, and, *2:*
349
nuclear weapons and, *1:* 31,
108
politics and, *1:* 102
Potsdam Conference and, *1:*
35–36; *2:* 431
retirement of, *1:* 108
Roosevelt, Franklin D., and, *1:*
105–6; *2:* 431
Soviet Union and, *1:* 108
Stalin, Joseph, and, *1:* 105–6,
107; *2:* 431
Tehran Conference and, *2:* 431
Truman, Harry S., and, *1:*
107–8; *2:* 457
World War I and, *1:* 102
World War II and, *1:* 27–28,
100, 102–6; *2:* 304–5, 349
Yalta Conference and, *1:* 65,
66; *2:* 431
CIA. *See* Central Intelligence
Agency (CIA)
CIS. *See* Commonwealth of Inde-
pendent States (CIS)
Civil rights
Allende, Salvador, and, *1:* 23
communism and, *2:* 385
democracy and, *2:* 385
Federal Bureau of Investigation
and, *1:* 187, 193
House Un-American Activities
Committee and, *2:* 333
Johnson, Lyndon B., and, *1:*
194, 196, 197, 198; *2:* 222
Kennedy, John F., and, *2:* 218,
221–22
McCarthy, Joseph R., and, *2:*
336
Nixon, Richard M., and, *2:* 357,
358–59
Red Scare and, *2:* 333
Rice, Condoleezza, and, *2:*
402–3
Civil Rights Act of 1957, *1:* 196
Civil Rights Act of 1964, *1:* 194,
197; *2:* 222
Civilian Conservation Corps
(CCC), *2:* 295, 323

Clifford, Clark M., *1:* 109 (ill.),
109–15, 112 (ill.)
Clifford-Elsey Report, *1:* 110–11
Clinton, Bill, *1:* 60, 81; *2:* 364,
403
Cohn, Roy, *2:* 334
Cold War
beginning of, *1:* 172; *2:* 212
capitalism and, *2:* 384–85
colonialism and, *1:* 180
communism and, *2:* 316–17,
384–85
democracy and, *2:* 316–17
description of, *1:* 42, 190
end of, *1:* 58; *2:* 265, 274, 421
Japan and, *2:* 298
Kennan, George F., on, *2:* 396
Macmillan, Harold, and, *2:* 303
Nixon, Richard M., and, *2:* 354
nuclear weapons and, *2:*
366–67
Reagan, Ronald, and, *2:* 387,
396
Shevardnadze, Eduard, and, *2:*
416
Truman, Harry S., and, *2:* 452,
458–59, 459–61, 462
Collectivism, *2:* 384, 409, 429,
448
Colombo Plan, *1:* 40
Colonialism, *1:* 177–79, 180; *2:*
309–10. *See also* Imperialism
Cominform, *2:* 434, 448
Comintern, *2:* 412, 446
Common Market, *1:* 14; *2:* 308–9
Commonwealth of Independent
States (CIS), *2:* 423
Communism. *See also* Collectivism; Communist Party
Berlin Wall and, *2:* 226
Bolshevik Revolution and, *1:*
187; *2:* 231, 380–81
capitalism and, *1:* 111, 150,
181, 186; *2:* 210–11, 237,
251, 272, 351, 357, 385,
433–34
Castro, Fidel, and, *1:* 86, 88; *2:*
223
Chiang Kai-shek, Madame,
and, *1:* 95
in China, *1:* 93–97, 117–23; *2:*
235, 312, 314–15, 317–18,
319, 360, 434

Churchill, Winston, and, *1:* 100, 107

civil rights and, *2:* 385

Clifford, Clark M., and, *1:* 110–11

Cold War and, *2:* 316–17, 384–85

collapse of, *1:* 53, 57–59, 122; *2:* 273–74, 396, 405, 421–22, 442

Communist Party and, *1:* 17–18, 26, 42, 82, 100, 110, 127, 159–60, 162, 168, 178, 186; *2:* 223, 231, 251, 278, 312, 340, 346, 366, 385, 410, 426, 445

in Cuba, *1:* 82, 88

definition of, *1:* 17–18

democracy and, *1:* 168, 186, 189; *2:* 251, 316–17, 366, 404

dictatorship and, *2:* 250

Dulles, John Foster, and, *1:* 127, 128–30

in East Germany, *2:* 268

in Eastern Bloc, *2:* 273–74

economy and, *1:* 3, 18, 26, 42, 82, 100, 110, 127, 150, 160, 168, 178, 186; *2:* 211, 223, 231, 250, 251, 278, 295, 312, 331, 340, 346, 366, 385, 389, 404, 410, 426, 445, 458, 464

Eisenhower, Dwight D., and, *1:* 140–41, 181

elections and, *1:* 162; *2:* 295

Federal Bureau of Investigation and, *1:* 186, 189–92

freedom and, *2:* 250, 381

Gorbachev, Mikhail, and, *1:* 150; *2:* 418, 422

Harriman, W. Averell, and, *1:* 168, 172

Hitler, Adolf, and, *1:* 104 (ill.)

Ho Chi Minh and, *1:* 176, 178–79, 181

Hoover, J. Edgar, and, *1:* 186, 187, 189–92; *2:* 333

Johnson, Lyndon B., and, *1:* 201

Kennan, George F., and, *2:* 211

Kennedy, John F., and, *2:* 340

Khrushchev, Nikita, and, *2:* 235, 236

Kirkpatrick, Jeane, and, *2:* 251

Lenin, Vladimir I., and, *1:* 179; *2:* 312

MacArthur, Douglas, and, *2:* 293

Macmillan, Harold, and, *2:* 307

Mao Zedong and, *2:* 312, 314–15, 317–18, 319

Marx, Karl, and, *2:* 312, 346, 445, 464

McCarthy, Joseph R., and, *2:* 329, 331

Molotov, Vyacheslav, and, *2:* 345

Nixon, Richard M., and, *2:* 354, 355–56

in North Korea, *2:* 247

Oppenheimer, J. Robert, and, *2:* 370, 376–77

in Poland, *1:* 36–37

property and, *1:* 3, 18, 26, 42, 82, 100, 110, 127, 150, 160, 168, 178, 186; *2:* 211, 223, 231, 278, 295, 312, 331, 340, 346, 366, 385, 389, 404, 410, 426, 445, 458, 464

Rand, Ayn, and, *2:* 379, 381, 384

Reagan, Ronald, and, *2:* 251, 387, 389

Red Scare and, *2:* 332–33, 376, 389

religion and, *2:* 385, 389

Rice, Condoleezza, and, *2:* 404

Roosevelt, Franklin D., and, *1:* 185–86, 189

Rusk, Dean, and, *1:* 201, 202

in Soviet Union, *1:* 26, 110, 127; *2:* 385, 410, 418

Stalin, Joseph, and, *2:* 236, 426–28, 433–34

Tito, Josip Broz, and, *2:* 445–46

Truman Doctrine and, *1:* 3–4

Zhou Enlai and, *2:* 464

Communist Party. *See also* Communism

Allende, Salvador, and, *1:* 18, 19

Andropov, Yuri, and, *2:* 417

Beria, Lavrenty, and, *2:* 433

Bolshevik Revolution and, *1:* 45

Brezhnev, Leonid, and, *1:* 41, 42, 43–46, 49–50

Central Committee of, *1:* 152–53, 162; *2:* 232, 279, 347, 417, 419, 429, 465

Chernenko, Konstantin, and, *1:* 45; *2:* 417

in Chile, *1:* 19

in China, *2:* 313, 315, 317, 318, 465, 465–66, 467

communism and, *1:* 17–18, 26, 42, 82, 100, 110, 127, 159–60, 162, 168, 178, 186; *2:* 223, 231, 251, 278, 312, 340, 346, 366, 385, 410, 426, 445

Council of Ministers in, *1:* 162, 163, 166; *2:* 240, 277, 279, 280, 282

in Cuba, *1:* 86

Deng Xiaoping and, *1:* 117, 118, 119, 122–23

end of, *2:* 422

formation of, *1:* 159

in France, *1:* 178

freedom and, *2:* 434

Gorbachev, Mikhail, and, *1:* 146, 150, 151, 152–53, 153–54, 157, 166; *2:* 418, 419

Great Terror and, *1:* 45

Gromyko, Andrey, and, *1:* 162–63, 165, 166–67

Ho Chi Minh and, *1:* 178, 179

in Indochina, *1:* 179

Khrushchev, Nikita, and, *2:* 231–32, 233, 234, 240

Kosygin, Aleksey, and, *1:* 46; *2:* 277, 278–79, 279–80, 282

Lenin, Vladimir I., and, *1:* 159

Mao Zedong and, *2:* 313, 315, 317, 318, 467

Molotov, Vyacheslav, and, *2:* 347, 353

Podgorny, Nikolay, and, *1:* 46

Politburo in, *1:* 118, 152, 162–63, 165; *2:* 232, 234, 240, 279, 280, 347, 352, 418, 465–66

Presidium in, *1:* 44, 163; *2:* 419

Sakharov, Andrey, and, *2:* 410

Secretariat of, *1:* 162

Shevardnadze, Eduard, and, *2:* 417

in Soviet Union, *1:* 41, 42, 43–46, 49–50, 153–54, 157, 162–63; *2:* 231–32, 233, 234,

239–40, 277, 278–79, 279–80, 347, 353, 410, 417–18, 419, 429, 430, 433

Stalin, Joseph, and, *2:* 429, 430

structure of, *1:* 162–63

Tito, Josip Broz, and, *2:* 445–46

in United States of America, *1:* 192

in Vietnam, *1:* 176

Yeltsin, Boris, and, *1:* 157; *2:* 419

in Yugoslavia, *2:* 445–46

Zhou Enlai and, *2:* 465–66

Conant, James B., *2:* 375

Conference on Security and Co-operation in Europe (CSCE), *1:* 75; *2:* 264–65

Confucianism, *1:* 92, 177

Congress of People's Deputies, *1:* 154, 157; *2:* 414–15

Congressional Medal of Honor, *2:* 296–97

Conkin, Paul K., *1:* 194

Connally, John B., *2:* 228

Conservative Party
  in Great Britain, *1:* 25, 27, 102; *2:* 443
  Macmillan, Harold, and, *2:* 304
  Thatcher, Margaret, and, *2:* 439

Containment
  Attlee, Clement R., and, *1:* 30–32
  Clifford, Clark M., and, *1:* 111
  Colombo Plan and, *1:* 40
  Dulles, John Foster, and, *1:* 128
  Eisenhower Doctrine and, *1:* 132, 142
  Eisenhower, Dwight D., and, *1:* 141, 142
  Germany and, *2:* 432
  Harriman, W. Averell, and, *1:* 168, 171–72
  Japan and, *1:* 128; *2:* 298
  Johnson, Lyndon B., and, *1:* 198
  Kennan, George F., and, *2:* 207, 212–13
  Kohl, Helmut, and, *2:* 272–73
  MacArthur, Douglas, and, *2:* 295, 297, 298, 299
  Marshall, George C., and, *2:* 325
  Marshall Plan and, *1:* 112–13, 172

military and, *2:* 213

North Atlantic Treaty Organization and, *1:* 4, 31, 58, 111, 113; *2:* 271, 327, 434, 437

nuclear weapons and, *2:* 272–73

politics and, *2:* 213

Reagan, Ronald, and, *2:* 395, 395–97

Southeast Asia Treaty Organization and, *1:* 130, 141

Stalin, Joseph, and, *2:* 433–34

Truman Doctrine and, *1:* 3–4, 29–30, 38, 112, 172

Truman, Harry S., and, *1:* 3–4, 29–30, 38, 128, 172; *2:* 458–59

Contras, *1:* 56; *2:* 398

Conventional Forces in Europe (CFE) treaty, *2:* 274

Council of Ministers

in Communist Party, *1:* 162, 163

Gromyko, Andrey, and, *1:* 166

Khrushchev, Nikita, and, *2:* 240

Kosygin, Aleksey, and, *2:* 277, 279, 280, 282

Council on Foreign Relations, *2:* 256

"Crimes of Stalin" speech, *2:* 236, 291, 436

Crusade in Europe, *1:* 139

CSCE. *See* Conference on Security and Cooperation in Europe (CSCE)

Cuba. *See also* Cuban Missile Crisis

26th of July Movement and, *1:* 85

agriculture in, *1:* 86

Bay of Pigs and, *1:* 87, 113, 144; *2:* 223, 340–41

blockade of, *1:* 90; *2:* 227, 238

Central Intelligence Agency and, *1:* 87, 88, 113, 144; *2:* 223

China and, *1:* 86

communism in, *1:* 82, 88

Communist Party in, *1:* 86

Cuban Missile Crisis and, *1:* 88–91

Cuban People's Party in, *1:* 84–85

democracy in, *1:* 86

dictatorship and, *1:* 84–85

Eastern Bloc and, *1:* 86

economy of, *1:* 84–85, 86–87, 88, 91

Eisenhower, Dwight D., and, *1:* 87, 143–44; *2:* 223

Gorbachev, Mikhail, and, *1:* 91

Kennedy, John F., and, *1:* 87, 88

nationalization in, *1:* 86

nuclear weapons and, *1:* 88–91

revolution in, *1:* 84–85, 143–44

Soviet Union and, *1:* 82, 86, 87, 88–91; *2:* 223, 226–27

Spain and, *1:* 83

United Nations and, *1:* 91

Cuban Missile Crisis, *1:* 89 (ill.)

Acheson, Dean G., and, *1:* 7

blockade and, *1:* 90; *2:* 227, 238

Castro, Fidel, and, *1:* 88–89, 90

Kennedy, John F., and, *1:* 7, 89–91; *2:* 218, 226–28, 238, 308

Kennedy, Robert F., and, *2:* 227

Khrushchev, Nikita, and, *1:* 90–91; *2:* 226–27, 227–28, 230, 238

Kosygin, Aleksey, and, *2:* 277

Macmillan, Harold, and, *2:* 308

nuclear war and, *2:* 227, 238, 394

nuclear weapons and, *1:* 88–91

reconnaissance and, *1:* 90; *2:* 227

Cuban People's Party, *1:* 84–85

Cultural Revolution, *1:* 119; *2:* 246, 318–20, 471–72

Cummings, Homer S., *1:* 190 (ill.)

Czechoslovakia

Brezhnev, Leonid, and, *1:* 43, 47; *2:* 282

freedom in, *1:* 47

Gromyko, Andrey, and, *1:* 164

Soviet Union and, *1:* 43, 47, 164, 204; *2:* 216, 281, 282, 449

Sovietization of, *1:* 43

Stalin, Joseph, and, *2:* 435

Yugoslavia and, *2:* 449

D

Dag Hammarskjold Honorary Medal, *2:* 343

Davies, Joseph, *2:* 209–10
De Gaulle, Charles, *1:* 14; *2:* 305, 308, 309
De Rivera, José Antonio Primo, *1:* 84
Death
    in Cultural Revolution, *2:* 318, 320
    in Great Terror, *1:* 42–43; *2:* 232, 236, 278, 370, 412, 430, 434–35
    Stalin, Joseph, on, *2:* 425
    in Vietnam War, *1:* 201; *2:* 258, 359
    in World War II, *2:* 458
DeBakey, Michael, *2:* 419
"The Demands of the Annamite People," *1:* 178
Demilitarized Zone (DMZ), *2:* 244
DeMille, Cecil B., *2:* 382–83
Democracy
    Allende, Salvador, and, *1:* 17
    Bonner, Yelena, and, *2:* 415
    capitalism and, *1:* 42
    Castro, Fidel, and, *1:* 86
    in China, *2:* 314
    civil rights and, *2:* 385
    Cold War and, *2:* 316–17
    communism and, *1:* 168, 186, 189; *2:* 251, 316–17, 366, 404
    Conference on Security and Cooperation in Europe and, *2:* 265
    in Cuba, *1:* 86
    in East Germany, *2:* 421
    economy and, *2:* 426
    elections and, *1:* 25–26, 42, 86, 127; *2:* 251, 271, 314, 385, 404, 426, 449
    facism and, *1:* 186, 189
    Federal Bureau of Investigation and, *1:* 186, 189–90
    Gorbachev, Mikhail, and, *1:* 154; *2:* 418
    Harriman, W. Averell, and, *1:* 168, 171
    Hoover, J. Edgar, and, *1:* 186, 189–90
    in Hungary, *2:* 421
    Kohl, Helmut, and, *2:* 271
    in Poland, *2:* 421
    property and, *2:* 426
    Rice, Condoleezza, and, *2:* 404
    Sakharov, Andrey, and, *2:* 415

socialism and, *1:* 17, 20
    in Soviet Union, *1:* 154; *2:* 408, 415, 418
    in United States of America, *1:* 25–26, 127; *2:* 271
    in West Germany, *2:* 268
Democratic National Committee (DNC), *1:* 55, 74; *2:* 262, 363
Democratic Party
    Carter, Jimmy, and, *1:* 73
    Eisenhower, Dwight D., and, *1:* 139
    Harriman, W. Averell, and, *1:* 169–70, 173
    Kirkpatrick, Jeane, and, *2:* 250
    Reagan, Ronald, and, *2:* 389
    Vietnam War and, *2:* 358
Democratic People's Republic of Korea (DPRK). *See* North Korea
Democratic Republic of Vietnam (DRV), *1:* 179
Deng Xiaoping, *1:* 116 (ill.), **116–23,** 120 (ill.); *2:* 472
Deng Yingchao, *2:* 465
Desert Storm, *1:* 60
Détente
    Brezhnev, Leonid, and, *1:* 48–49; *2:* 360–61
    Carter, Jimmy, and, *1:* 74–75
    Ford, Gerald, and, *1:* 49
    Gromyko, Andrey, and, *1:* 165–66
    Helsinki Accords and, *1:* 49; *2:* 264, 265, 413
    Kissinger, Henry, and, *2:* 255, 260–62, 264, 390
    Nixon, Richard M., and, *1:* 48–49; *2:* 354, 360–61
    nuclear weapons and, *1:* 48–49
    Reagan, Ronald, and, *2:* 390, 393
    Soviet Union and, *1:* 48–49
    Watergate scandal and, *2:* 264
Dewey, Thomas, *1:* 127–28; *2:* 459, 460
Dictatorship
    capitalism and, *1:* 84–85, 99
    Carter, Jimmy, and, *1:* 76
    in Chile, *2:* 263
    communism and, *2:* 250
    Cuba and, *1:* 84–85
    Reagan, Ronald, and, *2:* 395–97
    Republic of China and, *1:* 98

United States of America and, *1:* 76, 84–85; *2:* 250–51, 263
"Dictatorships and Double Standards," *2:* 250
Diplomacy, *1:* 1; *2:* 463, 467–70, 472
Discrimination, *1:* 73, 198; *2:* 402–3, 435. *See also* Racism; Segregation
Distinguished Flying Cross, *1:* 54
Dixiecrats, *2:* 460
DMZ. *See* Demilitarized Zone (DMZ)
DNC. *See* Democratic National Committee (DNC)
Dockers' Union, *1:* 34
Doctor Zhivago, 2: 234
Dole, Robert, *1:* 74
Dominican Republic, *1:* 203
Domino theory, *1:* 181, 198
Douglas, Helen Gahagan, *2:* 355
DPRK (Democratic People's Republic of Korea). *See* North Korea
Draft, *1:* 76
DRV. *See* Democratic Republic of Vietnam (DRV)
Dubcek, Alexander, *1:* 47; *2:* 449
Dukakis, Michael, *1:* 56
Dulles, Allen, *1:* 124
Dulles, Eleanor, *1:* 125
Dulles, John Foster, *1:* 7, 124 (ill.), **124–33,** 129 (ill.); *2:* 256, 307, 469
Dumbarton Oaks Conference, *1:* 161

E

Early warning systems, *2:* 421
East Berlin, *2:* 224, 235–36
East Germany
    Brandt, Willy, and, *1:* 15
    communism and, *2:* 268
    democracy and, *2:* 421
    economy of, *2:* 225, 272, 275
    Eisenhower, Dwight D., and, *1:* 130
    formation of, *1:* 12, 138; *2:* 224, 235, 268, 432
    Gorbachev, Mikhail, and, *1:* 58

Khrushchev, Nikita, and, *2:* 224–25
Kohl, Helmut, and, *2:* 271–72
Marshall Plan and, *2:* 272
Nixon, Richard M., and, *1:* 14
Ostpolitik and, *1:* 15
Soviet Union and, *1:* 58, 129–30; *2:* 224–25
West Germany and, *1:* 15; *2:* 271–72
Eastern Bloc
    Castro, Fidel, and, *1:* 86
    collapse of, *2:* 421–22
    communism in, *2:* 273–74
    Cuba and, *1:* 86
    economy of, *2:* 448
    Gorbachev, Mikhail, and, *2:* 421–22
    Helsinki Accords and, *2:* 265
    Marshall Plan and, *2:* 325
    Shevardnadze, Eduard, and, *2:* 421–22
    Soviet Union and, *2:* 351, 446–48, 458
    Stalin, Joseph, and, *2:* 425, 432, 446–48
ECA. *See* Economic Cooperation Administration (ECA)
Economic Cooperation Administration (ECA), *2:* 325
Economy. *See also* Agriculture; Industry
    Adenauer, Konrad, and, *1:* 9, 12, 14
    Andropov, Yuri, and, *2:* 417
    Attlee, Clement R., and, *1:* 28–29, 32
    Bevin, Ernest, and, *1:* 38
    Brezhnev, Leonid, and, *1:* 46, 51
    capitalism and, *1:* 3, 26, 42, 86, 111, 119, 127, 150, 178; *2:* 211, 237, 251–52, 313, 385, 404
    Carter, Jimmy, and, *1:* 76–77; *2:* 391
    Castro, Fidel, and, *1:* 86–87, 88, 91
    of Chile, *1:* 21–23; *2:* 263, 362
    of China, *1:* 96, 116, 118–19, 121–23; *2:* 313, 317–18, 470–71
    Colombo Plan and, *1:* 40
    Common Market and, *1:* 14

communism and, *1:* 3, 18, 26,
42, 82, 100, 110, 127, 150,
160, 168, 178, 186; *2:* 211,
223, 231, 250, 251, 278, 295,
312, 331, 340, 346, 366, 385,
389, 404, 410, 426, 445, 458,
464
of Cuba, *1:* 84–85, 86–87, 88,
91
democracy and, *2:* 426
Deng Xiaoping and, *1:* 116,
118–19, 121–23
of East Germany, *2:* 225, 272,
275
of Eastern Bloc, *2:* 448
of Europe, *1:* 14, 30–31, 38; *2:*
308–9, 324–26
of France, *1:* 12
Gorbachev, Mikhail, and, *1:* 56,
154–55, 157; *2:* 395, 414,
418, 442
of Great Britain, *1:* 28–29, 32,
38, 39, 170; *2:* 305–6, 308–9,
310, 439–40
Great Leap Forward and, *2:*
317–18
Harriman, W. Averell, and, *1:*
172
of Japan, *2:* 297, 298, 299
Khrushchev, Nikita, and, *2:* 239
Kim Il Sung and, *2:* 244–45,
247
Kohl, Helmut, and, *2:* 272
Kosygin, Aleksey, and, *2:* 277,
279, 280–81
Macmillan, Harold, and, *2:*
305–6, 310
Mao Zedong and, *1:* 118–19
Marshall, George C., and, *2:*
321, 324–26
Marshall Plan and, *1:* 4, 30–31,
38, 113
nationalization of, *1:* 21, 22,
23, 28–29, 86; *2:* 263, 362,
380–81
of North Korea, *2:* 244–45, 247
Reagan, Ronald, and, *2:* 392
Roosevelt, Franklin D., and, *1:*
64; *2:* 295, 389
of Russia, *1:* 58–59; *2:* 346, 380
Shevardnadze, Eduard, and, *2:*
418
socialism and, *1:* 86

of Soviet Union, *1:* 3, 46, 51,
56, 146, 154–55, 157; *2:* 239,
277, 279, 280–81, 361, 395,
396, 414, 417, 418, 429, 442,
448
Stalin, Joseph, and, *2:* 429
of Taiwan, *1:* 98
Thatcher, Margaret, and, *2:*
439–40
Tito, Josip Broz, and, *2:* 448,
451
Truman, Harry S., and, *2:* 459
of United States of America, *1:*
3, 4, 26, 60, 64, 71, 76–77,
84–85, 86–87, 204; *2:*
294–95, 323, 369–70, 389,
391, 392, 455, 459
Vietnam War and, *1:* 204
of West Germany, *1:* 9, 12, 14;
2: 272
Yeltsin, Boris, and, *1:* 58–59
of Yugoslavia, *2:* 448, 451
EDC. *See* European Defense Community (EDC)
Eden, Anthony, *2:* 305, 306, 306
(ill.)
EEC. *See* European Economic
Community (EEC)
Egypt
Brezhnev, Leonid, and, *1:* 50
Camp David Accords and, *2:*
263
independence of, *1:* 29
October War and, *1:* 50; *2:*
262–63
Six-Day War and, *1:* 203
Soviet Union and, *1:* 50; *2:*
262–63
Suez War and, *1:* 131–32, 142;
2: 306
Einstein, Albert, *2:* 369
Eisenhower Doctrine, *1:* 132, 142
Eisenhower, Dwight D., *1:* 129
(ill.), 134 (ill.), **134–45**, 137
(ill.), 138 (ill.)
Acheson, Dean G., and, *1:* 6, 7
"Atoms for Peace" plan of, *1:*
140–41
as author, *1:* 139, 144
Bay of Pigs and, *1:* 144
Berlin and, *1:* 137
Castro, Fidel, and, *1:* 87; *2:* 223
character of, *1:* 143
China and, *1:* 130

communism and, *1:* 140–41, 181
containment and, *1:* 141, 142
Cuba and, *1:* 87, 143–44; *2:* 223
death of, *1:* 144–45
Dulles, John Foster, and, *1:* 128–30, 131
early life of, *1:* 134–35
East Germany and, *1:* 130
Eisenhower Doctrine and, *1:* 142
election of, *1:* 128, 139–40, 141–42, 143; *2:* 302, 334, 356, 389, 461
espionage and, *1:* 144; *2:* 308
Germany and, *1:* 138
Guatemala and, *1:* 141
Hungary and, *1:* 130, 142
imperialism and, *1:* 87, 141, 144; *2:* 223
Iran and, *1:* 141
Kennan, George F., and, *2:* 215
Khrushchev, Nikita, and, *1:* 141, 144; *2:* 230, 237, 238, 308
Korean War and, *1:* 134, 140, 143
MacArthur, Douglas, and, *1:* 135
Macmillan, Harold, and, *2:* 305, 307, 308
McCarthy, Joseph R., and, *1:* 140; *2:* 334
military and, *1:* 134, 135–39
missiles and, *2:* 307
Nixon, Richard M., and, *1:* 139–40; *2:* 356, 358
North Atlantic Treaty Organization and, *1:* 139
nuclear weapons and, *1:* 140, 144; *2:* 215
"Open Skies" plan of, *1:* 140–41
Oppenheimer, J. Robert, and, *2:* 376
peace and, *1:* 134
popularity of, *1:* 143
presidency of, *1:* 139–44
Reagan, Ronald, and, *2:* 389
Republic of China and, *1:* 141
retirement of, *1:* 144
Roosevelt, Franklin D., and, *1:* 136
Southeast Asia Treaty Organization and, *1:* 141
Soviet Union and, *1:* 137, 138, 140–41, 142, 143

space race and, *1:* 142
Stalin, Joseph, and, *1:* 138
Suez War and, *1:* 131–32, 142; *2:* 306
Taiwan and, *1:* 130
television and, *1:* 143
Third World and, *1:* 141
Truman, Harry S., and, *1:* 139
Vietnam and, *1:* 141
Vietnam War and, *1:* 198
West Berlin and, *1:* 132; *2:* 237
World War I and, *1:* 135
World War II and, *1:* 134, 135–38
Elections
of 1932, *1:* 2, 64, 170
of 1944, *2:* 456
of 1948, *1:* 139; *2:* 389, 459, 460
of 1952, *1:* 128, 139–40, 143 (ill.); *2:* 301–2, 334, 356, 389, 461
of 1956, *1:* 141–42, 143
of 1958, *2:* 389
of 1960, *1:* 113, 197; *2:* 221, 358, 390
of 1964, *1:* 199–200; *2:* 358, 390
of 1968, *1:* 204; *2:* 257, 358, 390
of 1972, *2:* 259, 362, 390
of 1976, *1:* 55, 74; *2:* 390
of 1980, *1:* 55–56, 79; *2:* 251
of 1984, *1:* 56; *2:* 395
of 1988, *1:* 56; *2:* 399
of 1992, *1:* 60
of 2000, *1:* 61; *2:* 406
Carter, Jimmy, monitors, *1:* 80–81
in Chile, *1:* 19, 20–21
communism and, *1:* 162; *2:* 295
democracy and, *1:* 25–26, 42, 86, 127; *2:* 251, 271, 314, 385, 404, 426, 449
in France, *1:* 14
in Germany, *2:* 274
in Great Britain, *1:* 27, 28, 33, 40, 106, 107; *2:* 304, 305, 306, 308, 437
in North Korea, *2:* 247
in Poland, *1:* 36–37, 66, 171; *2:* 431
in Soviet Union, *1:* 41, 44, 45, 152–53, 157, 163, 166; *2:* 210–11, 232

Stalin, Joseph, and, *1:* 138
in United States of America, *1:* 25–26
in West Germany, *1:* 12, 15; *2:* 271
in Yugoslavia, *2:* 450
Elizabeth II, *1:* 100–101
Elsey, George, *1:* 111
Emergency Powers Act, *1:* 35
Energy, *1:* 76–77. *See also* Nuclear energy
Enrico Fermi Award, *2:* 377
Espionage. *See also* Reconnaissance
Eisenhower, Dwight D., and, *1:* 144; *2:* 308
Johnson, Lyndon B., and, *1:* 203
Khrushchev, Nikita, and, *1:* 144; *2:* 238, 308
Manhattan Project and, *1:* 191–92; *2:* 285, 287, 351
North Korea and, *1:* 203
nuclear weapons and, *1:* 191–92; *2:* 285, 287, 333, 351
space race and, *1:* 142
Watergate scandal and, *2:* 363, 364
Ethiopia, *1:* 50, 164
Europe
Brezhnev, Leonid, on, *1:* 41
economy of, *1:* 14, 30–31, 38; *2:* 308–9, 324–26
Marshall Plan and, *2:* 324–25
military and, *2:* 262
unification of, *2:* 269–70, 272, 273
European Advisory Commission, *2:* 210
European Common Market. *See* Common Market
European Defense Community (EDC), *1:* 12
European Economic Community (EEC). *See* Common Market
Execution. *See* Death

F

Fabian Society, *1:* 26
Facism, *1:* 185–86, 189–90
Fair Deal, *2:* 459

Farrell, Thomas, *2:* 372
FBI. *See* Federal Bureau of Investigation (FBI)
February Revolution, *2:* 347. *See also* Bolshevik Revolution
Federal Bureau of Investigation (FBI)
civil rights and, *1:* 187, 193
communism and, *1:* 186, 189–92
corruption and, *1:* 188
democracy and, *1:* 186, 189–90
facism and, *1:* 189–90
Great Depression and, *1:* 188–89
Hoover, J. Edgar, becomes director of, *1:* 187–88
Manhattan Project and, *1:* 191–92
organized crime and, *1:* 189
Prohibition Era and, *1:* 185
Red Scare and, *1:* 189–92
science and, *1:* 188
Watergate scandal and, *2:* 363
World War II and, *1:* 189–90
Federal Council of Churches of Christ in America, *1:* 126
Federal Republic of Germany. *See* West Germany
Federalism, *2:* 450
Felix, Antonia, *2:* 403, 404, 407
"Feminine factor," *2:* 439
Ferguson, Francis, *2:* 368
Fermi, Enrico, *2:* 284, 371, 375, 377
Fission, *2:* 284–85, 409
Ford, Gerald, *1:* 49 (ill.)
Brezhnev, Leonid, and, *1:* 48–49
Bush, George, and, *1:* 55
détente and, *1:* 49
election of 1976 and, *1:* 74
Kissinger, Henry, and, *2:* 264–65
Nixon, Richard M., and, *1:* 74; *2:* 364
nuclear weapons and, *1:* 166
Reagan, Ronald, and, *2:* 266, 390
Rockefeller, Nelson A., and, *1:* 55
Strategic Arms Limitation Talks and, *1:* 166
Ford Motor Company, *2:* 339, 342

Foreign Intelligence Advisory
   Board, *1:* 113
Foreign Service, *2:* 208
The Fountainhead, 2: 383
Four Modernizations, *2:* 320
France
   Adenauer, Konrad, and, *1:* 12,
      14
   colonialism and, *1:* 177–78,
      180
   Communist Party in, *1:* 178
   economy of, *1:* 12
   elections in, *1:* 14
   Great Britain and, *2:* 308
   Ho Chi Minh and, *1:* 177–78,
      180; *2:* 257
   Indochina and, *1:* 177–78, 180
   Suez War and, *1:* 131–32, 142;
      2: 306
   Vietminh and, *1:* 180
   Vietnam and, *1:* 141, 177–78,
      179, 180, 198; *2:* 257, 469
   West Germany and, *1:* 12, 13,
      14
Franco, Francisco, *1:* 84
Franco-German Friendship Treaty,
   1: 14
Frankfurter, Felix, *1:* 2
Franklin Delano Roosevelt Free-
   dom from Want Medal, *2:*
   343
FRAP. *See* Popular Revolutionary
   Action Front (FRAP)
Freedom. *See also* specific free-
   doms
   Brezhnev, Leonid, and, *1:* 46,
      47
   communism and, *2:* 250, 381
   Communist Party and, *2:* 434
   in Czechoslovakia, *1:* 47
   Helsinki Accords and, *2:*
      264–65
   Ho Chi Minh and, *1:* 181–82
   KGB (Soviet secret police) and,
      1: 46
   Khrushchev, Nikita, and, *2:*
      233, 234
   Mao Zedong and, *2:* 312, 314,
      318, 320
   McNamara, Robert S., and, *2:*
      337
   Reagan, Ronald, on, *2:* 387
   Red Scare and, *2:* 384

Sakharov, Andrey, and, *2:* 408,
   412
Shevardnadze, Eduard, on, *2:*
   416
in Soviet Union, *2:* 233, 234, 408
Thatcher, Margaret, and, *2:*
   437, 442–43
Tito, Josip Broz, and, *2:* 451
in Vietnam, *1:* 181–82
in Yugoslavia, *2:* 451
Freedom March, *2:* 222
Freedom of assembly, *1:* 193
Freedom of religion, *2:* 385, 389
Freedom of speech, *1:* 193
Fuchs, Klaus, *1:* 192; *2:* 287
Fusion, *2:* 409

G

Gamsakhurdia, Zviad, *2:* 422
Gang of Four, *1:* 119, 120; *2:* 320
GDR. *See* German Democratic Re-
   public (GDR)
General Electric, *2:* 389
General Intelligence Division
   (GID), *1:* 187
Geneva Conference, *2:* 469
George Bush Presidential Library,
   1: 61
Georgia (USSR), *2:* 417, 422–23
German Democratic Republic
   (GDR). *See* East Germany
Germany. *See also* East Germany;
   West Germany
   Bush, George, and, *2:* 405
   Byrnes, James F., and, *1:* 67
   Christian Democratic Union in,
      2: 274
   containment and, *2:* 432
   division of, *1:* 12, 66, 105,
      106–7, 138, 161; *2:* 224, 235,
      268, 351–52, 432
   Eisenhower, Dwight D., and, *1:*
      138
   elections in, *2:* 274
   Gorbachev, Mikhail, and, *1:* 58;
      2: 405
   government of, *1:* 138
   Harriman, W. Averell, and, *1:* 172
   Kennan, George F., and, *2:* 210
   Molotov, Vyacheslav, and, *2:*
      348–50, 351

North Atlantic Treaty Organization and, *1:* 58; *2:* 274
nuclear energy and, *2:* 284–85
nuclear weapons and, *2:* 370, 371
Poland and, *2:* 431
reparations and, *1:* 66
reunification of, *1:* 12, 13–14, 53, 58; *2:* 268, 272, 273–74, 351, 401, 405
Rice, Condoleezza, and, *2:* 401
Soviet Union and, *1:* 58, 106–7, 172; *2:* 348, 351, 431, 432
Stalin, Joseph, and, *2:* 432
treaties concerning, *1:* 37; *2:* 274
Truman, Harry S., and, *1:* 107
World War II and, *1:* 102–5, 106–7, 136–37, 161; *2:* 348, 431
GID. *See* General Intelligence Division (GID)
Glasnost
  Gorbachev, Mikhail, and, *1:* 56, 146, 153; *2:* 274, 395, 414, 416, 418
  Shevardnadze, Eduard, and, *2:* 416
Glassboro Summit, *2:* 281
G-Men, *1:* 188–89
Goebbels, Joseph, *2:* 273
Goldwater, Barry, *1:* 54, 199–200; *2:* 358, 390
Goncz, H. E. Arpad, *2:* 253
Gopkalo, Pantelei Yefimovich, *1:* 147
Gorbachev, Andrei Moiseyevich, *1:* 147–48
Gorbachev, Mikhail, *1:* 120 (ill.), 146 (ill.), **146–58,** 156 (ill.); *2:* 397 (ill.)
  Afghanistan and, *1:* 156; *2:* 420
  Andropov, Yuri, and, *1:* 152–53; *2:* 417
  Brezhnev, Leonid, and, *1:* 152
  Bush, George, and, *1:* 57, 58, 157; *2:* 405
  Castro, Fidel, and, *1:* 91
  Chernobyl disaster and, *1:* 153
  communism and, *1:* 150; *2:* 418, 422
  Communist Party and, *1:* 146, 150, 151, 152–53, 153–54, 157, 166; *2:* 418, 419

Conference on Security and Cooperation in Europe and, *2:* 265
coup attempt on, *1:* 58, 157; *2:* 419, 422
Cuba and, *1:* 91
democracy and, *1:* 154; *2:* 418
early life of, *1:* 147–51
East Germany and, *1:* 58
Eastern Bloc and, *2:* 421–22
economy and, *1:* 56, 154–55, 157; *2:* 395, 414, 418, 442
education of, *1:* 148–51
election of, *1:* 45, 152–53, 157, 166; *2:* 418
as general secretary, *1:* 153–57, 166
Germany and, *1:* 58; *2:* 405
glasnost and, *1:* 56, 146, 153; *2:* 274, 395, 414, 416, 418
governmental reform by, *1:* 153–54
Great Terror and, *1:* 147–48
Gromyko, Andrey, and, *1:* 154, 166
honors for, *1:* 149–50, 157; *2:* 421
Kennan, George F., and, *2:* 216, 217, 396
Khrushchev, Nikita, and, *1:* 151
Kissinger, Henry, and, *2:* 266
Kohl, Helmut, and, *2:* 273, 274
Komsomol and, *1:* 150, 151
marriage of, *1:* 151
Memoirs of, *1:* 147, 148, 149
military and, *1:* 57, 58
nuclear weapons and, *1:* 56, 58, 154–55; *2:* 395–96, 418
perestroika and, *1:* 56, 121, 146, 153; *2:* 395, 414, 416, 418
Persian Gulf War and, *2:* 421
Reagan, Ronald, and, *1:* 56, 57, 155–56; *2:* 395–96, 418
resignation of, *1:* 146, 157
retirement of, *1:* 157
Sakharov, Andrey, and, *1:* 155; *2:* 414
Shevardnadze, Eduard, and, *1:* 151, 154, 166; *2:* 395, 418
Stalin, Joseph, and, *1:* 150
Strategic Defense Initiative and, *1:* 155; *2:* 395–96
Thatcher, Margaret, and, *2:* 442
United Nations and, *1:* 156

World War II and, *1:* 148

Yeltsin, Boris, and, *1:* 157; *2:* 418, 419

Gorbachev, Raisa, *1:* 120 (ill.), 151–52, 153, 156 (ill.), 157

Gore, Al, *1:* 61

Government Operations Committee, *2:* 334

Great Britain. *See also* British Commonwealth of Nations; British Empire

  Acheson, Dean G., and, *1:* 2

  Attlee, Clement R., and, *1:* 25, 27–32

  Bevin, Ernest, and, *1:* 33, 35–40

  Chamberlain, Neville, and, *1:* 27

  China and, *1:* 39; *2:* 307

  colonialism and, *2:* 309–10

  Conservative Party in, *1:* 25, 27, 102; *2:* 304, 439, 443

  Dockers' Union in, *1:* 34

  Dominican Republic and, *1:* 203

  economy of, *1:* 28–29, 32, 38, 39, 170; *2:* 305–6, 308–9, 310, 439–40

  elections in, *1:* 36, 40; *2:* 304, 305, 306, 308, 437

  European Common Market and, *2:* 308–9

  France and, *2:* 308

  Greece and, *1:* 29, 38, 112

  Independent Labour Party in, *1:* 26

  Israel and, *1:* 36–37

  Johnson, Lyndon B., and, *1:* 203

  Kurchatov, Igor, and, *2:* 291

  labor in, *1:* 34

  Labour Party in, *1:* 25, 27

  Lend-Lease program and, *1:* 170

  Liberal Party in, *1:* 102

  missiles and, *2:* 307

  Molotov, Vyacheslav, and, *2:* 348–49

  nationalization in, *1:* 28–29

  North Atlantic Treaty Organization and, *2:* 441–42

  nuclear energy and, *2:* 284, 291

  nuclear weapons and, *1:* 31, 38, 108; *2:* 307, 309, 440–41

  Palestine and, *1:* 36–37

  Reagan, Ronald, and, *2:* 441–42

  Republic of China and, *2:* 307

  socialism in, *1:* 25, 28–29; *2:* 439–40

  Soviet Union and, *1:* 35, 36–37, 108; *2:* 307–8, 348–49, 437–38

  Suez War and, *1:* 131–32, 142; *2:* 306

  Turkey and, *1:* 29, 38, 112

  Vietnam and, *1:* 141

  West Germany and, *2:* 308

  World War II and, *1:* 35, 100, 102–7; *2:* 219, 348–49, 438

Great Depression

  Byrnes, James F., and, *1:* 64

  Carter, Jimmy, and, *1:* 71–72

  Federal Bureau of Investigation and, *1:* 188–89

  Johnson, Lyndon B., and, *1:* 195–96

  MacArthur, Douglas, and, *2:* 294–95

  Marshall, George C., and, *2:* 323

  New Deal and, *2:* 455

  Oppenheimer, J. Robert, and, *2:* 369–70

  Roosevelt, Franklin D., and, *1:* 64; *2:* 295, 389

Great Leap Forward, *1:* 118–19; *2:* 317–18, 470–71

Great Society, *1:* 197–98, 201

Great Terror

  Brezhnev, Leonid, and, *1:* 42–43

  Communist Party and, *1:* 45

  execution during, *1:* 42–43; *2:* 232, 236, 278, 412, 430, 434–35

  Gorbachev, Mikhail, and, *1:* 147–48

  Gromyko, Andrey, and, *1:* 160

  Kennan, George F., and, *2:* 209

  Khrushchev, Nikita, and, *2:* 232, 236

  Kosygin, Aleksey, and, *2:* 278–79, 279–80

  Molotov, Vyacheslav, and, *2:* 348, 351, 352

  Sakharov, Andrey, and, *2:* 409–10

  Stalin, Joseph, and, *2:* 278, 370, 420, 430, 434–35

Tito, Josip Broz, and, *2:* 446
Great Wall of China, *2:* 361 (ill.)
Greece
    Attlee, Clement R., and, *1:* 29
    Bevin, Ernest, and, *1:* 38
    Great Britain and, *1:* 29, 38, 112
    Marshall, George C., and, *2:* 326
    Soviet Union and, *1:* 3–4; *2:* 326
    Truman Doctrine and, *1:* 112
    Truman, Harry S., and, *1:*
        29–30, 38; *2:* 326
    U.S. Congress and, *2:* 326
Greenglass, David, *2:* 287
Grenada, *2:* 395
Gromyko, Andrey, *1:* 131, 154,
    159 (ill.), **159–67,** 165 (ill.);
    2: 252 (ill.), 353
Groves, Leslie R., *2:* 371, 372
Guatemala, *1:* 141
Guevara, Che, *1:* 20, 85, 88
Gulag, *2:* 429, 433, 435
Gulf of Tonkin Resolution, *1:* 199

H

Haig, Alexander M., *2:* 261 (ill.)
Hall, Theodore Alvin, *2:* 287
Harriman, Mary, *1:* 170
Harriman, W. Averell, *1:* 168
    (ill.), **168–75,** 174 (ill.); *2:*
    210, 326 (ill.)
Havel, Václav, *2:* 253
Health care, *1:* 19, 198
Helms, Richard M., *2:* 261 (ill.)
Helsinki Accords, *1:* 49, 165–66;
    2: 264–65, 265–66, 413
Hero of Socialist Labor, *2:* 410
Hinckley, John, *2:* 392
Hiroshima
    deaths in, *2:* 458
    nuclear weapons and, *2:* 285,
        297, 371, 372, 409, 432
    Truman, Harry S., and, *2:* 458
Hiss, Alger, *2:* 333, 356
Hitler, Adolf
    Adenauer, Konrad, and, *1:* 11
    Chamberlain, Neville, and, *1:*
        103
    Churchill, Winston, and, *1:*
        102–3, 104
    Goebbels, Joseph, and, *2:* 273
    Molotov, Vyacheslav, and, *2:* 348

Nazi Party and, *1:* 126
rise of, *1:* 35, 189
Stalin, Joseph, and, *2:* 348, 431
Ho Chi Minh, *1:* 20, 176 (ill.),
    176–84, 178 (ill.); *2:* 239
    (ill.), 257, 465
Hoffman, Paul G., *2:* 326 (ill.)
Hollywood, *2:* 333, 384, 389
Hollywood Ten, *2:* 333
Hoover, Herbert, *2:* 294
Hoover, J. Edgar, *1:* 185 (ill.),
    185–93, 190 (ill.); *2:* 333, 376
Hot Line Agreement, *1:* 91; *2:* 238
An Hour Before Daylight, 1: 71
House Un-American Activities
    Committee (HUAC), *1:* 191;
    2: 332–33, 335 (ill.), 356,
    384, 389
*How Far We Slaves Have Come:
    South Africa and Cuba in
    Today's World, 1:* 91
"How to Fight Communism," *1:*
    191
Hu Yaobang, *1:* 120
Hua Guofeng, *1:* 119, 120
HUAC. *See* House Un-American
    Activities Committee
    (HUAC)
Hugo, Victor, *2:* 383
Human rights
    Bonner, Yelena, and, *2:* 408,
        412–13, 415
    Brezhnev, Leonid, and, *1:* 75
    Carter, Jimmy, and, *1:* 70,
        71–72, 75–76, 80–81
    definition of, *1:* 75
    in Japan, *2:* 297
    Kissinger, Henry, and, *2:* 264
    Kurchatov, Igor, and, *2:* 410–11
    Oppenheimer, J. Robert, and, *2:*
        410–11
    radio and, *1:* 75
    Sakharov, Andrey, and, *2:*
        410–12, 412–13
    in Soviet Union, *1:* 75
Humphrey, Hubert, *1:* 204; *2:* 358
Hungary, *1:* 129–30, 142; *2:* 236,
    421, 449
Hussein, Saddam, *2:* 421
Hydrogen bombs. *See also* Nuclear
    weapons
    development of, *1:* 6, 108, 150;
        2: 290, 375, 376, 409, 410

Oppenheimer, J. Robert, and, *2:* 375, 376

Sakharov, Andrey, and, *2:* 290, 375, 409, 410

testing of, *2:* 290, 307, 375, 410

I

IAS. *See* Institute for Advanced Study (IAS)

Ibáñez del Campa, Carlos, *1:* 19

ICBMs. *See* Intercontinental ballistic missiles (ICBMs)

IMF. *See* International Monetary Fund (IMF)

Imperialism. *See also* Colonialism
Bush, George, and, *1:* 59
Castro, Fidel, and, *1:* 82–83, 87
Central Intelligence Agency and, *1:* 24, 87, 88, 141, 144; *2:* 223, 398
Eisenhower, Dwight D., and, *1:* 87, 141, 144; *2:* 223
Kennedy, John F., and, *1:* 87, 88; *2:* 223, 226
Kissinger, Henry, and, *2:* 263–64
Nixon, Richard M., and, *2:* 361–62
Reagan, Ronald, and, *2:* 395–97
United States of America and, *1:* 82–83, 87, 88, 141; *2:* 223, 263, 395–97

Independent Labour Party, *1:* 26

India, *1:* 29; *2:* 470

Individualism, *2:* 383–84

Indochina, *1:* 177–78, 179, 180, 181

Industry, *2:* 429. *See also* Economy

INF. *See* Intermediate-range Nuclear Force (INF) treaty

Institute for Advanced Study (IAS), *2:* 213, 214–15, 375–76, 376–77

Intercontinental ballistic missiles (ICBMs), *2:* 361

Intermediate-range Nuclear Force (INF) treaty, *1:* 155; *2:* 396, 420

International Atomic Energy Agency, *2:* 352–53

International Bank for Reconstruction and Development. *See* World Bank

International Monetary Fund (IMF), *1:* 2–3

Ioffe, Abram, *2:* 284

Iran
Central Intelligence Agency and, *1:* 141
Eisenhower, Dwight D., and, *1:* 141
hostage crisis in, *1:* 70, 79; *2:* 391
Iran-Contra scandal, *1:* 56, 60; *2:* 398
Reagan, Ronald, and, *2:* 399

Iraq, *1:* 60; *2:* 421

Iron Curtain, *1:* 100, 107

Isolationism
China and, *1:* 116, 121
Harriman, W. Averell, and, *1:* 170
Kennan, George F., and, *2:* 211
Kim Il Sung and, *2:* 241, 245
Mao Zedong and, *1:* 116
North Korea and, *2:* 241, 245, 247
Republican Party and, *1:* 170
United States of America and, *1:* 170; *2:* 211

Israel
Bevin, Ernest, and, *1:* 36–37
Brezhnev, Leonid, and, *1:* 50
Camp David Accords and, *2:* 263
formation of, *1:* 36–37; *2:* 326–27
Great Britain and, *1:* 36–37
Marshall, George C., and, *2:* 326–27
October War and, *1:* 50; *2:* 262–63, 363
Palestine and, *1:* 36–37
Six-Day War and, *1:* 203
Soviet Union and, *1:* 50
Suez War and, *1:* 131–32, 142; *2:* 306
Truman, Harry S., and, *1:* 37; *2:* 326–27, 460

J

Japan
Chiang Kai-shek and, *1:* 94–96
China and, *1:* 94–96, 117; *2:* 467

Cold War and, *2:* 298
constitution of, *2:* 297
containment and, *1:* 128; *2:* 298
Dulles, John Foster, and, *1:* 128
economy of, *2:* 297, 298, 299
human rights in, *2:* 297
Indochina and, *1:* 179
Korea and, *2:* 241–42
MacArthur, Douglas, and, *2:* 293, 295–97, 298, 299
military of, *2:* 297
Roosevelt, Franklin D., and, *2:* 432
Soviet Union and, *1:* 66; *2:* 432
Stalin, Joseph, and, *1:* 66; *2:* 432
Truman, Harry S., and, *1:* 128
Vietnam and, *1:* 179
World War II and, *1:* 105, 106, 135–36, 179; *2:* 242, 285, 295–97, 370–71, 372, 409, 432, 458
Zhou Enlai and, *1:* 94–96
Jews, *1:* 36–37, 75; *2:* 435
Jiang Qing, *1:* 119; *2:* 320
Jiang Zemin, *1:* 121, 122
Jimmy Carter Library, *1:* 80
Joe-1, *2:* 410
Johnson, Lady Bird, *1:* 195
Johnson, Lyndon B., *1:* 7 (ill.), 194 (ill.), **194–205,** 199 (ill.); *2:* 222 (ill.), 281 (ill.)
Acheson, Dean G., and, *1:* 7–8
character of, *1:* 196
China and, *1:* 201
civil rights and, *1:* 194, 196, 197, 198; *2:* 222
Clifford, Clark M., and, *1:* 109, 113, 114
communism and, *1:* 201
containment and, *1:* 198
death of, *1:* 204–5
Dominican Republic and, *1:* 203
early life of, *1:* 195–96
election of, *1:* 199–200
espionage and, *1:* 203
Goldwater, Barry, and, *1:* 199–200
Great Britain and, *1:* 203
Great Depression and, *1:* 195–96
Great Society of, *1:* 197–98, 201

Harriman, W. Averell, and, *1:* 174–75
health care and, *1:* 198
Ho Chi Minh and, *1:* 182
Kennedy, John F., and, *1:* 197; *2:* 221, 228
Kissinger, Henry, and, *2:* 257
Kleberg, Richard, and, *1:* 195
Kosygin, Aleksey, and, *2:* 281
MacArthur, Douglas, and, *2:* 302
McNamara, Robert S., and, *2:* 337, 342
North Korea and, *1:* 203
nuclear weapons and, *1:* 204
Oppenheimer, J. Robert, and, *2:* 377
peace and, *1:* 200, 204
poverty and, *1:* 195, 197–98, 201
Rayburn, Sam, and, *1:* 195
retirement of, *1:* 204
Rusk, Dean, and, *1:* 201, 202
Six-Day War and, *1:* 203
Soviet Union and, *2:* 281
Strategic Arms Limitation Talks and, *1:* 204
in U.S. Congress, *1:* 196
vice presidency of, *1:* 197
Vietnam War and, *1:* 7–8, 109, 114, 174–75, 182, 183, 194, 198–203, 203–4; *2:* 281, 302, 342, 358, 359
World War II and, *1:* 196
Joliot-Curie Medal, *2:* 291
Jordan, *1:* 29, 203; *2:* 307

K

Kádár, János, *2:* 239 (ill.)
Kaganovich, Lazar, *2:* 231–32, 234, 236
Keenan, Joseph B., *1:* 190 (ill.)
Keep, John L., *1:* 41
Keeping Faith: Memoirs of a President, *1:* 79–80
Kennan, George F., *2:* 207 (ill.), **207–17,** 214 (ill.), 396
Kennan Institute for Advanced Russian Studies, *2:* 208
Kennedy, Jacqueline "Jackie" Lee Bouvier, *2:* 220, 221

Kennedy, John F., *1:* 112 (ill.),
174 (ill.); *2:* 218 (ill.),
218–29, 222 (ill.), 224 (ill.),
228 (ill.), 340 (ill.)
Acheson, Dean G., and, *1:* 7
Adenauer, Konrad, and, *1:* 15
as author, *2:* 219
Bay of Pigs and, *1:* 87, 144; *2:*
223, 340
Berlin Wall and, *1:* 15; *2:* 218,
226, 275
Churchill, Winston, and, *1:*
101
civil rights and, *2:* 218, 221–22
Clifford, Clark M., and, *1:* 113
communism and, *2:* 340
Cuba and, *1:* 87, 88
Cuban Missile Crisis and, *1:* 7,
89–91; *2:* 218, 226–28, 238,
308
death of, *1:* 113, 194, 197; *2:*
218, 222, 228–29
Dulles, John Foster, and, *1:* 131
early life of, *2:* 218–19, 230–31
election of, *1:* 113, 197; *2:* 220,
221, 358, 390
Harriman, W. Averell, and, *1:*
173
honors for, *2:* 219
Hoover, J. Edgar, and, *1:* 192
imperialism and, *1:* 87, 88; *2:*
223, 226
inaugural address of, *2:* 222
Johnson, Lyndon B., and, *1:*
197; *2:* 221, 228
Kennan, George F., and, *2:* 215
Khrushchev, Nikita, and, *2:*
223–26, 227–28, 230
Kissinger, Henry, and, *2:* 256,
257
Macmillan, Harold, and, *2:*
225, 308–9
McCarthy, Joseph R., and, *2:*
220
McNamara, Robert S., and, *2:*
337, 339–40, 341
military and, *2:* 225
nuclear weapons and, *2:*
226–27, 227–28, 341
Operation Mongoose and, *1:*
88; *2:* 226
Oppenheimer, J. Robert, and, *2:*
377
peace and, *2:* 221

Peace Corps and, *2:* 221
Reagan, Ronald, and, *2:* 216
Rusk, Dean, and, *1:* 202
segregation and, *2:* 221–22
Soviet Union and, *2:* 227–28,
340
submarines and, *2:* 309
Truman, Harry S., and, *2:* 220
Ulbricht, Walter, and, *2:* 225
in U.S. Congress, *2:* 219–21
Vietnam War and, *1:* 198
West Berlin and, *2:* 224–25
World War II and, *2:* 219
Kennedy, Robert F., *1:* 204; *2:* 227,
228 (ill.), 358
Kent State University, *2:* 359
KGB (Soviet secret police), *1:* 46;
2: 240, 433
Khomeini, Ayatollah Ruhollah, *1:*
79
Khrushchev, Nikita, *2:* 224 (ill.),
230 (ill.), **230–40,** 237 (ill.),
239 (ill.), 290 (ill.), 357 (ill.),
449 (ill.)
agriculture and, *2:* 238, 239
Berlin Wall and, *1:* 14; *2:*
225–26, 237, 275
Bolshevik Revolution and, *2:*
231
Brezhnev, Leonid, and, *1:* 43,
44–46; *2:* 238
Bulganin, Nikolay, and, *2:* 233,
234
Castro, Fidel, and, *2:* 223
character of, *1:* 46; *2:* 233–34
China and, *1:* 118; *2:* 235
communism and, *2:* 235, 236
Communist Party and, *2:*
231–32, 233, 234, 239–40
coup d'état and, *1:* 45–46
"Crimes of Stalin" speech and,
2: 236, 291, 436
Cuban Missile Crisis and, *1:*
90–91; *2:* 226–27, 227–28,
230, 238
death of, *1:* 41; *2:* 240
Deng Xiaoping and, *1:* 118
de-Stalinization and, *1:* 118; *2:*
233, 236
East Germany and, *2:* 224–25
economy and, *2:* 239
Eisenhower, Dwight D., and, *1:*
141, 144; *2:* 230, 237, 238,
308

election of, *1:* 150–51
espionage and, *1:* 144; *2:* 238, 308
as first secretary, *2:* 233–39
freedom and, *2:* 233, 234
Gorbachev, Mikhail, and, *1:* 151
Great Terror and, *2:* 232, 236
Gromyko, Andrey, and, *1:* 162, 164
Harriman, W. Averell, and, *1:* 171
Hungary and, *2:* 236
Kaganovich, Lazar, and, *2:* 231–32, 234, 236
Kennedy, John F., and, *2:* 223–26, 227–28, 230
KGB (Soviet secret police) and, *1:* 46; *2:* 240
"kitchen debate" and, *2:* 237 (ill.), 238, 357
Kosygin, Aleksey, and, *2:* 280
Kurchatov, Igor, and, *2:* 290–91
Limited Test-Ban Treaty of 1963, *2:* 238–39
Macmillan, Harold, and, *2:* 307, 308
Malenkov, Georgy M., and, *2:* 233, 234, 236
military and, *2:* 239–40
Molotov, Vyacheslav, and, *2:* 234, 236, 352–53
Nixon, Richard M., and, *2:* 238, 357
nuclear weapons and, *1:* 144; *2:* 227–28, 235, 238–39, 411
peace and, *2:* 352
religion and, *2:* 234
retirement of, *2:* 240
Sakharov, Andrey, and, *2:* 411
space race and, *2:* 235
Stalin, Joseph, and, *1:* 46, 118; *2:* 230, 231–32, 233, 236, 291, 352, 419, 435–36, 471
Tito, Josip Broz, and, *2:* 448–49
United Nations and, *2:* 233–34, 238
Virgin Land program and, *2:* 238
West Berlin and, *1:* 132; *2:* 224–25, 235–37
World War II and, *2:* 233
Yeltsin, Boris, and, *2:* 419
Zhou Enlai and, *2:* 471

Kim Il Sung, *2:* 241 (ill.), **241–48**
Kim Jong Il, *2:* 248
King, Martin Luther, Jr., *1:* 192, 204
Kirkpatrick, Jeane, *2:* 249 (ill.), **249–54,** 252 (ill.)
Kissinger, Henry, *2:* 255 (ill.), **255–67,** 259 (ill.), 261 (ill.)
Acheson, Dean G., and, *1:* 8
Allende, Salvador, and, *2:* 263–64
as author, *2:* 255, 256
Brezhnev, Leonid, and, *2:* 261–62
Bush, George, and, *2:* 266
Camp David Accords and, *2:* 263
Carter, Jimmy, and, *2:* 266
Chile and, *2:* 263–64
China and, *2:* 255, 260, 360, 470
Council on Foreign Relations and, *2:* 256
détente and, *2:* 255, 260–62, 264, 390
early life of, *2:* 255–56
Ford, Gerald, and, *2:* 264–65
as foreign affairs consultant, *2:* 256–57, 266
Gorbachev, Mikhail, and, *2:* 266
Helsinki Accords and, *2:* 264, 265–66
honors for, *2:* 255, 259–60
human rights and, *2:* 264
imperialism and, *2:* 263–64
Johnson, Lyndon B., and, *2:* 257
Kennedy, John F., and, *2:* 256, 257
as lecturer, *2:* 256
mutual assured destruction and, *2:* 260–61
as national security advisor, *2:* 257–65
National Security Council and, *2:* 257
Nixon, Richard M., and, *2:* 257, 259, 261–62, 262–63, 359
nuclear weapons and, *2:* 256, 260–62
October War and, *2:* 262–63, 363

Reagan, Ronald, and, *2:* 266,
390
Republic of China and, *2:* 260
reputation of, *2:* 258, 263,
264–65, 266
Rockefeller, Nelson A., and, *2:*
256
as secretary of state, *2:* 262–66
Soviet Union and, *2:* 255,
260–62, 264
Strategic Arms Limitation Talks
and, *2:* 261
U.S. Congress and, *2:* 264
Vietnam War and, *2:* 255,
257–60, 261–62, 264, 359
Vietnamization and, *2:* 258
Watergate scandal and, *2:* 363
World War II and, *2:* 255–56
Zhou Enlai and, *2:* 470
"Kitchen debate," *2:* 237 (ill.),
238, 357
Kleberg, Richard, *1:* 195
Klock, Augustus, *2:* 368
Kohl, Hans, *2:* 269
Kohl, Helmut, *1:* 58; *2:* 268 (ill.),
268–76
Komsomol
Andropov, Yuri, and, *1:* 45
Brezhnev, Leonid, and, *1:* 42
Gorbachev, Mikhail, and, *1:*
150, 151
Kosygin, Aleksey, and, *2:* 278
Shevardnadze, Eduard, and, *2:*
417
Korbel, Josef, *2:* 403
Korea, *2:* 241–42, 243, 244,
297–98. *See also* North Korea;
South Korea
Korean Airlines tragedy, *2:* 246,
394
Korean War
Acheson, Dean G., and, *1:* 5
Attlee, Clement R., and, *1:* 32
beginning of, *2:* 434
Bevin, Ernest, and, *1:* 40
Byrnes, James F., and, *1:* 68
Chiang Kai-shek and, *1:* 98
China and, *1:* 5, 98; *2:* 243–44,
299–300, 469
conduct of, *1:* 5
Eisenhower, Dwight D., and, *1:*
134, 140, 143
end of, *2:* 244
Kim Il Sung and, *2:* 243–44

MacArthur, Douglas, and, *1:* 5,
40; *2:* 243, 293, 299–301,
327, 461
Mao Zedong and, *2:* 299
Marshall, George C., and, *2:*
327
Rusk, Dean, and, *1:* 202
Soviet Union and, *1:* 5
Truman, Harry S., and, *1:* 5, 98,
139–40; *2:* 299–301, 461
United Nations and, *1:* 5; *2:*
243, 299
Zhou Enlai and, *2:* 469
Korean Workers' Party, *2:* 242,
247
Kosygin, Aleksey, *1:* 46; *2:* 277
(ill.), **277–82,** 281 (ill.)
Ku Klux Klan, *1:* 63, 192
Kurchatov, Igor, *2:* 283 (ill.),
283–92, 290 (ill.), 373,
410–11, 433
Kuwait, *1:* 60; *2:* 421

L

La Follette, Robert M., Jr., *2:* 331
Labor, *1:* 34, 35
Labour Party, *1:* 25, 27
Laird, Melvin R., *2:* 261 (ill.)
Latin America, *1:* 76; *2:* 327,
361–62
Le Duc Tho, *2:* 259 (ill.), 260
League for the Independence of
Vietnam. *See* Vietminh
League of Nations, *1:* 126, 127
Lebanon, *1:* 132; *2:* 307
Legion of Honor, *2:* 377
Lend-Lease program, *1:* 2, 170,
171
Lenin, Vladimir I., *2:* 428 (ill.)
Allende, Salvador, and, *1:* 18
Bolshevik Revolution and, *1:*
159; *2:* 278, 347, 427
communism and, *1:* 179; *2:*
312
Communist Party and, *1:* 159
death of, *2:* 381, 428–29
Molotov, Vyacheslav, and, *2:*
347
Stalin, Joseph, and, *2:* 427,
428–29
Li Peng, *2:* 465

Liberal Party, *1:* 102
Libya, *2:* 398–99
Limited Test-Ban Treaty of 1963, *1:* 91, 173; *2:* 227–28, 238–39, 309
The Little Red Book, 2: 318
Liu Bocheng, *1:* 119
Lodge, Henry Cabot, *2:* 221
Long March, *1:* 94, 117; *2:* 316, 466–67
"Long Telegram," *2:* 210–12
Looking Forward, 1: 61
Los Alamos National Laboratory, *2:* 285, 287, 368, 371, 409
Lossky, Nicolas O., *2:* 381–82
Lovett, Robert A., *2:* 338, 339

M

MacArthur, Douglas, *2:* 293 (ill.), **293–302,** 296 (ill.), 300 (ill.), 301 (ill.)
as author, *2:* 302
Bevin, Ernest, and, *1:* 40
character of, *2:* 294, 298
China and, *2:* 298–99, 299–300
Civilian Conservation Corps and, *2:* 295
communism and, *2:* 293
containment and, *2:* 295, 297, 298, 299
death of, *2:* 302
early life of, *2:* 293–94
Eisenhower, Dwight D., and, *1:* 135
election of 1952 and, *2:* 301–2
Great Depression and, *2:* 294–95
honors for, *2:* 294, 296–97
Japan and, *2:* 293, 295–97, 298, 299
Johnson, Lyndon B., and, *2:* 302
Korean War and, *1:* 5, 40; *2:* 243, 293, 299–301, 327, 461
Marshall, George C., and, *2:* 327
McCarthy, Joseph R., and, *2:* 299–300
as military advisor, *2:* 295
Philippines and, *2:* 295, 302
retirement of, *2:* 302

Roosevelt, Franklin D., and, *2:* 296–97
South Korea and, *2:* 297–98
Syngman Rhee and, *2:* 297–98
Truman, Harry S., and, *1:* 5, 40; *2:* 297, 298, 299–301, 327, 461
as U.S. Army chief of staff, *2:* 294–95
U.S. Congress and, *2:* 300–301
Vietnam War and, *2:* 302
World War I and, *2:* 294, 295
World War II and, *2:* 293, 295–97
Macmillan, Harold, *2:* 225, 303 (ill.), **303–11,** 309 (ill.)
Malenkov, Georgy M., *2:* 233, 234, 236
Malta Summit, *2:* 405
Mandela, Nelson, *1:* 91
Manhattan Project
development by, *1:* 31; *2:* 285, 409, 458
espionage and, *1:* 191–92; *2:* 285, 287, 351
Federal Bureau of Investigation and, *1:* 191–92
hydrogen bombs and, *2:* 375
Oppenheimer, J. Robert, and, *2:* 366, 368, 370–72
testing by, *2:* 285, 287, 458
Mao Zedong, *2:* 312 (ill.), **312–20,** 315 (ill.), 317 (ill.), 319 (ill.), 468 (ill.)
as author, *2:* 318–19
capitalism and, *2:* 313
communism and, *2:* 312, 314–15, 317–18, 319
Communist Party and, *2:* 313, 315, 317, 318, 467
Cultural Revolution of, *1:* 119; *2:* 246, 318–20, 471–72
death of, *1:* 119; *2:* 320, 472
Deng Xiaoping and, *1:* 118–19, 119–20
early life of, *2:* 313–15
economy and, *1:* 118–19
freedom and, *2:* 312, 314, 318, 320
Gang of Four and, *2:* 320
Great Leap Forward of, *1:* 118–19; *2:* 317–18, 470–71
health of, *2:* 319–20
Ho Chi Minh and, *1:* 179

isolationism and, *1:* 116
Korean War and, *2:* 299
Long March and, *2:* 316, 466–67
Maoism of, *2:* 312–13
Marxism and, *2:* 312, 314–15
May Fourth Movement and, *2:* 314
Nixon, Richard M., and, *2:* 313, 470
revolution and, *1:* 5–6, 93, 96, 117; *2:* 243, 298–99, 313, 315–16, 324, 466–67
Sino-Soviet Treaty and, *2:* 316–17
Soviet Union and, *2:* 313, 316–18
swimming and, *2:* 318
World War II and, *2:* 316
Zhou Enlai and, *2:* 470–72
Zhu De and, *2:* 316
Mao Zedong on People's War, 2: 318
Maoism, *2:* 312–13
Marshall, George C., *1:* 30 (ill.); *2:* 321 (ill.), **321–28,** 326 (ill.), 468 (ill.)
Berlin airlift and, *2:* 327
character of, *2:* 322
China and, *2:* 324, 467
Civilian Conservation Corps and, *2:* 323
containment and, *2:* 325
death of, *2:* 327
early life of, *2:* 321–22
economy and, *2:* 321, 324–26
as general, *2:* 321, 323–24
Great Depression and, *2:* 323
Greece and, *2:* 326
honors for, *2:* 321, 324, 325, 327
Israel and, *2:* 326–27
Kennan, George F., and, *2:* 212
Korea and, *2:* 243
Korean War and, *2:* 327
Latin America and, *2:* 327
as lecturer, *2:* 323
MacArthur, Douglas, and, *2:* 327
Marshall Plan and, *1:* 4, 113; *2:* 324–25
McCarthy, Joseph R., and, *2:* 324, 333–34
National Security Council and, *2:* 324

North Atlantic Treaty Organization and, *2:* 327
Organization of American States and, *2:* 327
Pershing, John J., and, *2:* 322
replacement of, *1:* 138–39
retirement of, *2:* 327
Rio Pact and, *2:* 327
Roosevelt, Franklin D., and, *2:* 323
as secretary of defense, *2:* 321, 327
as secretary of state, *1:* 3, 68; *2:* 321, 324–27
Soviet Union and, *2:* 324
Truman, Harry S., and, *2:* 324, 326–27
Turkey and, *2:* 326
U.S. Congress and, *2:* 326
U.S. State Department and, *2:* 324
World War I and, *2:* 322
World War II and, *2:* 323–24
Marshall Plan
Acheson, Dean G., and, *1:* 4
Attlee, Clement R., and, *1:* 30–31
Bevin, Ernest, and, *1:* 38
Clifford, Clark M., and, *1:* 112–13
containment and, *1:* 112–13, 172
East Germany and, *2:* 272
Eastern Bloc and, *2:* 325
economy and, *1:* 4, 113
Europe and, *2:* 324–25
Harriman, W. Averell, and, *1:* 172
Marshall, George C., and, *1:* 4, 113; *2:* 324–25
military and, *1:* 113
Soviet Union and, *2:* 272, 325
Truman, Harry S., and, *2:* 459
Martí, José, *1:* 84
Marx, Karl. *See also* Marxism
Allende, Salvador, and, *1:* 18
communism and, *2:* 312, 346, 445, 464
Ho Chi Minh and, *1:* 181
Marxism, *2:* 228–29, 312, 314–15, 346
Masters of Deceit, 1: 192
May Fourth Movement, *2:* 314, 464

McCarthy Committee, *2:* 334–35
McCarthy, Joseph R., *2:* 329
(ill.), **329–36,** 335 (ill.)
Acheson, Dean G., and, *1:* 6; *2:*
334
censure of, *2:* 220, 335
character of, *2:* 331
civil rights and, *2:* 336
Cohn, Roy, and, *2:* 334
communism and, *2:* 329, 331
death of, *2:* 335
early life of, *2:* 329–30
Eisenhower, Dwight D., and, *1:*
140; *2:* 334
election of, *2:* 331, 334
House Un-American Activities
Committee and, *2:* 333
Kennedy, John F., and, *2:* 220
La Follette, Robert M., Jr., and,
2: 331
MacArthur, Douglas, and, *2:*
299–300
Marshall, George C., and, *2:*
324, 333–34
McCarthyism and, *2:* 332–33
Permanent Subcommittee on
Investigations and, *2:* 334–35
Red Scare and, *2:* 329, 331–36,
376
Truman, Harry S., and, *1:* 140;
2: 299–300, 334, 460, 461
U.S. Army and, *1:* 140; *2:*
334–35
U.S. State Department and, *1:*
6; *2:* 331–32, 334
Voice of America and, *2:* 334
Welch, Joseph N., and, *2:* 329,
335
Wiley, Alexander, and, *2:*
330–31
World War II and, *2:* 330
McCarthyism, *2:* 332–33
McCone, John, *1:* 199 (ill.)
McGovern, George, *2:* 362
McMahon Act, *1:* 108
McNamara, Robert S., *1:* 199
(ill.); *2:* 337 (ill.), **337–44,**
340 (ill.)
The Medical-Social Reality in Chile,
1: 19
The Memoirs of Richard Nixon, 2:
364
Mensheviks, *2:* 427
Middle East, *2:* 363

Military. *See also* U.S. Army
Acheson, Dean G., and, *1:* 1, 4,
6
Adenauer, Konrad, and, *1:* 9,
12–14
Bevin, Ernest, and, *1:* 35, 38–39
Brezhnev, Leonid, and, *1:* 47,
51
buildup of, *1:* 51
Bush, George, and, *1:* 54, 58
Churchill, Winston, and, *1:*
101
Clifford, Clark M., and, *1:* 109,
111
containment and, *2:* 213
draft, *1:* 76
Eisenhower, Dwight D., and, *1:*
134, 135–39
Europe and, *2:* 262
Gorbachev, Mikhail, and, *1:* 57,
58
in Japan, *2:* 297
Kennedy, John F., and, *2:* 225
Khrushchev, Nikita, and, *2:*
239–40
Kim Il Sung and, *2:* 247
Kissinger, Henry, and, *2:* 256
Marshall Plan and, *1:* 113
in North Korea, *2:* 247
NSC-68 and, *1:* 6
Reagan, Ronald, and, *1:* 51; *2:*
392, 393
in Soviet Union, *1:* 47, 51, 58;
2: 213, 239–40
Stalin, Joseph, and, *2:* 431
Missiles, *1:* 155; *2:* 307, 309, 361,
393
Mitterrand, François, *2:* 272
Moldavia, *1:* 43–44
Molotov Cocktail, *2:* 350, 350
(ill.)
Molotov, Vyacheslav, *2:* 345
(ill.), **345–53,** 349 (ill.)
agriculture and, *2:* 348
Berlin blockade and, *2:* 352
Bolshevik Revolution and, *2:*
346–47
Churchill, Winston, and, *2:* 349
communism and, *2:* 345
Communist Party and, *2:* 347,
353
death of, *2:* 353
early life of, *2:* 345–47
as foreign minister, *2:* 348–52

Germany and, *2:* 348–50, 351
Great Britain and, *2:* 348–49
Great Terror and, *2:* 348, 351, 352
Gromyko, Andrey, and, *1:* 160, 162; *2:* 353
Harriman, W. Averell, and, *1:* 171
Hitler, Adolf, and, *2:* 348
Khrushchev, Nikita, and, *2:* 234, 236, 352–53
Lenin, Vladimir I., and, *2:* 347
Marxism and, *2:* 346
Molotov Cocktail and, *2:* 350
nuclear weapons and, *2:* 351
Potsdam Conference and, *2:* 351
Pravda and, *2:* 346–47
retirement of, *2:* 353
Roosevelt, Franklin D., and, *2:* 348–50
Stalin, Joseph, and, *2:* 345, 346, 347–48, 351, 352
Tehran Conference and, *2:* 349
Truman, Harry S., and, *2:* 350–51
World War II and, *2:* 348–50
Yalta Conference and, *2:* 349–50
Monarchy, *2:* 345–46, 380
Mondale, Walter, *1:* 74
Moorer, Thomas H., *2:* 261 (ill.)
Movies, *1:* 189, 192
Murrow, Edward R., *2:* 334
Mutual assured destruction, *2:* 260–61
My African Journey, 1: 102
The Mysterious Valley, 2: 383
Mzhevandze, Vassily, *2:* 417

N

Nagasaki
deaths in, *2:* 458
nuclear weapons and, *2:* 285, 297, 371, 372, 409, 432
Truman, Harry S., and, *2:* 458
NASA. *See* National Aeronautics and Space Administration (NASA)
Nasser, Gamal Abdel, *1:* 131; *2:* 306, 450

Nathaniel Branden Institute, *2:* 384
Nation building
in Africa, *2:* 310, 470
Brezhnev, Leonid, and, *1:* 50
Castro, Fidel, and, *1:* 83, 88
China and, *2:* 470
Gromyko, Andrey, and, *1:* 164
Soviet Union and, *1:* 50, 164
in Third World, *1:* 50, 83
Zhou Enlai and, *2:* 470
National Academy of Sciences, *2:* 371
National Aeronautics and Space Administration (NASA), *1:* 142
National Guard, *2:* 222
National Press Club, *1:* 5
National Security Act, *1:* 109
National Security Council (NSC)
formation of, *1:* 109
Kirkpatrick, Jeane, and, *2:* 251
Kissinger, Henry, and, *2:* 257
Marshall, George C., and, *2:* 324
NSC-68, *1:* 6
Rice, Condoleezza, and, *2:* 404–5
National Youth Administration (NYA), *1:* 195–96
Nationalism, *2:* 428
Nationalists
Chiang Kai-shek and, *1:* 93–97; *2:* 465, 466, 467
revolution and, *1:* 117; *2:* 315–16, 324, 465, 466, 467
Nationalization
by Attlee, Clement R., *1:* 28–29
in Chile, *1:* 21, 22, 23; *2:* 263, 362
in Cuba, *1:* 86
in Great Britain, *1:* 28–29
in Soviet Union, *2:* 380–81
of Suez Canal, *2:* 306
NATO. *See* North Atlantic Treaty Organization (NATO)
Nazi Party, *1:* 126
The Necessity for Choice, 2: 256
Nehru, Jawaharlal, *2:* 450, 470
New Deal, *1:* 64; *2:* 389, 455
New Life Movement, *1:* 94
New Look, *1:* 129
Ngo Dinh Diem, *1:* 129 (ill.)
Nicaragua, *1:* 56, 81; *2:* 398

Nichols, K. D., *2:* 374 (ill.)
9/11. *See* September 11, 2001, terrorist attacks
Nitze, Paul H., *1:* 6
Nixon Center for Peace and Freedom, *2:* 365
Nixon, Richard M., *1:* 48 (ill.), 165 (ill.); *2:* 237 (ill.), 261 (ill.), 354 (ill.), **354–65,** 357 (ill.), 361 (ill.), 362 (ill.)
 ABM treaty and, *2:* 262
 Acheson, Dean G., and, *1:* 8
 Allende, Salvador, and, *1:* 22–23; *2:* 362
 as attorney, *2:* 355, 358
 as author, *2:* 358, 364
 Brezhnev, Leonid, and, *1:* 48–49, 50; *2:* 261–62, 360–61
 Bush, George, and, *1:* 55; *2:* 364
 character of, *2:* 355
 "Checkers Speech" and, *2:* 356
 Chile and, *1:* 22–23; *2:* 362
 China and, *1:* 98–99; *2:* 260, 313, 354, 359, 360, 470
 Christmas bombing and, *2:* 359
 civil rights and, *2:* 357, 358–59
 Clinton, Bill, and, *2:* 364
 Cold War and, *2:* 354
 comebacks of, *2:* 358, 364
 communism and, *2:* 354, 355–56
 death of, *2:* 365
 détente and, *1:* 48–49; *2:* 354, 360–61
 domestic agenda of, *2:* 358–59
 early life of, *2:* 354–55
 East Germany and, *1:* 14
 Eisenhower, Dwight D., and, *1:* 139–40; *2:* 356, 358
 elections of, *1:* 197, 204; *2:* 221, 257, 259, 355, 356, 358, 362, 390
 Ford, Gerald, and, *1:* 74; *2:* 364
 Gromyko, Andrey, and, *1:* 164–65
 Harriman, W. Averell, and, *1:* 175
 Hiss, Alger, and, *2:* 356
 House Un-American Activities Committee and, *2:* 332–33, 356
 imperialism and, *2:* 361–62
 Khrushchev, Nikita, and, *2:* 238, 357

 Kissinger, Henry, and, *2:* 257, 259, 261–62, 262–63, 359
 "kitchen debate" and, *2:* 237 (ill.), 238, 357
 Latin America and, *2:* 361–62
 Mao Zedong and, *2:* 313, 470
 Middle East and, *2:* 363
 North Korea and, *2:* 246
 nuclear weapons and, *1:* 48–49; *2:* 359, 360–61
 October War and, *1:* 50; *2:* 262, 363
 peace and, *2:* 359, 365
 presidency of, *2:* 358–64
 Reagan, Ronald, and, *2:* 364, 390
 Red Scare and, *2:* 332–33
 Republic of China and, *1:* 98–99; *2:* 260, 360, 470
 reputation of, *2:* 355
 resignation of, *2:* 264, 363–64
 retirement of, *2:* 364–65
 Russia and, *2:* 364–65
 Shanghai Communiqué and, *2:* 360
 Silent Majority and, *2:* 359
 Soviet Union and, *1:* 48–49, 164–65; *2:* 261–62, 354, 359, 360–61
 Strategic Arms Limitation Talks and, *1:* 164–65; *2:* 261, 360–61
 Taiwan and, *1:* 98–99
 in U.S. Congress, *2:* 355–56
 vice presidency of, *2:* 356–57
 Vietnam War and, *1:* 50, 175; *2:* 257, 259, 359–60, 362–63
 Vietnamization and, *2:* 359
 Watergate scandal and, *1:* 55, 74; *2:* 262, 264, 363–64
 World War II and, *2:* 355
 Zhou Enlai and, *2:* 470
Nobel Literature Prize, *1:* 101
Nobel Peace Prize
 Begin, Menachem, and, *1:* 79
 Brandt, Willy, and, *1:* 15
 Carter, Jimmy, and, *1:* 81
 Gorbachev, Mikhail, and, *1:* 157; *2:* 421
 Kissinger, Henry, and, *2:* 255, 259–60
 Marshall, George C., and, *2:* 321, 325
 Sadat, Anwar, and, *1:* 79

Sakharov, Andrey, and, *2:* 408, 412–13
Nonalignment, *2:* 444, 449–50
Noriega, Manuel, *1:* 59
North Atlantic Treaty Organization (NATO)
  Acheson, Dean G., and, *1:* 4, 6
  Adenauer, Konrad, and, *1:* 12–14
  Attlee, Clement R., and, *1:* 31
  Bevin, Ernest, and, *1:* 38
  China and, *2:* 317
  Clifford, Clark M., and, *1:* 111, 113
  containment and, *1:* 4, 31, 58, 111, 113; *2:* 271, 327, 434, 437
  Dulles, John Foster, and, *1:* 128
  Eisenhower, Dwight D., and, *1:* 139
  formation of, *1:* 4, 38, 113, 128, 139; *2:* 271, 434, 437
  Germany and, *1:* 58; *2:* 274
  Great Britain and, *2:* 441–42
  Kirkpatrick, Jeane, and, *2:* 253
  Kohl, Helmut, and, *2:* 271–72, 273
  Marshall, George C., and, *2:* 327
  nuclear weapons and, *2:* 273, 438, 440
  Soviet Union and, *1:* 113; *2:* 317, 441–42
  Stalin, Joseph, and, *2:* 317
  Thatcher, Margaret, and, *2:* 438, 440, 441–42
  Tito, Josip Broz, and, *2:* 448
  Truman, Harry S., and, *2:* 459
  Warsaw Pact and, *2:* 274
  West Germany and, *1:* 12–14; *2:* 271–72, 273
  Yugoslavia and, *2:* 448
North Korea
  Carter, Jimmy, and, *1:* 81; *2:* 248
  China and, *2:* 245–46
  communism in, *2:* 247
  economy of, *2:* 244–45, 247
  elections in, *2:* 247
  espionage and, *1:* 203
  formation of, *2:* 242–43, 244
  government of, *2:* 247
  isolationism and, *2:* 241, 245, 247

  Johnson, Lyndon B., and, *1:* 203
  Korean Workers' Party in, *2:* 242, 247
  military in, *2:* 247
  Nixon, Richard M., and, *2:* 246
  nuclear weapons and, *2:* 247–48
  society in, *2:* 245
  South Korea and, *2:* 246, 247
  Soviet Union and, *2:* 242, 243, 245–46
  terrorism and, *2:* 246
  Third World and, *2:* 246
  United Nations and, *2:* 247
North, Oliver, *2:* 398
North Vietnam, *2:* 257
NSC. *See* National Security Council (NSC)
Nuclear energy. *See also* Energy; Nuclear weapons
  Acheson, Dean G., and, *1:* 3
  Baruch, Bernard, and, *2:* 373
  Germany and, *2:* 284–85
  Great Britain and, *2:* 284, 291
  International Atomic Energy Agency and, *2:* 352–53
  international control of, *2:* 373
  Kurchatov, Igor, and, *2:* 283, 284–85, 289–91, 373
  Oppenheimer, J. Robert, and, *2:* 213–14, 283, 366, 373
  Soviet Union, *2:* 289–91
  United Nations and, *1:* 3; *2:* 373
Nuclear Nonproliferation Treaty, *2:* 248, 281
Nuclear war, *2:* 227, 238, 394
Nuclear weapons. *See also* Manhattan Project; Nuclear energy
  ABM treaty, *2:* 262
  Acheson, Dean G., and, *1:* 3, 6
  Attlee, Clement R., and, *1:* 31
  Baker, James, and, *2:* 421
  Beria, Lavrenty, and, *2:* 433
  Bevin, Ernest, and, *1:* 31, 38
  Brandt, Willy, and, *1:* 15
  Brezhnev, Leonid, and, *1:* 47, 48–49, 77–78, 166; *2:* 360–61
  brinkmanship and, *1:* 129
  Bush, George, and, *1:* 57, 58

Carter, Jimmy, and, *1:* 49, 70, 74–75, 77–78, 81, 166; *2:* 248, 392

China and, *2:* 318

Churchill, Winston, and, *1:* 31, 108

Cold War and, *2:* 366–67

Conference on Security and Cooperation in Europe and, *2:* 265

containment and, *2:* 272–73

Cuba and, *1:* 88–91

Cuban Missile Crisis and, *1:* 88–91

détente and, *1:* 48–49

deterrence and, *1:* 108, 140; *2:* 440–41

development of, *1:* 6, 31, 38, 150; *2:* 212, 283, 285–88, 351, 366, 371–72, 375, 409, 410, 432, 433, 458

Dulles, John Foster, and, *2:* 256

Eisenhower, Dwight D., and, *1:* 140, 144; *2:* 215

espionage and, *1:* 191–92; *2:* 285, 287, 333, 351

Ford, Gerald, and, *1:* 166

Germany and, *2:* 370, 371

Gorbachev, Mikhail, and, *1:* 56, 58, 154–55; *2:* 395–96, 418

Great Britain and, *1:* 31, 38, 108; *2:* 307, 309, 440–41

Gromyko, Andrey, and, *1:* 164–65, 166

Harriman, W. Averell, and, *1:* 173

hotline for, *1:* 91; *2:* 238

Intermediate-range Nuclear Force (INF) treaty, *2:* 396, 420

Johnson, Lyndon B., and, *1:* 204

Kennan, George F., and, *2:* 212, 213, 215

Kennedy, John F., and, *2:* 227–28, 341

Khrushchev, Nikita, and, *1:* 144; *2:* 226–27, 227–28, 235, 238–39, 411

Kim Il Sung and, *2:* 247–48

Kissinger, Henry, and, *2:* 256, 260–62

Kohl, Helmut, and, *2:* 272–73

Kurchatov, Igor, and, *2:* 285–88, 289–91, 373, 433

Limited Test-Ban Treaty of 1963, *1:* 91, 173; *2:* 227–28, 238–39, 309

Macmillan, Harold, and, *2:* 307, 309

McNamara, Robert S., and, *2:* 341

Molotov, Vyacheslav, and, *2:* 351

mutual assured destruction and, *2:* 260–61

negotiations concerning, *1:* 48–49, 56, 144, 155, 164–65, 166, 173, 204; *2:* 227–28, 238–39, 252, 261–62, 395–96

Nitze, Paul H., and, *1:* 6

Nixon, Richard M., and, *1:* 48–49; *2:* 359, 360–61

North Atlantic Treaty Organization and, *2:* 273, 438, 440

North Korea and, *2:* 247–48

Nuclear Nonproliferation Treaty, *2:* 248, 281

Oppenheimer, J. Robert, and, *2:* 366, 368, 370–72, 375

race for, *1:* 31, 51, 74–75, 154, 166; *2:* 213, 290, 341, 396, 410, 418, 432

Reagan, Ronald, and, *1:* 56, 78, 155; *2:* 252, 392, 395–96, 418

reconnaissance and, *2:* 288

Red Scare and, *2:* 333

Sakharov, Andrey, and, *2:* 290

Shevardnadze, Eduard, and, *2:* 418–20, 421

Shultz, George, and, *1:* 166; *2:* 418–20

Soviet Union and, *1:* 6, 47, 48–49, 50, 56, 58, 70, 77–78, 88–91, 154–55, 164–65, 166, 204; *2:* 213, 226–28, 235, 238–39, 283, 285–88, 289–91, 333, 351, 360–61, 373, 375, 395–96, 409, 410–11, 418, 421, 432, 433, 434, 440–41

Stalin, Joseph, and, *2:* 285, 351, 432

Strategic Arms Limitation Talks and, *1:* 48, 49, 50, 70, 77–78, 164–65, 166, 204; *2:* 255, 261, 360–61, 390

Strategic Defense Initiative and, *2:* 273, 393, 395–96

strength and, *2:* 409, 411

test bans and, *1:* 173; *2:* 238–39

testing of, *1:* 6, 31, 106, 108; *2:* 285, 287–88, 307, 333, 351, 366, 371, 372, 373, 375, 410, 434, 458

Thatcher, Margaret, and, *2:* 440–41

treaties concerning, *1:* 48, 50, 56, 58, 70, 77–78, 91, 155, 164–65, 166, 173, 204; *2:* 227–28, 238–39, 248, 255, 261–62, 265, 281, 309, 359, 360–61, 395–96, 420

Truman, Harry S., and, *1:* 3, 31, 108; *2:* 212, 288, 333, 351, 375, 458

U.S. Congress and, *1:* 108

use of, *1:* 3, 31; *2:* 285, 297, 371, 372, 409, 432, 458

West Germany and, *2:* 272–73

World War II and, *1:* 3, 31; *2:* 285, 297, 371, 409, 432, 458

Yeltsin, Boris, and, *1:* 58

Nuclear Weapons and Foreign Policy, *2:* 256

NYA. *See* National Youth Administration (NYA)

O

OAS. *See* Organization of American States (OAS)

Objectivism, *2:* 379, 382, 383, 384, 385

October Revolution, *2:* 347. *See also* Bolshevik Revolution

October War, *1:* 50; *2:* 262–63, 363

OEEC. *See* Organisation for European Economic Cooperation (OEEC)

Oil, *1:* 54, 76–77, 142; *2:* 262–63, 363

Olympics, *1:* 70, 78

One Day in the Life of Ivan Denisovich, *2:* 234

OPEC. *See* Organization of Petroleum Exporting Countries (OPEC)

"Open Skies" plan, *1:* 140–41

Operation Mongoose, *1:* 88; *2:* 226

Oppenheimer, J. Robert, *2:* 213–14, 283, 366 (ill.), **366–78,** 374 (ill.), 410–11

Order of Lenin, *1:* 149; *2:* 410

Order of Merit, *1:* 32

Order of Stalin, *2:* 410

Order of the Garter, *1:* 100–101

Order of the Red Banner of Labor, *1:* 149–50

Organisation for European Economic Cooperation (OEEC), *1:* 38; *2:* 325

Organization of American States (OAS), *1:* 60; *2:* 327, 377

Organization of Petroleum Exporting Countries (OPEC), *1:* 76; *2:* 363

Organized crime, *1:* 185, 189

Ortega, Daniel, *2:* 398

Ostopolitik, *1:* 15

Oswald, Lee Harvey, *2:* 228–29

P

Pace, Stephen, *1:* 72

Pahlavi, Mohammed Reza, *1:* 79; *2:* 391

Pakistan, *1:* 29

Palestine, *1:* 29, 36–37

Palestine Liberation Organization (PLO), *1:* 50

Palmer, A. Mitchell, *1:* 187

Palmer Raids, *1:* 187

Pan Am bombing, *2:* 399

Panama, *1:* 59–60, 77, 81

Panama Canal, *1:* 59, 77, 125

Partisans, *2:* 446

Pasternak, Boris, *2:* 234

Paul VI (pope), *1:* 164

Peace

Dulles, John Foster, and, *1:* 126

Eisenhower, Dwight D., and, *1:* 134

Johnson, Lyndon B., and, *1:* 200, 204

Kennedy, John F., and, *2:* 221

Khrushchev, Nikita, and, *2:* 352

Kirkpatrick, Jeane, on, *2:* 249

Kurchatov, Igor, and, *2:* 283, 289–91, 373

Nixon, Richard M., and, *2:* 359, 365

Oppenheimer, J. Robert, and, *2:* 213–14, 283, 373
Vietnam War and, *1:* 175, 204
World War II and, *1:* 106
Peace Corps, *2:* 221
Pearce, Robert, *1:* 25
Pearl Harbor, *1:* 105, 135–36; *2:* 296, 370–71
Pendergast, Thomas, *2:* 454
People's Republic of China (PRC), *1:* 96–97, 117; *2:* 243, 467. *See also* China; Republic of China (ROC); Taiwan
Perestroika
adoption of, *1:* 56
China and, *1:* 121
Gorbachev, Mikhail, and, *1:* 146, 153; *2:* 395, 414, 416, 418
Shevardnadze, Eduard, and, *2:* 416
Permanent Subcommittee on Investigations, *2:* 334–35
Pershing, John J., *2:* 322
Persian Gulf War, *1:* 60; *2:* 421
Phan Boi Chau, *1:* 177
Philippines, *2:* 295, 296–97, 302
Pinochet Ugarte, Augusto, *2:* 263, 362
PLO. *See* Palestine Liberation Organization (PLO)
Podgorny, Nikolay, *1:* 46
Poindexter, John, *2:* 398
Poland
boundary of, *1:* 66
Brandt, Willy, and, *1:* 15
Brezhnev, Leonid, and, *1:* 51
communism in, *1:* 36–37
democracy and, *2:* 421
elections in, *1:* 36–37, 66, 171; *2:* 431
Germany and, *2:* 431
Gromyko, Andrey, and, *1:* 166
Solidarity in, *2:* 394
Soviet Union and, *1:* 36–37, 51, 66, 161, 166, 171; *2:* 394, 431
Stalin, Joseph, and, *1:* 66
West Germany and, *1:* 15
World War II and, *1:* 106, 161, 171; *2:* 431
Policy Planning Staff (PPS), *2:* 212
Politburo. *See also* Presidium
in Communist Party, *1:* 162–63

Deng Xiaoping and, *1:* 118
Gorbachev, Mikhail, and, *1:* 152; *2:* 418
Gromyko, Andrey, and, *1:* 165
Khrushchev, Nikita, and, *2:* 232, 234, 240
Kosygin, Aleksey, and, *2:* 279, 280
Molotov, Vyacheslav, and, *2:* 347, 352
Zhou Enlai and, *2:* 465–66
Political Woman, 2: 250
Politics, *2:* 213
Popular Revolutionary Action Front (FRAP), *1:* 19
Popular Unity Coalition, *1:* 17, 20
Potsdam Conference
Attlee, Clement R., and, *1:* 28, 35–36, 66; *2:* 431
Bevin, Ernest, and, *1:* 35–37
Big Three and, *1:* 65, 66
Byrnes, James F., and, *1:* 65, 66
Churchill, Winston, and, *1:* 35–37
Gromyko, Andrey, and, *1:* 161
Molotov, Vyacheslav, and, *2:* 351
overview of, *1:* 106
Stalin, Joseph, and, *1:* 66; *2:* 431
Truman, Harry S., and, *1:* 65, 66; *2:* 457
Poverty, *1:* 195, 197–98, 201–3
Powell, Colin, *2:* 406 (ill.)
PPS. *See* Policy Planning Staff (PPS)
Pravda, 2: 346–47, 427
PRC. *See* People's Republic of China (PRC)
Present at the Creation: My Years in the State Department, 1: 8
Presidential Medal of Freedom, *1:* 109; *2:* 217, 249, 253, 343
Presidium, *1:* 44, 163; *2:* 419. *See also* Politburo
Profumo, John, *2:* 310
Prohibition Era, *1:* 185
Propaganda, *1:* 42, 45, 150, 159, 190
Property
capitalism and, *1:* 3, 42, 86, 111, 150, 178; *2:* 211, 237, 251–52, 313, 385, 404
collectivism and, *2:* 409

communism and, *1:* 3, 18, 26, 42, 82, 100, 110, 127, 150, 160, 168, 178, 186; *2:* 211, 223, 231, 278, 295, 312, 331, 340, 346, 366, 385, 389, 404, 410, 426, 445, 458, 464

democracy and, *2:* 426

Pulitzer Prize, *1:* 8

Purple Heart, *2:* 219

Putin, Vladimir, *2:* 419

Q

Quarantine, *1:* 90; *2:* 227, 238

R

Rabi, I. I., *2:* 375

Racism, *1:* 63, 68. *See also* Discrimination; Segregation

Radical Party, *1:* 18

Radio, *1:* 75; *2:* 334

Radio Free Europe, *1:* 75

Radio Liberty, *1:* 75

Rajk, Laszlo, *2:* 434

Rand, Ayn, *2:* 379 (ill.), **379–86,** 384 (ill.)

Rayburn, Sam, *1:* 195

Reagan Doctrine, *2:* 397–98

Reagan, Nancy, *1:* 156 (ill.); *2:* 389, 441 (ill.)

Reagan, Ronald, *1:* 156 (ill.); *2:* 252 (ill.), 387 (ill.), **387–400,** 391 (ill.), 394 (ill.), 397 (ill.), 441 (ill.)

as actor, *2:* 388–89

Afghanistan and, *2:* 392–93

Andropov, Yuri, and, *1:* 155

assassination attempt of, *2:* 392

as author, *2:* 399

Brezhnev, Leonid, and, *1:* 51

Bush, George, and, *2:* 391

Carter, Jimmy, and, *2:* 391–92

character of, *2:* 387

Cold War and, *2:* 387, 396

communism and, *2:* 251, 387, 389

containment and, *2:* 395, 395–97

Democratic Party and, *2:* 389

détente and, *2:* 390, 393

dictatorship and, *2:* 395–97

early life of, *2:* 387–88

economy and, *2:* 392

Eisenhower, Dwight D., and, *2:* 389

elections of, *1:* 55–56, 79; *2:* 251, 390–92, 395

Ford, Gerald, and, *2:* 266, 390

on freedom, *2:* 387

General Electric and, *2:* 389

Goldwater, Barry, and, *2:* 390

Gorbachev, Mikhail, and, *1:* 56, 57, 155–56; *2:* 395–96

as governor, *2:* 390

Great Britain and, *2:* 441–42

Grenada and, *2:* 395

Gromyko, Andrey, and, *1:* 166

Harriman, W. Averell, and, *1:* 175

health of, *2:* 399

honors for, *2:* 399

House Un-American Activities Committee and, *2:* 389

imperialism and, *2:* 395–97

Iran and, *2:* 399

Iran-Contra scandal and, *1:* 56, 60; *2:* 398

Kennan, George F., and, *2:* 216, 396

Kirkpatrick, Jeane, and, *2:* 251

Kissinger, Henry, and, *2:* 266, 390

Kohl, Helmut, and, *2:* 272

Korean Airlines tragedy and, *2:* 394

Libya and, *2:* 398–99

military and, *1:* 51; *2:* 392, 393

Nicaragua and, *2:* 398

Nixon, Richard M., and, *2:* 364, 390

nuclear war and, *2:* 394

nuclear weapons and, *1:* 56, 78, 155; *2:* 252, 392, 395–96, 418

as radio broadcaster, *2:* 388

Reagan Doctrine and, *2:* 397–98

Reaganomics and, *2:* 392

Red Scare and, *2:* 389

retirement of, *2:* 399

Screen Actors Guild and, *2:* 388–89

Soviet Union and, *1:* 56,
  155–56, 166, 175; *2:* 216,
  252, 392–93, 395–96
Strategic Arms Limitation Talks
  and, *1:* 78; *2:* 390, 392
Strategic Defense Initiative and,
  1: 155; *2:* 273, 393, 395–96
Thatcher, Margaret, and, *2:*
  441–42
Third World and, *2:* 397–99
Truman, Harry S., and, *2:* 389
United Nations and, *2:* 395
Vietnam War and, *2:* 390
World War II and, *2:* 388
Reaganomics, *2:* 392
Reconnaissance, *1:* 90; *2:* 227,
  288. *See also* Espionage
Red Army, *2:* 316, 466
Red Guard, *2:* 318, 472
Red Scare
  blacklisting and, *2:* 384, 389
  China and, *2:* 333
  civil rights and, *2:* 333
  communism and, *2:* 332–33,
    376, 389
  Federal Bureau of Investigation
    and, *1:* 189–92
  freedom and, *2:* 384
  Harriman, W. Averell, and, *1:*
    172
  Hiss, Alger, and, *2:* 333
  Hollywood and, *2:* 333, 384,
    389
  Hoover, J. Edgar, and, *1:*
    189–92; *2:* 333
  House Un-American Activities
    Committee and, *2:* 332–33
  McCarthy, Joseph R., and, *2:*
    329, 331–36, 376
  Nixon, Richard M., and, *2:*
    332–33
  nuclear weapons and, *2:* 333
  Oppenheimer, J. Robert, and, *2:*
    375–77
  overview of, *2:* 332–33
  Rand, Ayn, and, *2:* 384
  Reagan, Ronald, and, *2:* 389
  World War I and, *2:* 332
  World War II and, *2:* 332
Religion, *2:* 234, 422
Reparations, *1:* 66, 105, 126
Republic of China (ROC). *See also*
  China; People's Republic of
  China (PRC); Taiwan

Chiang Kai-shek and, *1:* 118
Chiang Kai-shek, Madame,
  and, *1:* 95 (ill.)
dictatorship and, *1:* 98
Eisenhower, Dwight D., and, *1:*
  141
formation of, *1:* 39, 92, 97–98,
  118; *2:* 298–99, 467
Great Britain and, *2:* 307
Kissinger, Henry, and, *2:* 260
Nixon, Richard M., and, *1:*
  98–99; *2:* 260, 360, 470
Truman, Harry S., and, *1:* 39,
  98, 118
United Nations and, *1:* 98–99;
  2: 469
Republic of Korea. *See* South
  Korea
Republican National Committee
  (RNC), *1:* 55
Republican Party
  Bush, George, and, *1:* 54, 55
  Eisenhower, Dwight D., and, *1:*
    139
  House Un-American Activities
    Committee and, *1:* 191
  isolationism and, *1:* 170
  Kirkpatrick, Jeane, and, *2:* 253
  Watergate scandal and, *2:* 363
Ribbentrop, Joachim von, *2:* 348
Ribbentrop-Molotov Pact. *See* So-
  viet-German Nonaggression
  Treaty
Rice, Condoleezza, *2:* 401 (ill.),
  401–7
Rickover, Hyman G., *1:* 72–73
Rio Pact, *2:* 327, 459
RNC. *See* Republican National
  Committee (RNC)
Robertson, David, *1:* 62
ROC. *See* Republic of China
  (ROC)
Roca, Blas, *2:* 239 (ill.)
Rockefeller, Nelson A., *1:* 55, 173;
  2: 256
Rogers, William P., *2:* 261 (ill.)
Romania, *1:* 43
Ronald Reagan Washington Na-
  tional Airport, *1:* 37
Roosevelt, Eleanor, *1:* 170
Roosevelt, Franklin D., *1:* 190
  (ill.)
  Acheson, Dean G., and, *1:* 2
  Bullitt, William C., and, *2:* 209

Byrnes, James F., and, *1:* 62, 63–64, 64–65
Churchill, Winston, and, *1:* 105–6; *2:* 431
Civilian Conservation Corps and, *2:* 295
communism and, *1:* 185–86, 189
Davies, Joseph, and, *2:* 209–10
death of, *1:* 3, 65, 66, 106, 127, 171; *2:* 350, 452, 457
Eisenhower, Dwight D., and, *1:* 136
election of, *1:* 2, 64, 170; *2:* 456
facism and, *1:* 185–86, 189
Great Depression and, *1:* 64; *2:* 295, 389
Harriman, W. Averell, and, *1:* 170–71
Hiss, Alger, and, *2:* 356
Hoover, J. Edgar, and, *1:* 189
Japan and, *2:* 432
Kennan, George F., and, *2:* 209–10
MacArthur, Douglas, and, *2:* 296–97
Marshall, George C., and, *2:* 323
Molotov, Vyacheslav, and, *2:* 348–50
New Deal of, *1:* 64; *2:* 389, 455
Soviet Union and, *2:* 209
Stalin, Joseph, and, *1:* 105–6; *2:* 430, 431–32
Tehran Conference and, *2:* 431
Truman, Harry S., and, *1:* 65; *2:* 455, 456
World War II and, *1:* 105–6, 136, 170–71, 196; *2:* 348–50
Yalta Conference and, *1:* 65, 66; *2:* 431, 432
Rosenbaum, Alissa Zinovievna. *See* Rand, Ayn
Rosenberg, Ethel, *1:* 192
Rosenberg, Julius, *1:* 192
Royal, Denise, *2:* 371–72
Ruby, Jack, *2:* 228
Rusk, Dean, *1:* 7 (ill.), 199 (ill.), 201, 202
Russia
  Bolshevik Revolution in, *1:* 42, 45, 159–60, 187; *2:* 231, 277–78, 346–47, 380–81, 427–28, 445

Bush, George, and, *1:* 58–59
economy of, *1:* 58–59; *2:* 346, 380
Kennan, George F., and, *2:* 207, 208
Mensheviks in, *2:* 427
monarchy in, *2:* 345–46, 380
Nixon, Richard M., and, *2:* 364–65
Russian Research Centre Kurchatov Institute, *2:* 286, 286 (ill.)
Ruz Gonzalez, Lina, *1:* 83

S

Sadat, Anwar, *1:* 78 (ill.), 79
Sakharov, Andrey, *1:* 75, 155; *2:* 290, 375, 408 (ill.), **408–15**
SALT. *See* Strategic Arms Limitation Talks (SALT)
Schlesinger, James, *2:* 262
Schmidt, Helmut, *2:* 271
Schuman Plan, *1:* 12
Scowcroft, Brent, *2:* 404–5
Screen Actors Guild, *2:* 388–89
SDI. *See* Strategic Defense Initiative (SDI)
Seaborg, Glenn T., *2:* 374 (ill.)
SEATO. *See* Southeast Asia Treaty Organization (SEATO)
Segregation. *See also* Discrimination; Racism
  African Americans and, *1:* 68, 71, 73; *2:* 221–22
  Byrnes, James F., and, *1:* 68
  Carter, Jimmy, and, *1:* 73
  Carter, Lillian Gordy, and, *1:* 71
  Civil Rights Act of 1964 and, *1:* 197
  Kennedy, John F., and, *2:* 221–22
  Rice, Condoleezza, *2:* 402–3
September 11, 2001, terrorist attacks, *2:* 407
Shanghai Communiqué, *2:* 360
Shevardnadze, Eduard, *2:* 416 (ill.), **416–24**
  Afghanistan and, *2:* 420
  Andropov, Yuri, and, *2:* 417
  as author, *2:* 423
  Baker, James, and, *1:* 57; *2:* 420–21
  Cold War and, *2:* 416

Commonwealth of Independent States and, *2:* 423
Communist Party and, *2:* 417
coup attempt and, *2:* 422
early life of, *2:* 416–17
early warning systems and, *2:* 421
Eastern Bloc and, *2:* 421–22
economy and, *2:* 418
election of, *2:* 422, 423
as foreign minister, *2:* 422
on freedom, *2:* 416
Georgia and, *2:* 417, 422–23
glasnost and, *2:* 416
Gorbachev, Mikhail, and, *1:* 151, 154, 166; *2:* 395, 418
Intermediate-range Nuclear Force treaty and, *2:* 420
nuclear weapons and, *2:* 418–20, 421
perestroika and, *2:* 416
Persian Gulf War and, *2:* 421
religion and, *2:* 422
resignation of, *2:* 422
Shultz, George, and, *2:* 418–20
Strategic Defense Initiative and, *2:* 421
Shevardnadze, Nanuli, *2:* 423
Shultz, George, *1:* 166; *2:* 418–20
Sian Incident, *1:* 94–96
Silent Majority, *2:* 359
Sino-Soviet Treaty, *2:* 316–17
Six Pillars of Peace, 1: 126
Six-Day War, *1:* 203
Slansky, Rudolf, *2:* 434–35
Smith, Herbert, *2:* 367–68
Smythe, H. D., *2:* 374 (ill.)
Socialism
    Allende, Salvador, and, *1:* 17, 18, 19–20, 21–22
    Attlee, Clement R., and, *1:* 26, 28–29
    in Chile, *1:* 21–22; *2:* 263
    definition of, *1:* 17
    democracy and, *1:* 17, 20
    economy and, *1:* 86
    in Great Britain, *1:* 25, 28–29; *2:* 439–40
Socialist Party, *1:* 18, 19
Socialist Republic of Vietnam (SRV), *1:* 182
Society for Ethical Culture, *2:* 367
Solidarity, *2:* 394

Solzhenitsyn, Aleksandr, *2:* 234, 413
Somalia, *1:* 50, 60
Song of Russia, 2: 384
Soong Ch'ing'ling, *1:* 95
Soong Mei-ling. *See* Chiang Kai-shek, Madame
"The Sources of Soviet Conduct," *2:* 212
South Africa, *1:* 91; *2:* 310
South Korea, *2:* 242–43, 244, 246, 247, 297–98
South Vietnam, *2:* 257
Southeast Asia Treaty Organization (SEATO), *1:* 130, 141
Soviet Academy of Sciences, *2:* 410
Soviet-German Nonaggression Treaty, *2:* 348
Soviet Union
    Adenauer, Konrad, and, *1:* 12, 13–14
    Afghanistan and, *1:* 50, 70, 78, 156, 164; *2:* 252, 392–93, 413, 420
    agriculture in, *1:* 44, 46; *2:* 232, 238, 239, 278, 348, 429
    Angola and, *1:* 50
    Berlin and, *1:* 137
    Bevin, Ernest, and, *1:* 36–37
    Brandt, Willy, and, *1:* 15, 48
    Bush, George, and, *1:* 57, 58; *2:* 420, 421
    Byrnes, James F., and, *1:* 62, 65–68
    capitalism and, *2:* 280–82
    Carter, Jimmy, and, *1:* 50, 70, 74–75, 77–78; *2:* 393
    Castro, Fidel, and, *1:* 86, 87, 88–89, 91
    Castro, Raúl, and, *1:* 88
    Chiang Kai-shek and, *1:* 93
    China and, *1:* 47, 93, 116, 118; *2:* 235, 280, 316–18, 471
    Churchill, Winston, and, *1:* 108
    Clifford, Clark M., and, *1:* 110–11
    collectivism in, *2:* 429
    communism in, *1:* 26, 110, 127; *2:* 385, 410, 418
    Communist Party in, *1:* 41, 42, 43–46, 49–50, 153–54, 157, 162–63; *2:* 231–32, 233, 234,

239–40, 277, 278–79,
279–80, 347, 353, 410,
417–18, 419, 429, 430, 433
Congress of People's Deputies
in, *1:* 154, 157
constitution of, *1:* 154
Council of the Federation in, *1:*
154
coup d'état in, *1:* 45–46, 58,
157; *2:* 419, 422
Cuba and, *1:* 82, 86, 87, 88–91;
2: 223, 226–27
Czechoslovakia and, *1:* 43, 47,
164, 204; *2:* 216, 281, 282,
449
democracy in, *1:* 154; *2:* 408,
415, 418
Deng Xiaoping and, *1:* 118
de-Stalinization of, *1:* 118; *2:*
233, 236
détente and, *1:* 48–49
Dubcek, Alexander, and, *1:* 47
East Germany and, *1:* 58,
129–30; *2:* 224–25
Eastern Bloc and, *2:* 351,
446–48, 458
economy of, *1:* 3, 46, 51, 56,
146, 154–55, 157; *2:* 239,
277, 279, 280–81, 361, 395,
396, 414, 417, 418, 429, 442,
448, 459
Egypt and, *1:* 50; *2:* 262–63
Eisenhower, Dwight D., and, *1:*
137, 138, 140–41, 142, 143
elections in, *1:* 44, 45, 152–53,
157, 163, 166; *2:* 210–11, 232
end of, *1:* 53, 57, 58, 146, 157;
2: 396, 401, 405, 415, 422,
442
Ethiopia and, *1:* 50
formation of, *1:* 42
freedom in, *2:* 233, 234, 408
Germany and, *1:* 58, 106–7,
172; *2:* 348, 351, 431, 432
glasnost in, *1:* 146, 153; *2:* 274,
414, 416, 418
government of, *1:* 153–54,
162–63
Great Britain and, *1:* 35, 36–37,
108; *2:* 307–8, 348–49,
437–38
Great Terror in, *1:* 42–43,
147–48, 160; *2:* 209, 232,
278, 279–80, 348, 351, 352,

370, 409–10, 412, 420, 430,
434–35
Greece and, *1:* 3–4; *2:* 326
Guevara, Che, and, *1:* 88
Harriman, W. Averell, and, *1:*
170–72, 175
Helsinki Accords and, *2:* 265,
413
human rights in, *1:* 75
Hungary and, *1:* 129–30, 142;
2: 236, 449
industry in, *2:* 429
Israel and, *1:* 50
Japan and, *1:* 66; *2:* 432
Jews in, *1:* 75
Johnson, Lyndon B., and, *2:*
281
Kennan, George F., and, *2:*
209–10, 210–14, 215, 216
Kennedy, John F., and, *2:* 340
Kim Il Sung and, *2:* 245–46
Kirkpatrick, Jeane, and, *2:* 252
Kissinger, Henry, and, *2:* 255,
260–62, 264
Kohl, Helmut, and, *1:* 58; *2:*
271–72, 273
Korea and, *2:* 242
Korean Airlines tragedy and, *2:*
394
Korean War and, *1:* 5
Macmillan, Harold, and, *2:*
307–8
Mao Zedong and, *2:* 313,
316–18
Marshall, George C., and, *2:*
324
Marshall Plan and, *2:* 272, 325
military of, *1:* 47, 51, 58; *2:*
213, 239–40
nation building and, *1:* 50, 164
nationalization in, *2:* 380–81
Nixon, Richard M., and, *1:*
48–49, 164–65; *2:* 261–62,
354, 359, 360–61
North Atlantic Treaty Organization and, *1:* 113; *2:* 317,
441–42
North Korea and, *2:* 242, 243,
245–46
North Vietnam and, *2:* 257
nuclear energy and, *2:* 289–91
nuclear weapons and, *1:* 6, 47,
48–49, 50, 56, 58, 70, 77–78,
88–91, 154–55, 164–65, 166,

204; *2:* 213, 226–28, 235,
238–39, 283, 285–88,
289–91, 333, 351, 360–61,
373, 375, 395–96, 409,
410–11, 418, 421, 432, 433,
434, 440–41
October War and, *1:* 50; *2:*
262–63
oil and, *2:* 262–63
Palestine Liberation Organization and, *1:* 50
perestroika in, *1:* 146, 153; *2:*
414, 416, 418
Poland and, *1:* 36–37, 51, 66,
161, 166, 171; *2:* 394, 431
Presidential Council in, *1:* 154
Reagan, Ronald, and, *1:* 56,
155–56, 166, 175; *2:* 216,
252, 392–93, 395–96
religion in, *2:* 234
reparations and, *1:* 66
republics of, *2:* 417, 420–21,
422
Rice, Condoleezza, and, *2:* 401,
403–5
Romania and, *1:* 43
Roosevelt, Franklin D., and, *2:*
209
school in, *1:* 148–49
Sino-Soviet Treaty and, *2:*
316–17
Six-Day War and, *1:* 203
Somalia and, *1:* 50
space programs and, *1:* 47, 142;
2: 235, 307
Strategic Arms Limitation Talks
and, *1:* 204
Strategic Defense Initiative and,
2: 393, 421
Suez War and, *1:* 132, 142
as superpower, *1:* 111; *2:* 432
Syria and, *1:* 50
Thatcher, Margaret, and, *2:*
438, 440–43
Third World and, *1:* 50, 164; *2:*
440
Truman, Harry S., and, *1:*
171–72; *2:* 288, 333
Turkey and, *1:* 3–4; *2:* 326
United Nations and, *1:* 5, 66
Vietnam War and, *1:* 50; *2:*
261–62, 281
Virgin Land program in, *1:* 44;
2: 238

Warsaw Pact and, *1:* 47–48
Watergate scandal and, *2:* 264
West Berlin and, *2:* 224–25,
235–37
West Germany and, *1:* 13–14,
15, 47–48, 165; *2:* 271–72
World War II and, *1:* 104–7,
148, 161, 170–71; *2:* 232–33,
242, 279, 348–50, 430–32
Yugoslavia and, *2:* 434, 444,
446–49
Zhou Enlai and, *2:* 471
Sovietization, *1:* 43
Space race, *1:* 47, 142; *2:* 235
Spain, *1:* 83
Spanish-American War, *1:* 83
Sputnik I, 2: 235, 307
SRV. *See* Socialist Republic of Viet-
nam (SRV)
Stalin, Joseph, *2:* 425 (ill.),
425–36, 427 (ill.), 428 (ill.)
agriculture and, *2:* 348, 429
Beria, Lavrenty, and, *2:* 286,
351, 432, 433, 435
Bevin, Ernest, and, *1:* 35
Bolshevik Revolution and, *2:*
346, 347, 427–28
Brezhnev, Leonid, and, *1:* 44
capitalism and, *2:* 210–11, 351
China and, *2:* 317
Churchill, Winston, and, *1:*
105–6, 107; *2:* 431
collectivism and, *2:* 429, 448
Cominform and, *2:* 434
communism and, *2:* 236,
426–28, 433–34
Communist Party and, *2:* 429,
430
containment and, *2:* 433–34
Czechoslovakia and, *2:* 435
on death, *2:* 425
death of, *1:* 44, 150; *2:* 280,
352, 435
early life of, *2:* 426
Eastern Bloc and, *2:* 425, 432,
446–48
economy and, *2:* 429
Eisenhower, Dwight D., and, *1:*
138
elections and, *1:* 138
as general secretary, *2:* 429
Germany and, *2:* 432
Gorbachev, Mikhail, and, *1:*
150

Great Terror of, *1:* 42–43, 45,
147–48, 160; *2:* 209, 232,
236, 278, 279–80, 348, 351,
352, 370, 409–10, 412, 420,
430, 434–35
Harriman, W. Averell, and, *1:*
170, 171
Hitler, Adolf, and, *2:* 348, 431
Ho Chi Minh and, *1:* 183
Japan and, *1:* 66; *2:* 432
Jews and, *2:* 435
Kennan, George F., and, *2:*
209–10, 211
Khrushchev, Nikita, and, *1:* 46,
118; *2:* 230, 231–32, 233,
236, 291, 352, 419, 435–36,
471
Kim Il Sung and, *2:* 243
Kosygin, Aleksey, and, *2:*
278–79, 279–80
Kurchatov, Igor, and, *2:* 285–86
Lenin, Vladimir I., and, *2:* 427,
428–29
military and, *2:* 431
Molotov, Vyacheslav, and, *2:*
345, 346, 347–48, 351, 352
nationalism of, *2:* 428
North Atlantic Treaty Organiza-
tion and, *2:* 317
nuclear weapons and, *2:* 285,
351, 432
paranoia of, *2:* 434, 435
Poland and, *1:* 66
Potsdam Conference and, *1:*
66; *2:* 351, 431
reputation of, *2:* 430
Roosevelt, Franklin D., and, *1:*
105–6; *2:* 430, 431–32
as secretary, *2:* 347–48
Sino-Soviet Treaty and, *2:* 317
Tehran Conference and, *2:* 431
Tito, Josip Broz, and, *2:* 434,
444, 446–48
Trotsky, Leon, and, *2:* 429
Truman, Harry S., and, *2:* 351,
452, 457
World War II and, *1:* 170; *2:*
348, 349, 425, 430–32
Yalta Conference and, *1:* 65,
66; *2:* 431, 432
Zhou Enlai, *2:* 471
Star Wars. *See* Strategic Defense
Initiative (SDI)
Stephens, Mark, *1:* 33

Stevenson, Adlai, *1:* 140, 141–42,
173; *2:* 461
Stone, Harlan Fiske, *2:* 456 (ill.)
Strategic Arms Limitation Talks
(SALT)
Brezhnev, Leonid, and, *1:* 48,
49, 50, 77–78, 166; *2:* 261,
360–61
Carter, Jimmy, and, *1:* 49, 70,
77–78, 166; *2:* 392
Ford, Gerald, and, *1:* 166
Gromyko, Andrey, and, *1:*
164–65, 166
Johnson, Lyndon B., and, *1:*
204
Kissinger, Henry, and, *2:* 255,
261
Nixon, Richard M., and, *1:* 48,
164–65; *2:* 261, 360–61
Reagan, Ronald, and, *1:* 78; *2:*
390, 392
Soviet Union and, *1:* 204
U.S. Congress and, *1:* 77–78
Strategic Defense Initiative (SDI)
Baker, James, and, *2:* 421
Gorbachev, Mikhail, and, *1:*
155; *2:* 395–96
Kohl, Helmut, and, *2:* 273
Reagan, Ronald, and, *1:* 155; *2:*
273, 393, 395–96
Shevardnadze, Eduard, and, *2:*
421
Soviet Union and, *2:* 421
Strauss, Lewis, *2:* 376
Strength, *1:* 1; *2:* 409, 411
Submarines, *1:* 72; *2:* 309
Subversives, *2:* 333
Suez War, *1:* 131–32, 142; *2:*
306–7
Sun Yat-sen, *1:* 93, 95; *2:* 315
Supreme Soviet, *1:* 163
Swimming, *2:* 318
Syngman Rhee, *2:* 297–98
Syria, *1:* 50, 203

T

Taiwan, *1:* 98–99, 130; *2:* 469. *See
also* China; People's Republic
of China (PRC); Republic of
China (ROC)

Tehran Conference, *1:* 105, 161;
　　2: 349, 431, 446
Telegraph, *2:* 208
Television, *1:* 143
Teller, Edward, *2:* 375
Terrorism, *2:* 246, 264–65,
　　398–99, 407
Tet Offensive, *1:* 114, 183, 203–4
Texas, *1:* 54–55
Thatcher, Denis, *2:* 441 (ill.)
Thatcher, Margaret, *2:* 272, 437
　　(ill.), **437–43,** 441 (ill.)
Thatcher's Law, *2:* 440
Third World
　　Brezhnev, Leonid, and, *1:* 50
　　Eisenhower, Dwight D., and, *1:*
　　　141
　　Gromyko, Andrey, and, *1:* 164
　　Kim Il Sung and, *2:* 246
　　Maoism and, *2:* 312–13
　　nation building in, *1:* 50, 83
　　North Korea and, *2:* 246
　　Reagan, Ronald, and, *2:* 397–99
　　Soviet Union and, *1:* 50, 164; *2:*
　　　440
Threats, *1:* 42, 150, 190; *2:* 263
Thurmond, Strom, *2:* 460
Tiananmen Square, *1:* 121; *2:*
　　314, 315 (ill.)
Time, *2:* 324
Tito, Josip Broz, *2:* 214 (ill.),
　　215–16, 434, 444 (ill.),
　　444–51, 447 (ill.), 449 (ill.)
Titoism, *2:* 448
Trades Union Congress (TUC), *1:*
　　35
Transport and General Workers'
　　Union, *1:* 35
Transportation, *2:* 455
Travel, *2:* 225
Treaty of Versailles, *1:* 126; *2:* 464
Treaty on the Final Settlement
　　with Respect to Germany, *2:*
　　274
Trinity, *2:* 371, 372
Trotsky, Leon, *2:* 429
Truman, Bess, *2:* 456 (ill.)
Truman Committee, *2:* 455–56
Truman Doctrine
　　Acheson, Dean G., and, *1:* 3–4
　　Clifford, Clark M., and, *1:* 109,
　　　111–12
　　communism and, *1:* 3–4

containment and, *1:* 3–4,
　　29–30, 38, 112, 172
Greece and, *1:* 112
Kennan, George F., and, *2:* 212
"Long Telegram" and, *2:* 212
Truman, Harry S., and, *1:* 112,
　　172; *2:* 458–59
Turkey and, *1:* 112
Truman, Harry S., *1:* 30 (ill.), 67
　　(ill.); *2:* 300 (ill.), 326 (ill.),
　　452 (ill.), **452–62,** 456 (ill.),
　　457 (ill.)
Acheson, Dean G., and, *1:* 3
African Americans and, *2:* 460
Attlee, Clement R., and, *1:* 31
Berlin airlift and, *2:* 459
Byrnes, James F., and, *1:* 62, 65,
　　67–68, 127
character of, *2:* 455, 461
Chiang Kai-shek and, *1:* 96, 98
China and, *1:* 96, 98, 139; *2:*
　　298, 324, 467
Churchill, Winston, and, *1:*
　　107–8; *2:* 457
Clifford, Clark M., and, *1:* 109,
　　110
Cold War and, *2:* 452, 458–59,
　　459–61, 462
containment and, *1:* 3–4,
　　29–30, 38, 128, 172; *2:*
　　458–59
death of, *2:* 461
Dulles, John Foster, and, *1:*
　　127, 128
early life of, *2:* 453–54
economy and, *2:* 459
Eisenhower, Dwight D., and, *1:*
　　139
election of, *2:* 389, 455, 456,
　　459, 460
Fair Deal of, *2:* 459
Germany and, *1:* 107
Greece and, *1:* 29–30, 38; *2:*
　　326
Israel and, *1:* 37; *2:* 326–27, 460
Japan and, *1:* 128
Kennan, George F., and, *2:* 212
Kennedy, John F., and, *2:* 220
Korea and, *2:* 242
Korean War and, *1:* 5, 98,
　　139–40; *2:* 299–301, 461
Lend-Lease program and, *1:*
　　171
"Long Telegram" and, *2:* 212

MacArthur, Douglas, and, *1:* 5, 40; *2:* 297, 298, 299–301, 327, 461

Marshall, George C., and, *2:* 324, 326–27

Marshall Plan and, *2:* 459

McCarthy, Joseph R., and, *1:* 140; *2:* 299–300, 334, 460, 461

middle initial of, *2:* 453

Molotov, Vyacheslav, and, *2:* 350–51

North Atlantic Treaty Organization and, *2:* 459

nuclear weapons and, *1:* 3, 31, 108; *2:* 212, 288, 333, 351, 375, 458

Oppenheimer, J. Robert, and, *2:* 373

Pendergast, Thomas, and, *2:* 454

political beginnings of, *2:* 454–55

popularity of, *2:* 459, 460, 461, 462

Potsdam Conference and, *1:* 65, 66; *2:* 351, 431, 457

presidency of, *2:* 452, 456–62

Reagan, Ronald, and, *2:* 389

Republic of China and, *1:* 39, 98, 118

retirement of, *2:* 461

Rio Pact and, *2:* 459

Roosevelt, Franklin D., and, *1:* 65; *2:* 455, 456

Rusk, Dean, and, *1:* 202

as senator, *2:* 455–56

Soviet Union and, *1:* 171–72; *2:* 288, 333

Stalin, Joseph, and, *2:* 351, 452, 457

Tito, Josip Broz, and, *2:* 448

transportation and, *2:* 455

Truman Committee and, *2:* 455–56

Truman Doctrine and, *1:* 29–30, 38, 112, 172; *2:* 212, 458–59

Turkey and, *1:* 29–30, 38; *2:* 326

United Nations and, *2:* 457

Wallace, Henry A., *2:* 461

World War I and, *2:* 454

World War II and, *1:* 106–7; *2:* 455–56, 457–58

Yalta Conference and, *1:* 65

Zhou Enlai and, *2:* 468–69

TUC. *See* Trades Union Congress (TUC)

Tupolev, A. N., *2:* 290 (ill.)

Turkey, *1:* 3–4, 29–30, 38, 112; *2:* 326

26th of July Movement, *1:* 85

U

Ukraine, *1:* 58

Ulbricht, Walter, *2:* 225

UN. *See* United Nations (UN)

Union of Soviet Socialist Republics (U.S.S.R.). *See* Soviet Union

United Front, *1:* 96

United Fruit Company, *1:* 86

United Nations Security Council
Cuba and, *1:* 91
formation of, *1:* 161

United Nations (UN)
Attlee, Clement R., and, *1:* 28
Bush, George, and, *1:* 55, 60
China and, *1:* 98–99, 119; *2:* 313, 360, 469
Cuba and, *1:* 91
Deng Xiaoping and, *1:* 119
Dulles, John Foster, and, *1:* 127
formation of, *1:* 28, 105, 127, 161; *2:* 457
Gorbachev, Mikhail, and, *1:* 156
Grenada and, *2:* 395
Gromyko, Andrey, and, *1:* 161, 166
Khrushchev, Nikita, and, *2:* 233–34, 238
Kirkpatrick, Jeane, and, *2:* 249, 251–52, 253
Korea and, *2:* 243
Korean War and, *1:* 5; *2:* 243, 299
North Korea and, *2:* 247
nuclear energy and, *1:* 3; *2:* 373
October War and, *2:* 263
Panama invasion and, *1:* 60
proposal for, *1:* 161
Reagan, Ronald, and, *2:* 395

Republic of China and, *1:* 98–99; *2:* 469
Six-Day War and, *1:* 203
South Korea and, *2:* 247
Soviet Union and, *1:* 5, 66
Suez War and, *1:* 132, 142
Truman, Harry S., and, *2:* 457
voting in, *1:* 66, 161
United States of America Medal of Merit, *2:* 373
United States of America (USA). *See also* specific presidents, officials, and agencies
Bush, George, on, *1:* 53
capitalism in, *1:* 86, 127
Communist Party in, *1:* 192
democracy in, *1:* 25–26, 127; *2:* 271
dictatorship and, *1:* 76, 84–85; *2:* 250–51, 263
economy of, *1:* 3, 4, 26, 60, 64, 71, 76–77, 84–85, 86–87, 204; *2:* 294–95, 323, 369–70, 389, 391, 392, 455
elections in, *1:* 25–26
Ho Chi Minh and, *1:* 181–82
imperialism and, *1:* 82–83, 87, 88, 141; *2:* 223, 263, 395–97
Indochina and, *1:* 181
isolationism and, *1:* 170; *2:* 211
as superpower, *1:* 111; *2:* 324, 432
Vietnam and, *1:* 181–82
U.S. Army, *1:* 140; *2:* 244 (ill.), 323, 327, 334–35
U.S. Congress
Greece and, *2:* 326
Johnson, Lyndon B., in, *1:* 196
Kennedy, John F., in, *2:* 219–21
Kirkpatrick, Jeane, and, *2:* 249
Kissinger, Henry, and, *2:* 264
MacArthur, Douglas, and, *2:* 300–301
Marshall, George C., and, *2:* 326
Nicaragua and, *2:* 398
Nixon, Richard M., in, *2:* 355–56
NSC-68 and, *1:* 6
nuclear weapons and, *1:* 108
Strategic Arms Limitation Talks and, *1:* 77–78
Turkey and, *2:* 326
veterans and, *2:* 295

Vietnam War and, *1:* 199, 201
U.S. Department of Defense, *1:* 109
U.S. Department of Education, *1:* 76
U.S. Department of Energy, *1:* 76
U.S. Senate, *1:* 193; *2:* 220
U.S. State Department, *1:* 6; *2:* 324, 331–32, 334
USA. *See* United States of America (USA).
USS *Pueblo, 1:* 203; *2:* 246
U.S.S.R. *See* Soviet Union

V

Vance, Cyrus, *1:* 74
Vardaman, James, *1:* 110
Versailles Peace Conference, *1:* 126, 178
Veterans, *2:* 295
Vietcong, *1:* 183, 203; *2:* 258
Vietminh, *1:* 179, 180
Vietnam. *See also* North Vietnam; South Vietnam
China and, *2:* 469
colonialism and, *1:* 177–78
Communist Party in, *1:* 176
Declaration of Independence in, *1:* 181–82
division of, *1:* 130, 141, 180, 198; *2:* 257
domino theory and, *1:* 181, 198
Dulles, John Foster, and, *1:* 130
Eisenhower, Dwight D., and, *1:* 141
France and, *1:* 141, 177–78, 179, 180, 198; *2:* 257, 469
freedom in, *1:* 181–82
Great Britain and, *1:* 141
Japan and, *1:* 179
names in, *1:* 180
reunification of, *1:* 182
United States of America and, *1:* 181–82
Zhou Enlai and, *2:* 469
Vietnam War, *1:* 200 (ill.)
Acheson, Dean G., and, *1:* 7–8
Brezhnev, Leonid, and, *1:* 50
Carter, Jimmy, and, *1:* 76
Christmas bombing, *2:* 259, 359
Clifford, Clark M., and, *1:* 109, 114–15

death in, *1:* 201; *2:* 258, 359
Democratic Party and, *2:* 358
economy and, *1:* 204
Eisenhower, Dwight D., and, *1:* 198
end of, *1:* 182; *2:* 260
Gulf of Tonkin Resolution and, *1:* 199
Harriman, W. Averell, and, *1:* 174–75
Ho Chi Minh and, *1:* 182
Hoover, J. Edgar, and, *1:* 192
Johnson, Lyndon B., and, *1:* 7–8, 109, 114, 174–75, 182, 183, 194, 198–203, 203–4; *2:* 281, 302, 342, 358, 359
Kennan, George F., and, *2:* 216
Kennedy, John F., and, *1:* 198
Kissinger, Henry, and, *2:* 255, 257–60, 261–62, 264, 359
Kosygin, Aleksey, and, *2:* 277, 281
MacArthur, Douglas, and, *2:* 302
McNamara, Robert S., and, *2:* 337–38, 341–43
Nixon, Richard M., and, *1:* 50, 175; *2:* 257, 259, 359–60, 362–63
opposition to, *1:* 175, 192, 201, 202, 204; *2:* 258, 342, 343, 358, 359, 390
peace and, *1:* 175, 204
Reagan, Ronald, and, *2:* 390
Rusk, Dean, and, *1:* 201, 202
Soviet Union and, *1:* 50; *2:* 261–62, 281
Tet Offensive, *1:* 114, 183, 203–4
U.S. Congress and, *1:* 199, 201
Vietcong and, *1:* 183, 203; *2:* 258
Vietnamization, *2:* 258, 359
Virgin Land program, *1:* 44; *2:* 238
Voice of America, *1:* 75; *2:* 334
Voorhis, Jerry, *2:* 355
Voting Rights Act of 1965, *1:* 198

W

Wagner, Robert, *1:* 127–28
Wallace, Henry A., *1:* 64; *2:* 456, 460, 461

Warren Commission, *2:* 229
Warsaw Pact, *1:* 47–48; *2:* 271, 274
Washington Dulles International Airport, *1:* 131
Watergate scandal, *1:* 55, 74; *2:* 262, 264, 363–64
We the Living, *2:* 383
Weapons, *1:* 42, 150, 190. *See also* Missiles; Nuclear weapons
Weinberger, Caspar, *1:* 60
Welch, Joseph N., *2:* 329, 335, 335 (ill.)
West Berlin, *1:* 132; *2:* 224–25, 235–37
West Germany
    Acheson, Dean G., and, *1:* 4–5
    Adenauer, Konrad, and, *1:* 9, 11–16
    Brandt, Willy, and, *1:* 15
    Brezhnev, Leonid, and, *1:* 47–48
    capitalism and, *2:* 268
    Christian Democratic Union in, *2:* 270, 271
    constitution of, *1:* 11–12
    democracy and, *2:* 268
    Dulles, John Foster, and, *1:* 131
    East Germany and, *1:* 15; *2:* 271–72
    economy of, *1:* 9, 12, 14; *2:* 272
    elections in, *1:* 12, 15; *2:* 271
    formation of, *1:* 4–5, 12, 138; *2:* 224, 235, 268, 432
    France and, *1:* 12, 13, 14
    Great Britain and, *2:* 308
    Gromyko, Andrey, and, *1:* 165
    independence of, *1:* 13
    North Atlantic Treaty Organization and, *1:* 12–14; *2:* 271–72, 273
    nuclear weapons and, *2:* 272–73
    Poland and, *1:* 15
    Soviet Union and, *1:* 13–14, 15, 47–48, 165; *2:* 271–72
Western Union, *2:* 208
Westmoreland, William C., *2:* 342
White Citizen's Council, *1:* 73
The White House Years, *1:* 144
"Whiz Kids," *2:* 339
Why England Slept, *2:* 219
Wiley, Alexander, *2:* 330–31
Will, George F., *2:* 345

Wilson, Woodrow, *1:* 125
Women's rights, *1:* 63
World Bank, *1:* 2–3; *2:* 342
World Peace Council, *2:* 291
A World Transformed, 1: 61
World War I
  Attlee, Clement R., and, *1:* 27
  Baruch, Bernard, and, *1:* 126
  Bevin, Ernest, and, *1:* 34
  Churchill, Winston, and, *1:* 102
  Dulles, John Foster, and, *1:* 125–26
  Eisenhower, Dwight D., and, *1:* 135
  end of, *2:* 464
  Harriman, W. Averell, and, *1:* 169
  Hoover, J. Edgar, and, *1:* 187
  MacArthur, Douglas, and, *2:* 294, 295
  Macmillan, Harold, and, *2:* 304
  Marshall, George C., and, *2:* 322
  Panama Canal and, *1:* 125
  Red Scare and, *2:* 332
  reparations and, *1:* 126
  Tito, Josip Broz, and, *2:* 445
  Treaty of Versailles and, *1:* 126; *2:* 464
  Truman, Harry S., and, *2:* 454
  Versailles Peace Conference and, *1:* 178
  veterans of, *2:* 295
World War II
  Acheson, Dean G., and, *1:* 2–3
  Adenauer, Konrad, and, *1:* 11
  Attlee, Clement R., and, *1:* 27–28
  beginning of, *1:* 102–3; *2:* 323
  Berlin and, *1:* 137
  Bevin, Ernest, and, *1:* 35
  Big Three and, *1:* 65, 66, 104–7; *2:* 349, 431–32, 446
  Brezhnev, Leonid, and, *1:* 43
  Bush, George, and, *1:* 54
  Byrnes, James F., and, *1:* 64–65
  Chiang Kai-shek and, *1:* 96
  China and, *1:* 96; *2:* 316
  Churchill, Winston, and, *1:* 27–28, 100, 102–6; *2:* 304–5, 349
  Clifford, Clark M., and, *1:* 110
  conduct of, *1:* 136–37
  death in, *2:* 458
  Deng Xiaoping and, *1:* 117

  Eisenhower, Dwight D., and, *1:* 134, 135–38
  end of, *1:* 37, 49; *2:* 274, 285, 371, 372, 467
  "Europe first" strategy in, *1:* 136
  Federal Bureau of Investigation and, *1:* 189–90
  Germany and, *1:* 102–5, 106–7, 136–37, 161; *2:* 348, 431
  Gorbachev, Mikhail, and, *1:* 148
  Great Britain and, *1:* 35, 100, 102–7; *2:* 219, 348–49, 438
  Gromyko, Andrey, and, *1:* 161
  Harriman, W. Averell, and, *1:* 170–71
  Hoover, J. Edgar, and, *1:* 189–90
  Japan and, *1:* 105, 106, 135–36, 179; *2:* 242, 285, 295–97, 370–71, 372, 409, 432, 458
  Johnson, Lyndon B., and, *1:* 196
  Kennan, George F., and, *2:* 210
  Kennedy, John F., and, *2:* 219
  Khrushchev, Nikita, and, *2:* 233
  Kim Il Sung and, *2:* 242
  Kissinger, Henry, and, *2:* 255–56
  Kohl, Helmut, and, *2:* 269, 274
  Kosygin, Aleksey, and, *2:* 279
  Kurchatov, Igor, and, *2:* 285
  Lend-Lease program and, *1:* 170
  MacArthur, Douglas, and, *2:* 293, 295–97
  Macmillan, Harold, and, *2:* 303, 304–5
  Mao Zedong and, *2:* 316
  Marshall, George C., and, *2:* 323–24
  McCarthy, Joseph R., and, *2:* 330
  McNamara, Robert S., and, *2:* 338–39
  Molotov, Vyacheslav, and, *2:* 348–50
  Nazi Party and, *1:* 126
  Nixon, Richard M., and, *2:* 355
  nuclear weapons and, *1:* 3, 31; *2:* 285, 297, 371, 409, 432, 458
  Paris Peace Conference and, *2:* 351
  peace and, *1:* 106

Philippines and, *2:* 296–97
Poland and, *1:* 106, 161, 171; *2:*
431
Potsdam Conference and, *1:*
28, 35–37, 65, 66, 106, 161;
2: 351, 431, 457
Reagan, Ronald, and, *2:* 388
Red Scare and, *2:* 332
reparations and, *1:* 66, 105
Roosevelt, Franklin D., and, *1:*
105–6, 136, 170–71, 196; *2:*
348–50
Soviet Union and, *1:* 104–7,
148, 161, 170–71; *2:* 232–33,
242, 279, 348–50, 430–32
Stalin, Joseph, and, *1:* 170; *2:*
348, 349, 425, 430–32
Tehran Conference and, *1:* 105,
161; *2:* 349, 431, 446
Thatcher, Margaret, and, *2:* 438
Tito, Josip Broz, and, *2:* 446
Treaty on the Final Settlement
with Respect to Germany, *2:*
274
Truman, Harry S., and, *1:*
106–7; *2:* 455–56, 457–58
Yalta Conference and, *1:* 65,
66, 105–6, 161; *2:* 349, 431,
432
Yugoslavia and, *2:* 446

Y

Yalta Conference
Big Three and, *1:* 65, 66
Byrnes, James F., and, *1:* 65, 66
Churchill, Winston, and, *1:* 65,
66
Gromyko, Andrey, and, *1:* 161
Molotov, Vyacheslav, and, *2:*
349
overview of, *1:* 105–6
Roosevelt, Franklin D., and, *1:*
65, 66
Stalin, Joseph, and, *1:* 65, 66; *2:*
431, 432
Truman, Harry S., and, *1:* 65
Yeltsin, Boris, *1:* 58–59, 59 (ill.),
157; *2:* 418, 419, 419 (ill.),
422
Yom Kippur War. *See* October War

Young Communist League. *See*
Komsomol
Yo-Yo Ma, *2:* 407
Yüan Shih-k'ai, *1:* 93
Yugoslavia
breakup of, *2:* 450, 451
Cominform and, *2:* 448
Communist Party in, *2:* 445–46
Czechoslovakia and, *2:* 449
economy of, *2:* 448, 451
elections in, *2:* 450
freedom in, *2:* 451
Hungary and, *2:* 449
Kennan, George F., and, *2:*
215–16
most-favored-nation trade sta-
tus of, *2:* 216
North Atlantic Treaty Organiza-
tion and, *2:* 448
Partisans in, *2:* 446
republics of, *2:* 450
Soviet Union and, *2:* 434, 444,
446–49
World War II and, *2:* 446

Z

Zhao Ziyang, *1:* 120, 121
Zhou Enlai, *2:* 463 (ill.), **463–73**,
468 (ill.), 470 (ill.)
character of, *2:* 472
Chiang Kai-shek and, *1:* 94–96
communism and, *2:* 464
Communist Party and, *2:*
465–66
Cultural Revolution and, *2:*
471–72
death of, *1:* 119; *2:* 472
Deng Xiaoping and, *1:* 116,
118, 119
on diplomacy, *2:* 463
Dulles, John Foster, and, *1:*
130; *2:* 469
early life of, *2:* 463–65
as foreign minister, *2:* 463,
467–70
Great Leap Forward and, *2:*
470–71
Ho Chi Minh and, *2:* 465
Japan and, *1:* 94–96
Khrushchev, Nikita, and, *2:* 471
Kissinger, Henry, and, *2:* 470

Korean War and, *2:* 469
Long March and, *2:* 466–67
Mao Zedong and, *2:* 470–72
May Fourth Movement and, *2:* 464
nation building and, *2:* 470
Nehru, Jawaharlal, and, *2:* 470
Nixon, Richard M., and, *2:* 470
as premier, *2:* 463, 467–72
Red Guard and, *2:* 472

reputation of, *2:* 463, 472
revolution and, *1:* 93, 94–96; *2:* 464–67
Soviet Union and, *2:* 471
Stalin, Joseph, and, *2:* 471
Taiwan and, *2:* 469
Truman, Harry S., and, *2:* 468–69
Vietnam and, *2:* 469
Zhu De, *2:* 316
Zionists, *1:* 37